Breads

by
THE EDITORS OF TIME-LIFE BOOKS

TIME-LIFE BOOKS·AMSTERDAM

TIME-LIFE BOOKS
EUROPEAN EDITOR: Kit van Tulleken
Design Director: Louis Klein
Photography Director: Pamela Marke
Chief of Research: Vanessa Kramer
Chief Sub-Editor: Ilse Grav

THE GOOD COOK
Series Editor: Alan Lothian
Series Co-ordinator: Liz Timothy
Head Designer: Rick Bowring

Editorial Staff for *Breads*
Text Editor: Norman Kolpas
Anthology Editor: Josephine Bacon
Staff Writers: Alexandra Carlier, Jay Ferguson,
Ellen Galford, Thom Henvey
Designer: Mary Staples
Researcher: Tim Fraser
Sub-Editors: Katie Lloyd, Sally Rowland
Anthology Researcher: Deborah Litton
Anthology Assistant: Debra Dick
Design Assistants: Sally Curnock, Ian Midson
Proofreader: Aquila Kegan
Editorial Assistant: Molly Sutherland

EDITORIAL PRODUCTION FOR THE SERIES
Chief: Ellen Brush
Quality Control: Douglas Whitworth
Traffic Co-ordinators: Helen Whitehorn,
Linda Mallett
Picture Co-ordinators: Kate Cann, Philip Garner
Art Department: Julia West
Editorial Department: Beverley Doe, Lesley
Kinahan

TIME
LIFE
BOOKS
PEOPLES OF THE WILD
THE EPIC OF FLIGHT
THE SEAFARERS
WORLD WAR II
THE GOOD COOK
THE TIME-LIFE ENCYCLOPAEDIA OF GARDENING
HUMAN BEHAVIOUR
THE GREAT CITIES
THE ART OF SEWING
THE OLD WEST
THE WORLD'S WILD PLACES
THE EMERGENCE OF MAN
LIFE LIBRARY OF PHOTOGRAPHY
THIS FABULOUS CENTURY
TIME-LIFE LIBRARY OF ART
FOODS OF THE WORLD
GREAT AGES OF MAN
LIFE SCIENCE LIBRARY
LIFE NATURE LIBRARY
YOUNG READERS LIBRARY
LIFE WORLD LIBRARY
THE TIME-LIFE BOOK OF BOATING
TECHNIQUES OF PHOTOGRAPHY
LIFE AT WAR
LIFE GOES TO THE MOVIES
BEST OF LIFE

Cover: A cylindrical loaf of yeast-leavened white bread is
cut into thick slices, revealing a fine, light crumb that results
from thorough kneading and two slow risings (*pages 14-
17*). Before baking, the loaf was scored in a chequerboard
pattern, to increase the bread's crust, and brushed with
egg white to give it a light glaze.

THE CHIEF CONSULTANT:
Richard Olney, an American, has lived and worked since 1951
in France, where he is a highly regarded authority on food and
wine. He is the author of *The French Menu Cookbook* and the
award-winning *Simple French Food,* and has contributed to
numerous gastronomic magazines in France and the United
States, including the influential journals *Cuisine et Vins de
France* and *La Revue du Vin de France.* He has directed
cooking courses in France and the United States and is a
member of several distinguished gastronomic and oenologi-
cal societies, including *L'Académie Internationale du Vin, La
Confrérie des Chevaliers du Tastevin* and *La Commanderie
du Bontemps de Médoc et des Graves.*

THE PHOTOGRAPHERS:
Tom Belshaw was born near London and started his working career in films. He now has
his own studio in London. He specializes in food and still-life photography, undertaking
both editorial and advertising assignments.
Alan Duns was born in 1943 in the north of England and studied at the Ealing School of
Photography. He has undertaken many advertising assignments, but specializes in
food photography. His work has appeared in major British publications.

THE INTERNATIONAL CONSULTANTS:
Great Britain: *Jane Grigson* was born in Gloucester and brought up in the north of
England. She is a graduate of Cambridge University. Her first book on food, *Charcu-
terie and French Pork Cookery,* was published in 1967; since then, she has published a
number of cookery books, including *Good Things, English Food* and *Jane Grigson's
Vegetable Book.* She became cookery correspondent for the colour magazine of the
London *Observer* in 1968. *Alan Davidson* is the author of *Fish and Fish Dishes of Laos,
Mediterranean Seafood* and *North Atlantic Seafood.* He is the founder of Prospect
Books, which specializes in scholarly publications on food and cookery. *Pat Alburey* is a
Member of the Association of Home Economists of Great Britain. Her wide experience
includes preparing foods for photography, teaching cookery and creating recipes. She
has been responsible for many of the step-by-step photographic sequences in this
volume. *Jean Reynolds,* who also prepared many of the breads in this volume, is an
American from San Francisco. She trained as a cook in the kitchens of several of
France's great restaurants. **France:** *Michel Lemonnier* was born in Normandy. He
began contributing to the magazine *Cuisine et Vins de France* in 1960, and also writes
for several other important French food and wine periodicals. The co-founder and vice-
president of the society *Les Amitiés Gastronomiques Internationales,* he is a frequent
lecturer on wine and academies, and a member of most of the vinicultural confraterni-
ties in France. **Germany:** *Jochen Kuchenbecker* trained as a chef, but worked for 10
years as a food photographer in many European countries before opening his own
restaurant in Hamburg. *Anne Brakemeier,* who also lives in Hamburg, has published
articles on food and cooking in many German periodicals. She is the co-author of three
cookery books. **Italy:** *Massimo Alberini* divides his time between Milan and Venice. He
is a well-known food writer and journalist, with a particular interest in culinary history.
Among his 14 books are *Storia del Pranzo all'Italiana, 4000 Anni a Tavola* and *100
Ricette Storiche.* **The Netherlands:** *Hugh Jans,* a resident of Amsterdam, has been
translating cookery books and articles for more than 25 years. He has also published
several books of his own, including *Bistro Koken* and *Sla, Slaatjes, Snacks,* and his
recipes are published in many Dutch magazines. **The United States:** *Carol Cutler,* who
lives in Washington, DC, is the author of three cookery books, including the award-
winning *The Six-Minute Soufflé and Other Culinary Delights.* Julie Dannenbaum has
directed a cooking school in Philadelphia, Pa., for many years and is the author of two
cookery books and numerous magazine articles. *Judith Olney* received her culinary
training in England and France and has written two cookery books. *Robert Shoffner* has
been wine and food editor of the *Washingtonian* magazine since 1975.

Valuable help was given in the preparation of this volume by the following members of
Time-Life Books: *Maria Vincenza Aloisi, Joséphine du Brusle* (Paris); *Janny Hovinga,*
(Amsterdam); *Elisabeth Kraemer* (Bonn); *Ann Natanson* (Rome); *Bona Schmid*
(Milan).

CONTENTS

INTRODUCTION 5 — The symbol of sustenance/
A range of flours and meals
for bread-making/A wheat
grain revealed/A guide
to yeast leavens

BASIC YEAST BREADS 13

1

Diverse results from simple techniques/The fundamental loaf/
Variations on the round/Moulding an even cylinder/Stretching dough/
Plaiting a loaf/Flattening dough to unusual effect/Rolls: quickly
shaped and baked/Cigars: tapering neatly/Baking in moulds and tins/
Rolls moulded in a cluster/Crumpets/Intricate shapes cooked by steam

FLAVOURED AND FILLED BREADS 45

2

Elaborations simple and substantial/
Moist toppings for thin breads/Enclosing ample
fillings/Vegetables for flavour and colour/
An amalgam of elements in a rich, dark loaf/
A fruit and nut bun in a plain wrapper

RICH BREADS 57

3

Special effects from butter and eggs/A simple egg and butter ring/
An elaborate construction from a firm mixture/Brioche: replete with
butter and eggs/Wrapping a sausage in brioche dough/Layering for
a marbled crumb/Flaky pastry interleaved with butter/Individual pastries/
Large yeast puff shapes/Bagels: poached, then baked

BREADS WITHOUT YEAST 81

4

Alternative ways to leaven batters and doughs/
Puffing up an unleavened dough/Spoonbread: gently
raised with egg whites/Doughs leavened with soda/
Batters: airy or substantial/Puréed fruit for a
cake-like crumb/A marbled finish for cornmeal

ANTHOLOGY OF RECIPES 93 — Basic breads 94/Flavoured and
filled breads 107/Egg breads
128/Yeast puff pastry 150/
Breads without yeast 155/
Standard preparations 170

RECIPE INDEX 174

GENERAL INDEX AND GLOSSARY 178

RECIPE CREDITS 181

ACKNOWLEDGEMENTS AND PICTURE CREDITS 184

The Symbol of Sustenance

Think of eating and you think of bread: the heady aroma of a loaf fresh from the oven, the crispness of its golden crust, the lightness of its crumb. No meal is really complete without bread to accompany it; a few vegetables, some cheese, meat or broth need only bread to make a meal. Bread's elemental importance was summed up by the 18th-century French agronomist Antoine-Auguste Parmentier: "Bread is a generous gift of nature, a food that can be replaced by no other. . . . It is suitable to every time of day, every age of life, and every temperament. . . . It is so perfectly adapted to men that we turn our hearts to it almost as soon as we are born and never tire of it to the hour of our death."

Not the least of bread's pleasures is its variety. Bread as most people know it is a dough of wheat flour and water, seasoned with a little salt, leavened—raised—by the action of yeast, then baked in an oven. Yet each element and stage in the basics of bread-making is open to exciting alteration. The bread can be made of rye flour, barley flour or cornmeal instead of wheat. It can be spiced or sweetened, flavoured or filled, enriched with butter or eggs. It may be unleavened and pancake-flat, or it can be lightened by beaten egg whites or baking soda instead of yeast. It can be fried on a griddle or cooked by steam.

This volume is a guide to the preparation of bread in all its forms. The book begins by explaining the fundamentals—the various flours and meals (*page 8*) used to make bread, and the yeast leavens (*page 10*) that figure in many bread recipes. These introductory pages are followed by four chapters of practical demonstrations on every aspect of bread-making. The first chapter shows, from start to finish, how to make a simple, yeast-leavened loaf of wheat flour (*pages 14-17*) and how to shape dough into all kinds of loaves and rolls. Chapter 2 describes how to elaborate basic bread dough with flavourings and fillings. The third chapter deals with the realm of cake-like breads enriched with eggs and butter—including moist, tender brioche (*pages 62-65*) and light, yeast puff pastries (*pages 70-77*). The demonstrations conclude with a chapter devoted to breads made without yeast. With the guidance of the lessons in the first half of the book, you will have the confidence and skill to prepare any of the 204 recipes that comprise the Anthology on pages 94-173.

The evolution of bread and baking

Bread has served as a mainstay of the human diet for nearly 8,000 years. Wheat and barley were first cultivated by Stone Age men in the "fertile crescent"—the land curving from the western part of present-day Iran through Iraq and Syria to the Valley of the Nile. These primitive farmers probably cooked porridges of coarsely ground grain on top of large, flat stones that had been heated over an open fire, to make the first crude flatbreads.

Early in bread's evolution came two important discoveries. One was the oven. Only thin breads can be cooked on an open surface. Large breads of any substantial thickness require all-round heat to cook evenly. As early as the Bronze Age, some 5,000 years ago, simple ovens were contrived by inverting pots over heated stones to trap the rising heat. Present-day campers still use the same method to bake bread over outdoor fires.

The other major discovery was yeast fermentation. Early cooks found that an uncooked grain porridge left in the open for a few hours would develop bubbles and give off a sour smell. If the porridge was thin, this process produced a pleasantly tangy and intoxicating drink—beer. If the mixture was thicker and cooked after its fermentation, the bread was lighter and had a more palatable texture than bread made from fresh dough.

The cause of the fermentation, unknown to primitive man, was the yeast that is present in the air. Yeast exists in various strains, not all of which produce successful fermentation, and early bread-making was a hit-or-miss affair. The Egyptians eliminated much of the chance from bread-making more than 4,500 years ago. They discovered that if, before baking, a small piece was reserved from dough that had fermented favourably, the sample could be added to new, freshly mixed dough to start its fermentation, and good results could be achieved again and again. Some present-day cooks use the same principle to make their own yeast cultures, known as sourdough starters (*page 11*), as alternatives to commercial yeast.

The Egyptians left detailed hieroglyphic and pictorial records of their sophisticated baking techniques. Their pictures tell us that they had more than 50 different kinds of bread: loaves of different shapes, flavoured with poppy or sesame seeds or bitter, aromatic camphor, breads sweetened with honey or enriched with milk or eggs. Besides experimenting with ingredients, the Egyptians developed the first purpose-built ovens. These clay structures, shaped like beehives or barrels, had two compartments. The lower compartment was for the fire, whose heat, contained and absorbed by the oven walls, gradually rose to a high, steady level. The loaves were then placed in the upper chamber and the chamber was closed to let the bread bake.

Breads cooked in such an oven were much better than those baked by more makeshift methods. The intense, radiant heat of the thick clay walls produced an almost instantaneous surge in the dough, stepping up the activity of the yeast cells and converting much of the moisture in the dough into steam. As a result, the loaves expanded greatly. The steam also produced a humid atmosphere, which delayed the formation of a crust and thereby allowed the loaves to swell even more. Finally, as the bread went on baking, the air in the oven dried out, and a perfectly crisp, brown crust formed just as the crumb cooked through.

The Egyptians were the great bread-makers of the ancient world; they were known as "bread eaters". But the Greeks also ate bread, and extant fragments from works by the playwrights Antiphanes and Aristophanes, who lived in the 4th century B.C., specifically mention Attic breads and baking. But Greek loaves were less elaborate than Egyptian bread.

The Romans not only ate bread but made further advances in bread-making. They perfected the first large-scale mills for turning grain into fine bread flour. These mills—examples of which were found in the ruins of Pompeii—consisted of two large stones, shaped like shallow cones. One stone, its apex uppermost, was stationary; around it, slaves—or a team of horses or mules—turned the other, downward-pointing stone; and between the two stones the grain was trickled and ground. The flour could then be sifted through closely woven baskets to produce a finer texture. The Romans also invented a machine to mix and knead dough. An ox or a slave walked around a large stone bowl, turning wooden paddles that did all the work.

Such mechanization helped turn milling and baking into full-time professions. By the end of the 2nd century A.D., specialists in these fields had been organized by the Roman government into guilds or "colleges", the main purpose of which was to ensure that the number of people practising the trades did not dwindle; eventually, milling and baking became hereditary obligations.

With little alteration, Roman milling and baking techniques were used throughout Europe until the 19th century. Village bakers used large ovens, usually tunnel-shaped and made of brick. A brick oven was heated by building a fire directly on its floor. When the fire died down, its embers were swept out and the loaves were placed on the floor to bake. Few homes had ovens: any domestic baking was done at the hearth, in covered iron pots or on griddles. Some villages maintained communal ovens that were

used once a week for baking breads. Or professional bakers offered oven space for home-prepared loaves—for a small fee.

Brown bread versus white bread

Until the 19th century, most bread was coarse, dark and heavy. Light, fine, white loaves require the whitest of flours. These flours are obtained from the starchy endosperm of the wheat grain, freed of the husk or "bran" and the embryo or "germ" (the anatomy and properties of wheat and other grains are explained on page 8). Wheat was once relatively scarce, and most people relied on darker flours—rye or barley, for example—for their daily bread. As agriculture became more sophisticated, wheat-grow-

ing increased, but the grinding method—essentially the same as that used in Roman times—made it difficult to achieve a pure endosperm flour. The stones crushed the whole grain, and although the flour could be sifted through a series of progressively finer cloths—a laborious and costly process called "bolting"—small particles of bran and most of the pale yellow germ remained. To achieve a semblance of snowy purity, flours were sometimes adulterated with white, powdery alum or chalk.

In the 1830s, however, Swiss millers revolutionized the production of white flour with roller milling, the process still used today. Wheat grains are first cleaned and then passed through a series of high-speed rollers. The first set crack open the grains, causing the endosperm—broken into coarse granules, known as semolina—to separate from the bran and the germ. Progressively finer rolling and bolting ultimately result in a white flour that is virtually pure endosperm. Finally, to make it even whiter, the flour is bleached, usually with chlorine gas.

While roller milling has made white bread commonplace, it has also produced controversy about both taste and nutrition, and engendered a new awareness of brown bread's virtues. Any bread that contains some bran and germ, or other flours or meals, certainly has more flavour than pure white bread. But a more important issue is the question of health and nutrition.

Purists claim that the processing of white flour takes away much of its nutritional value. In fact, brown bread is not markedly more nutritious than white bread. The real advantage of wholemeal breads is that they can easily supplement diets that are deficient in the B vitamins that are essential to the body's efficient use of carbohydrates for energy. The endosperm of wheat does contain a small amount of vitamin B2, and the vitamin content of commercial wheat flour is always boosted in the factory. But the wheat's germ and, to a lesser degree, its bran, have a higher concentration of the B vitamins. And the bran provides dietary fibre—roughage. But, in the end, your choice of white or brown bread is simply a question of taste.

The advantages of baking at home

Because most bread is produced commercially, a mystique has developed around bread-making: kneading, people fear, is too strenuous, the working of yeast too capricious, the resulting loaves or rolls not as conveniently uniform as store-bought bread. These fears will disappear with the first bread you make. As the 19th-century cookery writer Eliza Acton remarked somewhat tetchily in *The English Bread Book*: "A very exaggerated idea of the difficulty and trouble of breadmaking prevails amongst people who are entirely ignorant of the process."

The advantages of baking bread at home are numerous. You can mix your dough with whatever combinations of flours, meals, flavourings, enrichments and leavens you desire. You can shape the dough as you like. And the bread-making process is sufficiently flexible for the schedule of even the busiest of home bakers. Mix and knead a bread dough in the evening, for example, then let it rise and shape it into rolls. Leave the rolls in the refrigerator to rise again overnight (cold slows down the action of the yeast). The next morning, bake the rolls and enjoy your own fresh bread for breakfast.

You need very little equipment to prepare most breads. Baking sheets are necessary to hold free-form loaves that have been shaped by hand. Moulds and tins contain doughs and shape them while they bake—and they make it possible to fit more bread in the oven for baking at one time.

By working with your oven, you will become familiar with its specific qualities and learn how you can best use it for baking bread. You may, for example, find that you must re-position loaves during baking to ensure even rising: because heat rises, most ovens are hotter at the top than at the bottom, unless there is a fan to keep the heat in constant circulation; the back of an oven, farthest from the door, may be warmer than its front.

Any home oven can be modified to simulate the ideal conditions of an old-fashioned, professional baker's brick oven. To

achieve the even, radiant heat of brick, you can line your oven's shelves with clean, unglazed quarry tiles; once the oven has been preheated for baking, shaped bread dough can be slid directly on to the hot tiles. The direct contact with the heat will stimulate the dough to increase in volume before its crust forms, producing a lighter crumb. To delay crust formation further, for an even fuller and lighter loaf, you can place a pan of hot water on the floor of the oven or on its lowest shelf; to supplement the humid atmosphere that results, you can spray in fresh water from a plant sprayer as soon as the dough is put in.

Serving and storing bread
Appealing as the aroma of hot, freshly baked bread may be, it is generally better to leave loaves of bread to cool for several hours or overnight before you eat them. The wait is necessary to let the bread's flavour mature and to allow the crumb to firm up so that the bread can be sliced without tearing or crumbling. There are, of course, exceptions: topped or filled breads such as an onion and anchovy *pissaladiera* (*page 46*) or a sausage wrapped in rich brioche dough (*page 66*) are meant to be eaten warm; a spoon-bread leavened with beaten egg whites (*page 84*) would fall flat were it not served straight from the oven; and small bread rolls would simply dry out if they were not served soon after baking.

Cooling should be done on a wire rack (loaves baked in tins should, of course, be unmoulded first). The rack will ensure a full circulation of air round the bread, so that any steam given off will not collect, condense and spoil the crispness of the crust.

If bread is to be kept more than 24 hours, put it in a dry, well-ventilated metal or earthenware bread bin. The length of time bread will stay fresh is determined by its size and ingredients: large, thick loaves give up moisture more slowly than small thin breads; breads rich with egg and butter—which retain moisture—keep longer than plain breads. Kept in a bin, a 1 kg (2 lb) plain loaf will stay in good condition for at least a week, and an enriched loaf of the same size will keep a few days more. Wash out and dry your bin once a week to prevent the growth of mould.

Bread freezes well if wrapped tightly in a double thickness of plastic film or aluminium foil. Frozen bread will keep for several months. Before you serve the bread, unwrap it and allow it to thaw for 3 to 6 hours; or heat it, wrapped in foil, for 45 minutes in a 200°C (400°F or Mark 6) oven.

Bread transformed
In time, any bread stales. In its early stages, staling is caused by the bread's starch undergoing a chemical change and becoming firmer; eventually, the bread loses moisture. To revive partly staled bread that is still fairly moist, heat it in a 230°C (450°F or Mark 8) oven: 5 minutes for rolls, 10 minutes for a loaf.

A partly stale loaf is ideal for making toast and the origins of toast—though unrecorded—must surely lie in attempts to make stale bread edible. Today, of course, toast is made for its own sake and everyone has his own preference. Modern grills can prepare toast to meet almost any requirements, although some people may still prefer to spear their bread on a toasting fork and brown it before an open fire. In any event, the aims of toasting are two-fold: as the bread browns, the flavour of the grain is intensified and the texture of the bread becomes crisper. Bread quickly toasted at a high temperature will be browned and crisp on the outside, but still soft within; longer, more gentle toasting will give more evenly crisp results.

Toast is by no means the only transformation already-baked bread can undergo. Bread that is three to four days old, firm and slightly dry, is an invaluable source of garnishes. Cut into small cubes and gently fried in butter or oil until crisp, the bread becomes croûtons, to be scattered over salads, soups, scrambled eggs or stews. Stale bread can also be turned into breadcrumbs—grated, crusts and all, by hand or in an electric blender or a processor. Use breadcrumbs in stuffing mixtures, to coat foods for frying, or as a crisp topping for baked casseroles.

Aside from being an adjunct to other ingredients, bread can become a featured element. Many countries have traditional soups based on rough, peasant bread, moistened with stock or boiling water. Baked savoury casseroles are easily improvised around slices of stale bread, layered with a sauce, scraps of left-over meat and some shredded or grated cheese. And desserts of great diversity are based on bread. Almost every Western cuisine offers some version of the sweet known in England as Poor Knights of Windsor, in America as French toast and in France as *pain perdu*, "lost bread". Slices of stale bread are soaked in beaten egg and milk, then fried in butter and sprinkled with sugar and spices—cinnamon is especially good—or served with a dollop of jam. And the homeliest bread dessert of all is probably the basic "bread pudding", made by baking slices or torn pieces of bread with milk, butter, sugar, eggs and a hint of nutmeg.

These multiple culinary uses are really only a bonus. The bread you bake for yourself, from ingredients you have chosen and prepared exactly to your taste, is an entirely worthy end in itself—as much so as any food humankind has ever dreamed up. Elizabeth David, an authority on bread-making, states the case with perfect simplicity when she says that good bread is equally at home "in the background, in the foreground, in the hand of the diner, on the plate, on the table."

A Range of Flours and Meals for Bread-Making

The fine flours and coarser meals shown here are the raw materials of bread. Any of them can be used alone in a loaf; each may also be mixed with another flour or meal for variety in flavour and texture.

All flours and meals are ground from seeds: wheat, rye, barley, corn (maize) and oats come from cereal plants; buckwheat seeds come from a relative of rhubarb. According to type, the seeds differ in size and shape, but all have the same basic anatomy as the wheat grain illustrated in the box below. The grain is covered by a protective husk; inside are the plant's embryo—the "germ"—and the starchy endosperm, food for the infant plant.

Until just over a century ago, all grains were ground between heavy millstones.

Today, most flours and meals are milled with high-speed metal rollers. Unlike millstones, which grind the whole grain, rollers extract the husk and germ, which can be returned to the flour or meal in varying proportions.

Wheat is the source of most bread flour—with good reason. It is especially rich in the complex proteins that, when wetted, form the elastic substance known as gluten. When dough is kneaded, the gluten develops into a web, which traps the gas produced by yeast fermentation. During baking, the gluten sets, producing firm, well-aerated bread.

White flour is made from the endosperm, which has all the gluten-forming proteins, and produces a full-volumed loaf. There are many commercial varieties of white flour: strong or soft, plain or self-raising, unbleached or bleached.

For bread-making, strong plain flour, sometimes labelled "bread flour", is best. Strong flour is milled largely from so-called "hard" wheats—varieties with a high gluten potential. Soft plain flour, made from low-gluten wheat, produces a more tender texture than strong flour. Soft flour absorbs less water than strong flour, and breads made from it stale more quickly. Self-raising flour is a soft flour that contains baking powder (*Chapter 4*), a chemical leaven. White flours naturally turn whiter, or bleach, with age but may be bleached during manufacture.

Wholemeal flours (also called whole wheat) contain all of the grain, not just the endosperm, and are therefore darker.

A Wheat Grain Revealed

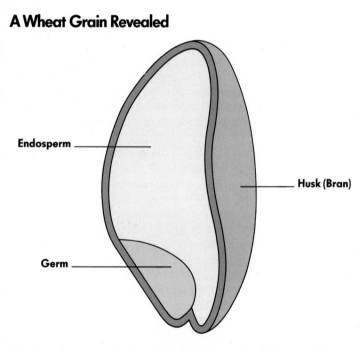

Endosperm

Husk (Bran)

Germ

Ovoid in shape, a wheat grain is about 6 mm (¼ inch) long and 3 mm (⅛ inch) wide. Its outer coating—or husk—is made up of four layers of cellulose, collectively known as bran. At the stem end of the grain is the oil-rich germ, the embryo of the future plant; it has a nut-like flavour and is a concentrated source of protein, iron and vitamins B and E. The bulk of the grain—over 80 per cent of its weight—is the endosperm, the germ's food source. It contains about 67 per cent starch and 10 per cent gluten-forming proteins; the remainder is made up of water and minerals.

Plain wheat flour

Wholemeal flour

Bread made from them has a nut-like flavour and contains vitamins and oils from the germ and dietary fibre from the husk. But the germ and husk lower the gluten potential, so that wholemeal breads are heavier than white breads.

Many excellent wheat flours lie between the extremes of wholemeal and white. Wheatmeal flours, for example, contain some husk and germ, and make a relatively light brown loaf.

Rye flour contains gum-like substances that inhibit gluten development, and bread made solely from rye flour is very dense. Dark rye flour contains some or all of the husk and germ, and has a strong savour. Light rye flour, mostly endosperm, is milder and paler. Bread made from either rye flour often includes wheat flour, for lightness. A little rye flour may be added to a white wheat flour dough, giving extra flavour without making the dough significantly heavier.

Barley flour, largely endosperm, is deficient in gluten-forming proteins, and makes a flat, greyish loaf that stales quickly. Its merit is the good, earthy flavour it can give to wheat breads.

Cornmeal, ground from dried, whole grains, is slightly sweet. Because cornmeal entirely lacks any gluten proteins, breads made from it are raised by egg white, which supplies its own air bubbles to lighten the dough, or by bicarbonate of soda or baking powder, which both leaven rapidly by the pressure of carbon dioxide gas. To be leavened by yeast, cornmeal breads must include a large proportion of wheat flour, so as to supply the gluten.

Oatmeal, made from husked grains, also lacks gluten. It is used chiefly to flavour other doughs and to give bread a coarse, crunchy texture.

Buckwheat flour is slightly bitter. The sample shown was milled from whole grain, but lighter buckwheat flours are made without husk. Although it too lacks gluten, buckwheat flour makes an interesting addition to white wheat dough.

The keeping qualities of a flour or meal depend on how much germ it includes: the oils in the germ eventually turn rancid. White wheat flour and light rye flour keep for at least a year in a cool, dry, well-ventilated place. Flours and all meals that contain germ keep for two to three months in similar conditions but away from light, which speeds oil's spoilage.

Dark rye flour

Cornmeal

Oatmeal

Light rye flour

Barley flour

Buckwheat flour

A Guide to Yeast Leavens

Leavens raise dough by releasing gas that causes it to swell. Yeast is the most widely used leaven in bread-making (non-yeast leavens are discussed in Chapter 4). An organism present in the air, yeast thrives in contact with moist, sweet or starchy food, such as sugar, potatoes or flour. As a by-product of its growth, yeast slowly releases carbon dioxide gas. Gas trapped in a dough's network of gluten stretches the gluten fibres and raises the bread. The gradual action of the yeast allows the dough's flavour to mature and its texture to develop evenly.

Most of the yeast used today is cultivated commercially and sold as fresh yeast compressed into blocks or as dried yeast granules. Fresh yeast should feel cold and be smooth, compact and creamy-fawn in colour. If dark or crumbling, it may not be capable of leavening a dough. Fresh yeast does not keep well. Small blocks can be stored for up to three weeks, wrapped in plastic film and refrigerated.

Dried yeast is more concentrated than fresh yeast; by weight, it has at least twice the potency. Dried yeast will keep in a cool, dry place for up to six months.

To prepare fresh yeast and most dried yeasts for use, mix them with tepid water (*boxes, below*). Gentle warmth stimulates the yeast; too much heat slows it down and temperatures that are above 43°C (110°F) kill it. A new variety of dried yeast—called by its patent name "fermipan"—is composed of fine particles that can be mixed directly with flour.

Temperature also affects the rate at which a yeast dough rises. The process is fastest in a warm room, where it takes about 2 hours. However, dough that is allowed to rise more slowly will produce bread with a better flavour and texture; whenever possible, leave the dough for 4 to 5 hours in a cool place or even overnight in a refrigerator. If it is more convenient, you can also slow the rising by using half as much yeast as a recipe requires.

Commercial yeasts are convenient, but you can cultivate your own by providing a medium in which wild yeast can feed and grow. Such cultures, known as sourdough starters because of their tart flavour and aroma, give bread a pleasant, acid tang. You can substitute sourdough starter for commercial yeast in the proportion of one part by weight for every four parts of flour. Sourdough starters are useful for leavening rye breads; their acid breaks down the gums that inhibit gluten development in rye flour.

A starter culture is made by combining a starchy ingredient, such as flour or potatoes, with water and, perhaps, sugar (*recipes, page 170*). It is wisest to mix in some commercial yeast to ensure a good culture (*opposite page, above*). Wild yeasts can be cultivated on their own (*opposite page, below*) but are more temperamental.

Sourdough starters can last indefinitely if replenished with flour and water after each use. If a starter is not used at least once a week, stir it every three to four weeks to redistribute the ingredients evenly; discard half of the starter and add an equivalent amount of flour and water to give the yeast more food.

Moistening Fresh Yeast

Mashing the yeast. Pour a little tepid water into a small bowl and add the fresh yeast. With a fork, mash the yeast with the water (*above*) until they form a smooth, thoroughly blended paste.

Reconstituting Dried Yeast

1 **Moistening the yeast.** Put tepid water into a bowl. Sprinkle the required amount of dried yeast granules into the water (*above*). To allow the yeast to absorb water, leave it for 15 to 20 minutes.

2 **Whisking the yeast.** Immediately before using the yeast, whisk it vigorously until it forms a smooth, thin cream that will combine evenly when added to the other bread dough ingredients.

A Simple Sourdough Starter

1 **Mixing flour and yeast.** In a large bowl, mix fresh or dried yeast with tepid water (*boxes, opposite page*). Whisk in enough flour—here, strong plain flour—to form a thick, pourable mixture. The mixture need not be absolutely smooth: any lumps will be broken down by the yeast's action.

2 **Fermenting the mixture.** Cover the bowl tightly with plastic film (*above*). Leave the mixture undisturbed to ferment at room temperature. It will be ready to use after 24 hours, but the sourdough flavour will need about three days to develop fully.

3 **Using the leaven.** To leaven bread, ladle the starter into the other ingredients. To replenish the remaining leaven, whisk in equal parts of flour and water. Cover the bowl and leave the mixture to ferment again at room temperature for a day, until it is risen and bubbly (*above*). If you do not use the starter regularly, keep it in the refrigerator, covered with plastic film.

A Natural Sourdough Starter

1 **Mixing the ingredients.** Boil potatoes, drain them and peel them, reserving the cooking liquid. Mash the potatoes. In a large bowl, put flour—here, rye flour—sugar, the mashed potatoes and the reserved liquid. Stir the ingredients together to make a thick batter.

2 **Fermenting the leaven.** Cover the bowl tightly with plastic film (*above*). To ensure a constant temperature and to protect the culture from draughts, wrap the bowl in a thick towel. Set it in a warm place to ferment for at least three days.

3 **Replenishing the starter.** The leaven is ready when it is bubbly and smells strong and sour when unwrapped. Before use, stir the starter then ladle it into the other ingredients. Replenish the starter with equal parts of flour and water. Leave it to ferment for a day before use.

1
Basic Yeast Breads
Diverse Results from Simple Techniques

Mixing and kneading dough

Scoring for more crust

Shaping plain and fancy loaves

Adding light enrichments

Soft or crusty flatbreads

Five forms for rolls

Pretzels and breadsticks

Cooking on a griddle

Improvising a steamer

"All that bread wants is time and warmth", goes an old English saying. The preparation of a yeast-leavened loaf does indeed depend upon these two factors. With time, gluten develops and the yeast raises the dough; with warmth, yeast thrives. Yet every stage of bread-making, from mixing the dough to cooking it, can be adapted to your taste and timetable.

The basic ingredients of a yeast-leavened bread are flour, yeast, water and salt; the flours (*page 8*) and yeast leavens (*page 10*) that you select will affect flavour and texture. The ingredients are mixed into a dough, which is kneaded to develop the gluten that will support the risen loaf. A good method of kneading is shown on page 15, but the only real requirement is that the dough be stretched repeatedly until it is smooth and elastic. If you like, you can use an electric mixer fitted with a dough hook.

The kneaded dough must be allowed to rise. The number of risings you give the dough will depend on the flour you have used. Doughs made from wholemeal flour are inhibited in their rising by particles of husk. The doughs are sometimes shaped into loaves or moulded as soon as they are mixed and they are left to rise just once before baking. Other doughs benefit in flavour and texture from second—and even third—risings, and should not be shaped until after the dough has risen at least once.

Whatever the dough and however many risings you give it, the process can be arranged to suit your schedule. Left at room temperature (18° to 20°C or 65° to 70°F), dough usually doubles in bulk in 1½ to 2 hours. If you are in a hurry, you can leave it in a warmer place, at up to 29°C (85°F), to hasten rising, although the results will not be as good as those from slower rising. Leaving the dough in a cool place for several hours or refrigerating it overnight will give bread a finer texture and flavour.

The choices are even wider when it comes to shaping the dough. You can form large rounds (*page 18*) or small rolls and sticks (*pages 30-35*), stretch the dough into long loaves (*page 24*), flatten it (*page 28*), divide it into strands and plait it (*page 26*), or—for neat contours—put the dough in a mould and let it shape itself (*pages 36-39*).

Shaped and risen, a dough is ready to be cooked. Yeast-leavened bread is usually baked, of course. But even in cooking, there are alternatives. You can steam bread dough (*page 42*), and a yeast-leavened batter may be cooked on a griddle to make pancake-like crumpets (*page 40*).

A moulded loaf of small rounds of bread (*page 38*) is torn apart into individual rolls. A yeast-leavened dough—lightly enriched with butter and milk—was first formed into balls (*page 30*). The balls were placed in a round baking tin, in which they were left to rise and join together. They were then glazed with egg, sprinkled with poppy seeds and baked.

The Fundamental Loaf from Start to Finish

Bread-making requires more patience than hard labour. It takes about 4½ hours to produce a basic, yeast-leavened loaf, but for most of this time the dough is set to one side to allow the yeast to act and the gluten to develop.

Bread is most often made from a simple mixture of flour, yeast, a moistening agent and usually a seasoning. The most readily available and commonly used ingredients are plain white wheat flour, commercial yeast, water and salt, as in this demonstration (*recipe, page 171*). For more flavour and a better texture, you may vary this mixture by adding other flours (*box, page 17*) and a sourdough leaven (*page 10*), but the basic steps of preparation remain unchanged.

The ingredients are mixed together into a shaggy-textured dough, which is kneaded (*Step 4*) to form a network of gluten—the substance that gives dough its elasticity (*page 8*). When the dough is supple and smooth, it is covered and set aside to "prove": the yeast produces bubbles of carbon dioxide gas which gently stretch the gluten, raising the dough.

If baked after this first rising, the bread would have a loose, cottony texture and be full of large holes. To redistribute the yeast cells and to expel large gas bubbles, for a finer, more even crumb, the dough is next kneaded into a round (*Step 7*). After a short rest to relax the gluten, the dough can be handled further without tearing and moulded into its final shape.

To give lightness to the finished bread and to mature its flavour, the shaped loaf must then be left to rise briefly once more before it is baked. At any time during this final rising, the surface may be slashed or scored (*Step 9, overleaf*). The slashes enhance and increase the area of the crust; the earlier the slashes are made, the more they will open as the loaf rises.

When the loaf is placed in a preheated oven, it expands even more during the first 20 minutes or so, until the yeast dies and the crust forms. To delay the crust's formation and thereby promote the loaf's expansion, make the oven humid during this critical period. Place a wide dish of hot water on the floor of the oven while it preheats and, when the loaf goes into the oven, spray in fresh water.

1 Combining the ingredients. Place the flour—in this case, white wheat flour—in a mixing bowl and put the bowl in an oven at its lowest setting for 3 to 5 minutes; warming the flour will help the dough to rise. Add fine salt to the flour. Mix yeast in a little tepid water (*page 10*) and pour it with the remaining water into the centre of the bowl (*above*).

2 Mixing the dough. With one hand, hold the bowl steady. With the other, mix the flour and liquid together, scooping and turning them until they are thoroughly combined, forming a shaggy mass.

5 Leaving the dough to rise. Replace the dough in the mixing bowl. To keep the dough moist, cover the bowl with plastic film. Set aside in a warm place, until the dough has doubled in bulk—from 1½ to 2½ hours. To test that the dough has risen enough, press a finger into it: if the indentation remains, filling in only very slowly, the dough is ready.

6 Dividing the dough. Turn the risen dough out on to the work surface. If, as here, you have made enough for two loaves, use a knife to divide the dough in half. Cover one portion of dough with a damp cloth or plastic film to keep it from drying, and set it aside while you work with the other.

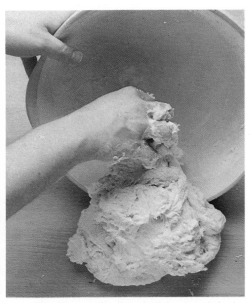

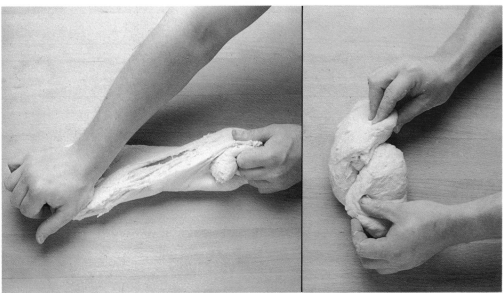

3 **Tipping out the dough.** If the dough feels very dry and stiff, mix in a little more water; if it is too loose and wet, work in some more flour. Empty the dough from the bowl on to the work surface. Wash out and dry the mixing bowl.

4 **Kneading the dough.** Hold the dough with one hand. With the heel of the other hand, push the dough away from you until it begins to tear (*above, left*). At first, the dough will be sticky and will tear very easily. Fold the dough back and at the same time give the mass of dough a slight turn (*above, right*). Continue to push, fold and turn the dough with a regular, rhythmic motion for 10 to 15 minutes. To develop the gluten further, occasionally lift up the dough and throw it down on to the work surface. The dough is ready when it is no longer sticky, is easy to stretch and feels smooth.

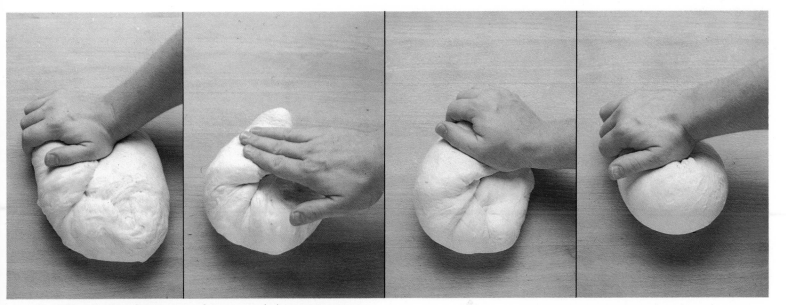

7 **Kneading the dough into a round.** Exerting a light, even pressure with the heel of your hand, push away a corner of dough; at the same time, give the corner a slight anti-clockwise twist (*far left*) to turn the whole mass of dough slightly. Fold the pushed-out piece of dough back into the middle (*centre, left*) and begin the process again with the adjacent section (*centre, right*). Repeat the process with a regular, rhythmic motion until the loaf is rounded (*far right*). Turn over the dough so that its pleats are on the bottom. Cover the round and repeat the process with the other piece of dough. ▶

8 **Leaving the dough to rise a final time.** Cover and rest the loaves for 10 to 15 minutes. Repeat the rhythmic kneading motion (*Step 7*) to mould the loaves into neat rounds. Place them on boards sprinkled with semolina; cover with a cloth and leave to rise for about 50 minutes. Set the oven to 230°C (450°F or Mark 8); to produce a steamy atmosphere, place a wide dish at the bottom of the oven and fill with hot water. Place a baking sheet in the oven.

9 **Slashing the loaves.** Test with your finger to see if the loaves are fully risen. With a razor blade, make a long, shallow slash across the top of one loaf; at right angles to the first, make two additional slashes from the edge to the centre. For variety, give the other loaf extra crust by slashing it more deeply (*above, right*). With a sharp, pushing movement, slide each loaf from its board on to the baking sheet. Spray fresh water into the oven from a plant sprayer.

10 **Baking the loaves.** After 20 minutes, remove the dish of water. After a further 15 minutes, if the loaves are browning too quickly, lower the heat to 200°C (400°F or Mark 6). When the loaves have baked for about 45 minutes, test for doneness: rap the bottom of each loaf with your knuckle. The loaf should sound hollow; if not, bake 10 minutes more and test again. Put the loaves on a wire rack to cool.

A Rustic Sourdough Loaf

1 **Mixing the dough.** Put white flour and salt in a mixing bowl and add a couple of handfuls of wholemeal flour and rye flour. Warm the bowl for a few minutes in an oven at its lowest setting. Ladle sourdough leaven (*page 11*) into the flour mixture (*above*). Adding enough tepid water to hold the dough together, combine and knead the dough as shown on the preceding pages, and leave it to rise.

2 **Slicing the finished loaf.** Knead the dough into a round and let it rest; mould it, leave it to rise and slash it. Bake for 45 minutes to 1 hour in an oven preheated to 230°C (450°F or Mark 8), lowering the temperature if necessary to control the loaf's browning. Transfer the bread to a rack; when it has cooled thoroughly, slice the loaf with a sharp knife.

11 **Slicing the bread.** Leave the bread to cool for several hours or overnight before serving. Use a very sharp knife to cut the loaves into thick or thin slices, whichever you prefer. □

Variations on the Round

A simple moulded round of dough (*page 14*) is the starting point for a range of different-looking loaves. It is easy to create variety: round loaves may be scored in different patterns or they can be stacked one on top of the other. Scoring and stacking both increase the amount of crust, which many consider the best part of any loaf. Scoring also produces a soft, pale crust within the cuts, which contrasts nicely with the crisp, brown exterior. In the demonstration here, these strategies for variation are seen in two traditional forms—a double-tiered cottage loaf and a simple chequerboard.

The cottage loaf on the right is made by stacking unequal-sized rounds of dough: the upper piece, or topknot, is about half the size of the base. To ensure that the two rounds are joined evenly and securely, the dough has to be shaped carefully; otherwise, the rounds may come apart in the oven or the baked loaf might be very lopsided. First, each round is deeply indented by pushing firmly down into its centre. This process is aptly known as "bashing" and forms the rounds into slightly flattened rings. They are then rested and bashed once again to re-emphasize their shapes. Finally, the topknot is placed on top of the base, and they are indented a third time to bind them. To further increase the amount of crust, the cottage loaf may be scored vertically, as here.

The particular charm of the chequerboard loaf (*opposite page, below*) is its combination of lightly floured squares of dark crust on top of a pale gridwork pattern of inner crust. To achieve this effect, the risen round is first dusted with flour and then scored. A brief, final rising allows the cuts to open, exposing the contrasting, unfloured interior.

A Notched Cottage Loaf

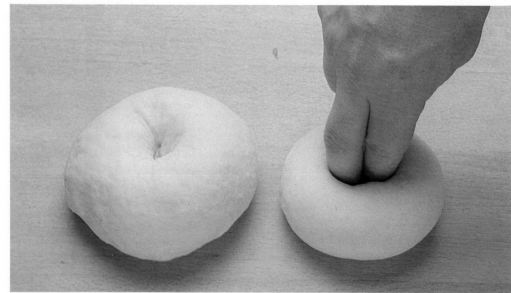

1 **Bashing the dough.** Divide a risen dough into two pieces, one twice the size of the other. Knead both pieces into rounds (*pages 14-16*). Place the rounds well apart on a clean board, cover them with a damp cloth and leave them to rest for 5 to 10 minutes. Bash the larger round, pressing three fingers and a thumb straight down through its centre to the board. Use two fingers to bash the smaller round—which will form the loaf's topknot—in the same way.

5 **Baking the loaf.** Bake the cottage loaf in a preheated 230°C (450°F or Mark 8) oven for about 40 minutes until it is evenly browned and sounds hollow when it is rapped with a knuckle. Cool the loaf on a wire rack (*right*). To serve, slice the loaf from top to bottom or, if it is particularly large, pull apart the two pieces and slice the two pieces separately. □

2 **Joining the two rounds.** Cover both rounds of dough and leave them to rest for 15 minutes, then bash each one once more. Place the topknot on top of the larger round; both rounds should be bashed-side-up. With two fingers, bash the combined loaf through to its bottom.

3 **Notching the loaf.** Position the loaf so that it slightly overhangs the edge of a table or board. With a razor blade, score the overhanging portion of the loaf all the way from top to bottom, making a notch about 5 mm (¼ inch) deep. Rotate the loaf and repeat the scoring at 2.5 to 4 cm (1 to 1½ inch) intervals all round the sides.

4 **Proving the loaf.** Put the loaf directly on to a baking sheet and cover it; or you can put the loaf on a board and leave it covered while you preheat the oven and baking sheet (*Step 8, page 16*). Either way, leave the loaf to prove for about 50 minutes, until doubled in bulk. Bash the risen loaf once more (*above*) to ensure that the rounds are securely joined.

A Flour-Dusted Chequerboard

1 **Flouring the loaf.** Knead a risen bread dough into a round (*pages 14-16*). Place the loaf on a baking sheet that has been dusted with semolina or greased, cover it with a damp cloth and leave the loaf to rise until almost doubled in bulk. Sprinkle the surface of the loaf with flour (*above*).

2 **Scoring the loaf.** With a razor blade, make shallow, parallel cuts 4 to 5 cm (1½ to 2 inches) apart across the top of the loaf. To divide the surface of the loaf into squares, make further cuts at right angles to the first cuts. For a very crusty effect, make the cuts up to 1 cm (½ inch) deep.

3 **Baking the loaf.** Set the oven to 230°C (450°F or Mark 8). To allow the cuts to open slightly, leave the chequerboard loaf to rise for a further 10 minutes. Bake the loaf for about 40 minutes until it is evenly browned and it sounds hollow when its base is rapped. Cool it on a rack before slicing and serving.□

Moulding an Even Cylinder

A round of dough can readily be moulded into a cylinder—either evenly formed (*demonstration, right*) or tapered (*page 22*)—which will hold its shape well during baking. The kneaded round must first be rested for about 10 minutes so that it loses some of its elasticity and becomes easy to handle again. Then it is moulded in gradual stages, each of which brings it nearer to a cylindrical shape. The repeated folding and stretching of the dough in different directions develops its gluten into an especially tight-knit network, which maintains the loaf's well-defined form during baking and gives the bread's crumb a fine, firm texture.

Before baking the cylinder, you can impose a decorative pattern on its surface. The cylindrical loaf here, for example, is repeatedly cut with scissors, yielding a series of crusty ridges that appeal to the eye—and also make the loaf simple to tear apart by hand. Two other possibilities are shown on pages 22-23.

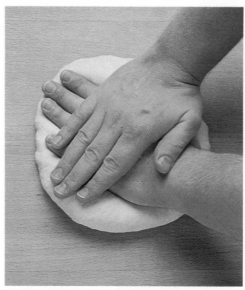

1 Flattening a round of dough. Knead a risen yeast dough into a round (*page 15*). Cover the dough with a damp cloth and leave it to rest for 10 to 15 minutes. With crossed hands—or a rolling pin—firmly press down on the dough (*above*) to flatten it less than 2.5 cm (1 inch) thick.

2 Rolling the dough. Starting at the far edge of the flattened round of dough, roll up the dough towards yourself, using your thumbs to steady the cylinder and maintain an even shape (*above*).

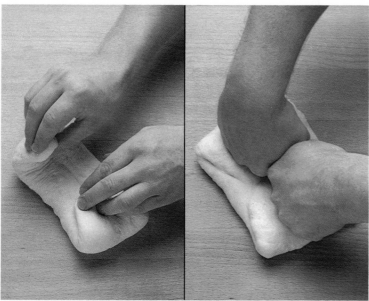

5 Folding up the dough. Fold in both ends of the elongated dough so that they meet at the middle (*above, left*). With your knuckles, or with a rolling pin, press down firmly on the dough (*above, right*) in order to spread it out into a rectangle that is slightly thicker at the end furthest away from you.

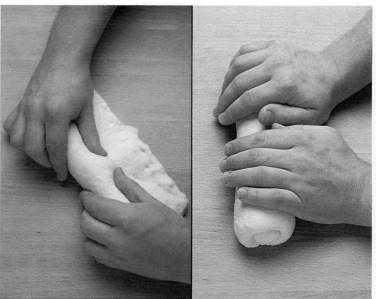

6 Finishing the shaping. Roll up the dough rectangle as shown in Step 2, but this time more tightly, pushing in firmly with your thumbs (*above, left*), to produce a compact cylinder. To even out its shape, gently roll the cylinder backwards and forwards beneath the palms of your hands (*above, right*).

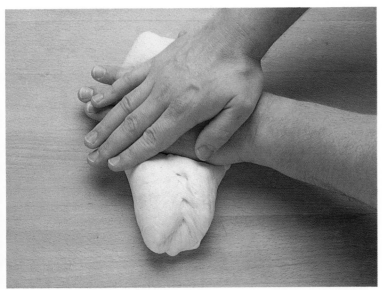

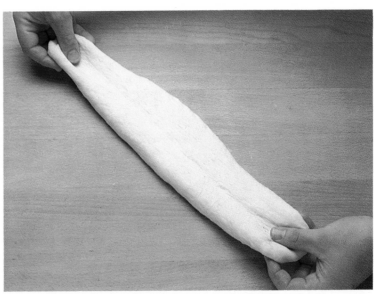

3 **Flattening the rolled dough.** With your crossed palms, press down on the dough (*above*). Repeat, moving your hands along the length of the dough roll and exerting an even pressure, to flatten the dough to a thickness of less than 2.5 cm (1 inch). Alternatively, flatten the dough with a rolling pin.

4 **Stretching the dough.** Take one end of the flattened dough in each hand and lift both ends slightly off the work surface. Gently flap the dough up and down and at the same time pull on its ends (*above*). Continue this movement until you have stretched the dough to almost twice its original length.

7 **Cutting the loaf.** Place the loaf on a baking sheet that has been dusted with semolina or greased. Sprinkle the loaf's surface with flour. Leave the loaf unslashed or, as here, cut its surface decoratively. With kitchen scissors make a zigzag pattern of very deep diagonal cuts (*above*) along the length of the loaf.

8 **Baking and cooling the loaf.** Cover the loaf and leave it to rise for about 50 minutes—until an indentation made in the dough remains, filling in only very slowly. Place the loaf in an oven preheated to 230°C (450°F or Mark 8) and bake it for about 40 minutes, until it is evenly browned and sounds hollow when rapped with a knuckle. Transfer the loaf to a rack to cool. To serve the loaf, tear it apart along its ridged crust or slice it in the usual way.□

Rolling a Tapered Cylinder

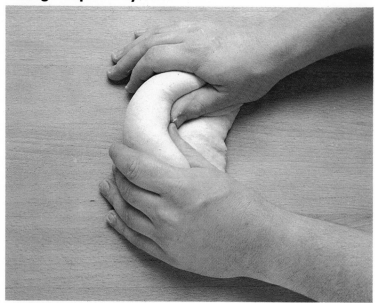

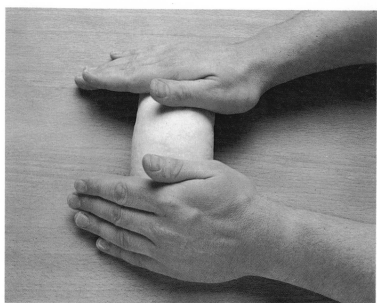

1 **Tapering the loaf.** Mould a risen yeast dough into a cylindrical loaf (*page 20*). As you roll up the dough for the final time, angle your hands at either end. Exert pressure with your hands while pushing the dough towards the centre with your thumbs (*above*) to make a tapered, curved cylinder of dough.

2 **Completing the shaping.** To straighten the loaf and accentuate its tapering, place the palms of your hands at either end of the dough and gently roll the dough backwards and forwards, keeping your hands in the same position (*above*). Continue to roll the cylinder in this way until the desired shape is achieved.

A Neat Pattern of Diagonal Slashes

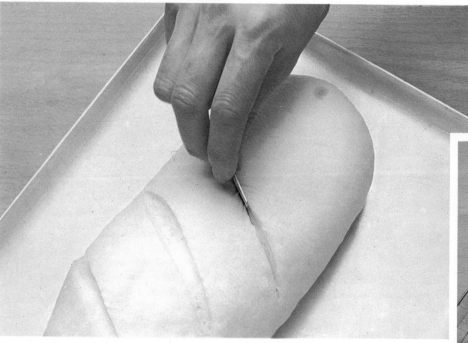

Slashing and baking the loaf. Cover the shaped loaf and leave it to rise for about 50 minutes. With a razor blade held vertically, make four parallel diagonal cuts about 1 cm (½ inch) deep across the loaf's top (*left*). To allow the cuts to open slightly, cover the loaf and leave it for about 5 minutes. Bake the loaf and transfer it to a rack to cool.

3 **Garnishing the loaf.** Grease a baking sheet or sprinkle it with semolina; place the shaped loaf on the sheet. For a decorative finish, brush the loaf with milk and then scatter poppy seeds over its surface. Alternatively, you can brush the loaf with beaten egg and sprinkle it with sesame seeds.

4 **Slashing the loaf.** With a razor blade held almost flat, make three long, shallow, irregular slashes along the top of the loaf (*above*). To cover the loaf without disturbing the poppy seeds, invert a large bowl over it; leave the dough to rise for about 50 minutes, or until it has nearly doubled in bulk.

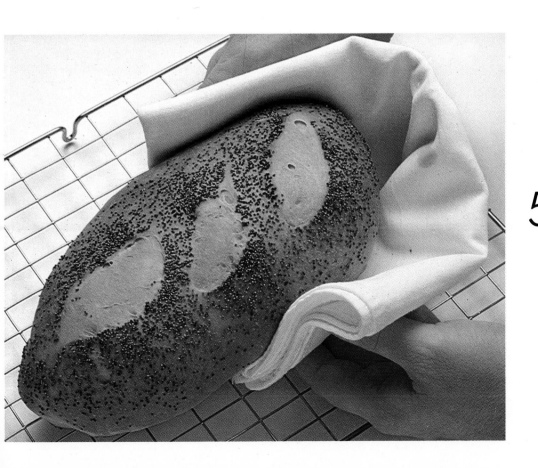

5 **Baking and cooling the loaf.** Place the loaf in an oven preheated to 230°C (450°F or Mark 8). Bake it for about 40 minutes, or until its surface is evenly browned and the loaf sounds hollow when rapped. Transfer the loaf to a wire rack (*left*) to cool before you slice it.□

Stretching Dough to Make Long Loaves

By repeatedly rolling a shaped cylinder of dough (*page 20*), you can extend it into a thin, elongated shape (*demonstration, right*) reminiscent of the classic French loaf. The loaf can be as long as you wish: the only limiting factor is the size of your baking sheet and oven.

Like all of the basic dough shapes, the long loaf is open to all kinds of variations. For example, if you roll the cylinder out very thinly, then coil it neatly, you can make a spiral, turban-shaped loaf (*box, below*). To ensure that the spiral has a compact, circular outline, taper one end of the cylinder as you roll out the dough so that the tip will merge smoothly into the side of the loaf.

A more elaborate version of the basic long loaf is shown on the opposite page, below. The surface of the elongated cylinder of dough is deeply cut with scissors and shaped into a knobbly pattern that is easily torn apart by hand. The baked loaf's form inspires its common French name, *épi*, which means "ear of wheat".

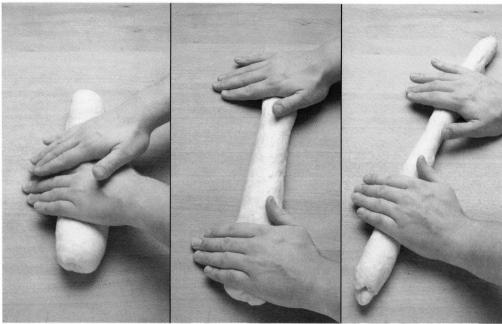

1 Lengthening the dough. Make a basic dough (*page 14*) and knead it into a round. Cover the dough and leave it to rest for 10 to 15 minutes, then shape it into a cylinder (*page 20*). Rest the dough again. Roll the cylinder back and forth under your palms with a steady pressure; to ensure that it lengthens evenly, place your hands at the centre, move them outwards as you roll, and repeat. If the dough resists, rest it for 5 to 10 minutes, then continue.

Coiling a Turban

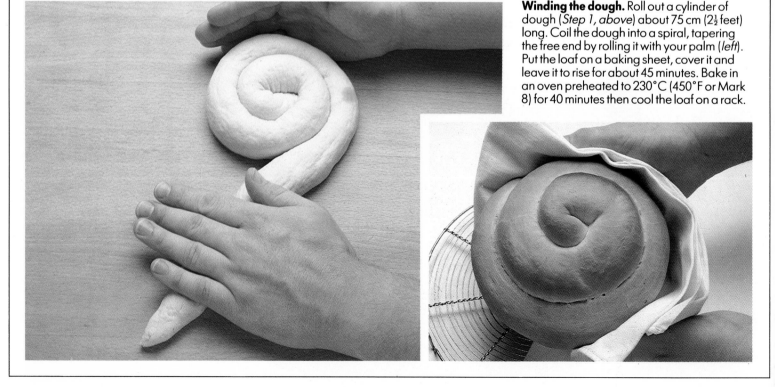

Winding the dough. Roll out a cylinder of dough (*Step 1, above*) about 75 cm (2½ feet) long. Coil the dough into a spiral, tapering the free end by rolling it with your palm (*left*). Put the loaf on a baking sheet, cover it and leave it to rise for about 45 minutes. Bake in an oven preheated to 230°C (450°F or Mark 8) for 40 minutes then cool the loaf on a rack.

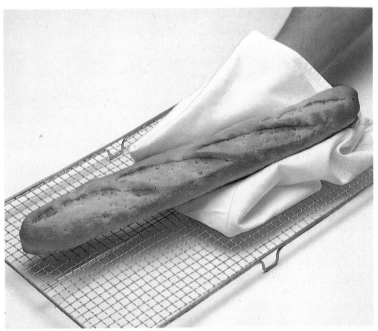

2 **Slashing the dough.** Put the shaped loaf on a baking sheet that has been sprinkled with semolina, as here, or greased. With a razor blade held almost horizontally, score the surface of the loaf: in this case, four long shallow, overlapping cuts are made almost parallel to the loaf's length (*above*).

3 **Baking the loaf.** Cover the loaf and leave it to rise in a warm place for about 45 minutes. Bake the loaf in an oven preheated to 230°C (450°F or Mark 8) for about 30 minutes, until well browned. Transfer the loaf to a wire rack and leave it to cool for an hour. Slice the bread for serving or break it apart by hand. □

Scissor Cuts for a Knobbly Crust

Cutting the dough. Roll out a thin cylinder of dough and put it on a baking sheet dusted with semolina. With a pair of scissors held almost horizontally, make cuts about three-quarters of the way through the dough's diameter and about 5 cm (2 inches) apart. As you cut, pull the sections to alternate sides (*left*). Leave the loaf to rise, then bake it in an oven preheated to 230°C (450°F or Mark 8).

Plaiting a Loaf from Three Strands

Several elongated strands of dough (*Step 1, page 24*) can be braided together to make a very decorative plaited loaf. The number of strands is variable: use two for the simplest of twists, or as many as nine to make an intricately patterned loaf. Three strands are used in this demonstration to make a classic plaited loaf.

Plaited loaves are traditionally made from a dough that has been enriched to some degree. To enrich a basic dough, a little softened butter is added to the dry ingredients, and milk or cream replaces some or all of the water (*box, opposite; recipe, page 171*). A little sugar may also be added to make a slightly sweeter loaf.

As well as giving a bread more flavour, butter and milk or cream considerably alter its texture. Their fat content produces a softer, moister crumb and a thinner, more tender crust. To complement these qualities, you can brush the bread with a mixture of beaten egg yolks and water so that the surface of the plaited loaf bakes to a deep brown glaze.

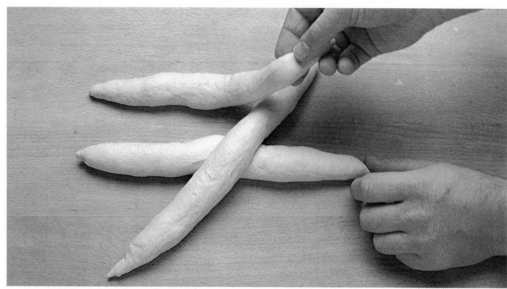

1 Arranging the dough strands. Prepare a lightly enriched dough (*box, opposite*)—in this case, enough for two loaves. Knead the dough and leave it to rise, then divide the risen dough into six equal portions. Set three of the pieces aside, covered. Shape the other three pieces into long strands (*page 24*) and taper their ends (*page 22*). To begin the plait, set one dough strand on the work surface and lay another strand across its middle. Place the third strand across the first two (*above*).

3 Turning over the plait. When you have finished plaiting half of the loaf, lift the plaited end and flip it upside-down and away from you (*above*), so that the unplaited strands now face you.

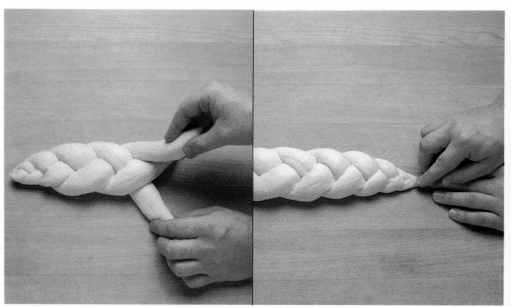

4 Finishing the plaiting. Braid the second half of the plait in the same way as the first half. Shape and plait the remaining three dough strands to make a second loaf. Place the loaves well apart on a greased or floured baking sheet, cover them with a damp cloth and leave them in a warm place to rise until they have nearly doubled in bulk. Preheat the oven to 230°C (450°F or Mark 8).

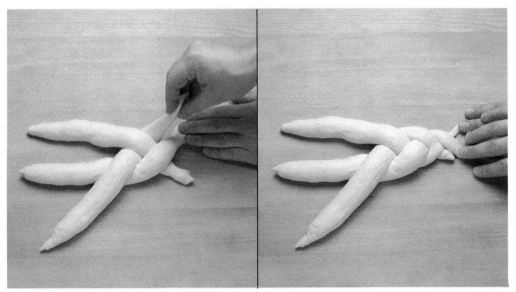

A Light Enrichment

Adding butter and milk. Put flour and salt in a large mixing bowl and add small pieces of softened butter. Mix the yeast in tepid milk and pour the liquid into the bowl (*above*). Mix and prepare the dough in the usual way (*page 14*).

2 **Plaiting the first half.** Starting at the centre and working towards yourself, cross the first strand over the third one, then move the second over the first (*above, left*); then cross the third strand over the second. Continue to plait the three strands in this order. To accentuate the tapering, so that the plaiting finishes in a neat point, gently pull on the tips of the strands as you braid them. Press the tips down on to the work surface as you near the end of the plait (*above, right*) to stretch them further and accentuate their shape.

5 **Glazing the loaves.** Brush the surface of each risen loaf with a mixture of beaten egg yolk and a little water (*above*). Put the baking sheet in the oven and bake the loaves for about 40 minutes, until they are well browned and sound hollow when rapped. Transfer the plaited loaves to a rack (*right*) to cool. To serve, slice the loaves or tear them apart by hand. □

Flattening Dough to Unusual Effect

Flatbreads, shaped by rolling a risen dough or spreading it out by hand, can be as different as the small, hollow breads in the demonstration on the right and the large, crusty free-form loaf shown below. Because of their thinness, all flatbreads cook quickly, but by varying the baking time, you can make them soft and chewy or dry and crisp, as you wish.

Middle-Eastern pittas (*right*), based on an oil-enriched dough (*recipe, page 171*), are baked in a very hot oven. The high temperature causes the flattened dough to puff up quickly, forming a hollow interior that can be spread with butter or stuffed with meat, cheese or salad. For soft pittas, only about 10 minutes' baking is needed; for a crisper effect, the breads can be cooked for almost twice as long.

For a very crisp flatbread, slash a large piece of rolled-out dough to increase its surface area (*Step 2, below*). When baked in a moderately hot oven for about 35 minutes, the bread will acquire a thick, deeply browned crust.

Pittas: Soft Pouches for Stuffing

 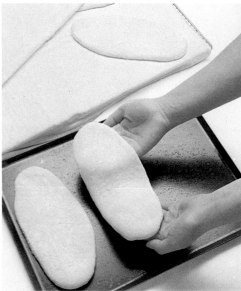

1 Rolling the dough. Make a basic dough enriched with olive oil; knead it and let it rise. Divide the dough into handfuls, and shape each into a ball (*page 30*). With a rolling pin, or by hand, flatten each ball into an oval or round about 5 mm ($\frac{1}{4}$ inch) thick. Put the dough on a floured cloth on a rack or tray; cover them and leave them for 20 minutes to rise slightly.

2 Baking the dough. Lightly oil baking sheets and heat them for 10 minutes in an oven preheated at its highest setting. Remove the sheets from the oven and place the risen dough on them at once. Return the sheets to the oven.

Deep Cuts for Maximum Crust

1 Flattening the dough. Prepare a basic dough and knead it (*page 15*). Leave the dough to rise, then knead it into a round and put it on a floured work surface. With a rolling pin, flatten the dough to a thickness of about 5 mm ($\frac{1}{4}$ inch). If the dough is too elastic and will not roll out easily, cover it and leave it to relax for 5 to 10 minutes before continuing to roll it to the required thickness.

2 Slashing the dough. With a sharp knife, make several slashes right through the dough, beginning and ending each cut about 2.5 cm (1 inch) from the edge of the dough (*above*). To ensure that the resulting bread has a large area of crust, the slashes should be made no more than 4 cm ($1\frac{1}{2}$ inches) apart.

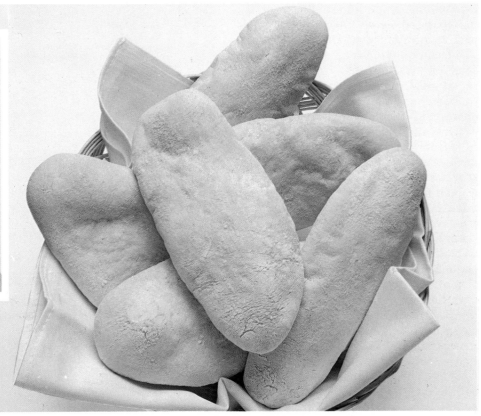

3 **Serving the bread.** After about 10 minutes—when the breads have puffed up—take them out of the oven. If you prefer a crisper texture, bake for an additional 5 to 10 minutes. Serve them warm in a napkin-lined basket (*right*). Tear the bread apart by hand; if you like, you can spoon a filling into its hollow.☐

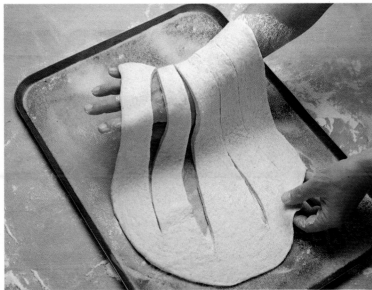

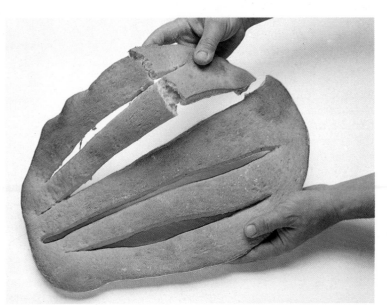

3 **Preparing the dough for baking.** Sprinkle a baking sheet with semolina, as here, or lightly smear it with oil. To transfer the large piece of dough on to the baking sheet without tearing it, fold one end over your arm and pick up the other end with your fingers, then quickly place it on the sheet (*above*). Gently rearrange the shape of the dough, pulling it to open the slits.

4 **Serving the bread.** Cover the dough with a cloth and leave it for about 20 minutes to rise slightly. Bake the dough in an oven preheated to 230°C (450°F or Mark 8) for about 35 minutes, until it is golden-brown. If, after about 25 minutes, the bread is browning too quickly, reduce the temperature to 190°C (375°F or Mark 5). Cool the bread on a rack; to serve it, break the bread apart by hand.☐

Rolls: Quickly Shaped and Speedily Baked

By dividing dough into small and easily manipulated pieces, the cook can form a wide range of bread rolls in a few minutes. The techniques for shaping five different kinds of small breads—cloverleaf rolls, round rolls, cigars, knots and wedge-shaped "Parker House" rolls—are demonstrated on the right and on pages 32-33.

All of these rolls can be made successfully from basic bread dough. However, to achieve a softer crust and richer flavour, they are more often prepared with a butter and milk dough (*box, page 27; recipe, page 171*). As with larger loaves, the crusts of bread rolls may be adorned with slashes, glazes and seed garnishes.

The most basic shape, the round, is fashioned by rotating your cupped hand on top of a flattened portion of dough until it gathers up into a ball (*demonstration, right*). Once shaped, the rolls may be scored to provide a wide area of softer crust. They can also be glazed with beaten egg, or sprinkled with seeds.

Cloverleaf rolls are formed from small balls of dough placed together in a triangular pattern (*right, below*). The balls are shaped even more simply than round rolls: they are squeezed from a large piece of dough through the space between the thumb and index finger of one hand. Before baking, cloverleaf rolls may be glazed with egg and sprinkled with seeds, or brushed with melted butter.

Cigar-shaped rolls (*page 32, above*) are made by rolling small rounds of dough backwards and forwards under your hand. Knot-shaped rolls begin similarly: the knots are formed from cylinders that are just long enough to tie.

Parker House rolls—which originated in the eponymous Boston hotel—are made from flat rounds of dough, brushed with butter and folded into semi-circles. When baked, the rolls retain their folded shape and have a rich, buttery crust.

Simple Rounds: Gathering Up by Hand

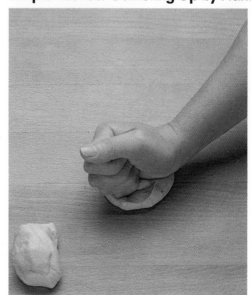

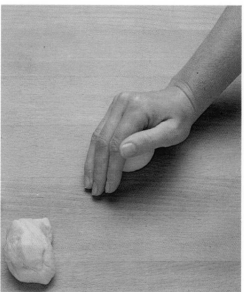

1 **Expelling air.** Mix and knead a butter and milk dough (*box, page 27*); let it rise. Cut the dough into small pieces, each weighing about 60 g (2 oz). With your clenched fist, press down on each piece several times to expel air (*above*).

2 **Shaping the dough.** To shape each piece of dough, cup the palm of your hand over it and rotate your hand continuously until the dough gathers up into a round ball. Repeat the process with each portion.

Cloverleaf Rolls: Joining Small Balls of Dough

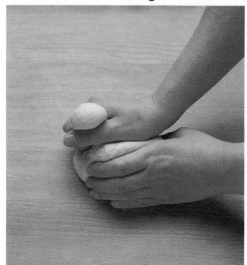

1 **Shaping the dough.** Mix and knead a butter and milk dough; let it rise and knead it again into a round (*page 15*). To shape each ball, squeeze off a walnut-sized piece of dough between the thumb and index finger of one hand (*above*).

2 **Assembling the rolls.** Grease a baking sheet with butter. On the sheet, spaced well apart, place the balls of dough in clusters of three to form a cloverleaf pattern. Cover them with a damp cloth.

3 **Scoring the dough.** Place the balls of dough, spaced well apart, on a greased or floured baking sheet. With a razor blade, cut a small, shallow cross on top of each roll. Cover the rolls with a damp cloth and leave them to rise for about 25 minutes, until they have doubled in bulk.

4 **Baking the rolls.** Preheat the oven to 230°C (450°F or Mark 8). To give the finished rolls a hard, lightly seasoned crust, brush them with salted water just before placing them in the oven. Bake the rolls for about 25 minutes, until they are well browned. Transfer the rolls to a wire rack to cool before serving.□

3 **Sprinkling on seeds.** Leave the rolls to rise until they have doubled in bulk, about 25 minutes. Brush them with a lightly beaten mixture of egg and a little water. Liberally sprinkle the glazed rolls with poppy seeds (*above*).

4 **Baking the rolls.** Preheat the oven to 230°C (450°F or Mark 8). Bake the cloverleaf rolls for about 25 minutes, until their crusts are shiny and well browned (*above*). Transfer the baked rolls from the baking sheet to a rack to cool before serving.□

Cigars: Tapering Neatly

1 **Shaping the dough.** Prepare a butter and milk dough, let it rise and divide it into small, equal portions—here, about 60 g (2 oz) each. Form each portion into a ball (*page 30, Steps 1 and 2, above*). To shape each round into a short, broad cigar shape, roll the dough backwards and forwards under your fingers (*above*). Place the cigar-shaped rolls well apart on a greased baking sheet.

2 **Dusting with flour.** With a razor, cut a shallow slash along each roll. Cover the rolls with a damp cloth and let them rise for about 25 minutes. For a mottled crust, lightly dust the rolls with flour.

3 **Baking the rolls.** Preheat the oven to 230°C (450°F or Mark 8). Bake the rolls for about 25 minutes, or until they are lightly browned. Transfer them to a wire rack to cool before serving (*above*). □

Parker House Rolls: Folding for a Double Crust

1 **Cutting out the dough.** Mix and knead a butter and milk dough and leave it to rise until doubled in bulk. Knead the dough into a round. With a rolling pin, roll it to a thickness of about 1 cm (½ inch). Using a 9 cm (3½ inch) floured pastry cutter, cut out circles from the dough (*above*).

2 **Scoring the circles.** Lift the trimmings away from the cut circles; gather the excess dough into a mass, roll it out again and cut more circles. Brush the surface of each circle with melted butter and then crease it along its diameter with the back of a small knife (*above*).

3 **Folding the circles.** Fold each circle of dough in half along its crease (*above*). Position the folded shapes well apart on a greased baking sheet, then cover them with a damp towel.

Knots: Tying Lengths of Dough

1 Rolling the dough. Prepare a butter and milk dough and then divide it into equal portions. Exerting an even pressure with both hands, roll each portion of dough backwards and forwards until it is about 30 to 40 cm (12 to 15 inches) in length and about 1 cm (½ inch) thick.

2 Tying the knots. Tie each strip of dough into a loose knot (*above*). Place the knotted rolls on a greased baking sheet, cover them with a damp cloth and let them rise until they have doubled in bulk—about 25 minutes.

3 Baking the knots. Glaze the rolls with a mixture of egg and water. Preheat the oven to 230°C (450°F or Mark 8). Bake the rolls for about 25 minutes, until they are evenly browned. Cool the rolls on a wire rack before serving.□

4 Glazing the rolls. Leave the shaped rolls to rise for about 25 minutes. For a matt finish, brush the tops of the risen rolls with melted butter (*above*). Preheat the oven to 230°C (450°F or Mark 8).

5 Cooling the rolls. Bake the Parker House rolls for about 25 minutes, until they are evenly browned. Transfer the rolls to a wire rack (*above*) to cool before serving.□

Thin Strips, Crisp Results

Pretzels: Loose Knots Briefly Risen

The crispest of breads are made from long strips of dough, rolled out so thin that, after baking, more crust will exist than crumb. The strips may be fashioned into many shapes: looped into pretzels, for example (*right*), or twisted into breadsticks (*opposite page, below*).

Because a deep surface crust and a firm texture are the major attractions of these breads, their preparation differs from that of normal breads. The dough pieces are often baked just after shaping; without a final rising they will have a denser crumb. For a lighter result, let the shaped dough rise briefly—about 10 minutes.

Traditionally, the strips of dough used to make pretzels are rolled out slowly and progressively from small balls (*Step 1, right*). So much handling can sometimes overdevelop the dough's gluten; if a dough strip becomes too elastic or tears, let it relax, covered, for 5 to 10 minutes.

A quicker way to shape strips is by slicing flattened dough. The flat-sided strips produced may be used for pretzels; more often, however, they are twisted into breadsticks (*opposite, Step 2, below*).

Whatever their shape, the small, thin breads are usually garnished before baking with coarse salt and, perhaps, seeds of cumin, caraway or fennel. Such piquant additions make the breads particularly suitable as an accompaniment to drinks.

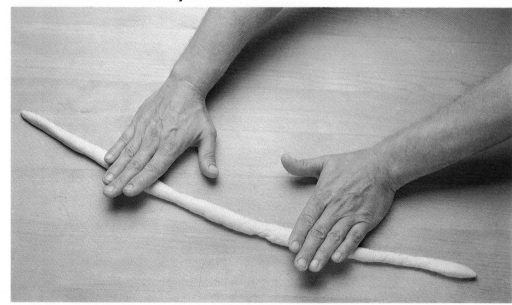

1 **Rolling out the dough.** Mix and knead a basic bread dough, and leave it to rise (*page 14*). Cut the dough into small pieces, each about 100 g (3½ oz). Shape each piece into a ball, then into an oval. Roll each oval back and forth beneath your fingers (*above*), moving them along its length to keep the shape even, until the dough is a strip about 1 cm (½ inch) thick and 60 cm (2 feet) long.

4 **Baking and serving.** Bake the pretzels in a preheated 230°C (450°F or Mark 8) oven for about 15 minutes, until golden-brown. Transfer the pretzels to a wire rack to cool; serve them warm or cold.□

2 **Shaping the dough.** Grease a baking sheet with butter, or sprinkle it with semolina. To form the pretzels, arrange each strip of dough into a loose horseshoe shape with the ends pointing towards you. Take hold of the ends, and cross them over twice; rest both ends on the resulting loop of dough (*above*). Place the pretzel on the sheet.

3 **Garnishing the dough.** For lighter-textured pretzels, cover them and leave them to rise for 10 minutes. To glaze the pretzels, beat an egg together with a little water and brush it over each piece of dough. Sprinkle the pretzels with coarse salt crystals (*above*). If you like, add a light sprinkle of aromatic seeds such as caraway.

Sticks: Sliced and Twisted

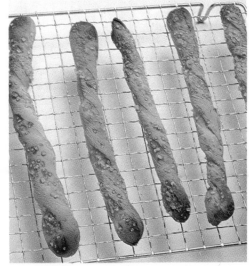

1 **Cutting dough strips.** Mix and knead a basic bread dough, leave it to rise and knead it into a round (*pages 14-15*). On a lightly floured work surface, use a rolling pin to flatten the dough into an oblong about 22 cm (9 inches) wide and 1 cm (½ inch) thick. With a long, sharp knife, cut the dough across its width into strips about 1 cm (½ inch) (*above*).

2 **Twisting the strips.** Sprinkle the work surface with coarse salt. Lay a strip on top of the salt. Place a hand at each end of the strip. Simultaneously, slide one hand forward and the other back to twist the strip and coat it with salt (*above*). Repeat this process with the other strips. Place them on a buttered baking sheet.

3 **Baking and serving.** Bake the sticks in an oven preheated to 230°C (450°F or Mark 8) for 10 to 15 minutes, or until they are golden-brown. Transfer the baked breadsticks to a wire rack (*above*) and serve them hot or cold, as you prefer.□

Baking in Moulds and Tins

By baking bread dough in a mould or a tin, you can neatly control its shape. Any dough, plain or elaborate, can be baked in this way—and in the case of a very soft dough or a batter a mould is essential.

The moulds shown on the right are specifically designed for bread-making. An open, rectangular bread tin (*upper demonstration*) sharply defines the base and sides of a loaf while allowing its top to rise freely and develop a crust. A bread mould that completely encloses dough— such as the cylinder used in the lower demonstration—stops the dough from rising to its full extent during baking. The result is a close-textured loaf with a crust that is pale, soft and thin.

Moulds can also be improvised from ordinary kitchen equipment for any kind of dough, or to suit specific needs; as demonstrated on pages 38-39. A wide cake tin, for example, makes a perfect container in which to place small rolls that will join together as they rise and bake, or a glazed earthenware dish can be used to contain a very thick batter (*recipe, page 95*).

To fill a mould's contours, place the dough in the mould before its final rising. The mould should be twice as large as the unrisen dough; if you warm the mould for 5 minutes in an oven preheated at its lowest setting before filling it, the dough will rise more readily.

After the bread has been baked, it should be unmoulded immediately on to a wire rack to cool. If it were left in the mould, steam would collect around the loaf and soften the crust. To make a moulded loaf's crust crisper, remove the bread from its container after about 30 minutes' cooking, then return the loaf to the oven to complete its baking.

An Open Container for a Crusty Top

1 **Greasing the tin.** Mix a basic dough (*page 14*). Knead the dough, cover it and leave it to rise. Using your fingers, smear the inside of a loaf tin liberally with butter—as here—or oil: this will prevent the dough from sticking to the tin.

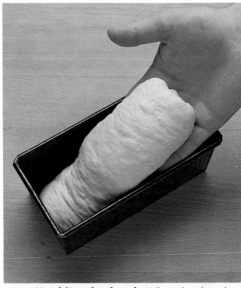

2 **Moulding the dough.** When the dough has risen to twice its original bulk, knead it into a round. Mould the round into a cylinder (*page 20*) that is the same length as the tin. Place it in the tin (*above*).

Complete Enclosure for a Compact Crumb

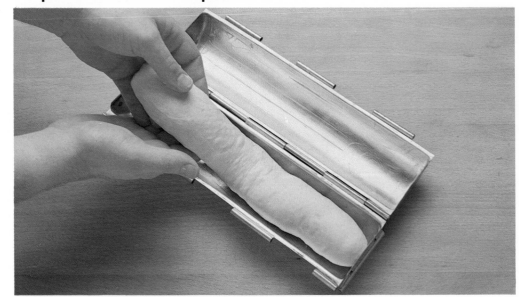

1 **Putting the dough in the mould.** Mix a dough enriched with a little butter and milk (*box, page 27*) or, if you prefer, prepare a basic dough (*page 14*). Knead the dough, cover it and leave it to rise. Shape the risen dough into an elongated cylinder (*page 24*) the same length as the mould. Rub both halves of the mould's interior with softened butter and place the cylinder of dough inside.

3 Scoring the loaf. Cover the tin with a cloth and leave the dough for at least 40 minutes, until it rises above the rim of the tin. With a razor blade, make a 5 mm ($\frac{1}{4}$ inch) deep slash along the loaf.

4 Baking the loaf. Put the tin in an oven preheated to 230°C (450°F or Mark 8). After 40 minutes, when the top of the loaf is well browned, remove the tin from the oven and tip the loaf on to a cloth held in one hand. Rap the base of the loaf with your knuckles: if the bread sounds hollow, it is cooked; if not, bake the loaf, without its mould, for 10 to 15 minutes more and then test again. Transfer the finished bread to a wire rack to cool before serving. □

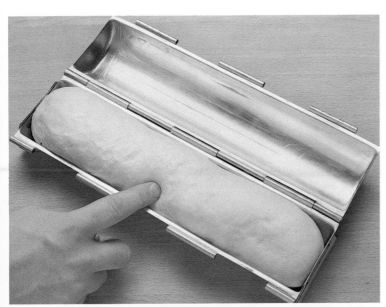

2 Leaving the dough to rise. Close the lid of the mould and leave the dough to rise in a warm place. After about 40 minutes, test the dough by poking a finger into it: if the indentation remains, filling in very slowly, the dough has risen enough and is ready for baking.

3 Baking and slicing. Close the mould securely and put it in an oven preheated to 230°C (450°F or Mark 8). Bake the loaf for about 40 minutes. Remove the mould from the oven, open it and tip out the loaf. Leave on a wire rack to cool for several hours before slicing. □

Rolls Moulded in a Cluster

1 **Filling the mould.** Mix a basic dough, enriched, if you like, with butter and milk (*box, page 27*). Knead the dough, cover it and let it rise. Shape the dough into small rounds (*page 30*). Grease the inside of a shallow, circular cake tin with softened butter. Distribute the rounds of dough evenly in the tin, placing them about 1 cm (½ inch) apart. Cover the tin with a cloth and leave the dough in a warm place to rise for about 30 minutes.

2 **Baking the bread.** With a pastry brush, glaze the rounds with a mixture of beaten egg and water; if you like, sprinkle them with poppy seeds. Bake in an oven preheated to 230°C (450°F or Mark 8) for about 40 minutes. Remove the tin from the oven. Protecting your hand with a cloth, support the base of the tin while you place a wire rack on top of the bread (*above*).

A Wholemeal Loaf Baked in Earthenware

1 **Moulding the batter.** Prepare a very thick wholemeal batter (*recipe, page 95*). Rub the inside of the mould—here, an ovenproof, glazed earthenware dish—with softened butter. With your hand, scoop the batter into the mould.

2 **Levelling the batter.** Firmly press down on the batter with your hand to pack the mould; smooth the surface of the batter as evenly as possible. Cover the dish with a cloth and put it in a warm place.

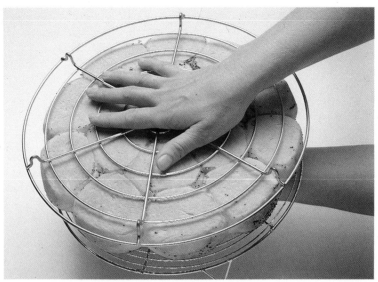

3 **Unmoulding the bread.** Holding the rack firmly in place, invert the tin so that the bread rests on the rack. Lift off the tin. Place another wire rack over the base of the bread (*above*) and invert the bread again, leaving it right-side up on the second rack.

4 **Serving the bread.** Leave the unmoulded bread to cool on the wire rack for several hours or overnight before serving. Present the cluster of rolls whole at table. To serve, tear away the rolls by hand, as required (*page 12*).☐

3 **Garnishing the loaf.** Leave the batter to rise for about 45 minutes, until it reaches the top of the mould. If you like, garnish the surface of the batter; cracked wheat kernels are used here.

4 **Slicing the bread.** Put the mould in an oven preheated to 200°C (400°F or Mark 6). After about 40 minutes, take it out and invert it on to a baking sheet. To allow the base and sides of the bread to become crisp, lift off the mould (*left*) and return the inverted loaf on the baking sheet to the oven for about 10 minutes. Cool the bread on a rack before slicing it.☐

Crumpets: Airy Batter Cooked on a Griddle

Thin, pancake-like breads are made by including more liquid in a yeast-leavened mixture to produce a pouring batter, and then cooking it on a hot cast-iron griddle or in a frying pan.

Obviously, a batter cannot be kneaded to develop its gluten—it must be beaten (*Step 2*). While the batter rises, the gases produced by the yeast will be trapped by the gluten, making the batter airy. By beating in bicarbonate of soda, you can increase the lightness to produce bread with a honeycombed crumb—as in the crumpets on the right (*recipes, pages 105-106*).

To achieve the desired porous effect, a crumpet batter should be thin enough to let some bubbles rise during cooking. Test the consistency with a sample crumpet: if no holes appear, add a little more milk or water to thin the batter.

The batter can be poured directly on to the griddle to make unevenly shaped breads of whatever size you like. If you prefer neat, uniform rounds, contain the batter in metal rings (*Step 4*).

1 Mixing the ingredients. Put flour and salt in a heatproof mixing bowl and warm them in an oven at its lowest setting for 5 minutes. Mix the yeast with the tepid liquid—in this case, milk. Make a well in the centre of the flour and pour in the yeast mixture. Hold the bowl steady with one hand and, with your other hand, combine the ingredients by stirring from the centre outwards (*above, left*), to produce a loose, lumpy batter (*above, right*).

4 Filling the rings. While the batter is resting, lightly grease the griddle and the inside of the crumpet rings with oil or lard. Warm the griddle over a low heat and set the rings on top. Ladle the batter into each ring (*above*), filling it to about half its depth.

5 Turning the crumpets. Cook the crumpets over a low heat for about 6 minutes, until their surfaces appear dry and are honeycombed with holes. Slide a palette knife under each crumpet and gently flip it over with its ring (*above*). Cook the other side very briefly—about 30 seconds—until it is lightly browned.

2 **Beating the batter.** Tilt the bowl with one hand. With the other hand, beat the batter by scooping it up and slapping it repeatedly against the side of the bowl in a vigorous, rhythmic motion. Continue beating for about 5 minutes, until the batter is smooth and elastic.

3 **Letting the batter rise.** Cover the bowl with plastic film. Leave the batter for about 1½ hours, until it rises to 2 to 3 times its original volume. Dissolve bicarbonate of soda in tepid water and add it to the batter (*above*). Beat with one hand for about a minute; cover the bowl and let the batter rest for 15 minutes.

6 **Serving the crumpets.** Using the palette knife, remove the crumpets and rings to a wire rack. Run the tip of a knife around the edge of each crumpet to ease it from its ring. Lift the rings away. Leave the crumpets to cool while you cook the remaining batter. Serve the crumpets as they are, or toast them under a grill and spread generously with butter.□

Intricate Shapes Cooked by Steam

Bread cooked in the moist heat of a steamer comes out soft, springy and crustless. The techniques and the results are the same whatever combination of ingredients you use. The dough can be moulded into large loaves or small rolls, simple shapes or more intricate ones such as the Chinese flower-rolls demonstrated here.

Made from a basic yeast dough (*page 14*), or a dough enriched with milk (*box, page 27*) or sweetened with a little sugar and filled with spring onions (*recipe, page 104*), these rolls traditionally accompany richly spiced and sauced dishes in Chinese meals. Their flower-like "petals" are formed by a simple process. The risen dough is flattened into a rectangle, then rolled up tightly and cut into slices. The slices are stacked edge to edge in pairs, and each pair is flattened with a chopstick, causing the layers of the rolled, cut surfaces to blossom out (*Step 3*).

To keep the petals separate, the flattened dough must be brushed with oil before it is rolled up. Sesame-seed oil adds an authentic Eastern touch, but melted butter or lard, or vegetable oil, could be used instead. If you like, before rolling the dough you can sprinkle it with flavourings—chopped spring onions or ham, perhaps, for savoury rolls, or dried fruits or candied citrus peels for sweet ones.

There is no need to buy a steamer to cook the dough: you can improvise an efficient substitute from ordinary kitchen equipment (*Step 4*). Use a large pan with a lid that fits snugly, and place a trivet on the bottom of the vessel. The trivet supports a plate which, in turn, holds the dough. To allow steam to circulate freely, the plate should be about 2.5 cm (1 inch) smaller in diameter than the pan itself. To keep the rolls from sticking to the plate, a dampened and folded kitchen towel is placed on top.

Rolls will cook by steaming in about 15 minutes; a loaf may take as long as 2 to 3 hours, depending on its size. To test for doneness, stick a small knife blade or a skewer into the centre of a roll or loaf. If it comes out clean, the bread is ready. Otherwise, replace the lid on the pan and steam a while longer before testing again: steamed breads will not suffer from overcooking. Serve the bread hot.

1 **Preparing the dough.** Mix and knead a basic dough (*page 14*). Let the dough rise, knead it into a round, cover and leave it to rest for 5 to 10 minutes. On a floured work surface, roll the dough into a rectangle about ½ cm (¼ inch) thick. Lightly brush the surface of the dough with oil. Starting at a long edge, roll the rectangle into a tight cylinder (*above*).

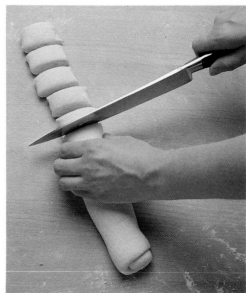

2 **Dividing the dough.** Steady the roll of dough with one hand. Using a sharp knife, slice the dough into an even number of uniform rounds, each about 2.5 cm (1 inch) thick (*above*).

4 **Assembling the steamer.** While the rolls are rising, prepare the steamer. Use a large pan with a tight-fitting lid. Centre a trivet in the bottom of the pan. Pour in water until it comes to within 1 cm (½ inch) of the top of the trivet. On top of the trivet place a plate that is slightly smaller than the diameter of the pan (*above*).

5 **Positioning the rolls.** Dampen a clean cloth with warm water; fold it to fit the plate and place it on the plate. Put the steamer on a high heat and bring the water to a boil. Place the rolls on the cloth at least 2.5 cm (1 inch) apart to permit the steam to circulate and to allow room for the rolls to expand.

3 **Fashioning flower shapes.** Place one round of dough on top of another (*above, left*). Lay a chopstick or skewer lengthwise along the top of the upper roll (*above, centre*). With both hands, press the chopstick down almost to the work surface to join the two slices together and shape the rolls (*above, right*). Repeat this process with the remaining rounds of dough. Place the shaped rolls on a lightly floured surface and cover them with a damp cloth. Leave them to rise for about 30 minutes, until doubled in bulk.

6 **Steaming the rolls.** Place the lid on the steamer and adjust the heat to maintain a steady boil. After 15 minutes, turn off the heat; uncover the steamer and test the rolls for doneness. Serve the rolls at once on a heated plate.☐

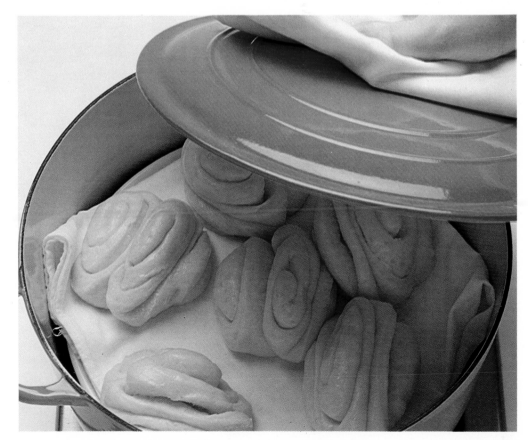

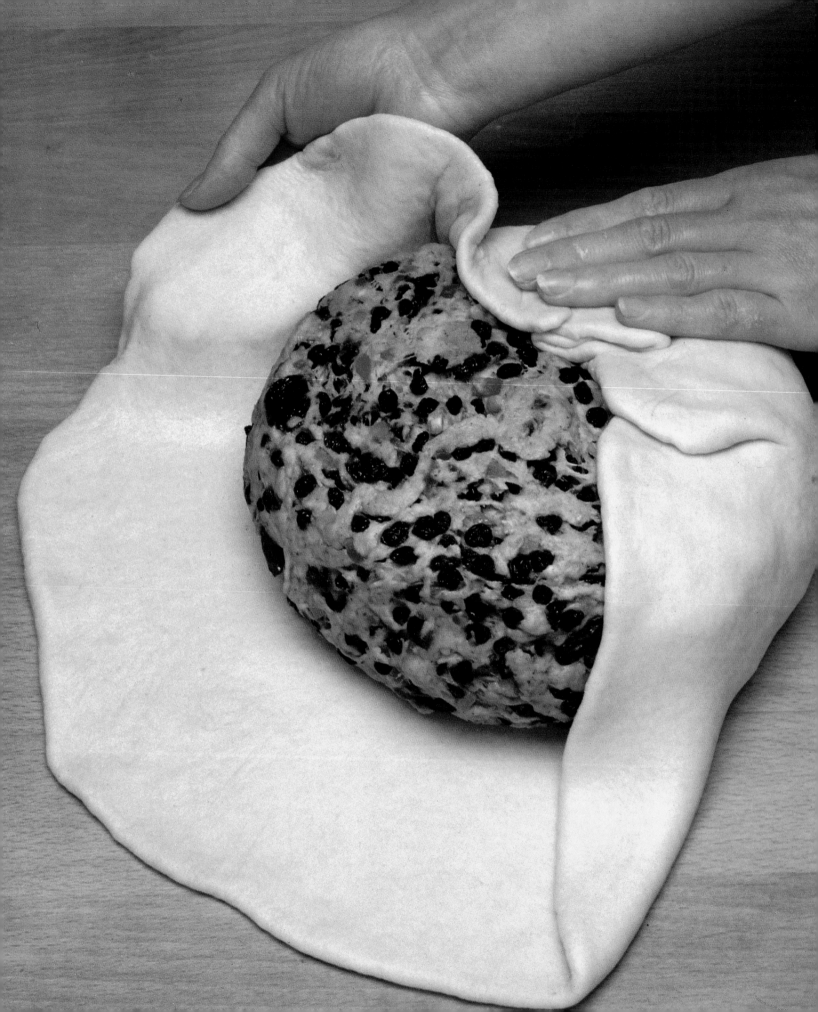

2
Flavoured and Filled Breads
Elaborations Simple and Substantial

Toppings for flattened dough
Two ways with fillings
Mixing in moist vegetables
Blending sticky mixtures
Kneading in fruits and nuts

Without fundamentally changing the basic techniques of bread-making, you can radically alter bread's taste, texture and colour by combining sweet or savoury ingredients with a yeast-leavened dough. Depending on their nature and the effect you want, these extra elements may either be included when the dough is being mixed or added to an already kneaded and risen dough. Products of this approach include filled pies and turnovers, loaves brightly coloured with vegetables, and moist, dark breads rich with chocolate and molasses.

To make open-faced, flavoured breads, pre-cooked or raw ingredients are spread on top of flattened dough just before it is baked. The topping can be as abundant as the anchovy, olive and onion mixture used in a Provençal *pissaladiera* (*page 46*) or as sparse as a few pieces of bacon and some cream (*page 47*). More substantial breads are produced by wrapping dough around a filling (*page 48*)—anything from a combination of several different kinds of cheese and chopped salami to a cooked mixture of endive, pine-nuts, sultanas and garlic.

The way you incorporate additional ingredients into a dough mixture will be determined by the weight, bulk and consistency of the ingredients themselves. Light, dry additions that will not inhibit the dough's rising— chopped herbs or grated cheese, for example—can be combined with the flour at the start of the mixing process. Likewise, moist vegetables such as courgette and pumpkin (*page 50*), which will supply some or all of a dough's liquid content, are added to the flour together with the yeast and just enough extra liquid to bind the dough.

Sweet, syrupy ingredients such as chocolate and molasses are usually difficult to work smoothly into a dough mixture. In the dark bread demonstrated on page 52, these flavourings are melted together in a warm cornmeal mush; only then are the yeast and flour stirred in to finish mixing the dough. And when a large quantity of dry, bulky ingredients are to be included in a dough, such as the fruits and nuts in the Scotch bun shown opposite, they should be kneaded in only after the dough has risen for the first time (*page 54*); if they were added at any earlier stage they would hinder the leavening action of the yeast.

A ball of yeast-leavened dough—scented with spices and packed with chopped almonds, citrus peels, raisins and currants—is wrapped in a piece of plain dough large enough to enclose it completely before baking (*recipe, page 127*). The dough wrapper helps to keep the bun's rich interior moist and disguises it until the moment of slicing.

Moist Toppings for Thin Breads

The simplest way to flavour a plain dough is to spread it out thinly—with a rolling pin or by hand—and cover it with a moist topping that will be partly absorbed by the bread as it bakes. Cooked quickly in a hot oven, the bread will develop a crisp bottom crust; its upper surface, shielded by the topping, will stay soft.

So that individual flavours will stand out, make the topping from just a few complementary ingredients. Any elements that take longer to cook than the 30 minutes or so required by the dough—meats and root vegetables, for example—should be pre-cooked. Otherwise, the choice of topping is limited only by your preferences and by what is available (*recipes, pages 108-113*).

The traditionally flavoured French breads demonstrated here exploit local produce from their respective regions. On the right, a Provençal *pissaladiera* (*recipe, page 108*), is covered with onions that have been stewed in olive oil and is garnished with salt anchovies (a substitute for *pissala*, a salted purée of fish that originally flavoured the bread) and black olives. On the opposite page, below, a time-honoured Lorraine variety of quiche, which differs markedly from the familiar filled pastry of today, is topped with bacon and bathed with cream.

Another good topping for this sort of bread is a thick sauce made from skinned and seeded fresh tomatoes or sieved, tinned tomatoes. Simmer them with garlic, onions or sweet peppers, and dried oregano or fresh basil. If you like, add cooked minced beef or lamb, or sliced sausage, to the sauce. Mashed soft or semi-soft cheeses—cream cheese, goat cheese or Roquefort—also make excellent toppings, alone or accompanied by a little cream. Or, for a sweet variation, cover the dough with fresh fruit—apricots, plums or cherries are especially suitable. Stone, and halve or slice the fruits; before baking, sprinkle them with sugar and, if you like, dust them with cinnamon.

A Neat Display of Onions, Anchovies and Olives

1 **Rolling out the dough.** Mix a dough, adding oil if you like, then knead it and let it rise. Stew chopped onions in olive oil until soft—about 40 minutes. Soak anchovies in water. Knead the dough into a round; rest it for 10 minutes. Break off a handful of it. With a rolling pin, or your hands, form the remaining dough into a rectangle 5 mm (¼ inch) thick.

2 **Flavouring the surface.** Place the rolled-out dough on to a lightly buttered or oiled baking sheet. Leaving a narrow margin round the edge of the dough, spread out the onions evenly over its surface. Fillet the anchovies, rinse them with water and dry them on paper towels. Arrange the anchovies on top of the onions in a regular criss-cross pattern (*above*).

6 **Baking and serving.** Leave the flattened and flavoured dough at warm room temperature to rise slightly for about 10 minutes. Bake it in an oven preheated to 220°C (425°F or Mark 7) for about 30 minutes, until the exposed dough is evenly browned. Serve hot, cut into squares, straight from the baking sheet (*above*). □

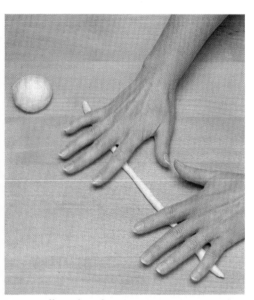

3 **Rolling dough strips.** Pull walnut-sized pieces from the reserved dough. With your fingers, roll each piece back and forth on a board to make a long, even strip the thickness of a pencil (*above*).

4 **Attaching the dough strips.** To make a decorative lattice-work effect, place the strips of dough on top of the flavourings to divide the surface into a series of neat squares—each one containing a pair of anchovy fillets. To secure each strip of dough, brush the underside of both ends with water (*above*), then press the ends into the rim of the dough base.

5 **Brushing with olive oil.** Complete the pattern by distributing black olives over the surface. To add more flavour and to help keep the surface moist, sprinkle olive oil over the flavourings. Brush the oil evenly over the exposed dough (*above*).

A Bacon and Cream Embellishment

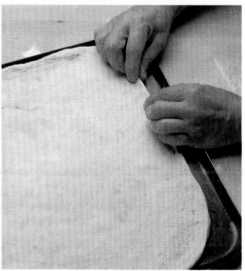

1 **Preparing the dough base.** Mix and knead a basic bread dough and let it rise. Transfer the dough to a lightly floured surface. Use the heels of your hands, or a rolling pin, to spread out the dough to a thickness of about 5 mm (¼ inch). Transfer it to an oiled baking sheet. To form a rim to contain the fairly liquid topping, pinch up the edge of the dough (*above*).

2 **Adding flavourings.** Cut rindless green bacon into pieces about 1 cm (½ inch) square and 2.5 cm (1 inch) long. Fry the pieces in a little oil over a low heat for 5 to 7 minutes, until lightly browned. Drain the bacon, then gently press the pieces into the dough at regular intervals. Spoon a thin coating of double cream over the dough and bacon (*above*).

3 **Baking and serving.** Put the bread in an oven preheated to 220°C (425°F or Mark 7). After about 15 minutes, when the cream has been absorbed, take out the bread and spoon over it another coating of cream. Return the bread to the oven and bake for 15 minutes more, until it is golden. Cut the bread into squares while still hot, and serve immediately.□

Enclosing Ample Fillings

A basic bread dough (*page 14*) is pliant enough to be wrapped round a substantial quantity of ingredients. After baking, such an assemblage is best served hot or warm and it can be eaten either by hand or with a knife and fork.

No rigid rules govern the size or contents of filled breads. The filling can be sandwiched between two rounds of dough and baked in a circular tin, like a pie (*right*); or enfolded by a circle of dough, turnover-fashion (*right, below*).

Savoury fillings may include meats, vegetables, cheese and seafood, alone or in simple combinations. In the upper demonstration here, the filling is based on cooked, shredded Batavian endive (*recipe, page 108*); spinach and chard are appropriate substitutes.

The bread turnover in the lower demonstration is filled with salami and three kinds of cheese (*recipe, page 113*), providing contrasts in flavour and texture. *Ricotta* and Parmesan are blended and bound together with egg to make a smooth, creamy paste on top of which a layer of salami is placed. A final layer of cubed *mozzarella* cheese melts during baking yet retains a supple consistency.

For sweet fillings, you could use tart fruit, such as plums, cherries or apples, lightly sprinkled with sugar and spices. But the easiest non-savoury filled bread to prepare—perhaps the most satisfying of all—may well be the French *petit pain au chocolat*: just wrap and seal a small rectangle of dough around some plain or bitter-sweet chocolate (*recipe, page 115*).

A Leaf Mixture Between Two Layers

1 Cooking the filling. Mix and knead a dough—enriched, if liked, with olive oil or butter (*box, page 27*). Let it rise. Heat olive oil in a pan over a medium heat; add shredded Batavian endive, reduce the heat and cook for 3 to 4 minutes. Add pine-nuts, sultanas, capers, black olives, garlic, parsley, salt and pepper. Remove the pan from the heat.

2 Adding the filling. Divide the risen dough in two; knead each piece into a round. Lightly grease a circular baking tin. Roll out one round of dough to make a circle slightly larger than the tin. Put the dough in the tin and press it into place: its edges should come half way up the sides of the tin. Spoon in the cooled filling.

A Turnover Stuffed with Cheese and Salami

1 Positioning the dough. On a floured surface, roll out a risen bread dough with a rolling pin to make a large circle about 5 mm (¼ inch) thick. Lift the dough by hand or loosely roll it round the pin, then transfer the dough to an oiled baking sheet, positioning it so that half of the circle lies on the baking sheet (*above*) and the other half on the work surface.

2 Preparing a ricotta mixture. To lighten and smooth the texture of *ricotta* cheese, press it with a pestle through a sieve held over a mixing bowl. Add an egg (*above*) and freshly grated Parmesan cheese and a little salt and pepper. Stir until the ingredients are thoroughly blended.

3 **Making a rim of dough.** With a palette knife, spread the filling evenly over the dough base. With the tip of the knife, turn the edge of the dough inwards, over the filling, to form a rim (*above*). Brush the rim of the dough with water to make it sticky.

4 **Enclosing the filling.** Roll out the rest of the dough and, using the base of the tin as a guide, trim it into a neat circle. Place the circle of dough on top of the filling (*above*). With your fingers, firmly press down the edges of the dough to seal in the filling. Brush the bread lightly with oil, then cover it with a damp cloth and leave it to rise for about 45 minutes.

5 **Baking and serving.** Brush the dough with a lightly beaten mixture of egg white and a little water to glaze it. For a decorative finish, score the bread lightly with a razor in a criss-cross pattern. Bake at 190°C (375°F or Mark 5) for 50 minutes until golden-brown. Turn the bread out on to a towel and invert it on to a plate. Serve warm, cut into wedges. □

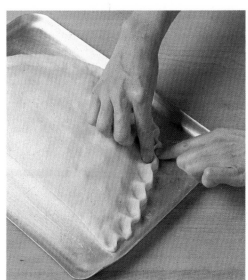

3 **Adding the filling.** Leaving a 2.5 cm (1 inch) margin at the outer edge, spread the cheese mixture over the semi-circle of dough on the baking sheet. Arrange thin slices of salami—peeled of any rind—on top. Finally, add a third layer consisting of small cubes of *mozzarella*.

4 **Sealing the bread.** Moisten the margin of the topped semi-circle of dough with water. Fold the plain half over the filling. To seal in the filling, crimp the circular edges of the dough firmly together: pinch the dough between the first finger and thumb of one hand and push into the dough between them with the first finger of your other hand (*above*).

5 **Baking and serving.** Lightly brush the surface of the dough with olive oil. Bake the bread in an oven preheated to 220°C (425°F or Mark 7) for 35 minutes, until golden-brown. Transfer the bread to a large plate or a slicing board. Cut the bread into wedges and serve it warm. □

Vegetables for Flavour and Colour

Vegetables, shredded or puréed and then mixed into a basic dough, can subtly alter a loaf's colour, texture and flavour. Because all vegetables have a high water content, they will provide some of the liquid needed to mix the dough: simply combine them with the flour and yeast and just enough additional liquid to make the dough hold together. The vegetables will not affect the basic procedure of bread-making (*pages 14-17*).

Virtually any vegetable can be included in the dough. The vegetable's preparation will depend largely on the effect you desire. Shreds of raw vegetable—such as the courgettes used in the top demonstration here (*recipe, page 124*)—will fleck the loaf with colour and provide a textural contrast to the loaf's crumb. Because they have an exceptionally high water content, the courgettes, once shredded, must then be salted and squeezed to rid them of excess moisture before they are mixed with the flour, yeast and water. The shreds will cook through in the time it takes for the loaf to bake. Other good vegetables for grating and adding raw are carrots and onions; neither requires the salting treatment given to the courgettes.

To suffuse a loaf with flavour and colour, add a cooked vegetable purée. In the lower demonstration, a loaf acquires a glowing hue, moist crumb and an elusive edge of sweetness from a pumpkin purée (*recipe, page 124*). Puréed root vegetables such as beetroot, turnips, swedes, parsnips and tubers—potatoes or sweet potatoes—are equally suitable additions (*recipe, page 116*). A thick tomato sauce will produce striking results.

You can add cooked whole grains such as white or brown rice, wheat, rye or barley to the dough mixture; like vegetables, the grains will contribute moistness, as well as distinctive texture.

Whatever cooked vegetable or grain you add to a dough, make sure it is first allowed to cool until it is tepid. If it is too hot, it may kill the yeast and prevent the dough from rising.

A Green-Flecked Crumb from Shredded Courgette

1 **Preparing the courgettes.** With a rotary shredder or a hand-held grater, shred the courgettes coarsely. Spread a layer of courgettes in a bowl; sprinkle it evenly with salt. Repeat until all the courgettes have been shredded and salted. After 30 minutes, tightly squeeze the shreds in handfuls to extract their liquid; transfer them to another bowl; discard the liquid.

2 **Mixing the dough.** Put the flour in a large mixing bowl and add the courgettes. Pour in yeast that has been creamed in a little water (*above*). Mix the ingredients by hand, adding just enough water to form the dough into a firm mass.

The Amber Hue of Puréed Pumpkin

1 **Sieving pumpkin.** Cut a pumpkin in half; use a spoon to scrape out its seeds and fibres. Cut the flesh into thick slices; peel them and cut them into 3.5 cm (1½ inch) pieces. Simmer in lightly salted water for 20 to 25 minutes, until tender; drain over a bowl and reserve the water. With a pestle, press the pumpkin through a fine-meshed sieve set over another bowl.

2 **Mixing the dough.** Allow the pumpkin purée to cool. In a large mixing bowl, add the puréed pumpkin to flour and salt. Mix them together lightly by hand. Add yeast, creamed in a little water, and mix thoroughly; if the dough is too dry, add some of the cooking water; if it is too sticky, sprinkle in more flour.

3 **Preparing for baking.** Knead the dough in the usual way and let it rise. Knead it into a round and mould it into the desired shape—here, an oval *(page 22)*. Place the loaf on a baking sheet that has been dusted with semolina or greased; leave the loaf to rise once more. To protect any shreds of courgette on the surface from burning, brush the loaf with a little oil.

4 **Slicing the loaf.** Bake the bread in an oven preheated to 220°C (425°F or Mark 7) for about 45 minutes, until it sounds hollow when its underside is rapped. Using a cloth to protect your hands, remove the bread from the oven and place it on a rack to cool for several hours or overnight before slicing and serving.□

3 **Shaping the loaf.** Knead the dough and let it rise. For a pumpkin-shaped loaf, knead the risen dough again and mould it into a round. Place it on a greased or floured baking sheet to rise. Just before baking, use a razor blade to score a circle round the top so that the loaf will develop a decorative crown as it bakes.

4 **Serving the bread.** Bake the pumpkin bread in a preheated 220°C (425°F or Mark 7) oven for 50 minutes to 1 hour until it is golden and sounds hollow when rapped. Remove the loaf from the oven and transfer it to a rack to cool overnight before slicing and serving.□

An Amalgam of Elements in a Rich, Dark Loaf

A combination of many different flavourings produces the rich taste, the dense, moist crumb and the depth of colour that are typical of dark breads. The strong-flavoured flours and meals are a natural starting point. Traditional German pumpernickel loaves, for example, are made entirely from rye flour; the American version of pumpernickel shown here contains a mixture of rye flour, wholemeal flour and cornmeal (*recipe, page 117*).

To add more flavour as well as colour to dark breads, the flour is blended with sweet, syrupy or malty ingredients such as molasses, treacle, plain chocolate or beer. The mixture may be scented with spices and citrus peel. For body and moistness, mashed potato is often added; potato also stimulates the yeast's activity.

Combining so many different ingredients, with their varying consistencies and textures, requires patience and a methodical approach. In this demonstration, the cornmeal used must be heated in water to soften it. The thin mush that results is a perfect medium in which to melt and blend the chocolate and molasses (*Step 1*); without this cornmeal mush, the flavourings would have to be melted very gently on their own in a heavy pan set in a bain-marie. The flavoured mixture is then left to cool until lukewarm: too much heat would kill the yeast. Cooled mashed potato and yeast are incorporated.

Only at this stage are the flours introduced, first stirred then worked in by hand (*Steps 3 and 4*). Because the resulting dough is very stiff and sticky, it needs more energetic kneading than usual to develop its gluten and give it the necessary smooth consistency. Heavier than an ordinary, unflavoured bread mixture, the dark dough is simply patted into loaf shapes rather than being moulded in the manner shown on page 14.

Dark breads should be prepared and baked at least one day before serving so that their flavours mingle and mature and the bread becomes easier to cut into the thin slices that best suit its richness. Dense as the crumb of the dark bread is, it will stay moist for several weeks if the bread is wrapped up airtight in foil.

1 Blending in flavourings. Sprinkle fine yellow cornmeal into a pan of boiling water, stirring all the time (*inset*). Reduce the heat and stir with a wooden spoon until the mixture forms a light porridge—2 to 3 minutes. Remove the pan from the heat, and add flavourings—in this case, molasses (*above*), small pieces of plain chocolate, butter, sugar, salt and caraway seeds. Stir until the chocolate and butter have melted and all the flavourings are combined.

5 Kneading the dough. Turn the dough out on to a board dusted with wholemeal flour and sprinkle it with more flour. Press the dough down and spread it out with the heel of your hand; gather it back together, give it a slight turn, and repeat; use a dough scraper to gather up any dough that sticks. Knead until the dough is no longer sticky—10 to 15 minutes.

6 Shaping the loaves. Put the dough into a buttered or oiled bowl and cover it with plastic film. Leave the dough in a warm place to rise until it increases in bulk by half—1½ to 2 hours. Turn the dough out on to a floured board and cut it in two. Knead each piece of dough again for a few minutes to expel air, then pat each piece into a smooth round (*above*).

2 **Adding mashed potato.** Transfer the flavoured cornmeal to a large mixing bowl; set it aside until it is lukewarm. Add some lukewarm mashed potato (*above*). Mix yeast in a little tepid water and stir it thoroughly into the mixture.

3 **Adding the flours.** A little at a time, sprinkle the flours—here, wholemeal and rye—into the flavoured cornmeal and potato mixture. Stir briefly with a wooden spoon after each addition.

4 **Mixing by hand.** Continue to add the flours to the dough until the mixture becomes too stiff to stir. Coat your hands lightly with oil to prevent sticking, and use them to work in the remaining flour.

7 **Glazing the loaves.** Set the loaves on a baking sheet dusted with cornmeal or semolina. Cover them with wax paper or a kitchen towel and leave them to rise again until they have increased in bulk by half—about 50 minutes. Glaze the loaves' surface with a lightly beaten mixture of egg white and water (*above*).

8 **Baking and slicing.** Bake the loaves in an oven preheated to 190°C (375°F or Mark 5). Check them after 45 minutes: if they are browning too quickly, cover them with foil. After about 1¼ hours, rap the bottom of each loaf: if it sounds hollow, the loaf is done. Cool the loaves on a rack overnight. To serve, slice the bread thinly. □

A Fruit and Nut Bun in a Plain Wrapper

A surprisingly large amount of dried fruit and nuts can be kneaded into a plain or enriched dough—as much as twice the weight of the dough itself—to produce a festive, cake-like bread. Such extra bulk, however, will interfere with a dough's normal rising process, so it is essential that the flavourings are incorporated only after the dough has risen.

The Scotch black bun demonstrated here (*recipe, page 127*) includes chopped almonds, currants, raisins, orange peel, lemon peel and spices. For extra flavour, these ingredients may be sprinkled with rum or brandy and left for an hour or two.

The flavoured dough is enclosed in a thin layer of plain dough, which gives the final loaf a deceptively modest, conventional appearance: only when the bun is cut is the dark, aromatic bread revealed. The dough wrapper also serves a more practical purpose: it helps to keep the fruity dough from drying out as it bakes. To allow the escape of steam that might otherwise separate the doughs during baking, the bun is pierced all over with a fork before it goes into the oven.

1 Preparing the flavourings. Mix a dough enriched with butter. Knead it and let it rise. Finely chop orange and lemon peel. Blanch almonds in boiling water; peel and chop them. In a bowl, mix raisins and currants with the peel and the almonds. Use a mortar and pestle to pound cloves, allspice and dried ginger root; add them to the bowl. Grate in a little nutmeg.

2 Flavouring the dough. Cut the risen dough into two portions, one twice the size of the other. With your fists, flatten the larger portion of dough into a roughly circular shape about 3 cm (1 inch) thick and tip the fruit mixture on to it.

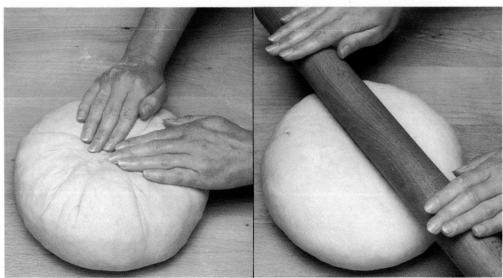

5 Sealing the bun. Lift the edges of the plain dough and fold them round the filling to enclose it completely. Press together the overlapping folds of dough (*above, left*). Turn the assembly over so that the folds are on the underside; with the rolling pin, lightly roll the bun to flatten it slightly (*above, right*).

6 Containing the bun. With a fork, pierce the bun deeply at intervals of about 4 cm (1½ inches). Grease and flour a baking sheet and place the bun on it. To ensure that the bun keeps its shape as it bakes, place a greased, expandable cake hoop round it (*above*). Tighten the hoop until it barely touches the bun.

3 **Kneading in the flavourings.** With your hands, lift the sides of the dough and fold them up and over the flavourings (*above, left*). Push the dough down into the flavourings. Continue to fold and push the dough to work in the flavourings; gather up any that fall away and press them back into the dough (*above, right*). When all the ingredients are evenly dispersed throughout the dough, mould it into an even round and flatten it so that its upper surface is level.

4 **Assembling the bun.** On a lightly floured work surface, use a rolling pin to roll out the smaller portion of dough into a circle large enough to wrap completely round the filling. Centre the flavoured dough on the rolled-out plain dough (*above*).

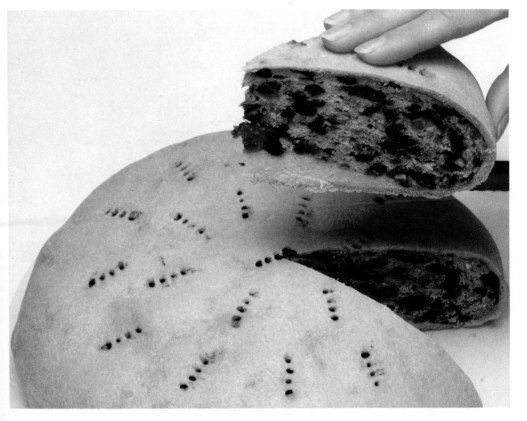

7 **Baking and serving the bun.** Put the bun in an oven preheated to 190°C (375°F or Mark 5). After 1 hour, remove the cake hoop so that the sides can brown, and bake the bun for another 30 minutes until it is golden-brown. Cool the bun on a wire rack for several hours or overnight; serve it cut into wedges. The bun will keep well for up to a week.□

Rich Breads
Special Effects from Butter and Eggs

Incorporating eggs in different ways
Moulding a free-form ring
Shaping a traditional brioche
Flavouring and filling rich doughs
Handling yeast puff pastry
Poaching small shapes

When eggs and butter are used as enrichments, yeast-leavened loaves take on cake-like qualities. Eggs make the bread lighter and more moist; butter can give it a tender, almost melting texture. Depending on the quantities you use of either ingredient, and on how you incorporate them, the transformations can be dramatic and diverse.

Mixing just a few whole eggs and a moderate amount of butter (*page 58*) into a dough will yield a loaf with a soft crust and a moist, yellow crumb. The more eggs and butter you add, the more pronounced these characteristics become. The classic brioche (*pages 62-65*), which contains a higher proportion of eggs and butter than any other bread, has an incomparable golden hue and silken texture.

Like any doughs, those prepared with eggs and butter are open to further elaboration. By adding a little extra flour when mixing it, for example, the dough can be made stiff enough to be rolled out, cut into shapes and stacked to make impressive constructions. A rich dough also provides an excellent background for flavourings. The bread demonstrated on page 60 combines both these variations: the saffron-scented, bright yellow dough, flavoured with raisins and almonds, is cut into rounds that are built up into an elaborate terraced loaf. An enriched dough lends itself to fillings, too; whether these are savoury, like the *cervelas* sausage encased in strips of brioche, on page 66, or sweet, like the fruit and nut mixture layered with brioche dough in a Viennese *kugelhopf* (*page 68*).

Spreading butter on dough, rather than mixing it in, will produce distinctive results. If a risen dough is rolled out, coated generously with butter, then repeatedly folded and flattened, it will puff up during baking into delicate, flaky layers (*page 70*). Such a yeast puff dough is often cut into a range of shapes—large or small, simple or elaborate—and folded around sweet or savoury fillings, making the breakfast or coffee breads that are usually known as Danish pastries (*pages 73-75*).

A relatively small amount of butter and the white of an egg also change a bread's character. Bagels—small, ring-shaped rolls (*page 78*)—are made from such a dough. After a brief rising, the dough is poached for a few seconds before baking, to promote the bagels' familiar chewy texture and absence of hard crust.

Dusted with sugar, a ring of yeast puff pastry is sliced for serving. The pastry, with its many delicate layers of butter and yeast-leavened dough, was rolled round a filling of currants and cinnamon-flavoured butter before it was shaped and baked (*page 76*).

A Simple Egg and Butter Ring

Adding eggs and butter to a basic yeast dough produces a rich bread with a more tender crust and a cake-like texture (*recipe, page 172*). Extra eggs and butter also make the uncooked dough very soft. But during rising and baking, the eggs will bind the dough, so that it can retain a neat, distinctive shape such as the freeform ring shown here or a plaited shape as demonstrated on page 26.

A large amount of fat in a dough can form a barrier between the flour grains and the yeast cells, which will slow down the leavening action. To allow the yeast to do its work unhindered by fat, the dough may be prepared in two stages, as demonstrated here. In the first stage, a preliminary batter is made from the yeast, milk, sugar and about a third of the flour; this batter is left to rise. In the second stage—when fermentation is well under way—the eggs, softened butter and the remaining flour are incorporated into the batter to make the dough.

Because an egg and butter dough is considerably softer than a plain dough, it is kneaded more gently (*Step 4*). To keep the butter from being melted by the warmth of your hands, which would make the dough looser and difficult to handle, do the kneading on a cool work surface—ideally, a marble slab. If the butter does begin to melt, chill the dough in the refrigerator for half an hour; then continue to knead it until it is smooth and elastic.

After it has risen and been kneaded into a round (*page 15, Step 7*), the dough is shaped. To form a ring—a shape that allows a large quantity of dough to cook quickly and evenly—begin by poking a small hole in the centre of the dough, then gently enlarge the hole with your fingers (*Step 5, below*). Thus opened up, the round is easy to stretch into a ring.

1 **Adding eggs.** Stir yeast into a pan of tepid milk. When the yeast has dissolved, pour the milk into a large mixing bowl. Add sugar and a few handfuls of flour and whisk vigorously to make a thick batter. Cover the batter and leave it to rise for about 1 hour in a warm place. Whisk in whole eggs (*above*).

5 **Forming a ring.** Put the dough in a large bowl, cover it with plastic film and leave it in a warm place to rise for at least 1½ hours, until it is three to four times its original bulk. Put the dough on a cool, lightly floured surface; knead it into a round (*page 15*). Press two fingers into the middle of the dough (*above, left*) and make gentle, circular movements to enlarge the hole. With both hands, stretch the dough round the hole, forming a ring (*above, right*). If the dough tears or resists stretching, let it rest, covered, for 10 minutes.

6 **Enlarging the ring.** With your hands held on each side of the ring, transfer it to a greased baking sheet. Continue to pat and stretch the dough into an even ring shape. Cover the dough with a large bowl or a cloth and let it rise for about 45 minutes, until doubled in bulk.

2 **Cutting out large rounds.** Knead the dough, cover it with plastic film and leave it to rise for about 2 hours, until it is two to three times its original bulk. On a cool, lightly floured work surface, knead the dough into a round. Roll it out to a thickness of 1 cm ($\frac{1}{2}$ inch). Place four inverted plates, of decreasing size, on the dough. With the tip of a table knife, cut round each plate (*above*). The large rounds so formed will be the lower tiers of the assembly.

3 **Cutting out smaller rounds.** Gather up the scraps of dough into a small ball; knead the dough gently to bind the scraps together. Roll the dough out again to a thickness of 1 cm ($\frac{1}{2}$ inch). Use small biscuit cutters of graduated sizes to cut out the small rounds that will form the uppermost tiers of the assembly.

6 **Baking and serving.** Bake the bread in a preheated 190°C (375°F or Mark 5) oven for about 1 hour. To test for doneness, insert a thin skewer into the centre of the loaf; it should come out clean. With two wide spatulas under opposite sides of the loaf, lift it from the baking sheet on to a wire rack. Leave it to cool for several hours. With a long knife, cut the bread into wedges (*left*). Serve it either warm or cold—with butter, if you like.□

Brioche: Replete with Butter and Eggs

Brioche is the richest of all yeast breads: for every 500 g (1 lb) of flour in its dough, it may include up to an equal weight of butter and six or more eggs (*demonstration, right; recipe, page 172*). Brioche also takes longer to produce than any other bread—12 to 14 hours in all. Most of this time, however, is taken up by three long, unhurried risings, which improve its flavour and give the brioche a silky texture to suit its richness.

As is the case with many egg and butter breads, the preparation of brioche begins with making a preliminary, butter-free dough of flour, yeast and eggs. The large quantity of eggs gives the dough an exceptionally loose consistency without the need for any additional liquid; the dough will spread out as it is kneaded, and a dough scraper must be used to gather it up repeatedly. When the dough is sufficiently softened, butter is folded in with the dough scraper. The dough is allowed to rise at room temperature, and afterwards is punched to expel any large gas bubbles, ensuring a fine texture.

Refinement of texture is also one of the objects of the second, longest rising. During this period, the dough is placed in the refrigerator. The cold slows down the rising, so that the dough's network of gluten is stretched more gently. The cold, risen dough will also be firm and easy to mould.

You can bake brioche dough in almost any size or shape, free-form or moulded. In the demonstration here, the dough is moulded into a traditional, top-knotted *brioche à tête*—literally, brioche with a head. Set in its mould, the dough is left to rise a final time before it is baked.

Brioche is best eaten warm, so that its buttery flavour and fine texture can be fully appreciated. But it may also be served cold. With its moistness and high fat content, it will keep for several days.

1 Mixing a preliminary dough. Put flour, sugar and salt into a large mixing bowl. Mix yeast with a little tepid water. Make a well in the centre of the flour and pour in the yeast. Break the eggs into the well; with your fingers, break the yolks and combine the eggs with the liquid. Stir the ingredients together by hand, gradually pulling in the flour from the sides of the bowl, to make a loose dough.

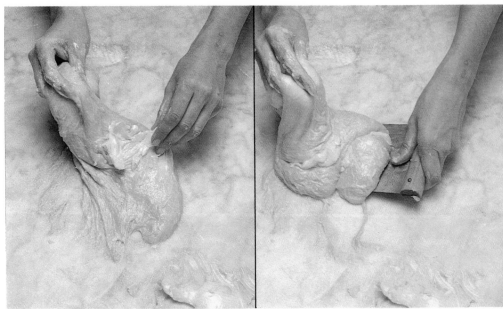

3 Folding in butter. On the cool work surface, soften butter by pressing and pushing it with the heel of your hand (*page 59, Step 2*). Pull the opposite sides of the kneaded dough slightly apart, and nestle into its centre a small piece of the softened butter (*above, left*). With a dough scraper, fold the butter and dough together, scraping and lifting with an up-and-over motion (*above, right*). Continue in this way, adding small pieces of butter to the dough until all the butter is incorporated.

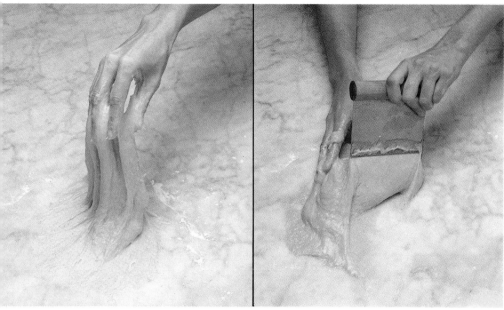

2 **Kneading the dough.** Turn the dough out on to a cool work surface—preferably marble—for kneading. Pull it up with one hand (*above, left*) and slap it back down on to the surface. Continue to knead in this manner for about 10 minutes, until the dough is elastic and pulls away from your hand. As the dough spreads, use a dough scraper to pull it together again (*above, right*). Should the dough be too loose to hold together, work a little sifted flour into it.

4 **Blending and rising.** With one hand, knead the dough; with the scraper in your other hand, gather up the dough as it spreads. Knead the dough until its ingredients are blended, 2 to 3 minutes (*above*). Put the dough in a bowl, cover and leave at room temperature to rise for 3 to 4 hours, until trebled in bulk.

5 **Punching the dough.** To expel excess gas from the dough, punch it several times (*above*). Cover the dough with plastic film and put it in the refrigerator to rise for 6 to 8 hours, until it has doubled in bulk. ▶

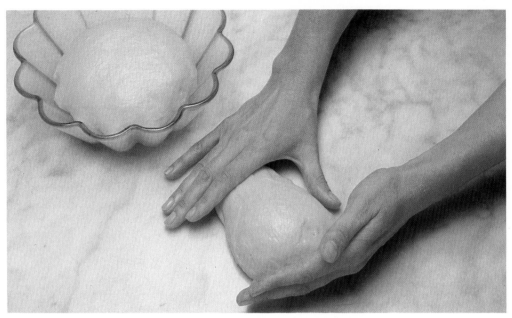

6 **Shaping the dough.** Turn out the dough on to a cool, lightly floured work surface. With a knife, cut off about one quarter of the dough and set it aside. Knead the larger piece of dough into a round and place it inside a well-buttered fluted mould that is twice the dough's volume. Shape the smaller piece of dough into a ball; then rest the ball against one hand and roll the dough back and forth with the other hand to make a teardrop shape (*above*).

7 **Indenting the dough.** With three fingers held closely together, press down into the centre of the large piece of dough in the mould (*above*) until they have reached the bottom. Enlarge the cavity by moving your hand in a circle until the hole is slightly larger than the tapered end of the smaller piece of dough.

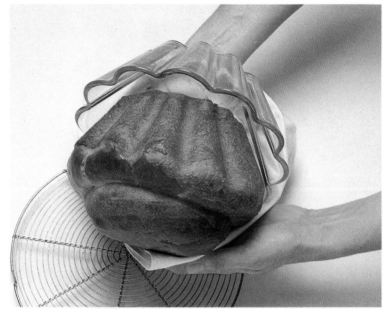

9 **Glazing the dough.** Beat an egg yolk with a little water. Brush the mixture over the surface of the dough; do not brush the seam between the topknot and the base, or the topknot will not rise freely during baking. To ensure a pronounced and even glaze, leave the coated surface to dry for several minutes, then brush the dough a second time. Put the brioche in a 220°C (425°F or Mark 7) oven.

10 **Baking and unmoulding.** After 10 minutes, reduce the heat to 190°C (375°F or Mark 5), then bake for 30 minutes more. If the brioche browns too quickly, cover with foil. To test for doneness, insert a toothpick or thin skewer into the centre of the brioche: it should emerge dry; if not, bake 10 minutes more and test again. To avoid spoiling the brioche's shape when unmoulding, invert it on to a cloth held in your palm and turn it over on to a rack.

8 **Assembling the brioche.** Lift up the small piece of dough and lower its tapered end into the cavity (*above, left*). Its rounded end will form a small head or topknot on top of the larger piece of dough. Pat the topknot with the fingers of both hands (*above, right*) to give it an even shape. Cover the filled mould with a large inverted bowl, or a cloth, and leave the dough to rise at room temperature for about 2 hours, until it has doubled in bulk.

11 **Serving the brioche.** Leave the brioche to cool for 15 minutes, then transfer it to a slicing board, as here, or a serving plate. Serve the brioche warm or cold, cut into vertical wedges (*right*), either on its own or spread with butter. □

Wrapping a Sausage in Brioche Dough

Brioche dough's richness and silken texture make it an excellent background for savoury ingredients. The sausage filling used in this demonstration is one of the most frequent companions of brioche, yielding a substantial hors-d'oeuvre or light main course. In Lyons, in southeastern France, a truffled *cervelas* sausage is often used (*recipe, page 142*), but any all-meat, poaching sausage will do. Other fillings include seasoned mixtures of rice and mushrooms or hard-boiled egg (*recipes, pages 148-149*).

Whatever the filling, the dough must be stiff enough to hold its shape during the final rising and baking; add a little more flour than usually called for in a brioche mixture. The stiffened dough is easily cut to a shape that will suit the filling—in this case, narrow strips that are coiled round the sausage. A rectangle or a circle of dough (*page 48*) would be necessary to contain a looser filling.

The filling should be cooked, if necessary before it is enclosed in the dough. The baking time required by the dough is sufficient only to heat the filling through.

1 Cooking the sausage. In a large pan, bring salted water or a light stock to the boil. With a needle, make a few punctures in the skin of a sausage—here, a 500 g (1 lb) pork sausage. Immerse the sausage in the liquid (*inset*), reduce the heat to a bare simmer and cook for about 40 minutes. With a slotted spoon, lift out the sausage and leave it to drain on a towel until it is cool enough to handle. With a sharp knife, make a shallow slash down the length of the sausage to cut its skin. Peel off the skin and discard it. Roll the sausage in flour until it is lightly coated (*above*).

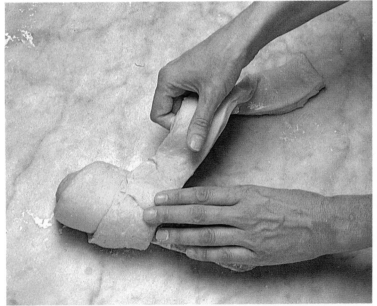

4 Joining the strip. When you have coiled most of the first strip, join its end to the remaining dough strip; overlap the ends and gently press them together. Continue to coil the dough round the sausage. If there is an excess length of dough, trim it away.

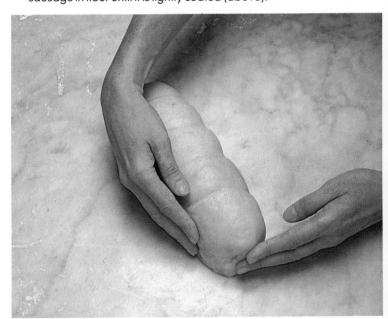

5 Sealing the ends. Gently press the open ends of the dough together to seal them (*above*). Place the sausage on a greased baking sheet, positioning the sausage so that the seam joining the two dough strips is underneath. Brush the entire surface of the dough with lightly beaten egg. Cover the wrapped sausage with an inverted bowl and leave it for about 2 hours, until the dough rises to almost double its bulk. Brush the dough again with beaten egg.

2 **Preparing the dough.** Make a brioche dough, using extra flour—an additional 50 g (2 oz) flour for each 500 g (1 lb) of dough—to produce a stiffer mixture. On a cool, floured surface, roll out the dough to a 1 cm (½ inch) thickness and trim it into two strips, each about 25 cm (10 inches) long and 5 cm (2 inches) wide. Lightly brush the dough with cold water (*above*).

3 **Wrapping the sausage.** Place the sausage at a slight angle to one of the dough strips, with the sausage's tip about 2.5 cm (1 inch) from one end of the strip. Tuck the end of dough neatly round the tip of the sausage. Roll the sausage to coil the dough round it, making sure that the edges of dough overlap by about 1 cm (½ inch).

6 **Baking and serving.** Bake the sausage in a preheated 220°C (425°F or Mark 7) oven for about 35 minutes, until its bread wrapping is golden-brown. Remove it from the oven and, to let the bread firm up, cool the sausage on a wire rack for about 10 minutes. Transfer it to a wooden board, as here (*left*), or to a serving platter. With a knife, slice the sausage into rounds and serve immediately. □

Layering for a Marbled Crumb

Like any bread, brioche gains variety in taste and texture from the addition of sweet or savoury ingredients. Depending on the quantity and consistency of these extra elements, you can either add them when you mix the dough or knead them in after the first rising. For a marbled effect, you can spread a prepared filling on slices of brioche dough and stack the slices in a mould—a technique that is used in the rich Viennese *kugelhopf* on the right.

The dessert *kugelhopf* here is made with a filling of chopped nuts and ginger (*recipe, page 146*); you could add dried fruit and candied citrus peels. For an even sweeter bread, include sugar dissolved over heat in a little milk and butter; a splash of liqueur or a spirit could also be added. For a savoury *kugelhopf*, you might use a seasoned soft cream cheese and some shredded ham.

To make small pieces of dough for layering, first shape the dough into a long cylinder; you then can cut it easily into thin, round slices. If the filling has been pre-cooked in any way, be sure it is no warmer than tepid when you spread it on the slices, otherwise its heat would kill the yeast and prevent further rising.

The bread can be baked in a container of any shape, but *kugelhopf* is traditionally made in a round, fluted mould with a central tube. During baking, the tube permits the heat to penetrate the centre of the loaf, thus cooking it more quickly.

1 Preparing the filling. In a mixing bowl, put finely chopped walnuts and ground ginger. Pour a little milk into a small saucepan and add butter and caster sugar. Set the pan over a gentle heat and stir until the sugar dissolves; add a dash of rum. Pour the sugar mixture into the mixing bowl (*above*) and stir well. Set this filling aside to cool until tepid.

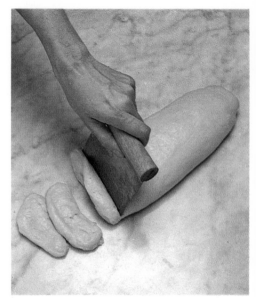

2 Slicing the dough. Prepare a brioche dough (*page 62*); if you like, include in it rum and grated lemon rind. On a cool work surface, pat the risen dough into a ball and roll it backwards and forwards beneath your hands until it is a cylinder about 40 cm (16 inches) long. With a dough scraper (*above*), slice the dough into pieces about 1 cm (½ inch) thick.

5 Compacting the layers. Press down on the dough with your knuckles (*right*). Cover the mould and leave the dough to rise for about 1 hour, until it reaches almost to the mould's rim. Bake in an oven preheated to 180°C (350°F or Mark 4) for about 50 minutes, until the loaf has browned and has come away slightly form the sides of the mould.

3 **Spreading the filling.** Place the slices of dough on the work surface. Spoon some of the cooled filling on to each slice of dough. With the back of the spoon, spread the filling evenly over each slice, pushing down gently to press the filling into the dough.

4 **Filling the mould.** Butter and lightly flour the inside walls and central tube of a fluted mould. Using both hands to avoid spilling the filling, lift the slices one by one and distribute them evenly inside the mould, overlapping them slightly to fill it to half its depth.

6 **Serving the loaf.** Unmould the loaf on to a wire rack. Allow the loaf to cool for at least an hour. Before serving, sieve icing sugar over the *kugelhopf (above)*, then cut the bread into wedges (*right*). □

Flaky Pastry Interleaved with Butter

A lightly enriched yeast dough interleaved with thin layers of butter produces a leavened puff dough—the raw material for a variety of delectable breads. The dough (*recipe, page 173*) is raised not only by yeast but also by the butter's moisture, which turns to steam during baking and separates the layers into light flakes. Croissants, favourites of the French breakfast table, are demonstrated here and on page 72; other shapes made from this dough are shown on pages 73-77.

The basic preparation of a leavened puff dough is shown here in Steps 1 to 5. The rolled dough is spread with softened butter, folded to enclose the butter, rolled out to compress the layers together, and folded once again. So that the leavened pastry will have enough layers to puff up handsomely, this folding and rolling-out sequence must be repeated at least once—more often if you wish.

Because the dough undergoes so much handling during its preparation, the initial kneading should be lighter than for an ordinary bread dough. Otherwise, the dough would become too elastic to work easily. In any case, to allow the dough to relax after each sequence of rolling and folding, it must be left to rest for an hour.

During the resting periods, the dough should be kept in the refrigerator, so that the butter remains firm enough to separate the layers of dough. Even with this precaution, the butter can easily become too soft, and the dough is best handled on a very cool work surface such as marble. If you only have a wooden board, you can cool it in the refrigerator or freezer.

After a final rolling-out, the dough is ready to be transformed into any shape. To make croissants, triangles of dough are rolled up tightly and curled into crescents. After a wait of about an hour—or overnight in the refrigerator—to allow the yeast to work, the croissants are ready to cook. Baking should begin in a very hot oven, which gives a thrust to the rising, then proceed at a slightly lower temperature so that the croissants do not burn.

1 **Adding butter to a dough.** Prepare a milk and butter dough (*page 27*), including, if you like, a little sugar; let the dough rise twice. Roll out the dough into a rectangle about 8 mm (⅜ inch) thick. Soften butter (*page 59*) and spread on the dough with a palette knife over two-thirds its length (*above*), leaving a 2 cm (¾ inch) wide margin round the edges.

2 **Folding the dough.** Fold the unbuttered third over half of the buttered dough, and bring over the remaining buttered section to cover these two layers. There are now two thicknesses of butter sandwiched between three layers of dough.

5 **Folding the dough.** Remove the dough from the refrigerator. Place the rectangle on the work surface with one of its short sides facing you. Roll out the dough lengthwise, fold it again (*above, left*), and give it a quarter turn. Roll it out into a rectangle and fold the dough into thirds once more (*above, right*). After the fourth folding, 54 thicknesses of butter are sandwiched between 55 layers of dough. Wrap the dough in plastic film and chill for another hour.

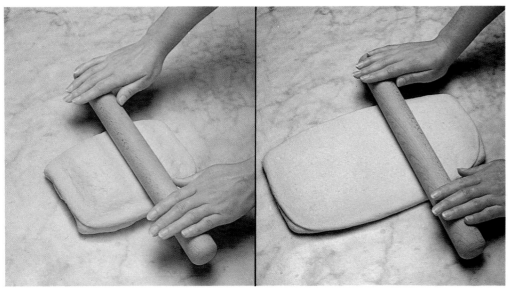

3 **Sealing the edges.** With a rolling pin, lightly squeeze together the three open sides of the rectangle (*above*). The gentle pressure will seal in the softened butter and prevent it from escaping when the dough is rolled out again.

4 **Turning and rolling out the dough.** Give the dough a quarter turn. Roll out the dough lightly (*above, left*): too much pressure would force out the softened butter enclosed within it. Continue to roll the dough until it is a rectangle twice as long as it is wide (*above, right*). Fold the dough into thirds again (*Step 2*). Six thicknesses of butter are now sandwiched between seven layers of dough. Wrap the dough in plastic film and chill it for an hour in the refrigerator.

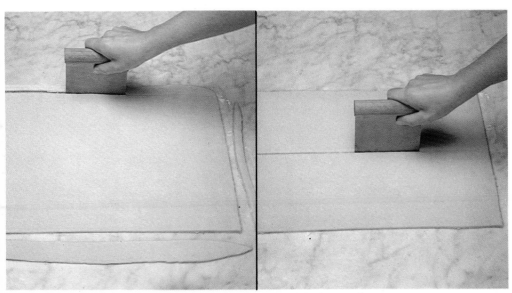

6 **Trimming the dough.** Roll out the layered dough to a thickness of about 3 mm (⅛ inch). Neatly trim the sides of the dough into a rectangle with a dough scraper (*above, left*), guiding the blade with a ruler if necessary. Cut the dough lengthwise into strips about 15 cm (6 inches) wide (*above, right*).

7 **Cutting out triangles.** With the dough scraper, mark points about 15 cm (6 inches) apart along one side of each strip, starting 15 cm from the end. On the opposite side of the strip, mark points 15 cm apart, but start 7.5 cm (3 inches) from the end. Make diagonal cuts between the marks to produce triangles (*above*). ▶

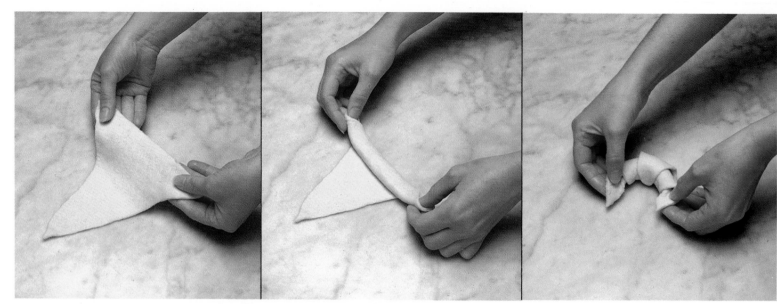

8 **Shaping the croissants.** Gently separate one triangle from the rest. Elongate the triangle slightly by giving it a light roll lengthwise with a rolling pin. Gently stretch the two corners of the triangle's base so that they are well defined (*above, left*). Starting at the base, roll up the triangle tightly (*above, centre*). Tuck the tip of the triangle just under the roll: it will emerge during baking. Shape the dough into a crescent by curling the ends of the roll so that they point inwards.

9 **Glazing the croissants.** Butter a baking sheet. Place the crescents on the sheet, leaving at least 2.5 cm (1 inch) between them to allow room for expansion. Cover the rolls with a cloth and leave them to rise for about 1 hour—or overnight in the refrigerator. Mix egg yolk with a little water and brush it over the croissants.

10 **Baking and serving.** Place the baking sheet of croissants in the centre of a 240°C (475°F or Mark 9) oven; after 2 minutes reduce the heat to 190°C (375°F or Mark 5) and bake for 15 to 20 minutes, until the croissants are golden-brown. Cool them on a rack for 10 to 15 minutes. Serve the croissants warm, in a napkin-lined basket. Pull them apart to eat them.□

Individual Pastries, Shaped and Filled with Flair

Envelopes Enclosing Almond Paste

Rolled out thin for the most dramatic increase in volume, leavened puff dough is easily cut and folded into a variety of shapes that increase in intricacy as the paper-thin layers of dough separate in the oven. Every folded shape will accommodate a filling, adding another element to the charm of this sort of pastry (*recipes, pages 150-155*). The four Danish pastries demonstrated here and on the next two pages show a few of the possibilities.

Envelopes (*right*) are formed by cutting the rolled-out dough into squares before adding a spoonful of filling to each piece; the corners are then folded over the filling and the pastries are baked. The same square sheets of dough can yield pinwheel shapes if they are cut and folded in a different way (*overleaf*).

The two other pastries demonstrated on the following pages are made from dough that is filled before it is shaped. In one, a double layer of dough sandwiching a filling is cut into squares and slit so that it opens out into cockscombs. In the other, a triple sandwich of dough and filling is sliced and twisted into helical strips.

The filling for any shape of dough can be as simple as a handful of currants or grated hard cheese. Richer, moister fillings include almond paste, sausage-meat or a mixture of egg with soft cheese. Both sweet and savoury pastries are usually glazed with egg yolk mixed with a little water; sweet ones may be topped with icing sugar or chopped nuts.

1 Mixing an almond-paste filling. Sieve castor sugar and icing sugar into a bowl. Add ground almonds to the sugar, and grate a little lemon rind into the bowl. Stir the ingredients with a spoon. Beat egg whites lightly and then add them to the bowl, stirring until all the ingredients are amalgamated into a stiff paste.

2 Dividing the dough. Prepare a yeast puff dough (*page 70*). On a lightly floured board, roll the dough about 5 mm (¼ inch) thick. Use a dough scraper to make a neat rectangle, and cut the rectangle into 12 cm (5 inch) squares (*above*).

3 Shaping the envelopes. Place a dollop of filling on the centre of each square. Fold one corner of the dough to half-cover the filling; bring over the opposite corner to overlap the first (*above*). Repeat this with the other corners to form an envelope. Seal the package by pressing the centre with one finger. Grease a baking sheet and place the envelopes on it.

4 Baking and serving. Cover the squares with a cloth; let them rise for 1 hour, or until almost doubled in bulk. Glaze the pastries with egg and water; place them in a preheated 240°C (475°F or Mark 9) oven. After 2 minutes, reduce the heat to 190°C (375°F or Mark 5). Bake for 15 to 20 minutes, until golden-brown. Cool on a rack; sieve castor sugar over them. □

Almond-Filled Pinwheels

1 **Cutting squares.** Prepare a yeast puff dough (*page 70*). Divide the dough into 12 cm (5 inch) squares. With a dough scraper, cut a diagonal line from each corner to about 1 cm (½ inch) from the centre of the square, so that you have four triangles joined in the middle. Place a teaspoonful of filling—here, almond paste—in the centre of the dough.

2 **Shaping pinwheels.** Folding in one direction, turn one bottom corner of each triangle over the filling. Leave the other half of each triangle unfolded (*above*). Lightly press the centre to seal the join. Repeat with the other dough pieces. Place the pastries on a buttered baking sheet and cover them. Let them rise for 1 hour, or until almost doubled in bulk.

3 **Baking and cooling.** Beat egg yolk with a little water, and glaze the pastries with this mixture. Place them in a preheated 240°C (475°F or Mark 9) oven for 2 minutes; reduce the heat to 190°C (375°F or Mark 5) and bake the pastries for 15 to 20 minutes, until golden-brown. Set the pinwheels on a rack to cool, and sieve icing sugar over them before serving. □

Twists of Pastry and Jam

1 **Layering dough with filling.** Prepare a yeast puff dough (*page 70*). Roll out the dough and, using a dough scraper, trim it into rectangles about 20 by 40 cm (8 by 16 inches). Heat apricot jam and pass it through a sieve. Spread a thin layer of the sieved jam over the dough, leaving a margin of about 1 cm (½ inch) around the edges. Fold the dough in thirds by bringing one third over to the middle, then folding the remaining third over it (*above*).

2 **Slicing the dough into strips.** With a dough scraper, slice the layered jam-filled dough into strips about 2.5 cm (1 inch) wide (*above*). For a straight line and even slices, you can place a ruler beside the dough to guide your hand as you cut.

Cockscombs with a Savoury Centre

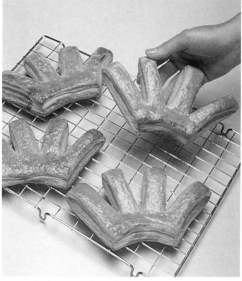

1 Filling the dough. Prepare a yeast puff dough (*page 70*). Divide the dough into rectangles about 20 cm (8 inches) wide. Prepare the filling—in this case, a mixture of *ricotta*, grated Parmesan cheese and egg—and spread it over half the width of each rectangle, leaving a 1 cm (½ inch) margin. Fold the uncovered half of the rectangle over the filling (*above*).

2 Cutting cockscombs. Using a dough scraper, divide the dough into squares. Make three cuts in the folded side of the dough, each one extending to within 1 cm (½ inch) of the opposite side (*above*). Place the pastries on a buttered baking sheet; spread their cut sections, so that they open out like a cockscomb.

3 Baking and cooling. Cover the pastries with a cloth; let them rise for 1 hour, or until almost doubled in bulk. Glaze them with egg beaten with water. Place them in a preheated 240°C (475°F or Mark 9) oven and reduce the heat to 190°C (375°F or Mark 5) after 2 minutes. Bake for 15 to 20 minutes, until the pastries are golden-brown. Cool them on a rack.□

3 Twisting the strips. Butter a baking sheet. Give each strip a half-twist as you place it on the sheet (*above*). Cover the twists with a cloth and let them rise for 1 hour, or until doubled in bulk. Glaze the strips with egg yolk beaten with water.

4 Baking and garnishing. Place the pastries in a preheated 240°C (475°F or Mark 9) oven for 2 minutes, then reduce the heat and bake for 15 to 20 minutes, or until the twists are golden-brown. Place the pastries on a rack to cool. Brush them with warm, puréed apricot jam and sprinkle with coarsely chopped walnuts (*above*).□

Large Yeast Puff Shapes

Yeast-leavened puff dough (*recipe, page 173*) need not be used exclusively for small pastries; it also lends itself to large, elaborate, filled shapes such as the long plait and the intricately twisted ring demonstrated on these two pages.

For the plait shown on the right, the long sides of a rectangle of dough are cut into a fringe of narrow strips, which are then criss-crossed over a filling. For the ring-shaped bread in the lower demonstration, the dough, spread with its filling, is first rolled into a tight cylinder and curved into a circle. The circle is then deeply notched and alternate sections flipped inwards to give a scalloped effect.

The choice of filling will depend on the capacity of the shape. If the bread can incorporate a substantial quantity of filling, the best choice is a firm mixture, such as the savoury blend of *ricotta*, Parmesan cheese and egg used in the plait. When the dough is to be spread only thinly with a flavouring, you can use a less cohesive mixture—as in the ring, with its layer of currants, cinnamon, butter and sugar.

A Plait Stuffed with Cheese

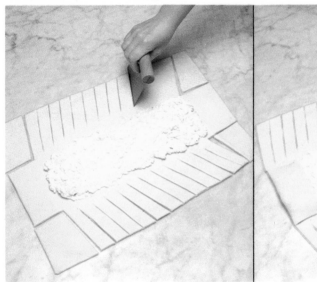

1 Filling and cutting. Roll out and trim a yeast puff dough (*page 70*) into a rectangle 1 cm (½ inch) thick. Spread a filling—here, cheese and egg—over the central third of the rectangle, leaving 5 cm (2 inches) uncovered at each end. Cut away the corners completely, leaving a rectangular flap of dough at each end of the filling. With a dough scraper, make slanting cuts, extending to within 1 cm (½ inch) of the filling at 2.5 cm (1 inch) intervals down the long sides of the dough (*above, left*). Remove the trimmed dough from the corners; fold the flaps over the filling (*above, right*).

A Fruit and Spice Circle

1 Filling the dough. Roll out a yeast puff dough (*page 70*) 3 mm (⅛ inch) thick; trim it into a rectangle. Spread a thin layer of filling over the dough with a palette knife, leaving 1 cm (½ inch) uncovered all round. Sprinkle dried fruits on the filling. Tightly roll the dough lengthwise into a cylinder.

2 Cutting the ring. Place the cylinder on a greased baking sheet, curving the dough into a ring as you set it down. With a pair of scissors, cut into the outside of the ring, at 2.5 cm (1 inch) intervals, to within 1 cm (½ inch) of the inner rim (*above*).

3 Shaping the ring. Moving in the same direction round the circle, turn alternate slices of the filled dough inwards, using your other hand to steady the preceding slice so that it stays in position, extending outwards. Cover the twisted ring with an inverted bowl or a cloth, and leave it to rest for about 1½ hours.

2 **Plaiting the dough.** Fold one of the topmost strips of dough over the filling. Cross the opposite strip over the first piece. Bring strips from alternate sides over the filling, forming a plait down the length of the dough. Tuck the loose ends of the last strips under the loaf.

3 **Baking and serving.** Place the loaf on a greased baking sheet and cover it with a cloth. Let it rise for about 1½ hours. Mix egg yolk with a little water and brush this glaze over the dough. Place the loaf in a preheated 240°C (475°F or Mark 9) oven for 2 minutes; reduce the heat to 190°C (375°F or Mark 5) and bake for a total of 30 minutes or until golden-brown. Cool the bread on a rack for 30 minutes if it is to be served warm. Place the loaf on a board and cut it into slices.□

4 **Glazing and baking.** Glaze the dough with egg yolk beaten with a little water (*above*). Place the ring in a preheated 240°C (475°F or Mark 9) oven and, after 2 minutes, reduce the heat to 190°C (375°F or Mark 5). Bake the ring for a total of 30 minutes, until golden-brown.

5 **Serving the ring.** Place the bread on a rack to cool. Let it rest for 30 minutes if you wish to serve it warm, or leave it for at least an hour if you prefer to serve it cold. Garnish the ring by sieving icing sugar over its surface (*above*). Place the ring on a board or plate and slice it into wedges for serving (*page 56*).□

Bagels: Poached, then Baked

When portions of barely risen dough are poached briefly in boiling water before baking, the result is close-textured rolls with a chewy crust. If each portion is first shaped into a ring to increase the area of crust, the result is known as the bagel of Jewish cookery (*demonstration, right*).

Bagels are usually made—as here—with a lightly enriched dough of flour, egg white, sugar, butter and milk (*recipe, page 149*); the enrichment enhances the bread's flavour and also makes its crust softer. To produce a dense crumb, the dough's first rising is limited to an hour and, once shaped, the dough is left to rise again only briefly before cooking. Shaping perfect rings is a straightforward process. Divide the dough into balls and use your finger to make and enlarge a hole in the centre of each (*Step 4, opposite*).

The bagels are poached only for about 15 seconds. The poaching moistens the outer dough and prevents the bagels from crisping when they are baked.

Before the bagels are baked, they can be brushed with egg to glaze them and, if you like, sprinkled with coarse salt, seeds of poppy, sesame or caraway or chopped onion. Bagels are traditionally eaten with cream cheese and smoked salmon.

1 Stirring in butter. In a small, heavy pan, heat milk until it boils. Remove the pan from the heat and add sugar and butter. With a spoon, stir the mixture until the sugar has thoroughly dissolved and the butter has melted (*above*).

2 Adding egg white. Pour the milk mixture into a large bowl and leave it to cool until tepid. Stir in yeast and leave it for about 10 minutes, until it is frothy. Over a small bowl, crack open an egg and separate the white from the yolk; add the white to the tepid milk (*above*) and reserve the yolk. Stir the mixture vigorously until all the ingredients are well combined.

5 Poaching the bagels. Heat a wide pan of water until it boils; adjust the heat to maintain a gentle boil. Carefully drop the bagels, a few at a time, into the water. Poach each batch, uncovered, for about 15 seconds, until they begin to puff up. Lift them out and drain them with a wide skimmer (*right*). Put the drained rings straight on to a greased baking sheet.

3 **Mixing in flour.** Stir a handful of flour and a little salt into the milk mixture; continue to add the flour in handfuls, stirring after each addition. When the dough is cohesive but still soft, turn it out on to a floured surface and knead it (*page 15*). Transfer the dough to a bowl, cover it and leave it to rise for about 1 hour, until it has increased in bulk by half.

4 **Shaping the dough.** Divide the dough into pieces weighing about 60 g (2 oz) each. Shape each piece into a ball (*page 30*). To form a ring, first poke your floured forefinger into the centre of a ball (*above, left*) and work your finger through the dough until it touches the work surface; move your finger in a circle to widen the hole. Twirl the bagel until the hole is about one-third of the roll's diameter (*above, right*). Place the bagels on a sheet, cover them with a cloth and let them rise—about 10 minutes.

6 **Baking the bagels.** Beat the reserved egg yolk with a little water and brush it over the bagels (*above*). Bake them in a preheated 200°C (400°F or Mark 6) oven for about 20 minutes, until golden-brown. With a palette knife, transfer the bagels to a rack to cool. Serve whole, or sliced horizontally and toasted.□

4
'Breads without Yeast
Alternative Ways to Leaven Batters and Doughs

Thin breads leavened by steam alone
Folding in whisked egg whites
Working with baking soda
Flavouring with fruit purées
Creating a custard-like topping

A loaf of banana bread is sliced for serving. Made from a thick batter leavened with baking powder and flavoured with puréed bananas, chopped nuts, raisins and spices, the bread has the moist and tender crumb typical of soda-leavened batters and doughs (*page 90*).

Breads that are made without yeast vary remarkably. They range from flat, thin loaves containing no leavening agent at all, to batter breads puffed up soufflé-light by beaten egg whites, to tender, cake-like breads leavened by bicarbonate of soda.

Although they lack the fine texture and the keeping qualities of most yeast-leavened breads, those leavened by other means have distinct advantages. The bread-making process is quick: non-yeast doughs do not require much, if any, of the kneading that develops the gluten network necessary to trap the gas slowly given off by the yeast. And because non-yeast leavens do not rely on gluten you can use flours and meals that have little or no gluten-forming potential—barley, oats and cornmeal, for example. In addition, no rising period is needed: whereas yeast must have time to act on the dough before baking, other leavens are triggered by the oven's heat and raise the dough or batter as it bakes.

Heat alone, without a leavening agent, is enough to raise light batters and soft, thinly flattened doughs. In the case of the flour and water paste used to make the Indian chapattis (*page 82*), for example, moisture in the dough is converted to steam and creates an expanding pocket that puffs up the bread. To incorporate more air in a batter you can use beaten egg whites; air trapped in the whites by whisking produces a light bread that is soft enough to serve with a spoon (*page 84*).

The most widely used of all non-yeast leavens, whether in a thin batter or a sturdy dough, is bicarbonate of soda. Moistened and subjected to heat, the soda gives off carbon dioxide, which expands during cooking and raises the bread mixture. However, the alkaline soda will give bread a soapy taste unless it is neutralized by the addition of some acidic element. In reacting with the soda, the acid also boosts the production of gas. Breads leavened by bicarbonate of soda (*pages 86-92*) are often made with some form of soured milk to supply the necessary acidity, but there is one kind of soda leaven, baking powder, that includes its own acid, in the form of cream of tartar. Baking powder also contains a little starch—usually cornflour—which keeps the mixture so dry that the bicarbonate of soda and the acid cannot react in storage.

Puffing Up an Unleavened Dough

In many parts of the world, the daily bread is no more than an unleavened dough of flour and water, shaped into thin rounds and cooked—often by the direct heat of a griddle. Elemental though they are, unleavened breads can be surprisingly varied. They can be made from any kind of flour or meal (*page 8*); wholemeal flour is the basis of the Indian chappatis in this demonstration (*recipe, page 163*). With equal success, you could make unleavened breads from cornmeal, oatmeal, barley, rye or buckwheat.

Different flavourings further extend the range of unleavened breads. At the very least, the dough mixture should be seasoned with salt, while ground spices or chopped herbs can make exciting additions. If you like, substitute milk for some or all of the water to make an enriched dough. You can produce flaky bread that is richer still by repeatedly brushing each round of dough with melted butter, folding it and then rolling it out again—a technique used for Indian *parathas* (*box, opposite page; recipe, page 163*). For a more substantial result, you can stuff the dough with puréed vegetables (*recipe, page 164*), or cooked minced meat, before cooking the bread.

The textures of unleavened doughs can vary markedly. The light, airy quality of the chappatis on the right is obtained by cooking the dough in two stages. First, each thin round is cooked briefly on a preheated griddle (*Step 4*). Then, the partially cooked bread is held over an open flame for a few seconds; the direct heat causes moisture in the dough to turn quickly to steam, puffing up the bread (*Step 5*) while the cooking is completed. For a crisper effect, unleavened dough could be cooked completely on the griddle, until well browned on both sides. To make a denser, softer bread, wrap thick, flattened rounds of unleavened dough in aluminium foil and bake them in the oven.

1 Mixing the dough. Put flour—here, wholemeal flour—and salt in a mixing bowl. With your hand, gradually mix in water to make a soft, slightly sticky dough. Turn out the dough on to a lightly floured work surface and knead for 5 to 10 minutes, until it is smooth and supple. Rinse and dry the bowl and put the dough back in; cover with a damp cloth.

2 Dividing up the dough. Leave the dough to rest for 30 minutes. Then, keeping the bulk of the dough covered, pull off 2 or 3 walnut-sized pieces at a time and put them on a floured work surface. Flour both your hands and roll each piece of dough between your palms to shape it into an even ball. Press down firmly on each ball (*above*) to flatten it into a circle.

3 Rolling out the dough. Sprinkle each round of dough with flour. Using a rolling pin, roll out each round: push the pin backwards and forwards with one hand and turn the dough gently with the other hand to make an even circle. Continue rolling and turning until the round of dough is about 2 mm ($\frac{1}{16}$ inch) thick.

4 Cooking the chappati. Preheat a griddle or a cast-iron pan over a medium heat. Put a round of dough on it. After 1 to 2 minutes, when bubbles caused by the steam appear on the surface, carefully turn the dough over with your fingertips. Cook the chappati for a further minute, until its underside begins to brown.

Melted Butter for a Flaky Texture

1 **Buttering the dough.** Prepare an unleavened dough of wholemeal flour (*Step 1, left*); replacing half of the water by milk. Divide up the dough into balls (*Step 2, left*). Roll each piece into a circle and brush its surface lightly with a little melted butter (*above*).

2 **Folding and rolling.** On a floured work surface, fold each circle of dough in half, then fold it again into a quarter circle. With a rolling pin, roll out the dough as evenly as possible to form a roughly circular shape. Butter, fold and roll out the dough three more times.

3 **Cooking and serving.** On a lightly buttered griddle over a low to medium heat, cook each round of dough for 3 to 5 minutes, until its underside is well browned. With a palette knife, carefully turn the bread over and cook it for a further 3 to 5 minutes. Stack the breads on a heated, napkin-lined plate and serve them immediately (*above*).

5 **Completing the cooking.** To puff up the chappati, rest it on a wire scoop or serving slice and hold it over an open, high heat. After a few seconds, when the bread puffs up (*left*), remove it from the heat. Place the cooked chappatis in a heated, napkin-lined dish; they should be eaten hot, torn apart by hand.☐

Spoonbread: Gently Raised with Egg Whites

Egg whites can leaven breads made from any flour or meal, including those, such as cornmeal and barley, which are too deficient in gluten-forming proteins to be raised effectively by yeast. Beaten egg whites form a honeycomb of tiny cells that enclose air and moisture. On heating, the air expands and the moisture turns to steam: the resulting increase in the egg whites' volume is enough to raise a loose mixture of flour or meal and a liquid. The bread produced is so moist and fluffy that it is served with a spoon.

In this demonstration, the whites are used to raise a cornmeal bread (*recipe, page 166*). The cornmeal is cooked with water to a porridge before being enriched with milk and egg yolks. The preliminary cooking softens the meal but does not obliterate its roughness; the resulting bread has an attractively grainy texture.

The basic mixture can be adapted to make either a sweet or a savoury bread. For a sweet bread, add sugar and a flavouring—for instance, a spoonful of rum or a little puréed fruit. For a savoury bread, include strong or sharp flavourings to balance the sweetish taste of the cornmeal. Here, bacon, garlic and Cheddar cheese are added. You could substitute any other strong cheese for Cheddar.

The bread's lightness depends on careful handling of the egg whites. When you separate the whites from the yolks, make certain that no trace of yolk spills into the whites: the fat in the yolks would prevent the whites from increasing in volume. For the same reason, be sure that the bowl in which you beat the whites is perfectly clean. Use a copper bowl if possible: a chemical reaction with the copper adds stability to the egg white foam. Finally, stir a spoonful of the whites into the batter before adding the bulk of the whites; this loosens the batter and enables the rest of the whites to be folded in gently.

If the bread is baked just long enough to colour its surface lightly, as here, it will have a moist, creamy consistency. For a drier bread, bake the mixture for 10 minutes longer and test it with the blade of a small knife: it should come out clean. With the lightness conferred by the egg whites, the bread will have an almost soufflé-like consistency.

1 **Making a cornmeal paste.** Pour cold water into a saucepan and then sprinkle cornmeal into it, stirring all the time with a wooden spoon to prevent lumps forming (*above*). Transfer the pan to a medium heat and, still stirring, bring the mixture to the boil. It will reach a thick, smooth consistency almost at once.

2 **Flavouring the cornmeal.** Remove the saucepan from the heat and immediately sprinkle in some grated Cheddar cheese (*above*). Add butter, salt and chopped garlic and stir until the cheese melts and blends thoroughly with the batter.

5 **Incorporating the egg whites.** Pour the batter into the bowl of beaten egg whites. With a wooden spoon, gently fold the cornmeal mixture and the whites together until they are just combined.

6 **Filling the baking dish.** Generously butter a shallow baking dish. Pour the batter into the dish (*above*) and then smooth its surface level with the back of the wooden spoon or with a spatula.

3 **Completing the basic batter.** Separate the whites from the yolks of three or four eggs; reserve the whites in a mixing bowl. Pour cold milk into the batter to cool it so that there is no risk of the yolks curdling when they are added. The milk will also thin the batter to a creamier consistency. Stir the yolks into the mixture. Add pieces of crisply fried bacon.

4 **Loosening the batter.** Using a wire whisk, beat the egg whites until they form soft peaks. To loosen the cornmeal batter slightly, fold a dollop of the beaten egg whites into the mixture (*above*).

7 **Baking and serving.** Bake in an oven preheated to 170°C (325°F or Mark 3) for about 1 hour—until puffy and golden (*left*). Serve the bread immediately, spooning it on to warmed plates. □

Doughs Leavened with Soda

When a dough is leavened with baking soda, there is no need to prove the dough; it can be shaped and baked at once. The oven's heat will cause the soda to release carbon dioxide that leavens the dough; the result is a moist, crumbly bread.

Soda will raise doughs based on any flour and can be used to leaven either large dough shapes, such as the Irish soda bread in the upper demonstration on the right, or small ones such as the scones in the lower demonstration. Because soda breads do not retain moisture well, they are best eaten fresh, on the same day they are baked, or toasted the following day.

The Irish soda bread here is made with a mixture of white flour and a little wholemeal flour, yielding a pale brown loaf with an agreeably coarse texture. The bread can also be made entirely with white flour (*recipe, page 156*). Buttermilk binds the ingredients and provides sufficient acidity to neutralize the flavour of the alkaline soda and to give a boost to the leavening action. Before baking, the loaf is scored with a deep cross to increase the amount of crust and to ensure the even penetration of heat.

The scone dough (*recipe, page 158*) is made with white wheat flour; a little butter is incorporated for flavour and to give a moister crumb. Sometimes, as in this demonstration, an egg is added to enrich the dough further; the egg also helps to retain moisture, and thus improves the keeping qualities of the scones. The scone dough is leavened with baking powder, which includes an acid—cream of tartar—as well as soda, so that there is no need for an acidic liquid; however, soured cream is included for its flavour.

The soda bread is best cooked in a preheated pot—preferably of cast iron, which holds heat well. The initial contact of the dough with the hot metal encourages rising. For the first part of baking, the pot is covered to trap steam, so that the formation of the crust is delayed and the dough is able to rise freely; then the lid is removed, to let the bread brown.

The thin scones cook quickly; you can bake them on a baking sheet in the oven or, as shown, cook them on top of the stove. Here, a griddle is used, but a heavy frying pan would work equally well.

A Loaf Baked in a Pot

1 Stirring in the liquid. Place all the dry ingredients—here, wholemeal flour, white flour, bicarbonate of soda and salt—in a large mixing bowl. Stir them together. Make a well in the centre and gradually pour in the liquid—in this case, buttermilk—while stirring with a fork.

2 Kneading the dough. Continue stirring, working outwards from the centre of the bowl, until a loose, soft dough is formed. Flour your hands and gather together the dough; turn it out on a floured work surface. Lightly and swiftly knead the dough for 2 to 3 minutes; pat it into a ball.

Griddle-Cooked Scones

1 Rubbing in the butter. Sieve white flour, baking powder and salt into a large mixing bowl. Add small pieces of butter. With your fingertips, rub the butter into the dry ingredients until the mixture has a uniform, crumbly texture. Make a well in the centre of the mixture.

2 Mixing the dough. In a separate bowl, prepare the liquid—here, soured cream whisked with an egg. Slowly pour the liquid into the well and, with your fingers, work the mixture into a soft dough. Draw the dough together, turn it out on a floured surface and briefly knead it until it is just smooth. Form the dough into a ball.

3 **Scoring the dough.** Oil a cast-iron pot. Heat the pot in a 200°C (400°F or Mark 6) oven for 10 minutes. Flatten the dough into a round slightly smaller than the diameter of the pot. Place the dough in the pot. With a sharp, floured knife, score a deep cross in the dough, taking care not to cut to the edges of the round. Cover the pot with its lid.

4 **Baking the bread.** Bake the bread in an oven preheated to 200°C (400°F or Mark 6) for 30 minutes; remove the lid and bake for a further 10 minutes to brown the crust. Protecting your hands with a towel, tip the bread out of the pot on to a rack to cool, for about 45 minutes. To serve, break the bread into wedges and slice it.□

3 **Cutting out the scones.** Sprinkle a little flour on the surface of the dough. With a rolling pin, lightly roll out the dough into a circle about 1 cm (½ inch) thick. Cut out rounds with a 5 cm (2 inch) pastry cutter (*above*) or an inverted glass. Gather together the trimmings, roll them out again and cut more rounds.

4 **Cooking the scones.** Place a griddle over a low to medium heat. When the griddle is hot, lightly grease it, using a clean cloth smeared with oil or lard. Place the scones, spaced well apart, on the griddle and cook them until they are browned on the underside—about 10 minutes. Turn the scones with a palette knife and brown the other side (*left*). To serve, break the scones open and butter them.□

Batters: Airy or Substantial

Batters of different consistencies need different leavening methods—as demonstrated by the two American tea breads here. A very light "popover" batter, which contains a lot of milk and beaten eggs (*right; recipe, page 162*), requires no additional leavening at all. The steam given off by the liquid during baking will be enough to lift the batter, and the eggs will set to hold the popovers' risen form. The thicker batter for American-style muffins (*right, below; recipe, page 161*) is heavy enough to need the assistance of baking powder or bicarbonate of soda.

Popovers, although they contain no leaven, will only achieve their maximum height if the batter is quickly set by hot moulds or supported by lined moulds. If you use cast-iron moulds, you can grease them and heat them in the oven before pouring in the batter. Or, as shown here, you can use buttered, unheated porcelain moulds and coat them with some grainy ingredient to which the batter can cling as it rises, thus preventing the popovers' thin walls from collapsing inwards. For plain popovers, coat the moulds with flour. To make savoury or sweet popovers, use grated cheese, as here, or sugar. If you like, you can add a little more of the flavourings to the batter as you fill the moulds (*Step 3*); or add complementary flavourings such as spices or finely chopped onion or herbs—they will be light enough not to weigh down the batter and prevent it from rising.

To ensure that a thick muffin batter has a tender texture, mix it only until it is roughly blended. Too much beating would overdevelop the gluten in the flour, and produce a tough muffin. Any lumps in the batter disappear during baking.

A muffin batter can support the weight of heavier additions than those which flavour popovers. In this demonstration, blueberries are used, but you could substitute redcurrants, cranberries, dried fruits, chopped nuts, pork cracklings or bits of crisply fried bacon. To prevent large morsels such as the berries from sinking to the bottom of the batter during baking, and to keep them from clustering together, they should be dusted with flour before they are added.

Popovers: Light and Puffy

1 Whisking the batter. Put plain flour and salt in a mixing bowl. Whisking continuously, gradually pour in enough milk to form a thin batter (*above, left*). Melt butter in a small pan and briefly whisk it into the batter (*above, centre*). One at a time, add eggs, whisking well after each addition (*above, right*).

Berry-Filled Muffins

1 Mixing the batter. Sieve together flour, salt, baking powder and tartaric acid into a mixing bowl; if you like, add a little sugar for sweeter muffins. In a separate bowl, whisk eggs and milk until they are thoroughly blended. Add melted butter to the liquid (*above*) and stir well. Pour the liquid into the flour and stir until the ingredients are only roughly blended.

2 Adding the fruit. Wash fresh blueberries and drain them on a towel. Put the berries in a strainer. Hold the strainer over a plate and sprinkle the berries with flour, tapping the strainer so that excess flour falls through. Add the floured berries to the muffin batter and stir them in with a few swift strokes.

2 **Lining the moulds.** Smear the insides of individual moulds with softened butter. Put freshly grated Parmesan cheese into each container; turn the container to coat its sides evenly (*above*). Empty out the excess cheese. Spoon a little batter into each container, then sprinkle in a teaspoonful of grated Parmesan cheese seasoned with paprika.

3 **Filling the moulds.** Add more batter until each mould is about three-quarters full. Put the moulds in an oven preheated to 230°C (450°F or Mark 8). After 15 minutes, reduce the heat to 180°C (350°F or Mark 4) and bake 20 minutes more, until the popovers are well risen, golden and firm.

4 **Serving the popovers.** The insides of the popovers will still be moist. If you want a drier texture, puncture the popovers with the tip of a small, sharp knife; turn off the oven and leave the popovers inside for 10 minutes more. Serve the popovers turned out into a napkin-lined basket.□

3 **Filling the muffin tins.** Spoon the batter into generously buttered muffin tins, filling them two-thirds full. Bake the muffins in an oven preheated to 200°C (400°F or Mark 6) for 20 to 25 minutes, until they are fully risen and light brown in colour.

4 **Serving the muffins.** Remove the muffins from the oven and leave them for about a minute so that they shrink slightly from the sides of the tins. To loosen each muffin, run a knife tip around its sides; invert the tins to unmould the muffins. Serve the muffins warm, in a napkin-lined basket. To eat them, break the muffins apart and spread them with butter.□

Puréed Fruit for a Cake-Like Crumb

A thick batter blended with puréed fruit and leavened with baking powder yields a mildly sweet bread with a moist, tender crumb. Such a fruit bread is best enjoyed cold, cut into thick slices, spread with butter and served with tea or coffee.

To combine easily with the other ingredients, the fruit purée must be fairly smooth. Some fruits can be puréed raw: the ripe bananas used in this demonstration (*recipe, page 162*) are simply peeled and mashed with either a fork or a potato masher. The same treatment would suit avocados or persimmons. Firmer fruits such as apricots, apples or pumpkin must be first cooked and then puréed.

The ingredients should be combined in a sequence that does not require persistent beating of the flour, which would make the bread tough. First butter and sugar are creamed together—beaten until they form a smooth, light mixture. The sugar used here has been flavoured by leaving a whole vanilla pod in a covered jar of sugar for a few days; this scented sugar does not have the aggressive edge of vanilla extract. Next, an egg is added to the creamed mixture. Then, in alternate spoonfuls, the puréed fruit and the dry ingredients—flour, baking powder, salt and nutmeg—are stirred in. Blending the ingredients in small batches ensures that no lumps form. Any solid additions—in this case, nuts and dried fruits—are folded in at the very end, before the batter is put into a tin and baked.

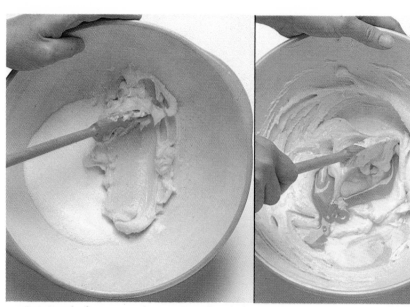

1 **Starting the batter.** In a large mixing bowl, use a wooden spoon to cream softened, unsalted butter with vanilla-flavoured sugar (*above, left*). When these two ingredients are thoroughly blended, add a raw egg and stir the mixture with a wooden spoon (*above, right*) until it has reached a smooth consistency.

4 **Adding other ingredients.** Coarsely chop nuts—here, pecans. Toss raisins in a sieve with a teaspoon of flour; the flour will keep the raisins separate by coating their moist surfaces and will prevent them from sinking to the bottom of the bread. Add the raisins and the pecans to the batter and stir briefly to mix them in.

5 **Filling the loaf tin.** Butter and flour a loaf tin that is twice the volume of the batter. Scrape the batter from the bowl into the tin (*above*), then level the surface of the batter with a spoon or a spatula.

2 **Mashing the bananas.** Peel large, ripe bananas, cut them into rough chunks and put them in a bowl. Using a potato masher, as here, or a fork, mash the bananas to a smooth pulp.

3 **Adding dry ingredients and fruit.** In a separate bowl, sieve together flour, salt, baking powder and grated nutmeg. A spoonful at a time, add the flour mixture (*above, left*) and the banana purée (*above, right*) alternately to the creamed mixture, stirring after each addition so that the ingredients are thoroughly blended.

6 **Baking the bread.** Bake the bread in an oven preheated to 180°C (350°F or Mark 4) for an hour. To test for doneness, push a skewer into the centre of the loaf; if the skewer comes out clean, the bread is ready; if not, bake 10 minutes more and test again. Unmould the bread and turn it right side up on to a wire rack to cool. Transfer it to a board for slicing. □

A Marbled Finish for Cornmeal

If the surface of a soda-leavened batter is dribbled with milk or cream just before baking, part of the liquid will seep into the batter as it cooks. The result is a bread marbled with soft, custard-like streaks.

The contrast of textures shows up best when the bread is based on a coarse flour or meal—cornmeal or oatmeal, for example. In this demonstration, a cornmeal batter is used (*recipe, page 166*), but to lighten the coarseness of the meal, some plain wheat flour is included. Bicarbonate of soda, buttermilk—which provides acid to balance the alkaline soda—and ordinary milk complete the mixture.

To provide an intense, immediate heat that will encourage the bread to rise to its fullest, the completed batter is poured into a preheated cast-iron vessel. The extra liquid is dribbled over the surface of the batter at once, before baking.

1 Mixing the batter. Preheat the oven to 180°C (350°F or Mark 4). Put butter or rendered bacon fat in a deep, heavy pan and set the pan in the oven to heat. In a mixing bowl, combine cornmeal, white flour, baking soda, sugar and salt. Pour in buttermilk, whisking continuously.

2 Adding the batter. Whisk in fresh milk to thin the batter to a smooth, pourable consistency. Take the hot pan from the oven and turn it to coat its sides with the melted fat. Pour in the batter (*above*).

3 Dribbling on milk. Gently pour more fresh milk in a thin stream all over the surface of the batter (*above*). Do not stir the batter after the milk has been added. Without delay, return the pan to the oven.

4 Serving the cornbread. Bake the bread for about an hour, until its surface is a deep golden colour. Remove the pan from the oven. Use a spoon to serve the hot bread on to warmed plates.□

Anthology
of Recipes

The recipes in this Anthology have been selected from among the best published during the past four centuries. They range from hearthbreads and flatbreads to the elaborate *kugelhopf* of France and central Europe. There are regional and national breads from 33 countries, including the cornbreads of the United States and Bulgaria, rye breads from German-speaking countries and Scandinavia, and flatbreads from Finland, the Middle East, India and Italy. Many recipes in the Anthology have been selected from rare and out-of-print books in private collections; a large number have never before been published in English.

Throughout the Anthology the emphasis is on techniques that are fully accessible to the home cook and do justice to the finest ingredients. Since many early recipe writers did not specify quantities, the missing information has been judiciously included and, where appropriate, introductory notes in italics have been added by the Editors. Modern terms have been substituted for archaic language, but to preserve the character of the original and create a true anthology, the authors' texts have been changed as little as possible. Some instructions have necessarily been expanded, but in cases where the method is somewhat vague, the reader need only refer to the appropriate demonstration in the front of the book to find the technique in question explained in words and pictures. Any cooking terms and ingredients that may be unfamiliar are explained in the combined Index and Glossary at the end of the book.

The type of yeast used has been standardized to give equivalent quantities for commercial fresh and dried yeasts. There is a recently developed variety of dried yeast which must be mixed directly with the flour; if you are using this yeast, follow the manufacturer's instructions. Wherever strong plain flour is indicated in the ingredients list, the reference is to white flour. Because flours vary in absorbency with the humidity of the atmosphere and the age and character of the flour, always add the liquid gradually, so that you can incorporate more or less to produce a dough of the required consistency.

Each recipe ingredients list is headed by the flour or flours and main ingredients; other ingredients are listed in order of use. Both metric and imperial weights for each ingredient are given in separate columns. The two sets of figures are not exact equivalents, but are consistent for each recipe. Working from either metric or imperial weights and measures will produce equally good results, but the two systems should not be mixed. Where only one dimension is given, it represents the diameter. All spoon measures are level. Recipes for standard preparations—sourdough starters, a selection of basic doughs and fillings—are listed at the end of the Anthology.

Basic Breads	94
Flavoured and Filled Breads	107
Egg Breads	128
Yeast Puff Pastry	150
Breads without Yeast	155
Standard Preparations	170

Basic Breads

Salt-Rising Bread

This salt-rising bread uses a natural, quick-fermenting leaven made from potatoes and cornmeal. The leaven must be kept at a constant temperature during fermentation.

To make four 20 by 10 cm (8 by 4 inch) loaves

2 kg	strong plain flour	5 lb
	bicarbonate of soda	
1 litre	milk	1¾ pints
40 g	sugar	1½ oz
	salt	
40 g	butter or lard, softened	1½ oz
	Salt-rising leaven	
2	medium-sized potatoes, peeled and thinly sliced	2
2 tbsp	cornmeal	2 tbsp
	bicarbonate of soda	
2 tbsp	sugar	2 tbsp
½ litre	boiling water	16 fl oz

At noon on the day before you make the bread, prepare the leaven by first putting the potatoes into a 1.25 litre (2 pint) jar and adding the cornmeal, sugar and a pinch of bicarbonate of soda. Pour the boiling water into the jar. Put on the lid, but do not screw it down. Wrap the jar in a blanket and set it in a warm place until morning, when there should be about 2.5 cm (1 inch) of foam on the surface of the mixture; you will notice an odd odour. If there is no foam, discard the mixture. The success of salt-rising bread depends upon the leaven.

Scald, but do not boil, the milk. Add 15 g (½ oz) of the sugar, a small pinch of bicarbonate of soda and ¼ litre (8 fl oz) of liquid drained from the jar containing the leaven.

Add enough flour to make a batter—about 250 g (8 oz)—and set this in a warm place to rise until it doubles its bulk. Add salt, the fat and the remainder of the sugar and flour, and knead for about 20 minutes. Pour the dough into four buttered 1 litre (2 lb) loaf tins and leave to rise for about 3 hours, or until the loaves have risen about 2 cm (¾ inch) above the tops of the tins. Bake in an oven preheated to 190°C (375°F or Mark 5) for 45 minutes or until the loaves are well risen and golden-brown.

BRITISH COLUMBIA WOMEN'S INSTITUTES
ADVENTURES IN COOKING

Home-Made Italian Milk Bread

Pane al Latte Fatto in Casa

To make two 20 cm (8 inch) loaves or 20 rolls

500 g	strong plain flour	1 lb
300 g	wholemeal flour	10 oz
80 g	fresh yeast or 2½ tbsp dried yeast	2½ oz
45 cl each	tepid milk and water, combined	¾ pint each
1 tsp	sugar	1 tsp
2 tsp	salt	2 tsp
	milk for glazing (optional)	

In a large bowl, dissolve the yeast and the sugar in 6 tablespoons of the milk and water mixture. Stir well, leave in a warm place until the yeast is foaming, then add the rest of the milk and water. Stir in the flours and the salt and knead to make a fairly soft dough, adding more tepid water if necessary. Turn the dough on to a working surface sprinkled with additional plain flour and knead it for 20 minutes, or until the dough is smooth and elastic. Shape the dough into balls, or into two large round loaves and place them on a buttered baking sheet. Cover the rolls or loaves with a cloth and leave them to rise in a warm place for about 1½ hours, or until a floured finger poked into the dough leaves a permanent dent. If you like, glaze the bread with a little milk.

Bake the dough in an oven preheated to 220°C (425°F or Mark 7)—about 30 minutes for the rolls or 1 hour for the loaves. Both the rolls and loaves should be golden-brown and sound slightly hollow when rapped. Cool them on wire racks.

MARIÙ SALVATORI DE ZULIANI
LA CUCINA DI VERSILIA E GARFAGNANA

Spanish Household Bread

Pan Casero

*To make three 20 by 10 cm
(8 by 4 inch) cylindrical loaves*

1.5 kg	wholemeal flour	3 lb
30 g	fresh yeast or 1 tbsp dried yeast	1 oz
¾ litre	tepid water (preferably spring water)	1¼ pints
1 tbsp	sea salt	1 tbsp
2 tbsp	oil	2 tbsp

Put the water and yeast into a bowl and stir to dissolve. Leave the yeast mixture in a warm place, until foaming, about 20 minutes. Put half the flour and the salt into a bowl, add the yeast and stir thoroughly with a wooden spoon or spatula. Work in the remaining flour with your hands. Remove the dough from the bowl to a floured work surface and knead well for about 5 minutes. Cover the dough with a cloth and put it in a warm place to rise, until it has doubled in bulk (1 hour or more). To see if it is ready, press the dough with a fingertip; if it leaves an indentation it has risen sufficiently.

Divide the dough into three pieces and knead them a little more. Then form them into cylindrical loaves. Place the loaves on a floured baking sheet and rub a little oil on the surface to glaze them. Leave the loaves to prove in a warm place for about 1 hour or until doubled in bulk. Bake them in a preheated 220°C (425°F or Mark 7) oven for 30 to 45 minutes, or until golden-brown.

MARIA ROSA SOLA FRANCH
DE QUÉ VA LA ALIMENTACIÓN NATURAL

The Grant Loaf

Should you want to make only one loaf, use 500 g (1 lb) of wholemeal flour, 2 teaspoons of fresh yeast or 1 teaspoon of dried yeast, about 35 cl (12 fl oz) of water, 1 teaspoon of salt and 1 teaspoon of sugar.

To make three 20 by 10 cm (8 by 4 inch) loaves

1.5 kg	stoneground wholemeal flour	3 lb
30 g	fresh yeast or 1 tbsp dried yeast	1 oz
2 tsp	salt	2 tsp
1.25 litres	tepid water	2 pints
3 tsp	soft brown sugar, honey or black molasses	3 tsp

Mix the salt with the flour. In very cold weather, warm the flour slightly—enough to take off the chill. Place in a cup 3 tablespoons of the tepid water, the fresh yeast and the sugar, honey or black molasses. If using dried yeast, sprinkle it on top of the water and leave for 2 minutes or so for the yeast to soften before adding the sweetener. In about 10 to 15 minutes this mixture should have produced a thick, creamy froth. Pour this into the flour and add the rest of the water. Mix well—by hand is best—for a minute or so, working from the sides to the middle, until the dough feels elastic and leaves the sides of the mixing bowl clean.

Butter three 1 litre (2 lb) loaf tins and leave them in a warm place. Divide the dough, which should be slippery but not wet, into the warmed tins. Put the tins in a warm place, cover them with a cloth and leave them for about 20 minutes or until the dough is within 1 cm (½ inch) of the rims of the tins. Bake the loaves in an oven preheated to 200°C (400°F or Mark 6) for approximately 35 to 40 minutes, or until they sound hollow when rapped on the bottom.

DORIS GRANT
YOUR DAILY FOOD: RECIPE FOR SURVIVAL

Sourdough Bread

Pain au Levain

When using a new starter, I add half water, half beer as liquid to increase sourness. I also stir in a bit of flavouring flours in place of strong plain, unbleached flour.

To make one 25 cm (10 inch) loaf or one 40 cm (16 inch) cylindrical loaf

1 kg	strong plain flour, unbleached	2 lb
2 tbsp	rye flour	2 tbsp
1 tbsp	buckwheat flour	1 tbsp
1 tbsp	bran	1 tbsp
250 g	sourdough starter (*page 170*)	8 oz
15 g	fresh yeast or 2 tsp dried yeast	½ oz
60 cl	tepid water	1 pint
2 tbsp	toasted, ground sesame seeds	2 tbsp
1 tbsp	malt extract (powdered or syrup)	1 tbsp
2 tsp	salt	2 tsp

To make the yeast sponge, empty the starter into a mixing bowl. Stir in ¼ litre (8 fl oz) of the tepid water and 250 g (8 oz) of the strong plain flour. Cover the sponge with a towel, place in a warm spot and leave for 24 to 36 hours. At the end of this time, stir down the yeast sponge and put half of it back into the container for your next baking.

Dissolve the yeast in the rest of the tepid water. Stir the dissolved yeast into the sponge and add the rye and buckwheat flours, the sesame seeds, bran, malt and salt. Add enough strong plain flour to form a soft dough, then turn the mass out on to a floured work surface and knead hard and well, pressing the entire weight of the upper body to the task. Knead for a good 12 minutes until the dough feels firm and elastic to the touch. Add only the minimum of flour necessary to reach this point, and keep in mind that the dough should above all remain malleable and soft enough to form easily. Place the dough in a lightly oiled bowl, cover it with a kitchen towel and let it rise until doubled in bulk. Remove it from the bowl, and shape it. Let the formed loaf rise, towel-covered, in a warm place until it has reached almost full size. This rising can be slowed by placing the bread in a cooler spot and it is often desirable to do so, because it allows the flavouring essences to develop more fully. In the case of full, bulky loaves, and particularly in winter, it will take a good hour at the very least for the bread to rise and expand enough, even in a warm place.

Bake the bread in a preheated 190° to 200°C (375° to 400°F or Mark 5 to 6) oven for 15 minutes, then reduce the heat to 180°C (350°F or Mark 4) for 20 minutes, and reduce the heat again to 170°C (325°F or Mark 3) until the bread is done, another 15 to 25 minutes, depending on the shape of the loaf.

JUDITH OLNEY
COMFORTING FOOD

Dutch Brown Bread

Bruin Brood

The method given below may also be followed for making white bread. Use 500 g (1 lb) strong plain flour and 30 cl (½ pint) of milk, sweetened with 2 teaspoons of sugar if desired. Mix the liquid with the yeast before pouring it into the flour. Leave the dough to rise for an extra 5 minutes at each proving.

To make one 20 by 10 cm (8 by 4 inch) loaf

350 g	wholemeal flour	12 oz
150 g	strong plain flour	5 oz
20 g	fresh yeast or 2 tsp dried yeast and 1 tsp sugar	¾ oz
About 30 cl	tepid milk or water	About ½ pint
1 tsp	salt	1 tsp
10 g	butter, softened (optional)	⅓ oz

Combine the wholemeal and plain flours in a mixing bowl and make a well in the centre. Pour the milk or water into the well. Stir the yeast into the liquid (if using dried yeast, dissolve it first with the sugar in half of the liquid). Gradually work in the flours, add the salt and finally the softened butter, if used. Knead the dough thoroughly for about 10 minutes, or until it is smooth and elastic. Cover the bowl with a damp cloth and leave the dough to rise in a warm place for 1½ to 2 hours, until it has doubled in bulk.

On a floured board, form the risen dough into a ball. Place the dough on a buttered baking sheet, cover it with a cloth, and leave it to prove for about 20 minutes. To test if the dough is well proved, push two fingertips into the top of the dough; if the impressions remain in the dough, it is ready.

Put the dough on a floured board. Knock it back and knead it for about 5 minutes. Form it into a ball again, return it to the baking sheet and let it rise for 10 minutes. Remove the dough to the floured board, knock it back again, and roll it out into an elongated triangle shape. Fold the corners towards the centre and shape the dough into a rectangle. Roll out the dough again and place it in a buttered 1 litre (2 lb) loaf tin. Cover and let it rise for a further 25 minutes.

Uncover the tin and bake the loaf in an oven preheated to 220°C (450°F or Mark 8) for 30 to 40 minutes or until the surface is brown and crisp. The loaf should sound hollow when rapped underneath. Allow it to cool on a wire rack.

C. A. H. HAITSMA MULIER-VAN BEUSEKOM (EDITOR)
CULINAIRE ENCYCLOPÉDIE

Household Bread

Pain de Ménage

If you like, add an egg, 2 pinches of sugar and 1 tablespoon of oil to the dough, and glaze the loaves with beaten egg.

To make two 45 cm (18 inch) or three 30 cm (12 inch) cylindrical loaves

1 kg	strong plain flour	2 to 2½ lb
80 g	fresh yeast or 2½ tbsp dried yeast	2½ oz
¾ litre	tepid water	1¼ pints
1 tsp	salt	1 tsp

Dissolve the yeast in 12.5 cl (4 fl oz) of the water. Add 250 g (8 oz) of the flour, kneading the mixture lightly. Cover it and leave it to rise in a warm place until it has doubled in bulk—about 30 minutes. Then add the rest of the flour and the salt and knead with the remaining water. Knead the dough for 5 to 10 minutes, until it is firm but elastic. Shape it into two or three cylindrical loaves, lay them on a buttered and floured baking sheet, and leave them to prove for about 2½ hours.

Bake the loaves in a preheated 180°C (350°F or Mark 4) oven for 40 minutes or until the loaves are golden-brown and sound hollow when rapped.

IRÈNE AND LUCIENNE KARSENTY
LA CUISINE PIED-NOIR

Black Rye Bread

Schwarzbrot

To make six 20 by 10 cm (8 by 4 inch) loaves

2.5 kg	wholemeal flour	5 lb
500 g	rye flour	1 lb
60 g	rye sourdough starter (*page 170*)	2 oz
15 g	fresh yeast or 2 tsp dried yeast	½ oz
About 1.5 litres	tepid water	About 2½ pints
1 tbsp	salt	1 tbsp
1 to 2 tbsp	caraway seeds (optional)	1 to 2 tbsp
4 to 5	potatoes, cooked and mashed (optional)	4 to 5

Mix the yeast with 12.5 cl (4 fl oz) of the water. Add 175 g (6 oz) wholemeal flour to make a sponge and leave overnight to rise.

The next day, warm the remaining flour and mix together with the sponge, the sourdough starter, the remaining water, the salt, and the caraway seeds and mashed potato if used. Knead the resulting stiff dough thoroughly until it comes away from your hands easily and contains air bubbles. Then sprinkle the dough thoroughly with flour, cover and leave it for 4 hours in a warm, but not too warm, place—the dough must prove slowly—until it doubles in bulk.

Divide the dough into six pieces and shape them into ovals. Butter six 1 litre (2 lb) loaf tins and half fill them with the dough; leave the loaves to rise in a warm place for a further 20 to 30 minutes so that they rise to the tops of the tins, then brush the tops with water.

Bake the loaves for 1 hour in an oven preheated to 200°C (400°F or Mark 6) until they are well browned. Brush them with warm water while they are hot, to give them a soft crust.

HERMINE KIEHNLE AND MARIA HÄDECKE
DAS NEUE KIEHNLE-KOCHBUCH

Sour Rye Bread with Caraway Seeds

Coarse semolina can be substituted for coarse cornmeal.

These tawny-crusted loaves have a crackled surface and the proper rye tang, enhanced with caraway seeds (which you can omit, if you like, but they lend much character to the bread). If you keep the bread for a few days (we think it improves in flavour for at least 24 hours after baking), restore the crispness of the crust by warming the loaf briefly in the oven before slicing it. The bread may be frozen.

To make two 30 cm (12 inch) cylindrical loaves

135 g	rye flour	4½ oz
500 g	strong plain flour	1 lb
450 g	rye sourdough starter (*page 170*) stirred down before measuring at room temperature	1 lb
30 g	fresh yeast or 1 tbsp dried yeast	1 oz
3 tbsp	caraway seeds	3 tbsp
30 cl	tepid water	½ pint
	sugar	
1 tbsp	salt	1 tbsp
	coarse cornmeal	
1 tsp	cornflour, cooked in 15 cl (5 fl oz) water until translucent (2 to 3 minutes) then cooled	1 tsp

Combine the yeast, 4 tablespoons of the water and the sugar and let the mixture stand until very foamy, about 10 minutes. Dissolve the salt in the remaining water and stir the mixture into the rye sourdough starter. Beat in the yeast mixture, then the caraway seeds. Beat in the rye flour, about 60 g (2 oz) at a time, then beat in 125 g (4 oz) of the strong plain flour.

Spread 175 g (6 oz) of the strong plain flour in a ring on a work surface and pour the dough into the centre of the ring. Mix roughly with a dough scraper or a palette knife, then knead just until thoroughly mixed, adding as much of the remaining strong plain flour as necessary to make a medium-stiff dough, not too heavy.

Scrape the work surface, dust it with additional rye flour, and knead the dough very thoroughly until it is elastic and smooth-surfaced. Don't overflour the board; keep the dough as close as possible to medium-stiff, not heavy.

Form the dough into a ball and place it in an ungreased bowl. Cover it with plastic film and leave it to rise until it has doubled in bulk, at least 1 hour.

Turn the dough out on to your work surface, dusted lightly with additional rye flour, then expel the air from the dough and form it into two smooth balls. Cover them with a towel and let them rest for 20 minutes. Meanwhile, sprinkle the cornmeal on a 27 by 42 cm (11 by 17 inch) baking sheet.

Flatten each ball of dough into an oval about 30 cm (12 inches) long and 2 cm (1 inch) thick. Beginning at a long edge, roll the dough up like a Swiss roll, and pinch the seam closed. Make a slightly pointed oval loaf about 30 cm (12 inches) long and higher than it is wide. Place it, seam down, on the cornmeal-covered baking sheet. Repeat with the other half of the dough, leaving ample space between the loaves.

Cover the baking sheet with a towel and let the loaves rise until they have not quite doubled in bulk. When they have reached this point, the light pressure of a finger should barely dent the side of each loaf.

While the loaves are rising, preheat the oven to 220°C (425°F or Mark 7) and put a large, shallow pan containing 5 cm (2 inches) of boiling water on the bottom (or on the lowest shelf, if yours is an electric oven).

Brush the loaves with the cooled cornflour glaze. With a single-edged razor blade or a very sharp knife, held almost parallel to the surface, cut three diagonal slashes about 5 mm (¼ inch) deep in the top of each loaf.

Bake for 15 minutes in the centre of the oven, then lower the heat to 180°C (350°F or Mark 4), remove the pan of water, and bake the bread for 30 minutes longer. Brush the loaves again with the glaze. Set them directly on the oven shelves for 10 to 15 minutes, or until there is a hollow sound when you rap the loaves on the bottom.

Cool the loaves on a rack, uncovered. Wrap them in plastic film and store them at room temperature.

HELEN WITTY AND ELIZABETH SCHNEIDER COLCHIE
BETTER THAN STORE-BOUGHT

Beer Bread

Øllebrød

These loaves can be baked in standard English 1 litre (2 lb) or ½ litre (1 lb) loaf tins or on a buttered and floured baking sheet.

To make one 28 by 18 cm (11 by 7 inch) loaf or three 20 by 10 cm (8 by 4 inch) loaves

500 g	rye flour	1 lb
700 g	strong plain flour	1½ lb
30 g	fresh yeast or 1 tbsp dried yeast	1 oz
35 cl	beer	12 fl oz
½ litre	tepid water	16 fl oz
17.5 cl	molasses, warmed	6 fl oz

Mix all but 1 tablespoon of the water with the beer and molasses. Soften the yeast in the tablespoon of water, then add this to the mixture. Add all the rye flour and 500 g (1 lb) of the plain flour. Mix well. Leave the dough to rise in a warm place until doubled in bulk, about 1½ hours. Knead on a floured board, using the remaining plain flour if necessary to make a stiff dough—about 10 minutes.

To make one loaf, place the dough in a floured cloth in a large bowl and let it rise again until doubled in bulk. For three loaves, divide the dough into three and leave to rise separately. Turn the dough upside down into a well-buttered tin or into three tins. Bake the single loaf in a preheated 200°C (400°F or Mark 6) oven for 10 minutes, then at 170°C (325°F or Mark 3) for 50 minutes. Proceed likewise for the three loaves, but at the lower temperature for only 35 to 40 minutes.

INGEBORG DAHL JENSEN
WONDERFUL, WONDERFUL DANISH COOKING

German Whole Rye Bread

Schrotbrot

The fine (light) and whole (dark) rye flour called for in this recipe are both obtainable at health food shops.

To make two 30 cm (12 inch) cylindrical loaves

450 g	whole rye flour	1 lb
200 g	fine rye flour	7 oz
450 g	wholemeal flour	1 lb
250 g	rye sourdough starter (*page 170*)	8 oz
60 cl	tepid water	1 pint
3 tsp	salt	3 tsp
3 tbsp	black coffee	3 tbsp

Blend the sourdough starter with ¼ litre (8 fl oz) of the water and the fine rye flour to make a smooth dough. Put the dough in a bowl, cover it and leave it overnight in a warm room.

On the following day, knead the other types of flour, the salt and the remaining water into the sponge. Knead the dough thoroughly for 10 minutes until it is smooth and has lost some of its stickiness. Leave the dough, covered, in a warm place to rise for 2 hours or until it has doubled in bulk. Knead it again for 10 minutes, then divide it into two equal portions and shape each into a cylindrical loaf about 30 cm (12 inches) long. Place the loaves on a buttered baking sheet, cover them with a cloth and let them rise again in a warm place for 1 to 2 hours, until almost doubled in bulk.

Make a lengthwise slash in each loaf and brush the tops of the loaves with the coffee. Put 30 cl (½ pint) of boiling water in a small pan in the bottom of a preheated 220°C (425°F or Mark 7) oven and bake the bread in the centre of the oven for 50 to 60 minutes.

MARGRET UHLE AND ANNE BRAKEMEIER
EIGENBRÖTLERS BROTBACKBUCH

Swedish Tin Loaves

The coarse rye meal called for in this recipe is available from health food shops. It is generally darker than fine rye flour.

To make two 20 by 10 cm (8 by 4 inch) loaves

400 g	strong plain flour	14 oz
850 g	coarse rye meal	1¾ lb
30 g	fresh yeast or 1 tbsp dried yeast	1 oz
1 litre	cold milk, 6 tbsp of it warmed to tepid	1¾ pints
2 tsp	salt	2 tsp
2 tbsp	pounded fennel seeds (optional)	2 tbsp
¼ litre	golden syrup	8 fl oz

Dissolve the yeast in the tepid milk. In a mixing bowl, sieve the flour and meal with the salt and pounded fennel seeds, if used. Add the rest of the milk and work the mixture into a smooth dough. Add the dissolved yeast and the golden syrup, and keep on kneading the dough. When it is quite smooth and glossy, cover it with a cloth and stand it in a fairly warm place to rise for about 24 hours.

Knead it again for about 5 minutes, and divide it in half. Put the dough in two 1 litre (2 lb) tins, making sure the tins are no more than half full. Stand the tins in a warm place until the dough rises to the tops of the tins. Bake the loaves in an oven preheated to 200°C (400°F or Mark 6) for 15 minutes, then reduce the temperature to 190°C (375°F or Mark 5) for the rest of the baking time, about 30 minutes. Test the loaves with a skewer to see if they are done: if they are, the skewer will come out clean. Remove the loaves from the oven, brush the surfaces lightly with warm water, and turn them out on to a wire rack to cool. Wrap them in a cloth until they are cold, to prevent them from becoming too crusty.

INGA NORBERG
GOOD FOOD FROM SWEDEN

German Malt Beer Bread

Malzbierbrot

If German malt beer is not available, a sweet stout or porter can be substituted.

To make one 30 cm (12 inch) loaf

500 g	strong plain flour	1 lb
500 g	rye flour	1 lb
250 g	rye sourdough starter (*page 170*)	8 oz
30 g	fresh yeast or 1 tbsp dried yeast	1 oz
30 cl	German malt beer	½ pint
1 tsp	salt	1 tsp
1 tsp	sugar	1 tsp
100 g	butter or lard, melted and cooled to tepid	3½ oz
30 cl	lager	½ pint

Sift the two kinds of flour into a warmed mixing bowl with the salt. Dissolve the yeast and sugar in half the malt beer and leave the mixture until foaming, about 20 minutes. Pour the butter or lard into the flour, add the lager and rest of the malt beer, saving 2 tablespoons of it for glazing. Mix the ingredients thoroughly, then add the rye sourdough starter and knead the mixture for 15 minutes or until the dough is smooth and elastic. Cover the dough and leave it in a warm place to rise until doubled in bulk—about 2 hours. Knock back the dough and knead it again for about 5 minutes, shape it into a ball and lay it on a buttered baking sheet. Leave the loaf to prove, covered, in a warm place for about 30 minutes. Brush the loaf with the rest of the malt beer and bake it in an oven preheated to 200°C (400°F or Mark 6) for 40 to 60 minutes.

JUTTA KÜRTZ
DAS BROT BACKBUCH

German Sourdough Rye Loaf

Feines Gesäuertes Roggenbrot

You may substitute buttermilk for the water, which will improve the quality of the bread. In this case, however, use only 60 g (2 oz) of the sourdough starter.

To make one 50 cm (20 inch) loaf

2.5 kg	rye flour	5 lb
125 g	rye sourdough starter (*page 170*)	4 oz
1 litre	tepid water	1¾ pints
2 tbsp	salt	2 tbsp

On the evening before baking day, make the yeast sponge. Mix together 250 g (8 oz) of the flour with the sourdough starter and ¼ litre (8 fl oz) of the water. Sprinkle on 2 table-spoons flour and leave the yeast sponge until the next morning in a warm place. If the sponge has not risen enough by the next morning, add another 15 g (½ oz) fresh yeast, or 2 teaspoons dried yeast, dissolved in 8 cl (3 fl oz) of tepid water.

Mix the salt with the remaining flour, add the yeast sponge and the rest of the water and knead thoroughly for about 15 minutes. Shape the dough into a long loaf, place it on a floured baking sheet and leave it in a warm place to rise for 2 to 3 hours, or until a finger pressed lightly into the dough leaves a dent. Bake the loaf in a preheated 200°C (400°F or Mark 6) oven for 2 hours or until it sounds hollow when rapped.

HENRIETTE DAVIDIS
HENRIETTE DAVIDIS ILLUSTRIERTES PRAKTISCHES KOCHBUCH

German Household Bread

Hausmannsbrot

To make one 35 cm (14 inch) cylindrical loaf

150 g	rye flour	5 oz
250 g	wholemeal flour	8 oz
600 g	strong plain flour	1¼ lb
50 g	rye sourdough starter (*page 170*)	2 oz
30 g	fresh yeast or 1 tbsp dried yeast	1 oz
30 cl	tepid water	½ pint
1 tsp	sugar	1 tsp
33 cl	buttermilk	11 fl oz
3 tsp	salt	3 tsp

Blend the starter with 20 cl (7 fl oz) of the water and the rye flour. Cover and leave overnight at room temperature.

Sieve the other flours into a bowl and make a well in the centre. Dissolve the yeast in the remaining water and pour it into the well with the sugar. Stir together about 6 tablespoons of flour from the edges and mix with the liquid to form a yeast sponge. Cover the bowl with a cloth and let the yeast sponge rise for 20 to 30 minutes or until it bubbles.

Add the sourdough starter, all but 2 tablespoons of the buttermilk, and the salt. Mix the sponge into the rest of the flour with the other ingredients, and knead well for about 10 minutes, until the dough is smooth and elastic. Cover the bowl with a cloth and let it rise in a warm place for 2 hours or until doubled in bulk.

Knead the dough again for 10 minutes, then form it into a cylindrical loaf. Place the loaf on a buttered baking sheet and, with a sharp knife or razor blade, make a shallow, lengthwise gash. Cover the loaf and prove it in a warm place for 2 hours.

Brush the loaf with the remaining buttermilk and bake in the centre of an oven preheated to 220°C (425°F or Mark 7) for 60 to 70 minutes.

MARGRET UHLE AND ANNE BRAKEMEIER
EIGENBRÖTLERS BROTBACKBUCH

Neapolitan Pepper Wreaths

Taralli a Sugna e Pepe

A popular variation of this recipe is to insert a few blanched, halved and toasted almonds between the braids.

To make about twenty 8 cm (3½ inch) wreaths

500 g	strong plain flour	1 lb
30 g	fresh yeast or 1 tbsp dried yeast and 1 tsp sugar	1 oz
1 tsp	freshly ground black pepper	1 tsp
30 cl	tepid water	½ pint
150 g	lard, coarsely chopped	5 oz
1 tsp	salt	1 tsp

Dissolve the yeast in the water. If using dried yeast, add 1 teaspoon of sugar to the mixture and leave in a warm place until foaming, about 15 minutes. Heap the flour on to a working surface, make a well in the centre and pour in the yeast mixture. Add the lard, salt and pepper. Mix the ingredients vigorously until they are thoroughly combined, and then knead the dough for 10 minutes. Divide the dough into four pieces; roll each piece into a sausage shape about 1 cm (½ inch) thick, making sure that the pieces are of equal length. Twist them in pairs (like the old electric cables) and then slice each pair into about 20 cm (8 inch) lengths. Join the ends of each length to form a wreath, using your thumb to press the ends firmly together. Arrange the wreaths on a tea towel, cover them with another tea towel, and leave them in a warm place to prove for at least 1 hour.

Bake the wreaths in an oven preheated to 180°C (350°F or Mark 4) for 1 hour; if they are not baked slowly, they will remain raw inside. When cooked, they should be crisp and golden. Serve the wreaths cold.

MARIA RIVIECCIO ZANIBONI
CUCINA E VINI DI NAPOLI E DELLA CAMPANIA

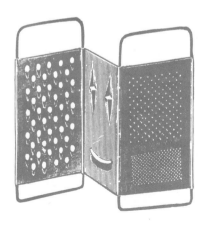

Salted Pretzels

Salzbrezeln

The technique of shaping pretzels is shown on page 34; boiling dough before baking it is demonstrated on page 78.

To make 15 large pretzels

500 g	strong plain flour	1 lb
15 g	fresh yeast or 2 tsp dried yeast	½ oz
20 cl	tepid water	7 fl oz
	sugar	
	salt	
20 g	butter, softened	¾ oz
15 cl	tepid milk	¼ pint
	coarse salt	

Dissolve the yeast in 2 tablespoons of the water with a pinch of sugar and leave until foaming, about 20 minutes. Sieve the flour and 1 teaspoon of salt into a bowl. Make a well in the centre and pour in the yeast mixture. Add 4 tablespoons of the water to the mixture and stir it in, drawing in a little of the flour from the edge of the well. Cover the mixture and leave it in a warm place for 10 minutes, or until the liquid foams.

Melt the butter, add it to the milk and combine this with the yeast mixture and the rest of the water. Then beat the flour into the yeast mixture until the dough cleans the sides of the bowl. Knead the dough on a well-floured board and leave it to rise until doubled in bulk.

Knead the dough again thoroughly for about 10 minutes and divide it into 15 pieces. Roll out each piece until it is the thickness of a pencil and about 30 cm (12 inches) long, tapering the dough at both ends. Keep flouring the work surface with additional flour, if the dough sticks to it. Form each piece of dough into a pretzel ring by forming a loop and folding the two ends over the loop.

Cover the pretzels with a towel and leave them to prove for 10 minutes. Preheat the oven to 230°C (450°F or Mark 8).

Fill a saucepan with 3 litres (5 pints) of water, add 2 tablespoons of salt, and bring to the boil. Put each pretzel into the boiling water, removing it with a slotted spoon as soon as it rises to the surface, which will happen almost immediately. Place the pretzels on kitchen towels to drain. With a sharp knife, make a notch in the thick part of each pretzel and sprinkle the notch with coarse salt. Transfer the pretzels to floured baking sheets. Just before putting them in the oven, sprinkle the rest of the tepid water on the oven floor and shut the door quickly to create steam. Reduce the oven temperature to 200°C (400°F or Mark 6) and bake the pretzels for 30 minutes or until well browned. Serve cold.

EVA AND ULRICH KLEVER
SELBER BROT BACKEN

German Sourdough Cornbread

Maisbrot mit Sauerteig

To make one 30 cm (12 inch) loaf

175 g	fine cornmeal	6 oz
600 g	strong plain flour	1¼ lb
250 g	sourdough starter (*page 170*)	8 oz
30 g	fresh yeast or 1 tbsp dried yeast	1 oz
50 g	butter or lard	2 oz
35 cl	milk	12 fl oz
1 tsp	sugar	1 tsp
¼ tsp	salt	¼ tsp
¼ litre	tepid water	8 fl oz

In a pan, add the butter or lard to the milk and bring the milk to the boil. Stir until the fat has dissolved. In a bowl, sieve the cornmeal, sugar and salt. Pour on the boiling milk and stir the mixture until it is smooth. Stir the sourdough starter with yeast and add the tepid water. Mix until very smooth. Mix the cornmeal and yeast mixtures thoroughly, gradually adding 500 g (1 lb) of the plain flour. Knead the dough well for about 10 minutes; it should be rather sticky. Leave the dough in a warm place to rise until it has doubled in bulk, about 1½ hours. Punch it down and knead it again for 5 minutes, adding the remaining flour to make a firmer dough, and shape it into a loaf. Leave the loaf on a buttered baking sheet in a warm place to prove for about 30 minutes. Bake it in an oven preheated to 220°C (425°F or Mark 7) for 40 to 45 minutes.

JUTTA KÜRTZ
DAS BROT BACKBUCH

Annadamma Bread

To make two 20 by 10 cm (8 by 4 inch) loaves

About 600 g	strong plain flour	About 1¼ lb
60 g	fine cornmeal	2 oz
30 g	fresh yeast or 1 tbsp dried yeast	1 oz
60 cl	water	1 pint
1 tsp	salt	1 tsp
30 g	butter	1 oz
175 g	molasses	6 oz

Stir ¼ litre (8 fl oz) of cold water into the cornmeal. Bring another ¼ litre (8 fl oz) of water to a rolling boil in a saucepan. Pour in the cornmeal mixture, stirring constantly. Cook the mixture until it is very thick—about 15 minutes—stirring from time to time. Add the salt, butter and molasses. Let the mixture cool slightly.

Warm the remaining water until it is tepid, and dissolve the yeast in it. Add this mixture to the cooled cornmeal and stir in the flour gradually, kneading to make a stiff dough. Knead well for about 10 minutes until the dough is springy; if it remains too sticky, it may be necessary to add more flour. Shape the dough into a ball, put it in a buttered bowl, cover and leave it to rise in a warm place for about 1½ hours or until doubled in bulk. Punch down the dough and divide it into two pieces. Put each piece in a 1 litre (2 lb) loaf tin, cover the tins with a cloth and leave them in a warm place until the dough has doubled in bulk again, about 30 minutes. Bake the loaves in an oven preheated to 220°C (425°F or Mark 7) for 1 hour or until the loaves sound hollow if rapped on the bottom.

MARIA CHAMBERLIN-HELLMAN (EDITOR)
FOOD NOTES

Corn Sandwich Muffins

Taloa

To make 8 large or 16 small muffins

250 g	strong plain flour	8 oz
280 g	cornmeal	9 oz
60 g	fresh yeast or 2 tbsp dried yeast	2 oz
2 tsp	salt	2 tsp
35 cl	tepid water	12 fl oz
1	egg white	1

In a large bowl, stir together half of the flour, the yeast, salt and water. Let the mixture stand for 3 minutes to allow the yeast to dissolve. Pour in the cornmeal and blend the ingredients with 25 strong strokes of a wooden spoon. Add the remaining flour, a little at a time, mixing first with the spoon and then with your hands to make a dough that cleans the sides of the bowl.

Turn out the dough on to a floured work surface, and knead with a push-turn-fold motion until the dough is smooth, soft and does not stick—about 10 minutes. Avoid making the dough dense with the addition of too much flour. Place the dough in a buttered bowl, cover with plastic film and leave at room temperature until doubled in volume—about 1 hour. Turn out the dough and knead for a moment to expel bubbles.

Divide the dough into pieces—8 for large muffins, or 16 for small. Pat the pieces flat with the palm of your hand and, with a rolling pin, roll each into a disc. Larger muffins will be about 15 cm (6 inches) in diameter and 1 cm (½ inch) thick; smaller ones will be about 10 cm (4 inches) by 1 cm (½ inch). Place the muffins on a baking sheet. Cover with a tea towel and allow them to rise for about 50 minutes. Preheat the oven to 230°C (450°F or Mark 8) 20 minutes before baking.

Brush the top of each *taloa* with the egg white. Place on the middle shelf of the oven. If the oven will only take one baking sheet, allow the reserved muffins to rise an additional time.

BERNARD CLAYTON, JR.
THE BREADS OF FRANCE

German Rusks

Zwieback

To make about 24 rusks

500 g	strong plain flour	1 lb
40 g	fresh yeast or 1½ tbsp dried yeast	1½ oz
15 cl	tepid milk	¼ pint
100 g	butter, melted and cooled to tepid	3½ oz
80 g	sugar	3 oz
½	lemon, rind grated	½
	salt	
	ground cinnamon (optional)	

Dissolve the yeast in the milk and leave until frothy—about 15 minutes. Sift the flour into a bowl and make a well in the centre. Pour the yeast mixture into the well and mix in about a quarter of the flour with a wooden spoon. Cover the bowl, leave it in a warm place for the yeast sponge to rise, about 20 minutes. Beat in 90 g (3 oz) of the butter, the sugar, the lemon rind, a generous pinch of salt and a pinch of cinnamon if desired. Mix together to form a fairly stiff dough and knead it thoroughly for about 10 minutes, or until smooth and elastic. Cover the dough with a tea towel and leave it to rise in a warm place until doubled in bulk, about 1½ hours.

Knead the dough again briefly on a floured board then divide it into six pieces and shape them into ovals about 5 cm (2 inches) thick. Flour two baking sheets, lay the ovals of dough on them and leave them to prove for about 30 minutes or until doubled in bulk again. Brush them with melted butter and bake them in an oven preheated to 180°C (350°F or Mark 4) for about 25 minutes or until pale golden. When they are completely cool, slice the loaves into 1 cm (½ inch) slices and toast them in the oven, on a hot plate or under a grill until golden-brown on both sides.

SOPHIE WILHELMINE SCHEIBLER
ALLGEMEINES DEUTSCHES KOCHBUCH FÜR ALLE STÄNDE

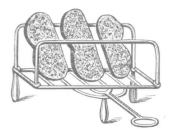

Hertfordshire Barley Bread
Made to Eat Like Wheaten Bread

This recipe, published in 1750, is said by the author to make a light, wholesome bread, instead of the heavy, indigestible loaf often produced by barley flour. The lightness is achieved by adding oatmeal. Barley bread was widely eaten in England in the 18th and early 19th centuries when wheat was expensive and only the wealthy could afford white wheaten bread.

To make four 20 by 10 cm (8 by 4 inch) loaves

1.5 kg	barley flour	3 lb
500 g	fine oatmeal, soaked in 90 cl (1½ pints) water overnight	1 lb
40 g	fresh yeast or 1½ tbsp dried yeast	1½ oz
30 cl	tepid water or milk	½ pint

Mix the yeast with the tepid water or milk and leave it in a warm place for about 10 minutes to froth. Combine the oatmeal, barley meal and yeast, and knead the mixture into a dough. The dough requires very little kneading. Leave it to rise in a warm place for 1½ hours or until doubled in bulk.

Divide the dough into four portions and knead them lightly on a floured work surface. Put each portion into a buttered 1 litre (2 lb) loaf tin. Leave the loaves in a warm place to prove for 20 minutes or until they have risen about 1 cm (½ inch) above the sides of the tins. Bake in an oven preheated to 200°C (400°F or Mark 6) for about 50 minutes or until the loaves sound slightly hollow when rapped. Thus a barley loaf may be made hollow, white and sweet, so as to be hardly known from coarse wheaten bread.

W. ELLIS
THE COUNTRY HOUSEWIFE'S FAMILY COMPANION

Polish Buckwheat Flatbread

Pyza z Hreczanej Mąki

To make one 25 cm (10 inch) flatbread

500 g	buckwheat flour	1 lb
125 g	strong plain flour	4 oz
30 g	fresh yeast or 1 tbsp dried yeast dissolved in 4 tbsp tepid water	1 oz
250 g	lard, melted	8 oz
1 tsp	salt	1 tsp
½ litre	tepid water	16 fl oz

Put the buckwheat flour into a bowl and gradually stir in the hot lard. Mix well. Add the plain flour, yeast and salt and the warm water. Beat the mixture then leave it to rise in a warm place for 1 hour or until it has doubled in bulk. Place the bread in a shallow, greased, 25 cm (10 inch) pie tin, and leave it to rise again for 30 minutes. Bake the bread for 1 hour in an oven preheated to 180°C (350°F or Mark 4) or until a skewer dipped into the centre comes out clean. Serve with soured cream.

MARIA DISSLOWA
JAK GOTOWAC

Bread with Rolled Oats

Kraftbrot mit Haferflocken

To make two 20 by 10 cm (8 by 4 inch) loaves

750 g	strong plain flour	1½ lb
250 g	rolled oats	8 oz
30 g	fresh yeast or 1 tbsp dried yeast	1 oz
35 cl	tepid milk or water	12 fl oz
250 g	potatoes, cooked and mashed (optional)	8 oz
15 g	butter or lard, softened	½ oz
1 tbsp	salt	1 tbsp

Dissolve the yeast in the milk or water. Sieve the flour, make a well in the centre and pour in the yeast mixture. Mix together to make a sponge and leave to rise in a warm place for about 1 hour or until doubled in bulk. Then work in the oats, potatoes and butter or lard, and knead the dough until bubbles appear in it—about 15 minutes. Butter two ½ litre (1 lb) loaf tins and lightly press the dough into them. Leave the loaves to rise for about 30 minutes in a warm place or until the top of the dough is about 1 cm (½ inch) above the rims of the tins. Bake in an oven preheated to 180°C (350°F or Mark 4) for 1 to 1¼ hours, or until golden-brown.

HERMINE KIEHNLE AND MARIA HÄDECKE
DAS NEUE KIEHNLE-KOCHBUCH

Oatmeal Bread

Kauraleipä

To make two 20 cm (8 inch) loaves

350 g	fine oatmeal	12 oz
350 g	strong plain flour	12 oz
30 g	fresh yeast or 1 tbsp dried yeast	1 oz
½ litre	tepid water, whey or vegetable stock	16 fl oz
1½ tsp	sea salt	1½ tsp
1 tbsp	honey	1 tbsp

Dissolve the yeast in the liquid. Stir in the salt and strong plain flour. Beat well until the mixture thickens. Then add the honey and oatmeal. Mix well to make an elastic, soft and silky dough. Knead the dough for about 20 minutes.

Put the dough into a bowl, cover it and let it rise in a warm place until it has doubled in bulk, about 1 hour. Punch down the dough and divide it into two 20 cm (8 inch) round loaves. Prick the loaves all over with a fork. Cover them and leave them to rise until almost doubled in bulk, about 30 minutes.

Bake the loaves in a preheated 220°C (425°F or Mark 7)

oven for 25 to 30 minutes. For a crisp crust, leave the loaves to cool, uncovered, on a wire rack. Eat the bread when fresh as it does not keep well.

ULLA KÄKÖNEN
NATURAL COOKING THE FINNISH WAY

Pitta Bread

Khubz (Eish Shami)

To make six 15 cm (6 inch) pittas

500 g	strong plain flour	1 lb
15 g	fresh yeast or 2 tsp dried yeast	½ oz
30 cl	tepid water	½ pint
	sugar	
½ tsp	salt	½ tsp
2 to 3 tbsp	oil	2 to 3 tbsp

Dissolve the yeast in about 6 tablespoons of the water. Add a pinch of sugar and leave in a warm place for about 10 minutes, or until the mixture becomes frothy.

Sift the flour and salt into a warmed mixing bowl. Make a well in the centre and pour in the yeast mixture. Knead well by hand, adding enough of the remaining water to make a firm, but not hard, dough. Knead the dough vigorously for about 15 minutes, until it is smooth and elastic, and no longer sticks to your fingers. Knead in 1 to 2 tablespoons of oil for a softer bread. Sprinkle the bottom of the bowl with 1 tablespoon of oil and roll the ball of dough round and round to grease it all over. This will prevent the surface from becoming dry and crusty. Cover the dough with a dampened cloth and leave it in a warm place for at least 2 hours, until nearly doubled in size.

Punch the dough down and knead it again for a few minutes. Divide the dough into six pieces. Flatten them on a lightly floured board with a dry rolling pin sprinkled with flour, or with the palm of your hand, until they are about 5 mm (¼ inch) thick. Dust them with flour and lay the rounds on a cloth sprinkled with more flour. Cover with another lightly floured cloth and allow the breads to rise again in a warm place for about 30 minutes.

Preheat the oven at its highest temperature for at least 20 minutes; oil the baking sheets and place them in the oven for the last 10 minutes to make them as hot as possible. Take care that the oil does not burn.

When the breads have doubled in bulk, slip them on to the hot baking sheets. Sprinkle them lightly with cold water to prevent them from browning too quickly and bake them for 6 to 10 minutes. Do not open the oven during this time.

Remove the breads from the baking sheets as soon as they come out of the oven and cool them on wire racks. The bread should be soft and white, with a pouch inside.

CLAUDIA RODEN
A BOOK OF MIDDLE EASTERN FOOD

Huffkins

To make ten 8 cm (3 inch) buns

500 g	strong plain flour	1 lb
30 g	fresh yeast or 1 tbsp dried yeast	1 oz
1 tsp	sugar	1 tsp
30 cl	tepid water	½ pint
1 tsp	salt	1 tsp

In a cup, mix the yeast with the sugar and half of the water. Leave the mixture in a warm place until it is frothy, about 15 minutes. Sieve the flour and salt together, mix in the yeast and the rest of the water. Knead the dough for about 10 minutes, or until it is smooth and elastic, and leave it to rise in a warm place for 1½ hours or until it has doubled in bulk. Shape it into 10 balls, and press a hole in the centre of each with your finger. Leave the huffkins to rise in a warm place for 20 minutes, or until well risen again. Bake them in a preheated, 200°C (400°F or Mark 6) oven for 15 minutes, or until golden-brown. Eat them on the day they are baked.

FLORENCE WHITE
GOOD ENGLISH FOOD

Split Rolls

Les Pistolets

These split rolls—small round milk rolls with a distinctive indentation across the top—are a speciality of eastern France. The groove is usually made with an oiled stick. The stick may also be used dry, provided the tops of the rolls have been moistened with a little oil.

To make about 40 rolls

1 kg	strong plain flour	2 to 2½ lb
15 g	fresh yeast or 2 tsp dried yeast	½ oz
15 g	malt extract	½ oz
½ litre	tepid water	16 fl oz
2 tsp	salt	2 tsp
40 g	sugar	1½ oz
40 g	dried milk	1½ oz
100 g	butter, softened	3½ oz
	oil	
	rye flour	

Cream the yeast with 6 tablespoons of the water and the malt extract. Leave it until it is foaming, about 10 minutes. Sieve the flour, salt, sugar and dried milk into a bowl and make a well in the centre. Pour in the yeast mixture and the rest of the water. Mix to form a dough. Turn the dough out on to a floured board, and knead it well for about 10 minutes, or until it is smooth and elastic, then leave it to rest for 15 minutes. Mix in the softened butter and knead vigorously for a further 5 minutes—the dough should be fairly firm. Put the dough in a bowl, cover it with a cloth or plastic film and leave it to rise at warm room temperature for about 3 hours or overnight in the refrigerator, until more than trebled in bulk.

Punch down the dough, turn it over and cover the bowl. Leave the dough to rise again until doubled in bulk, about 2 hours. Shape the dough into balls, each weighing about 40 g (1½ oz). Make a deep groove with an oiled stick across each ball and dust the surface with rye flour, to prevent the two halves of the roll sticking together during baking. Transfer the rolls, groove downwards, to a floured surface and leave them to rise again for about 30 minutes.

Preheat the oven to 220°C (425°F or Mark 7). Twenty minutes before baking, put a baking tin full of hot water on the bottom of the oven. Transfer the rolls with the groove uppermost to floured baking sheets. Bake the rolls for 25 to 30 minutes or until golden-brown and feel hard and hollow.

RAYMOND CALVEL
LA BOULANGERIE MODERNE

Flower Rolls

Huajuan

The technique for making Chinese steamed rolls is shown on page 42. The rolls can be made in advance and reheated in a steamer just before serving. Leftover rolls are also very good deep-fried in hot oil until golden.

To make about 24 rolls

375 g	strong plain flour	13 oz
2 tsp	fresh yeast or 1 tsp dried yeast	2 tsp
1 tbsp	sugar	1 tbsp
¼ litre	tepid water	8 fl oz
1 tsp	coarse salt	1 tsp
2 tbsp	lard	2 tbsp
4	spring onions, finely chopped	4

Mix the yeast, sugar and water together in a small bowl. Set the mixture aside for about 10 minutes until the yeast begins to bubble. Sift the flour into a large bowl. Slowly pour in the yeast and water mixture and stir it with a wooden spoon until it is thoroughly blended. (You may have to use your hands towards the end.)

Sprinkle some flour over a large wooden surface, set the dough on it and knead for 5 minutes. Put the dough back in the bowl, cover it with a barely damp cloth and set it aside to rise in a warm, draught-free place for 1½ to 2 hours. After that time, when the dough has just about doubled in bulk, put it back on the floured surface and knead it for another minute.

Put the dough back in the bowl to rise again, but this time for only about 30 minutes, until it has again doubled in bulk.

As soon as the dough has risen, separate it into two equal parts. Roll out one of the pieces into a large rectangle about 25 by 30 cm (10 by 12 inches). Sprinkle half of the salt evenly over the dough and press it in with your hands. Spread half of the lard over the dough, as if you were buttering a piece of bread. Finally, sprinkle half of the chopped spring onions over the dough, then roll it up, like a Swiss roll, into a long cylinder.

Using the rest of the salt and lard and the remaining spring onions, repeat the steps above with the other piece of dough. Slice each cylinder of dough into about 12 segments 2.5 cm (1 inch) thick. Then, using a chopstick, press down across the middle of each piece so that the inside layers flare out like a fan. Make sure that you press the dough hard enough so that the middle of each sliced segment sticks together and the layers don't fall out.

Lay the rolls on one or more large, warmed serving dish, spacing them well apart, and leave them to rise for a final hour before steaming.

Line the top part of a steamer with a piece of cheesecloth or a tea towel. Fill the bottom of the steamer with water and bring it to the boil over a high heat. Put the rolls in the top part of the steamer, cover and steam for 15 minutes.

ELLEN SCHRECKER
MRS. CHIANG'S SZECHWAN COOKBOOK

Crumpets

Crumpet rings or hoops are about 10 cm (4 inches) in diameter and 1 cm (½ inch) thick. The technique of making crumpets is demonstrated on page 40.

There is some truth in the idea that the more the crumpet batter is beaten when originally compounded, the more holes will result in the finished crumpet. Certainly the batter requires attacking with vivacious turbulence.

To make 45 to 50 crumpets		
2.25 kg	strong plain flour	4½ lb
60 g	fresh yeast or 2 tbsp dried yeast	2 oz
1 tsp	bicarbonate of soda mixed with 60 cl (1 pint) tepid water	1 tsp
2.25 litres	tepid water	4 pints
90 g	dried skimmed milk	3 oz
40 g	salt	1½ oz

Cream the yeast with 3 tablespoons of the water. Leave the flour in a bowl in a warm place.

Prepare a batter with the warmed flour, yeast, dried milk, salt and the rest of the water. Beat vigorously until the batter is smooth and elastic.

This batter sponge should be covered and placed in a warm, cosy situation for 1½ to 1¾ hours. Usually the ideal crumpet results if the batter is taken to its second stage, when the batter is on the verge of collapsing. There is plenty of warning, if one observes the signs. The bubbly stage is the first indication that the vital moment is not far away. Soon, fissures are noticed forming in the centre of the batter and this is the commencement of the "dropping" stage.

It is at this juncture that the bicarbonate of soda mixed with water is added and well distributed throughout the sponge. The batter now requires to be left for 10 to 15 minutes to recover from the handling, when it is ready for loading on to the hotplate or griddle.

Heat up a very shiny hotplate or griddle (greased or so shiny that greasing is not necessary) until very hot. Grease four crumpet rings lightly. When the hotplate or griddle is very hot, place the rings on it. (Do not do so prematurely, otherwise the rings get very dry and the crumpet tends to stick unduly.)

Now transfer the batter to the rings without spilling any on the hotplate, or, in fact, anywhere. (A measure may be used and a pan held underneath to catch the inevitable drippings, or the use of a lipped saucepan will be found a very quick way of transferring the batter.) The batter should quickly rise up to within 1.25 mm ($\frac{1}{16}$ inch) of the tops of the rings. If the batter is correctly fermented but fails to "hole" well, it may require a little more water, but a likely cause is draught or cold air playing over the tops, causing a binding effect which, again, is a legacy of chilling. The crumpets are turned over as soon as the glassy wetness disappears from the crumpet tops. At this stage the crumpet should still cling to the rings and so barely touch the plate after turning.

If the rings are over-greased, it is most likely that the crumpet will fall free from the ring and acquire a really healthy bloom. There is nothing unattractive about this, but a bright coloration is considered wrong because it is obtained by excessive ring greasing, in which case the crumpet will have suffered in other respects. Hence, crumpets are invariably anaemic-looking items, but a little colour takes away the "raw" look, and so this state should be the signal for removing the crumpets from the hotplate. Baking time is about 4 minutes. When the crumpets are cooked, keep them warm, and cook the rest of the batter in the same way.

WALTER T. BANFIELD
"MANNA". A COMPREHENSIVE TREATISE ON BREAD MANUFACTURE

Crumpets

Crumpet hoops or rings are about 10 cm (4 inches) in diameter and 1 cm ($\frac{1}{2}$ inch) deep. The technique of making crumpets is shown on page 40.

To make 8 to 10 crumpets

500 g	strong plain flour	1 lb
15 g	fresh yeast or 2 tsp dried yeast	$\frac{1}{2}$ oz
60 cl	tepid milk	1 pint
1 tsp	salt	1 tsp
1 tsp	bicarbonate of soda	1 tsp
About 4 tbsp	tepid water	About 4 tbsp
	melted lard or rendered suet	

Warm the flour in the plate-warming part of the stove, or stand it in a rack above the cooker. Fork up the yeast with 3 tablespoons of the milk. It will soon cream and swell into frothiness. Make a well in the centre of the flour and pour in both the yeast mixture and the rest of the tepid milk. Beat for a good 5 minutes. Cover the bowl and leave the dough to rise in a warm place for an hour. Dissolve the bicarbonate of soda in the tepid water, add it to the mixture, beating it in thoroughly, then leave it to rise for another hour.

Grease the griddle with lard or suet and grease the crumpet rings. Place the rings on the griddle and heat it when the dough is ready. Pour spoonfuls of mixture to half-fill the rings and leave to cook for about 5 minutes. Turn them over when the top part loses its liquid appearance and cook for a further 30 seconds. Ease the crumpets off the rings and start again with some more dough.

Eat these crumpets in the usual way, with plenty of butter. They make a good base for fried eggs, or scrambled eggs with anchovies. Some people like them with syrup and butter.

JANE GRIGSON
ENGLISH FOOD

Flannel Crumpets

To make eight to ten 10 cm (4 inch) crumpets

500 g	strong plain flour	1 lb
60 g	fresh yeast or 2 tsp dried yeast dissolved in 4 tbsp tepid milk	2 oz
1 tsp	salt	1 tsp
30 cl	tepid milk	$\frac{1}{2}$ pint
2	eggs, well beaten	2

Sieve the flour into a bowl with the salt and leave it in a warm place for 15 minutes. Mix the milk with the flour to make a smooth batter. Stir the eggs into the yeast and beat the mixture into the batter. If the mixture is too stiff, add a little

more milk. Cover the bowl with a cloth and leave it in a warm place for 1 hour or until doubled in bulk.

Heat a buttered griddle or baking iron, on a low heat. For each crumpet, pour on a ladleful of the batter and cook it slowly for 10 minutes on each side until brown. Serve the crumpets hot and buttered.

OSCAR TSCHIRKY
THE COOK BOOK BY "OSCAR" OF THE WALDORF

Pikelets

The thin, pancake-like pikelet is a relative of the crumpet. Pikelets can be made without rings, in which case the batter should be thicker.

To make about 25 pikelets

About 750 g	strong plain flour	About 1$\frac{1}{2}$ lb
15 g	fresh yeast, or 2 tsp dried yeast	$\frac{1}{2}$ oz
1.25 litres	tepid milk	2 pints
250 g	butter, melted and cooled to tepid	8 oz
2 tsp	salt	2 tsp

Dissolve the yeast in the milk. Then beat in sufficient flour to make a batter as thick as double cream. Set the batter in a warm place to rise for 1 hour, and shield it from draughts. Then add the butter and salt. Stir it well.

Grease and heat a hotplate or griddle, and place buttered metal rings on it. Pour the batter into the rings until three-quarters full and cook the pikelets until the tops have blistered with bubbles, about 7 to 10 minutes. Then turn them over and cook them for a further 5 minutes. They should be pale gold on both sides. Remove them from the rings and leave them to cool on a wire rack.

ALISON UTTLEY
RECIPES FROM AN OLD FARMHOUSE

Fried Flatbread

Bortellina Bettolese

To make about twenty 10 cm (4 inch) flatbreads

1 kg	strong plain flour	2 lb
20 g	fresh yeast or 2 tsp dried yeast	$\frac{3}{4}$ oz
60 cl	tepid water	1 pint
	salt	
100 g	lard for frying	3$\frac{1}{2}$ oz

Take 100 g (3$\frac{1}{2}$ oz) of the flour and mix it with half the yeast and half the water. Leave for 30 minutes or until foaming.

Put the rest of the flour into a bowl. Add the sponge, salt

and the rest of the yeast, if using fresh yeast. If using dried yeast, dissolve the rest of the yeast in 3 tablespoons of the water, then add to the sponge and dry ingredients. Mix the ingredients together, gradually adding enough water to make a firm dough. Knead until it forms a smooth, soft ball.

Leave the dough to rest for a further 10 minutes, then divide it into small pieces and flatten them into rounds about 10 cm (4 inches) in diameter.

In a heavy iron frying pan, heat the lard. Fry the rounds of flatbread in several batches until they are golden-brown, about 8 to 10 minutes on each side.

CARMEN ARTOCCHINI (EDITOR)
400 RICETTE DELLA CUCINA PIACENTINA

Swedish Salt Sticks

Saltstänger

To make 30 sticks

250 g	strong plain flour	8 oz
15 g	fresh yeast or 2 tsp dried yeast	$\frac{1}{2}$ oz
25 g	cold butter, cut into small pieces	1 oz
$\frac{1}{2}$ tsp	salt	$\frac{1}{2}$ tsp
1 tsp	sugar	1 tsp
2 or 3	cardamom pods, husks removed and seeds pounded	2 or 3
17.5 cl	cold milk	6 fl oz
	Salt topping	
1 tbsp	coarse salt	1 tbsp
4 tbsp	milk	4 tbsp
1 tbsp	caraway seeds (optional)	1 tbsp

Put the butter, flour and salt into a bowl. With your fingertips, rub the butter into the flour. Stir together the yeast, sugar and pounded cardamom seeds. Make a well in the centre of the flour and pour in the yeast mixture and the milk; mix thoroughly to make a firm dough.

Divide the dough into 30 small pieces and roll each piece into a stick the thickness of a finger, and about 8 cm (3 inches) long. Put the sticks on to buttered and floured baking sheets. Take a sharp knife or razor blade and make two or three diagonal incisions in each stick. Brush the sticks with the milk and sprinkle the coarse salt—mixed with caraway seeds if you like—over them. Leave the sticks in a warm place to rise until they have doubled in bulk—about 30 minutes—and bake them in an oven preheated to 180°C (350°F or Mark 4) for 20 minutes or until they are lightly browned.

JENNY AKERSTRÖM
PRINSESSORNAS KOKBOK

Flavoured and Filled Breads

Olive Tart

Tarte aux Olives

To make one 25 cm (10 inch) tart

400 g	strong plain flour	14 oz
30 g	fresh yeast or 1 tbsp dried yeast	1 oz
2 tbsp	tepid water	2 tbsp
	sugar	
	salt	
2 tbsp	oil	2 tbsp
	Cheese and olive filling	
200 g	Gruyère cheese, 150 g (5 oz) very thinly sliced, the rest grated	7 oz
250 g	green olives, stoned	8 oz
3	eggs, beaten	3
17.5 cl	milk	6 fl oz
50 g	butter	2 oz
$\frac{1}{2}$ tsp	salt	$\frac{1}{2}$ tsp
$\frac{1}{2}$ tsp	pepper	$\frac{1}{2}$ tsp

Dissolve the yeast in 1 tablespoon of the water, and mix it with 100 g (3½ oz) of the flour. Knead this yeast sponge gently and leave it in a warm place for 1 hour or until doubled in bulk. Add the rest of the flour, a pinch each of sugar and salt, the oil and the rest of the water. Knead the dough, adding more water if it is too stiff, then roll it out into a 25 cm (10 inch) circle about 5 mm ($\frac{1}{4}$ inch) thick. Butter a large baking sheet and slide the circle of dough on to it. Fold over the edges of the dough, so that a thick rim is formed. Leave the dough in a warm place to prove, about 1 hour.

To make the filling, combine the eggs and milk, then add the butter, sliced cheese, olives, salt and pepper. Pour the mixture over the dough and spread it out evenly. Sprinkle it with the grated cheese, then bake the tart in a preheated 180°C (350°F or Mark 4) oven for 30 minutes, or until the edge of the dough is browned and the cheese bubbling.

IRÈNE AND LUCIENNE KARSENTY
LA CUISINE PIED-NOIR

Neapolitan Batavia and Black Olive Bread

Tortino Ripieno di Scarole e Olive

The technique for making this bread is shown on page 48.

To make one 25 cm (10 inch) bread

250 g	strong plain flour, sieved	8 oz
15 g	fresh yeast or 2 tsp dried yeast	$\frac{1}{2}$ oz
$\frac{1}{2}$ tsp	sugar, dissolved in 4 tbsp tepid water	$\frac{1}{2}$ tsp
75 g	lard or butter, melted and cooled	$2\frac{1}{2}$ oz
1 tsp	salt	1 tsp
	freshly ground black pepper	
1	egg white, lightly beaten with 1 tsp water	1
	Batavian endive and olive filling	
3 or 4	very small Batavian endive heads or 1 large head, shredded	3 or 4
125 g	juicy black olives, rinsed, stoned and chopped	4 oz
5 tbsp	olive oil	5 tbsp
75 g	sultanas, soaked in warm water to cover for 20 minutes, drained and dried	$2\frac{1}{2}$ oz
60 g	pine-nuts	2 oz
1 tbsp	capers, rinsed and drained	1 tbsp
1	garlic clove, chopped	1
2 to 3 tbsp	chopped parsley	2 to 3 tbsp
	black pepper and salt	

Dissolve the yeast in the sugared tepid water. Set the mixture in a warm place until it is bubbly—about 15 minutes. Place the flour in a mixing bowl. Make a deep hollow in the centre. Add the bubbling yeast mixture, half the lard or butter, salt and a good pinch of freshly ground black pepper. Work and knead for about 10 minutes to form a smooth, elastic dough, adding more flour or tepid water as necessary. Cover the dough lightly with a damp tea towel and leave it to rise in a warm place for 1 hour or until doubled in bulk.

Meanwhile, in a large, heavy-based enamelled saucepan or casserole, heat 4 tablespoons of the olive oil. Add the shredded endive and cook it, stirring for several minutes until most of the liquid in the pan has evaporated. Add the olives, sultanas, pine-nuts, capers, garlic and parsley. Season well with black pepper and salt. Remove the mixture from the pan. Drain all excess liquid from it completely and leave it to cool to room temperature.

Punch down the dough in the bowl, turn it out on to a lightly floured board and knead it for 3 minutes. Work in the remaining lard or butter, and knead until the dough is smooth, about

5 minutes. Divide the dough into two equal parts. Roll out one piece to fit an oiled 25 cm (10 inch) cake or pie tin, and press it lightly into the tin. Spread the filling evenly over the dough and cover with the remaining piece of dough, rolled out to fit over the top. Press and push the dough to ensure that it covers the filling completely and pinch the top and bottom edges of the dough together with the fingers, to seal in the mixture. Brush the top with the remaining tablespoon of oil, cover the bread with a tea towel and let it rise a second time for about 20 minutes in a warm place, until almost doubled in bulk. Then brush the top of the bread with the egg white beaten with water. This will make a shiny crust. Bake the bread in an oven preheated to 190°C (375°F or Mark 5) for about 45 minutes or until golden-brown and well risen.

PAULA WOLFERT
MEDITERRANEAN COOKING

Provençal Pizza

Pissaladiera Niçoise

This Provençal version of the Italian pizza takes its name from pissala, *a salted purée of* poutines—*very young anchovies and sardines. However, since the fishing of these young fish in the Mediterranean is now illegal, salt anchovies are usually substituted. To prepare the anchovies for cooking, first soak them for a few minutes in cold water to remove the excess salt. Then split them in two, and remove the backbone and any other bones. Instead of using whole anchovy fillets, the anchovies can be puréed after simmering for a few minutes in 3 to 4 tablespoons of olive oil, and combined with the onion before spreading over the dough.*

The technique of making pissaladiera *is shown on page 46; the order in which the toppings are used is slightly different.*

To make one 25 cm (10 inch) pizza

600 g	basic bread dough with olive oil (*page 171*)	$1\frac{1}{4}$ lb
1 kg	onions, thinly sliced	2 lb
2 tbsp	olive oil	2 tbsp
6	salt anchovies, soaked, filleted, rinsed and dried	6
	pepper	
16	black olives, stoned	16

Fry the onions very slowly in the olive oil for about 40 minutes, until they are very soft but not browned. Take 500 g of the dough and roll it out to a thickness of 5 mm ($\frac{1}{4}$ inch). Line an oiled rectangular baking sheet with the dough. Arrange the anchovy fillets on the dough, cover them with the onion and season with pepper. Roll out the remaining piece of dough and slice it into thin strips each about 5 mm ($\frac{1}{4}$ inch) wide. Arrange these strips in criss-cross fashion over the onion and anchovies, as for a sweet tart. Place an olive in the centre of each of the squares formed by the crossed strips of dough.

Bake the *pissaladiera* in an oven preheated to 220°C (425°F or Mark 7) for 20 to 25 minutes or until the edges of the dough are golden-brown.

BENOÎT MASCARELLI
LA TABLE EN PROVENCE ET SUR LA CÔTE D'AZUR

Flatbread with Oil and Salt

Focaccia all'Olio con Sale

To make three 40 by 30 cm (16 by 12 inch) loaves

2 kg	strong plain flour	4 lb
150 g	fresh yeast or 5 tbsp dried yeast	5 oz
15 cl	olive oil	$\frac{1}{4}$ pint
	salt	
1.25 litres	tepid water	2 pints
$\frac{1}{4}$ litre	white wine	8 fl oz
5	sage leaves, very finely chopped	5

Dissolve the yeast in the water. Pour the flour into a large mixing bowl, make a well in the flour and pour in the yeast mixture. Knead the yeast with as much flour as has been wetted by the mixture, then cover this yeast and flour mixture with a layer of flour. Cover the bowl and leave the yeast sponge to rise for about 4 hours.

Make a hole in the flour layer covering the yeast sponge. Into it pour the white wine, 10 cl ($3\frac{1}{2}$ fl oz) of the oil, the sage leaves and a pinch of salt. Knead all the ingredients together to make a soft, elastic dough. If the dough is too stiff, add more tepid water, a little at a time, as you are kneading; if the dough is too soft, add more flour. Knead the dough for 10 minutes and leave it to rise in a warm place for 3 to 4 hours or until it has doubled in bulk.

Divide the dough into three. Oil three baking tins, put in the dough, press it down and spread it out until it completely fills the tins. Pinch the surface of the dough with your fingers. Sprinkle on a little salt and the rest of the oil and bake the loaves in an oven preheated to 200°C (400°F or Mark 6) for about 40 minutes, or until they sound hollow when rapped.

EMMANUELE ROSSI (EDITOR)
LA VERA CUCINIERA GENOVESE

Italian Flatbread with Butter

Schiacciata col Burro

To make one 25 cm (10 inch) flatbread

500 g	basic bread dough (*page 171*)	1 lb
125 g	butter, softened	4 oz
2 tsp	salt	2 tsp
30 g	fresh basil leaves	1 oz
2 tbsp	olive oil	2 tbsp

Knead the dough thoroughly, then incorporate the butter. Knead for a further 5 minutes, then leave the dough to prove in a warm place for 30 minutes.

Roll out the dough to fit a 25 cm (10 inch) flan tin or pizza plate, and press it here and there with your finger to dimple the surface. Sprinkle the dough generously with salt; then evenly distribute the basil leaves over the surface. Sprinkle the dough with olive oil.

Bake the flatbread in an oven preheated to 220°C (425°F or Mark 7) for about 30 minutes, or until golden in colour. Before serving, discard the basil leaves, which only flavour the bread. Serve hot.

MARIÙ SALVATORI DE ZULIANI
LA CUCINA DI VERSILIA E GARFAGNANA

Neapolitan Crackling Pizza

Tortano con i Cicoli o Pizza Stracciata

If pecorino cheese is not available, Gruyère or strong Cheddar cheese can be substituted. Pork cracklings are made by rendering down fresh pork fat. Sopressata is a pork and beef salami. Any good quality salami can be used instead.

To make two 30 cm (12 inch) pizzas

1 kg	basic bread dough (*page 171*)	2 lb
45 g	lard, softened	$1\frac{1}{2}$ oz
60 g	pork cracklings	2 oz
100 g	*pecorino* cheese, diced	$3\frac{1}{2}$ oz
100 g	*sopressata* salami, diced	$3\frac{1}{2}$ oz
	salt	

Knead the dough by pulling and tearing it apart very roughly, while gradually incorporating the lard, cracklings, cheese and salami. Then add a pinch of salt, and knead for a further 2 to 3 minutes. Divide the dough into two pieces. Roll each piece out in a circle about 1 cm ($\frac{1}{2}$ inch) thick and lay it on a greased baking sheet. Bake the pizzas in an oven preheated to 180°C (350°F or Mark 4) for about 30 minutes or until golden-brown. Serve while still warm.

MARIA RIVIECCIO ZANIBONI
CUCINA E VINI DI NAPOLI E DELLA CAMPANIA

Sage Flatbread

Focaccia alla Salvia

To make one 30 by 20 cm (12 by 8 inch) flatbread

350 g	strong plain flour	12 oz
15 g	fresh yeast or 2 tsp dried yeast	½ oz
10	sage leaves, finely chopped	10
3 tbsp	tepid milk	3 tbsp
15 g	sugar	½ oz
1 tsp	salt	1 tsp
60 g	butter, softened	2 oz

Dissolve the yeast in the tepid milk and leave in a warm place for about 15 minutes. Add the yeast mixture to the flour, with the sugar, half of the salt and all of the butter, and work the ingredients into a smooth, firm dough. Roll out the dough into a rectangle about 30 by 20 cm (12 by 8 inches) and place it on a buttered baking sheet or Swiss roll tin. Leave it to rise for 45 minutes, or until light and spongy.

Sprinkle the dough with the sage leaves and the rest of the salt. Bake the flatbread in an oven preheated to 180°C (350°F or Mark 4) for about 30 minutes, or until the surface is golden.

ILARIA RATTAZZI (EDITOR)
TANTE COSE CON IL PANE

Onion Cake

Zwiebelkuchen zum Neuen Wein

This cake is traditionally served with new wine in German-speaking countries.

To make one 25 cm (10 inch) cake

500 g	strong plain flour	1 lb
30 g	fresh yeast or 1 tbsp dried yeast	1 oz
1 kg	onions, finely chopped	2 lb
¼ litre	tepid water	8 fl oz
	sugar	
175 g	lard	6 oz
3	egg yolks, beaten	3
	salt	
200 g	lean bacon, finely chopped	7 oz
5	eggs, beaten	5
¼ litre	soured cream	8 fl oz
	caraway seeds	

Dissolve the yeast in a little of the tepid water with a pinch of sugar. Place the flour in a bowl and warm it. Make a well in the centre of the flour. Pour in the yeast mixture, and blend in the flour to make a thin dough, cover the dough with a cloth and leave it to rise until it has doubled in bulk—about 1 hour.

Melt 125 g (4 oz) of the lard and combine it with the egg yolks, a pinch of salt and the remaining water; add this mixture to the dough. Knead the dough until it becomes smooth and firm and no longer sticks to the bowl. Leave it to rise for another hour, or until it has doubled in bulk again, then roll it out into a round about 25 cm (10 inches) across, the thickness of a finger. Pinch the edge to make a raised rim about 2 cm (¾ inch) high and leave it to rise again.

Fry the onions in the rest of the lard until they are transparent; add three-quarters of the bacon and fry it until it is crisp. Remove the onions and bacon from the fat and leave them to cool, then spread them evenly over the dough. Beat the eggs lightly with the soured cream and a little salt and pour them over the onion and bacon topping. Sprinkle with the remaining bacon and with caraway seeds. Bake in an oven preheated to 190°C (375°F or Mark 5) for about 30 minutes, or until the filling is golden.

HANS KARL ADAM
DAS KOCHBUCH AUS SCHWABEN

Onion Flatbread

Schiacciata con la Cipolla

To make one 20 cm (8 inch) flatbread

400 g	basic bread dough (*page 171*)	14 oz
1	medium-sized onion, thinly sliced	1
30 g	lard or butter	1 oz
8 cl	oil	3 fl oz
3 tsp	salt	3 tsp
30 g	fresh sage leaves, chopped	1 oz

Work the lard or butter, half of the oil and 1 teaspoon of the salt into the risen bread dough, and knead it for about 5 minutes until the ingredients are well mixed. Roll out the dough into a round about 20 cm (8 inches) in diameter and lay it on a well-buttered baking sheet. Leave it to prove in a warm place for about 30 minutes, or until light and spongy. Meanwhile, put the onion in a shallow dish, sprinkle it with the remaining 2 teaspoons of salt, mix well and leave for about 10 minutes for the onion to absorb the salt.

Drain away the liquid given off by the onion; add the sage to the onion, mix well and cover the dough with this mixture. Sprinkle the bread with the remaining oil. Bake the bread in an oven preheated to 220°C (425°F or Mark 7) for 20 minutes or until the edges are golden-brown.

GUGLIELMA CORSI
UN SECOLO DI CUCINA UMBRA

Old-Fashioned Quiche Lorraine

Fiouse è lè Flemme

This bread dough flan was originally baked in the burning embers of the oven before they cooled sufficiently to make bread, hence its name, which in English means "Flame Cake". This version comes from Metz, the capital of Lorraine. The author recommends using a very light oil for the filling.

To make one 25 cm (10 inch) quiche

500 g	basic bread dough (*page 171*)	1 lb
1	egg	1
3 to 4 tbsp	walnut or rapeseed oil	3 to 4 tbsp
	salt	
125 g	streaky bacon, diced (optional)	4 oz
2	onions, finely chopped (optional)	2

To prepare the filling, beat the egg with the oil and a pinch of salt, and stir in the bacon and onions, if used.

Prepare the bread dough and let it rise once. Then roll it out into a fairly thick round about 25 cm (10 inches) across, and press it into a buttered tart tin or pizza plate. Pour in the filling. Bake the quiche in a preheated, 220°C (425°F or Mark 7) oven for 15 minutes; then reduce the temperature to 190°C (375°F or Mark 5), cover the quiche with buttered aluminium foil, and bake for a further 10 minutes. The dough should be browned and risen and the bacon and onions cooked through.

E. AURICOSTE DE LAZARQUE
CUISINE MESSINE

Oiled Pizza

Stiacciata con l'Olio

To make one 30 by 20 cm (12 by 8 inch) pizza

1 kg	basic bread dough (*page 171*)	2 lb
15 cl	olive oil	5 fl oz
1 tsp	salt	1 tsp

Knead 12.5 cl (4 fl oz) of the olive oil into the dough. Spread the dough on an oiled Swiss roll tin or similar baking sheet with a 3 cm (1 inch) rim. Prick the dough with a fork, sprinkle it with salt and the rest of the olive oil, and leave it to rise in a warm place for about 30 minutes or until doubled in bulk. Bake in an oven preheated to 220°C (425°F or Mark 7) for 30 minutes or until golden-brown. Serve hot or cold.

LOUIS MONOD
LA CUISINE FLORENTINE

Marrakesh "Pizza"

Khboz Bishemar

It may seem odd to stuff bread with fat and spices, but the idea is extremely ingenious; the fat runs out through holes pricked in the dough, becomes the medium in which the bread is fried, and leaves behind its flavour and an array of spices and herbs that make it taste strikingly like pizza crust.

To make four 35 by 20 cm (14 by 8 inch) flatbreads

250 g	strong plain flour	8 oz
15 g	fresh yeast, or 2 tsp dried yeast	½ oz
6 tbsp	tepid water	6 tbsp
125 g	mutton or beef suet	4 oz
3 tbsp	chopped parsley	3 tbsp
90 g	onion, finely chopped	3 oz
½ tsp	ground cumin	½ tsp
1	dried red chili pepper	1
2 tsp	paprika	2 tsp
1 tsp	salt	1 tsp
4 tsp	melted unsalted butter	4 tsp

Sprinkle the yeast over the tepid water. Stir to dissolve and let stand in a warm place for 10 minutes or until the yeast has become bubbly and doubled in volume.

Meanwhile, make the filling. Chop or mince the suet. Pound the parsley, onion and spices in a mortar or chop finely to a paste; mix with the suet and set aside.

Mix the flour with the salt and make a well in the centre. Pour in the yeast and enough tepid water to form a ball of dough. (Add more water if the dough seems hard to handle.) Knead the dough well until smooth and elastic, about 20 minutes. Separate the ball of dough into four equal parts.

Lightly flour a board. Begin patting the first ball of dough down to a disc shape, stretching and flattening it to make a rectangle approximately 35 by 20 cm (14 by 8 inches). Spread one-quarter of the filling in the centre. Fold the right and then the left side of the dough over the filling. Press down on this "package" and begin flattening and stretching it (with filling inside) until it is the same size as before. Repeat the folding, this time right side over centre and left side under. Repeat with the remaining three balls of dough. Set aside the breads, covered, in a warm place for 45 minutes to prove.

Heat the griddle. Prick each "package" with a fork six or seven times on both sides. Place them on the griddle—they will begin to fry in the fat released from their fillings. Fry the "packages" 10 minutes on each side, until crisp. Dot each package with a teaspoonful of melted butter before serving.

PAULA WOLFERT
COUSCOUS AND OTHER GOOD FOOD FROM MOROCCO

Italian Flatbread with Ham

Gnocco al Forno

To make one 35 cm (14 inch) flatbread

500 g	basic bread dough (*page 171*)	1 lb
125 g	prosciutto, diced	4 oz
4 tbsp	ham or pork stock	4 tbsp
2 tsp	coarse salt	2 tsp

After the bread dough has risen for the first time, knead it, adding the prosciutto and the stock to make a rather soft consistency. Roll the dough out in a circle about 2 cm ($\frac{3}{4}$ inch) thick and lay it on a buttered baking sheet. With a sharp knife, lightly score the surface to create a trellis pattern. Sprinkle the dough with the coarse salt. Leave the dough in a warm place to prove for 20 minutes. Bake it in an oven preheated to 220°C (425°F or Mark 7) for about 20 minutes or until brown. Eat while still warm.

GIORGIO CAVAZZUTI (EDITOR)
IL MANGIARFUORI: ALMANACCO DELLA CUCINA MODENESE

Neapolitan Endive Pie

Pizza di Scarola

To make one 25 cm (10 inch) pizza

500 g	strong plain flour	1 lb
30 g	fresh yeast or 1 tbsp dried yeast	1 oz
About 30 cl	tepid water	About $\frac{1}{2}$ pint
150 g	lard, softened	5 oz
	salt and freshly ground black pepper	
	Endive, olive and anchovy filling	
1.5 kg	endives, trimmed, washed and chopped	3 lb
100 g	black olives, stoned	3½ oz
100 g	salt anchovies, filleted and mashed	3½ oz
1	garlic clove, chopped	1
12.5 cl	olive oil	4 fl oz
60 g	capers	2 oz
	freshly ground black pepper	

Dissolve the yeast in 6 tablespoons of the tepid water. Stir in a handful of the flour to make a paste, and leave the mixture in a warm place for about 30 minutes to let the sponge develop.

Sieve the rest of the flour into a mound. Make a well in the centre and add the yeast sponge, lard, a little salt and a good pinch of freshly ground black pepper. Work these ingredients together, adding as much of the reserved water as necessary to make a rather soft dough. Knead the dough for about 10 minutes. Place it in a bowl, cover it, and leave it in a warm place to rise for 1 hour or until doubled in bulk.

Drop the chopped endives into a saucepan of boiling water and cook for about 2 minutes. Drain the endives in a strainer, pressing with a wooden spoon to extract any remaining liquid. Brown the garlic in the oil, and add the capers, olives and endives. Fry the vegetables briskly for 10 minutes. Then remove the pan from the heat and immediately add the anchovies. Leave the mixture to cool.

When the dough is well risen, divide it into two pieces, one slightly bigger than the other. Butter a flan tin or pizza plate and line it with the larger round of dough. Cover the dough with the endive mixture and roll out the remaining piece of dough to cover this pie.

Bake the endive pie in an oven preheated to 180°C (350°F or Mark 4) for about 45 minutes or until the pie is golden-brown and sounds slightly hollow when rapped.

JEANNE CARÒLA FRANCESCONI
LA CUCINA NAPOLETANA

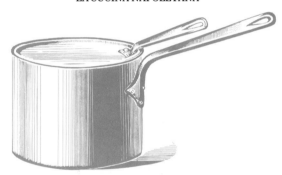

Country Pizza

Pizza Rustica

If pecorino cheese is not available, any hard yellow cheese such as Gruyère or strong Cheddar may be substituted.

To make one 25 cm (10 inch) pizza

500 g	basic bread dough (*page 171*)	1 lb
2	eggs, beaten	2
100 g	prosciutto, diced	3½ oz
60 g	*pecorino* cheese, diced	2 oz
90 g	Parmesan cheese, grated	3 oz
4 tbsp	olive oil	4 tbsp
	salt and freshly ground black pepper	

Mix the eggs, prosciutto, cheeses, oil and a pinch each of salt and pepper with the dough, and knead the mixture well for about 5 minutes. Then with your hands or a rolling pin, roll the dough into a circle about 25 cm (10 inches) in diameter and 5 mm ($\frac{1}{4}$ inch) thick. Place the dough on a well-oiled baking sheet and leave it to rest in a warm place, sheltered from draughts, for 1 hour or until it is light and puffy.

Prick the surface of the dough thoroughly with a fork and bake it in an oven preheated to 220°C (425°F or Mark 7) for about 20 minutes or until it is golden-brown.

GUGLIELMA CORSI
UN SECOLO DI CUCINA UMBRA

Neapolitan Turnover

Chausson à la Napolitaine

If mozzarella *cheese is unavailable, any semi-hard cheese such as Cheddar or Gruyère can be substituted. Ricotta may be replaced with curd cheese. The making of a Neapolitan turnover is shown on page 48, although the order in which the fillings are added is slightly different.*

The *calzone*, or turnover made with olive oil dough, is a speciality of the Campania region of Italy of which Naples is the chief town. Instead of one large turnover, several small ones may be made. In the latter case, the turnovers should be deep-fried in very hot olive oil for only 3 minutes.

To make one 38 cm (15 inch) turnover or 8 small turnovers

600 g	basic bread dough with olive oil (page 171)	1¼ lb
100 g	*mozzarella*, diced	3½ oz
200 g	*ricotta* cheese, sieved	7 oz
1	egg	1
	salt and pepper	
50 g	*pecorino* or Parmesan cheese, grated	2 oz
100 g	Italian salami, finely sliced, or prosciutto, cut into strips about 2 cm (1 inch) long	3½ oz

Put the sieved *ricotta* cheese into a bowl with the diced *mozzarella*, egg, salt and pepper, the *pecorino* or Parmesan cheese and the salami or prosciutto, and mix lightly.

Oil a large baking sheet. Roll out the dough in a round about 5 mm (¼ inch) thick and lay it on the sheet, slightly raising the edges of the dough to hold the filling. Spread the filling evenly over the dough. Moisten the edges of the dough. Then fold the dough in two to make a pasty or turnover shape. Stick the edges together securely so that the filling will not escape during cooking. Bake the turnover in an oven preheated to 220°C (425°F or Mark 7) for 30 minutes or until the pastry is golden-brown.

PIERRE ANDROUET
LA CUISINE AU FROMAGE

Swiss Cheese Flan

Käswähe

To make one 25 cm (10 inch) flan

400 g	strong plain flour	14 oz
20 g	fresh yeast or 2 tsp dried yeast	¾ oz
¼ litre	tepid water	8 fl oz
½ tsp	salt	½ tsp
75 g	butter, softened	2½ oz
	Cheese and onion topping	
300 g	Emmenthal cheese, grated, or 150 g (5 oz) Emmenthal cheese, grated, and 150 g (5 oz) Gruyère cheese, grated	10 oz
2	small onions, finely chopped	2
15 g	butter	½ oz
3	eggs, beaten	3
1 tsp	salt	1 tsp
	pepper	
15 cl	single cream	¼ pint

Sieve the flour and salt into a warm mixing bowl. Dissolve the yeast in about 6 tablespoons of the tepid water. Leave until slightly foaming, about 10 minutes. Pour the mixture into the flour and knead well, gradually adding the rest of the water. Knead the dough for about 10 minutes until it is smooth and elastic. Then work the butter into the dough with your fingertips. Knead the dough for 5 minutes, until the butter is well incorporated, and then leave it in a warm place to rise for about 1½ hours or until doubled in bulk.

Knock back the dough and roll it into a circle about 25 cm (10 inches) across and 1 cm (½ inch) thick. Place it in a buttered cake tin or on a pizza plate and leave it to rise for 30 minutes.

While the dough is rising, make the topping. Lightly fry the onions in the butter until they are transparent. Mix them with the grated cheese, eggs, salt, pepper and cream. Spread the mixture on the dough in a 1 to 2 cm (½ to 1 inch) thick layer and bake the flan in an oven preheated to 220°C (425°F or Mark 7) for about 30 minutes or until golden-brown.

GRETE WILLINSKY
KULINARISCHE WELTREISE

Cream Cheese Bread

Forron

This flan is traditional in the Dauphiné region of south-eastern France. The cream cheese can be made from cow's or goat's milk, or a mixture of both.

To make one 20 cm (8 inch) flan

150 g	basic bread dough with olive oil (*page 171*) 5 oz
300 g	cream cheese	10 oz
2 tsp	salt	2 tsp

Roll out the dough on a floured board, to fit a 20 cm (8 inch) flan tin, allowing for an extra 3 cm (1 inch) overlap of dough over the edge of the tin. Butter the tin and put the dough into it. Prick the dough with a fork.

Add the salt to the cream cheese and beat it in thoroughly. Spread the cheese evenly over the dough. Roll up the dough edge, and press it down round the edge of the flan. Bake in an oven preheated to 200°C (400°F or Mark 6) for about 30 minutes, or until the bread is golden-brown.

PIERRE ANDROUET
LA CUISINE AU FROMAGE

A Picnic Loaf

To make one 35 cm (14 inch) loaf

1 kg	basic bread dough (*page 171*)	2½ lb
300 g	Gruyère cheese, coarsely grated or sliced	10 oz
8	eggs, in the shell	8
500 g	Polish boiling sausage (*kielbasa*), cut into 4 pieces and pricked	1 lb
1	egg yolk, beaten	1

Let the dough rise once in a bowl. Divide it into two equal portions and roll one portion into a circle 35 cm (14 inches) in diameter. Place the circle of dough on an oiled baking sheet. Pile the cheese in the middle in a neat heap 15 cm (6 inches) wide. Roll out half of the remaining dough into a circle just large enough to cover the cheese topping. Lay this circle of dough on top of the cheese, sealing it on with a little water at the edges. Space the eggs and sections of sausage alternately around the edge of the large dough circle. Roll the remaining dough into narrow strips the width of a pencil and use them in a criss-cross pattern to bind the eggs and sausage to the bread base. Moisten the ends to help them stick. Let the loaf rise in a warm place for about 1 hour. Then glaze it with the egg yolk

and bake it in an oven preheated to 200°C (400°F or Mark 6) for 25 minutes. Then lower the heat to 180°C (350°F or Mark 4) and bake it for another 25 minutes. The eggs will cook, the sausage render its juices and the cheese melt succulently into the bread. Serve the loaf cut into wedges.

JUDITH OLNEY
SUMMER FOOD

Italian Sausage Bread

Pane con Salsicce

Olive bread can be made in the same way as this recipe except that 250 g (8 oz) of pitted black olives are kneaded into the dough instead of the sausages, and the sage is left out of the ingredients for the second rising. Because the sausages or olives make the dough heavier, extra yeast is added.

To make one 30 cm (12 inch) flatbread

1 kg	strong plain flour	2 lb
40 g	fresh yeast or 1½ tbsp dried yeast	1½ oz
250 g	pork frying sausages, cut into 2 cm (1 inch) slices	8 oz
2 tbsp	olive oil	2 tbsp
½ litre	tepid water	16 fl oz
	salt	
4 or 5	sage leaves, fresh or salted	4 or 5

Put the sausage slices, along with the olive oil, into a saucepan and sauté them very gently for about 10 minutes, until they are just beginning to brown. Remove them from the heat and set aside until needed.

Make a yeast sponge by dissolving the yeast in 4 tablespoons of the water in a small bowl. In a larger bowl, put 60 g (2 oz) of the flour. Add the dissolved yeast and mix with a wooden spoon until the flour is incorporated and a small ball of dough is formed. Sprinkle a little of the remaining flour over the ball of dough, then cover the bowl with a towel and put it in a warm place to rise, away from draughts. Let the sponge stand until it has doubled in size, about 1 hour.

Arrange the rest of the flour in a mound on a board, then make a well in the centre. Place the yeast sponge in the well, along with a pinch of salt and 12.5 cl (4 fl oz) of the water.

With a wooden spoon, carefully mix together all the ingredients in the well, then add the remaining water and start mixing with your hands, incorporating the flour from the inside rim of the well little by little. Keep mixing until all but 4 to 5 tablespoons of the flour are incorporated (about 15 minutes), then add the sage and knead the dough with the palms of your hands, in a folding motion, until it is homogeneous and smooth (about 20 minutes), incorporating the remaining flour, if necessary, to keep the dough from being sticky. Add the browned sausage slices to the dough and knead gently for 5 minutes more.

Lightly oil a 30 cm (12 inch) spring-form tin. Place the dough in the tin, cover it with a tea towel and put it in a warm place, away from draughts. Let the dough stand until doubled in size (about 1 hour); the time will vary a bit, depending on the weather. Remove the towel and immediately place the tin in an oven preheated to 200°C (400°F or Mark 6). Bake the bread for about 1 hour or until well browned. Do not open the oven door for at least 30 minutes after baking begins.

Remove the bread from the oven, allow it to cool for 5 minutes, then open the spring-form and transfer the bread to a board, standing the loaf at an angle, not lying flat. The bread must be allowed to cool for at least 3 hours before it will be at its best for eating.

GIULIANO BUGIALLI
THE FINE ART OF ITALIAN COOKING

Chocolate Rolls

Petits Pains aux Chocolat

To make 8 rolls

250 g	strong plain flour	8 oz
15 g	fresh yeast or 2 tsp dried yeast	½ oz
125 g	plain chocolate, broken into 8 pieces	4 oz
1 tsp	salt	1 tsp
About 15 cl	milk and water, mixed and warmed	About ¼ pint

Milk and sugar glaze		
2 tbsp	milk	2 tbsp
30 g	sugar	1 oz

Sift the salt into the flour, dissolve the yeast in the tepid milk and water mixture, see that it is well amalgamated, pour it on to the flour and mix lightly. If too stiff, add a little extra milk. Cover the bowl. Leave to rise for about 1½ hours.

When the dough has doubled in volume, break it down, knead it very little, divide it in half, then in quarters, then eighths. Roll or pat each piece out on a floured board, into rectangles of a size to fit round your chocolate pieces, which you place on your rectangle of dough. Fold over first the ends, then the sides, making a neat parcel of each. Press the joins carefully together and brush the rolls with milk. Leave them on a floured baking sheet to recover shape and volume; about 15 to 20 minutes should be sufficient.

Bake the rolls in an oven preheated to 200° to 220°C (400° to 425°F or Mark 6 or 7) for 15 to 20 minutes or until golden-brown. To make the rolls shiny, dissolve the sugar for the glaze in the milk, and brush the tops immediately the rolls are removed from the oven.

Chocolate rolls should be eaten warm, either immediately they are cooked or after reheating for a few minutes on the bottom shelf of a cool oven. The chocolate inside the roll must be just melting.

ELIZABETH DAVID
ENGLISH BREAD AND YEAST COOKERY

Nut Roll

Strucla Drożdżowa z Masą Orzechową

To make one 20 cm (8 inch) roll

275 g	strong plain flour	9 oz
15 g	fresh yeast or 2 tsp dried yeast	½ oz
90 g	sugar	3 oz
125 g	butter, softened and cut into pieces	4 oz
2 tbsp	tepid milk	2 tbsp
	milk or beaten egg yolk for brushing (optional)	
	icing sugar	
Nut filling		
400 g	walnuts or hazelnuts, finely ground	14 oz
200 g	sugar	7 oz
15 cl	water	¼ pint
15 g	butter	½ oz

Mix together the flour and sugar on a working surface; work in the butter with your fingertips. Dissolve the yeast in the tepid milk and leave it to rise for 10 minutes. Using your hands, work the yeast into the butter and flour mixture. Knead the dough for about 10 minutes, until smooth and elastic, then leave it, covered with a cloth, in a warm place to rise for approximately 1 hour.

To make the nut filling, bring the sugar and water to the boil and simmer them over a very low heat for 8 to 10 minutes. Stir the walnuts or hazelnuts into this syrup and remove the pan from the heat. Then stir in the butter until it dissolves, and leave the mixture to cool.

Roll out the dough into a rectangle about 25 by 20 cm (10 by 8 inches) and about 1 cm (½ inch) thick. Spread the filling over it, leaving a margin of about 3 cm (1 inch) at the edges. Roll up the dough like a Swiss roll and, if desired, brush it with the milk or egg yolk. Butter and flour a baking sheet and put the roll on it. Cover the roll with a cloth and leave it to prove for up to 1 hour or until doubled in bulk.

Bake the roll in an oven preheated to 220°C (425°F or Mark 7) for 10 minutes, then reduce the heat to 200°C (400°F or Mark 6) and bake for a further 20 minutes until pale golden. Leave it to cool and sprinkle with icing sugar.

LILI KOWALSKA
COOKING THE POLISH WAY

Vegetable Bread

Eliza Acton published her bread book in 1857, when the art of home bread-making was dying in England. Modern authors have noted how scrupulously she tested all her recipes, and what excellent tips she gives to the cook. She was one of the first cookery writers to advocate the eating of wholemeal or wheat-meal rather than white bread.

Many vegetables may be used in part for making bread; but, with the exception of potatoes and the seed of the French bean, all vegetables will impart their peculiar flavour to it, though their presence may not otherwise be perceptible. Parsnips, Swedish turnips and beetroot will all answer for dough (parsnips the best of any) if boiled tender, mashed to a smooth pulp (the beetroot, which may also be baked, must be grated), and stirred in a saucepan over a gentle fire until tolerably dry, and left to become cool before they are mixed with flour or meal for the purpose.

To make two 20 by 10 cm (8 by 4 inch) loaves

1 kg	strong plain or wheatmeal flour	2 lb
30 g	fresh yeast or 1 tbsp dried yeast	1 oz
500 g	cooked and puréed white haricot beans, parsnips, swedes or beetroot	1 lb
About ½ litre	tepid water	About 16 fl oz
2 tsp	salt	2 tsp

Dissolve the yeast in half the water. Mix the vegetable purée with the flour, adding the yeast and enough extra water to make a firm dough. Knead the dough thoroughly, then leave it to rise for 1½ hours or until well risen. Knock back the dough and knead it again. Half fill two buttered 1 litre (2 lb) loaf tins and leave them in a warm place for the dough to rise for 1 hour or until risen by one-third. Bake in an oven preheated to 220°C (425°F or Mark 7) for about 50 minutes or until golden-brown on top.

ELIZA ACTON
THE ENGLISH BREAD-BOOK FOR DOMESTIC USE

Potato Bread

This recipe is from an anonymous cookery book published in about 1827. Although excellent, the book was never republished and the identity of the author remains a mystery. For a lighter loaf, divide the dough between two 1 litre (2 lb) tins.

Some people put equal parts of potatoes and flour, and add to the warm milk and water 30 g (1 oz) of butter and a lump or two of sugar. If baked in a tin the crust will be more delicate, but the bread dries sooner.

To make one 30 cm (12 inch) loaf

750 g	strong plain flour, sifted	1½ lb
30 g	fresh yeast or 1 tbsp dried yeast	1 oz
250 g	floury potatoes, scrubbed, boiled or steamed, peeled and mashed	8 oz
45 cl	tepid milk and water in equal quantities	¾ pint
1 tsp	salt	1 tsp

Warm the flour in a bowl. Rub the potatoes while warm into the flour and mix thoroughly. Dissolve the yeast in 15 cl (¼ pint) of the milk and water and leave it in a warm place for about 10 minutes to froth. Put the yeast into the flour and potato mixture, with the salt and the rest of the milk and water, enough to work into a dough. Knead the dough thoroughly for about 10 minutes. Let it stand in a warm place to rise for 1½ hours. When it has risen, punch the dough down, knead it for 5 minutes and shape it into a ball. Leave the dough on a buttered baking sheet to prove for about 40 minutes. Then bake it in an oven preheated to 220°C (425°F or Mark 7) for 40 minutes or until golden-brown.

THE NEW LONDON COOKERY AND COMPLETE DOMESTIC GUIDE

Republican Potato Bread

Pain à la Pomme de Terre

This recipe comes from what is probably the only cookery book published during the French Revolution. The book, which appeared in Year 3 of the Republic (1795), consists of a selection of potato recipes. For bread-making purposes, it is best to boil the potatoes in their skins on a low heat, to ensure they do not disintegrate, then drain them thoroughly before peeling and mashing.

To make one 25 cm (10 inch) loaf

1 kg	strong plain flour	2 lb
30 g	fresh yeast or 1 tbsp dried yeast	1 oz
500 g	warm mashed potatoes, very smooth and dry	1 lb
60 cl	tepid milk and water, in equal quantities	1 pint
2 tsp	salt	2 tsp

Dissolve the yeast in 6 tablespoons of the milk and water. Sift the flour and salt together in a bowl. Rub the potato into the flour as if rubbing in fat, to make a smooth mixture. Add the yeast and the rest of the liquid. Knead thoroughly and leave to rise until doubled in bulk—about 2 hours.

Knock the dough back, knead it lightly, lay it on a floured baking sheet, and shape it into a round or oblong loaf. Cover the loaf with a damp cloth and leave it to prove for about 30 minutes, or until it has increased in bulk by half.

Bake the loaf in a preheated 220°C (425°F or Mark 7) oven for about 45 minutes, or until the crust is light brown.

MADAME MÉRIGOT
LA CUISINIÈRE RÉPUBLICAINE

Pumpernickel Bread

The technique of making this bread is shown on page 52.

*To make one 30 cm (12 inch) loaf
or two 20 cm (8 inch) loaves*

60 g	fine cornmeal	2 oz
400 g	rye flour	14 oz
125 g	wholemeal flour	4 oz
30 g	fresh yeast or 1 tbsp dried yeast	1 oz
50 cl	water	17 fl oz
17.5 cl	molasses	6 fl oz
15 g	butter	½ oz
1 tbsp	salt	1 tbsp
2 tsp	sugar	2 tsp
1½ tsp	caraway seeds, slightly crushed	1½ tsp
60 g	unsweetened chocolate, broken into pieces	2 oz
200 g	mashed potato	7 oz
	oil	
1	egg white, mixed with 1 tbsp cold water	1

Combine 45 cl (¾ pint) of the water with the cornmeal in a medium-sized saucepan and cook the mixture over a low heat, stirring with a wooden spoon until it has thickened—about 5 minutes. Remove the cornmeal from the heat and add the molasses, butter, salt, sugar, caraway seeds and chocolate. Stir until the mixture is well blended, then pour it into a large mixing bowl and set it aside until it has cooled to lukewarm.

Meanwhile, slightly warm the remaining water and dissolve the yeast in it. Add the yeast and the mashed potato to the mixture in the bowl. Blend them well and stir in the rye and wholemeal flours. The dough should be stiff and sticky. Turn the mixture out on to a work surface liberally sprinkled with additional wholemeal flour. Put a little oil on your hands before you start to knead, and keep the surface of the dough powdered with wholemeal flour. Have a scraper handy to remove the dough that accumulates on the work surface. The dough will require a lot of kneading before it begins to come away cleanly from the work surface and from your fingers.

Knead it until it is elastic, though stiff—about 15 minutes.

Place the dough in a buttered bowl, cover with a towel or plastic film and put it in a warm place to rise for about 1 hour or until it has doubled in bulk. Punch down the dough and form it into one or two round, smooth balls. Place the dough on a buttered baking sheet dusted with cornmeal or flour. Cover it with greaseproof paper and return it to a warm place for about 30 minutes to rise again.

Brush the dough with the egg white and water, and bake it in an oven preheated to 190°C (375°F or Mark 5) for about 50 minutes or until rapping the bottom crust yields a hard and hollow sound.

BERNARD CLAYTON, JR.
THE COMPLETE BOOK OF BREADS

The Hermit's Rice Bread

This recipe comes from a collection published in 1867 and was allegedly acquired by the authoress from a Welsh hermit. Rice bread is extremely light and has excellent keeping qualities. Any rice may be used, as long as it is very thoroughly cooked.

To make four 20 by 10 cm (8 by 4 inch) loaves

3 kg	strong plain flour	6 lb
60 g	fresh yeast or 2 tbsp dried yeast	2 oz
250 g	rice	8 oz
1.75 litres	salted water	3 pints
2 tsp	sugar	2 tsp
2 tsp	salt	2 tsp

Boil the rice in the water until it is soft, about 20 minutes. Drain the rice and reserve the cooking liquid. Put the liquid aside to cool until tepid.

Dissolve the yeast in 30 cl (½ pint) of the cooled rice cooking liquid, stir in the sugar and leave the mixture in a warm place until it foams, about 15 minutes. Sift the flour into a bowl and mix the rice with it thoroughly. Add the salt, the yeast mixture and the rest of the cooking liquid and knead the dough for about 5 minutes. Leave the dough to rise in a warm place, covered with a cloth, for about 1½ hours or until doubled in bulk. Knead the dough again and divide it between four buttered 1 litre (2 lb) loaf tins, so that the dough only comes half way up the sides of the tins. Leave the tins in a warm place, covered with a cloth, for the dough to prove for about 30 minutes, or until the dough reaches the rims of the tins.

Bake the loaves in an oven preheated to 230°C (450°F or Mark 8) for about 15 minutes, then lower the temperature to 200°C (400°F or Mark 6) and bake for a further 30 minutes, until the loaves are golden-brown and sound slightly hollow when they are rapped.

THE RIGHT HON. LADY LLANOVER
GOOD COOKERY

Sourdough Onion Bread

Sauerteig-Zwiebelbrot

To make two 35 cm (14 inch) cylindrical loaves

800 g	rye flour	1¾ lb
250 g	rye sourdough starter (*page 170*)	8 oz
100 g	rolled oats	3½ oz
5	onions, very finely chopped	5
20 cl	tepid water	7 fl oz
30 g	chives, very finely cut	1 oz
2 tbsp	olive oil	2 tbsp
3½ tsp	salt	3½ tsp
1 tsp	freshly ground white pepper	1 tsp
2 tbsp	wholemeal flour	2 tbsp

The night before, stir together the rye sourdough starter, water and 200 g (7 oz) of the rye flour until smooth. Cover the mixture with a cloth and leave overnight in a warm place.

Put 4 tablespoons of the onions in a heatproof dish and toast them under a hot grill until they are brown. Mix the remaining onions with the chives and fry them gently in the olive oil until they are transparent—about 10 minutes. Season with half a teaspoon of the salt and all the pepper, and allow the mixture to cool.

To the starter mixture, add the remaining rye flour, the rolled oats, the onion and chive mixture and the rest of the salt. Mix the ingredients into a dough and knead it for 15 minutes or until it is smooth and fairly elastic. Cover the dough with a cloth and let it rest for 2 hours in a warm place, until it has doubled in bulk.

Knead the dough again for 10 minutes, then divide it in half and shape it into two long, thin loaves. With a sharp knife or a razor blade, cut a few shallow, diagonal slashes in the tops of the loaves. Place the loaves on a greased and lightly floured baking sheet, cover them with a tea towel and leave them to prove in a warm place for 2 hours. Lightly press the toasted onions into the tops of the loaves. Sprinkle the loaves with the wholemeal flour and bake them in the centre of a preheated 220°C (425°F or Mark 7) oven for 40 to 50 minutes or until the loaves sound hollow when rapped on the bottom.

MARGRET UHLE AND ANNE BRAKEMEIER
EIGENBRÖTLERS BROTBACKBUCH

Rosemary Bread

Pane di Rosmarino

This bread is served at Easter in Florence and Tuscany. In Tuscany, it is shaped into long or round loaves; in Florence it is made into small rolls.

Some people like to add finely chopped fresh rosemary leaves to the oil and raisins to give the bread a much stronger flavour, but this is not traditional.

To make two 20 by 10 cm (8 by 4 inch) loaves or 20 rolls

800 g	basic bread dough (*page 171*)	1¾ lb
1	large sprig rosemary	1
250 g	raisins	8 oz
4 tbsp	oil	4 tbsp
1 tsp	salt	1 tsp
1 tbsp	castor sugar	1 tbsp
2 tbsp	sugar, dissolved in 4 tbsp tepid water	2 tbsp

Fry the raisins and rosemary in the oil until the rosemary is lightly browned, about 5 minutes. Remove the pan from the heat and discard the rosemary. Knead the dough for a further 5 minutes, then knead in the cooled oil and the raisins, the salt and castor sugar. Let the dough rise for 30 minutes in a warm place. Shape it into two circular or cylindrical loaves or 20 balls. Lay these on buttered baking sheets and leave them in a warm place to prove for about 30 minutes. Bake the loaves or rolls in an oven preheated to 220°C (425°F or Mark 7)— approximately 30 minutes for the loaves, or 20 minutes for the rolls. Half way through the cooking time, brush the tops with the sugar and water to make them shine. Leave the bread to cool on wire racks.

MARIÙ SALVATORI DE ZULIANI
LA CUCINA DI VERSILIA E GARFAGNANA

Ulm Bread

Ulmer Brot

To make 4 or 5 small, cylindrical loaves about 20 cm (8 inches) long

1.5 kg	strong plain flour	3 lb
60 g	fresh yeast or 2 tbsp dried yeast	2 oz
About ¾ litre	tepid milk	About 1¼ pints
125 g	butter	4 oz
250 g	sugar	8 oz
30 g	candied lemon peel, diced	1 oz
	aniseeds	
	fennel seeds	
30 g	vanilla sugar or 1 tsp vanilla extract	1 oz
1	egg, beaten	1

Dissolve the yeast in the milk and leave it in a warm place for about 20 minutes to froth. Add the flour, butter, sugar, lemon peel, a pinch each of aniseeds and fennel seeds and the vanilla sugar or vanilla extract, to make a firm dough, adding more milk if necessary. Knead the dough well and divide it into four or five equal portions. Shape each portion into a cylindrical loaf. With a sharp knife or a razor blade, make a long gash down the centre of each loaf.

Butter two or three baking sheets and place the loaves on them; leave them to rise for 20 minutes. Then brush the loaves with beaten egg, but do not brush the egg into the gashes. Bake in an oven preheated to 220°C (425°F or Mark 7) for 40 minutes or until the loaves sound hollow when tapped.

HANS KARL ADAM
DAS KOCHBUCH AUS SCHWABEN

Walnut Wholemeal Bread

Le Pain de Noix

To make two 20 by 10 cm (8 by 4 inch) loaves

375 g	strong plain flour	13 oz
375 g	wholemeal flour	13 oz
30 g	fresh yeast or 1 tbsp dried yeast	1 oz
400 g	walnuts, 175 g (6 oz) grated or coarsely ground	14 oz
4 tbsp	tepid water	4 tbsp
About 40 cl	milk	About 14 fl oz
4 tbsp	liquid honey	4 tbsp
40 g	butter	1½ oz
2 tsp	salt	2 tsp
¼ tsp	ground ginger	¼ tsp
30 g	wheat germ	1 oz
1	egg yolk, beaten with 1 tsp milk	1

Combine the yeast with the tepid water and set aside. Bring the milk almost to boiling, then remove it from the heat, stir in the honey, 30 g (1 oz) of the butter, the salt and ginger, and leave to cool. Then, in a large mixing bowl, combine the now bubbly liquid yeast with the milk and honey mixture. Add one-third of the strong plain flour, the wholemeal flour, the wheat germ and the grated or ground walnuts. Stir thoroughly before adding another third of the strong plain flour. The dough at this point should be somewhat sticky and too stiff to stir easily. Add more flour if necessary.

Spread the rest of the strong plain flour on a flat surface and turn the dough out on to it. Knead it vigorously until the dough is elastic and no longer sticky, usually in 10 to 15 minutes. Clean and lightly butter the bowl and return the dough to it. Set it aside, covered, in a warm place until doubled in bulk, in 1½ to 2 hours.

Then punch the dough down and divide it in half. Roll each half into a ball, cover the balls and let them rest on the lightly

floured work surface for about 20 minutes, before flattening each ball to a large pancake. Scatter the rest of the walnuts over the rounds of dough, pressing the nuts in slightly, then roll each pancake into a loaf shape by rolling it up like a Swiss roll and tucking in the ends. Pinch at the seam to seal and place the loaves in two 1 litre (2 lb) loaf tins with the seam underneath. Leave them to rise in a warm place until again nearly doubled in bulk, usually in about 1 hour.

Bake the loaves in an oven preheated to 190°C (375°F or Mark 5). After 35 minutes, brush the tops with the egg yolk and milk glaze, then continue baking until browned and a knife inserted in the centre of the loaves comes out clean, usually in about 10 minutes more.

ROY ANDRIES DE GROOT
THE AUBERGE OF THE FLOWERING HEARTH

Raisin Nut Bread

This recipe was written by Anne Glass, the compiler of the first edition of An American Cook in Turkey.

To make one 17 by 9 cm (7 by 3½ inch) loaf

250 g	strong plain flour, sifted	8 oz
30 g	fresh yeast or 1 tbsp dried yeast	1 oz
175 g	raisins, chopped or minced	6 oz
60 g	walnuts, chopped	2 oz
35 cl	tepid water	12 fl oz
90 g	sugar	3 oz
90 g	butter or lard, cut into pieces	3 oz
2 tsp	salt	2 tsp

Dissolve the yeast in the water with 1 teaspoon of the sugar. Cover and let the mixture stand in a warm place until foaming. In a large bowl, combine 200 g (7 oz) of the flour with the yeast mixture and mix well. Cover the dough with a cloth and leave it in a warm place until the mixture is spongy. Then work in the butter or lard, the salt, the rest of the sugar, the raisins and the walnuts. Add the rest of the flour and knead well to make a stiff, smooth dough. Leave the dough to rise in a warm place until doubled in bulk. Punch it down then leave it to rise again until doubled in bulk.

Put the dough into a ½ litre (1 lb) buttered loaf tin. Leave it for about an hour to prove. Bake the loaf in an oven preheated to 200°C (400°F or Mark 6) for about 15 minutes. Then reduce the heat to 190°C (375°F or Mark 5). The original recipe said to bake the bread for 50 minutes to 1 hour in all, but it often takes only 30 minutes, so be careful. The loaf is ready when it is golden-brown and sounds hollow when rapped.

ANNA G. EDMONDS (EDITOR)
AN AMERICAN COOK IN TURKEY

Walnut and Onion Bread

Le Salé du Bugey

To make one 25 cm (10 inch) bread

500 g	basic bread dough (*page 171*)	1 lb
2 to 3 tbsp	finely chopped walnuts	2 to 3 tbsp
2	onions, sliced into thick rounds	2
	salt and pepper	
	walnut oil	

Make the bread dough in the usual way, and leave it to rise until doubled in bulk. Punch it down and divide it into two pieces, one twice as big as the other. Roll out the larger piece in a circle about 1 cm (½ inch) thick to fit a round or square baking sheet. Butter the sheet and lay the dough on it.

Divide the remaining dough into five or six pieces and roll them into sausage shapes about the thickness of a finger. Bend these pieces of dough into 5 cm (2 inch) rings, pinching the ends firmly together. Arrange the rings on top of the dough on the baking sheet. Lay an onion round in the centre of each dough ring, then cover the bread and leave it to prove for about 1 hour. Season the bread with salt and pepper, sprinkle it with the oil and scatter the walnuts over the surface. Bake in an oven preheated to 180°C (350°F or Mark 4) for about 40 minutes, or until the bread sounds slightly hollow when tapped on the bottom. Allow to cool before serving.

LUCIEN TENDRET
LA TABLE AU PAYS DE BRILLAT-SAVARIN

Portuguese Crackling Loaf

Broas de Torresmos de Souzel

The cracklings can be made by rendering pork rinds with fat attached, or frying fat pork belly.

To make one 20 by 10 cm (8 by 4 inch) loaf

250 g	basic bread dough (*page 171*)	8 oz
250 g	strong plain flour	8 oz
250 g	pork cracklings, finely chopped	8 oz
250 g	sugar	8 oz
2	eggs, beaten	2
1 tsp	ground cinnamon	1 tsp
2 tsp	ground aniseeds	2 tsp
15 cl	brandy	¼ pint
1	egg yolk, lightly beaten	1

Leave the bread dough to rise until doubled in bulk, about 1½ hours. Fry the cracklings lightly. Pour the flour over them and brown, stirring with a wooden spoon. Remove from the heat and add all the remaining ingredients except the egg yolk. Mix them together, then work them into the bread dough. Sprinkle a 1 litre (2 lb) loaf tin with extra flour and spoon in the mixture. Leave it in a warm place to prove for 30 minutes, or until the dough rises to just above the rim of the tin. Glaze the loaf with the beaten egg yolk and sprinkle it with extra sugar. Bake it in an oven preheated to 200°C (400°F or Mark 6) for about 50 minutes or until the loaf sounds slightly hollow when rapped.

MARIA ODETTE CORTES VALENTE
COZINHA REGIONAL PORTUGUESA

Crustless Caraway Bread

Kümmelbrot (Ohne Rinde)

This bread is cooked by steaming instead of baking in the oven. A pain de mie tin is a loaf tin with a tight-fitting lid; it produces a crustless sandwich loaf suitable for sandwiches or canapés.

To make one 25 by 10 cm (10 by 4 inch) loaf

375 g	strong plain flour	13 oz
15 g	fresh yeast or 2 tsp dried yeast	½ oz
1 tbsp	caraway seeds	1 tbsp
12.5 cl	tepid milk	4 fl oz
½ tsp	salt	½ tsp
30 g	butter or lard	1 oz

Dissolve the yeast in the milk and leave until foaming, about 20 minutes. Sieve the flour into a bowl, make a well in the middle and pour in the yeast mixture. Mix together to make a dough and leave for 30 minutes to rise about half as much again. Then mix in the remaining ingredients and knead well into a soft dough—about 10 minutes. Leave the dough in a warm place until it has doubled in bulk—1½ to 2 hours.

Butter a *pain de mie* loaf tin or other baking dish with a tight-fitting lid. If neither is available, a deep pudding basin can be used, tightly covered with foil. Knead the dough well and place it in the tin; it should only half fill the container, so that it has room to rise and does not spill over. Cover the container tightly and cook the loaf on a trivet in a gently simmering bain-marie for about 1½ hours or until the loaf is firm to the touch and sounds hollow when tapped. Turn the bread out of the tin, leave it to cool and store it in a dry place until you are ready to use it.

HERMINE KIEHNLE AND MARIA HÄDECKE
DAS NEUE KIEHNLE-KOCHBUCH

Swedish Limpé

Limpé or limpa is a rye bread flavoured with caraway and fennel seeds that is eaten throughout Scandinavia.

To make two 20 by 10 cm (8 by 4 inch) loaves

700 g	strong plain flour, sifted	1½ lb
200 g	rye flour	7 oz
20 g	fresh yeast or 2 tsp dried yeast	¾ oz
90 cl	water	1½ pints
150 g	soft brown sugar	5 oz
1½ tsp	caraway seeds	1½ tsp
2 tbsp	fennel seeds	2 tbsp
20 g	butter	¾ oz
2 tsp	grated orange rind	2 tsp
2 tsp	salt	2 tsp

Boil the water, sugar, caraway seeds, fennel seeds, butter and orange rind for 3 minutes. Cool the mixture to tepid and add the yeast to it. Stir the mixture thoroughly. Add the plain flour, mix and knead for 10 minutes to make a soft dough. Place the dough in a buttered bowl, cover the bowl with a cloth and leave the dough to rise in a warm place until doubled in bulk, about 1½ hours. Then punch the dough down and work in the rye flour and salt, kneading for 5 minutes to make a stiff dough. Let the dough rise again until doubled, about 2 hours.

Knead it down and shape the dough into two large loaves. Place the loaves in two buttered 1 litre (2 lb) loaf tins and prove them in a warm place for about 45 minutes, or until the dough has risen to just above the rims of the tins. Bake the bread in an oven preheated to 180°C (350°F or Mark 4) for 1 hour or until the loaves sound hollow when rapped.

DOLORES CASELLA
A WORLD OF BREADS

Fennel Rings

Taralli con i Finocchietti

To make 24 rings

400 g	strong plain flour	14 oz
30 g	fresh yeast or 1 tbsp dried yeast	1 oz
2 tsp	fennel seeds	2 tsp
¼ litre	tepid water	8 fl oz
1 tsp	salt	1 tsp

Dissolve the yeast in the water. Sift the flour on to a working surface, make a well in the centre and add the yeast. Then add the salt and fennel seeds. Work them into the flour and knead the resulting dough for 10 minutes. Divide the dough into 24 pieces. Roll each piece into a sausage shape about the width of a finger and 10 cm (4 inches) long. Bring the two ends of each sausage shape together to make a ring and seal the join with a little water. Lay these rings on a cloth sprinkled with flour and leave them to rise, uncovered, in a warm place for about 1½ hours or until doubled in bulk.

In a large saucepan, bring some water to a rapid boil. Drop the well-risen rings into the water one by one. Turn them over with a slotted spoon as they rise to the surface and remove them from the water immediately. Drain the rings on a kitchen towel. Transfer the rings to buttered baking sheets. Do not preheat the oven, but set it to 190°C (375°F or Mark 5) and bake the rings for 45 minutes or until crisp and golden.

JEANNE CARÒLA FRANCESCONI
LA CUCINA NAPOLETANA

Miniature Cornmeal Loaves

Gialletti

To make 15 or 16 miniature loaves

100 g	cornmeal	3½ oz
100 g	strong plain flour	3½ oz
20 g	fresh yeast or 2 tsp dried yeast	¾ oz
About 20 cl	tepid water	About 7 fl oz
60 g	sugar	2 oz
30 g	butter	1 oz
30 g	lard	1 oz
	salt	
100 g	raisins	3½ oz

Mix the yeast, half of the flour and enough of the tepid water to make a loose sponge; leave it to rise in a warm place for 1 hour or until foaming. Meanwhile, make a dough from the cornmeal, the rest of the flour, the sugar, butter, lard, a pinch of salt and the rest of the water.

When the yeast sponge is ready, mix it with the cornmeal dough and knead thoroughly. Then work in the raisins.

Divide the dough into 15 or 16 tiny, torpedo-shaped loaves, and use the point of a sharp knife to incise a diamond-patterned grid on the top surface of each one. Leave the loaves to rise on a buttered baking sheet in a warm place for about 1½ hours, or until slightly risen.

Bake the tiny loaves in an oven preheated to 220°C (425°F or Mark 7) for about 20 minutes only. They must remain soft and should be lightly browned.

PELLEGRINO ARTUSI
LA SCIENZA IN CUCINA E L'ARTE DI MANGIAR BENE

Sheep's Cheese Bread

Schafskäsebrot

To make one 30 cm (12 inch) cylindrical loaf

1 kg	strong plain flour	2 lb
30 g	fresh yeast or 1 tbsp dried yeast	1 oz
250 g	*feta* or other sheep's cheese	8 oz
1 tsp	sugar	1 tsp
½ litre	tepid water	16 fl oz
1 tsp	salt	1 tsp
3	large onions, chopped	3
1 tbsp	oil	1 tbsp

Cream the yeast with the sugar and all but 3 tablespoons of the tepid water. Leave the mixture in a warm place until it is foaming, about 15 minutes. Sift the flour and salt into a warmed mixing bowl and add the onions. Stir in the cheese and the yeast mixture and knead the dough thoroughly for about 10 minutes. Cover the bowl and leave the dough to rise in a warm place for about 1½ hours or until doubled in bulk.

Knock back the dough and knead it again for about 5 minutes, dusting it with flour if it sticks to your fingers. Shape the dough into an oval 30 cm (12 inches) long and leave it to prove on a buttered baking sheet for about 30 minutes, or until it has doubled in bulk again. With a very sharp knife, make three shallow diagonal slashes in the top of the loaf. Brush the loaf with the oil, but do not brush the oil into the gashes. Bake the loaf in a preheated 200°C (400°F or Mark 6) oven for 50 minutes to 1 hour or until golden-brown.

JUTTA KÜRTZ
DAS BROT BACKBUCH

Cheese Bread

To make two 17 by 9 cm (7 by 3½ inch) loaves

600 g	strong plain flour	1¼ lb
30 g	fresh yeast or 1 tbsp dried yeast	1 oz
125 g	Cheddar cheese, grated	4 oz
¼ litre	milk, scalded	8 fl oz
3 tbsp	sugar	3 tbsp
1 tbsp	salt	1 tbsp
40 g	butter, melted	1½ oz
¼ tsp	ground ginger (optional)	¼ tsp
¼ litre	tepid water	8 fl oz

To the scalded milk, add the sugar, salt, 30 g (1 oz) of the butter and, if you wish, the ground ginger. Cool to lukewarm. Meanwhile, put the water into a large mixing bowl, add the

yeast and let it stand for at least 5 minutes. Add the milk mixture, the cheese and the flour, then beat with an electric mixer for about 2 minutes or with a large wooden spoon for about 300 strokes. This is too soft a dough to be kneaded.

Let the dough rise, covered, until more than doubled in bulk—45 to 60 minutes. There is a large proportion of yeast to flour, so the dough will rise faster than bread ordinarily does. Stir it down, then beat it for about half a minute.

Place the dough in two buttered ½ litre (1 lb) loaf tins. Let the bread rise until it comes almost to the top of the tins, about 30 minutes. Bake in an oven preheated to 180°C (350°F or Mark 4) for about 30 to 35 minutes, until golden-brown. If the tops brown too quickly, cover them with foil. Remove the loaves from the oven. Use the remaining melted butter to brush the tops of the loaves. Turn them out of the tins immediately. Let them cool on a wire rack before cutting.

ANN ROE ROBBINS
THE SEVEN-INGREDIENTS COOKBOOK

Anchovy and Tomato Flan

Sardenaira

To make one 30 cm (12 inch) flan

500 g	strong plain flour	1 lb
40 g	fresh yeast or 1½ tbsp dried yeast	1½ oz
15 cl	tepid water	¼ pint
15 cl	milk	¼ pint
3 tbsp	olive oil	3 tbsp
	Anchovy and tomato filling	
500 g	salt anchovies, filleted, soaked, drained and chopped	1 lb
1 kg	fresh tomatoes, skinned, seeded and sieved or 800 g (1 lb 10 oz) tomato sauce	2 lb
1 tbsp	capers	1 tbsp
3 tbsp	olive oil	3 tbsp
12	black olives, stoned and halved	12
3	garlic cloves, unpeeled	3
1 tbsp	crumbled, dried oregano	1 tbsp

Dissolve yeast in 2 tablespoons of the water. Put the flour on a board, make a well in the centre, add the yeast and mix to make a dough, gradually adding the remaining water, the milk and the olive oil. Knead the dough and leave it to rise, covered, for 1 hour, or until it has doubled in bulk.

Meanwhile, prepare the filling. In a large bowl, mix the chopped anchovies, tomatoes, capers and olive oil. When the dough has risen well, take a heavy, shallow pie tin or pizza plate, or best of all, the Italian copper pan known as a *testo*, and oil it thoroughly. Spread the dough out in the dish with your hands, pressing it down with your fingers in a layer no more than 1 cm (½ inch) thick. Spread a generous layer of filling over the dough. Dot it haphazardly with the olive halves, pressing them down lightly. Finally, stick in the garlic cloves here and there and finish with a light sprinkling of oregano. Bake in an oven preheated to 230°C (450°F or Mark 8) for 45 minutes to 1 hour.

LUIGI VOLPICELLI AND SECONDINO FREDA (EDITORS)
L'ANTIARTUSI: 1000 RICETTE

Mallorcan Onion and Tomato Flan

Coca de Trampó Mallorquina

Trampó is a Mallorcan word for a mixture of aromatic vegetables such as onions, tomatoes, peppers and garlic. The coca de trampó *is a pizza-like flan, as popular in the Balearics as pizzas are in Italy.*

To make two 30 cm (12 inch) or eight 10 cm (4 inch) flans		
1 kg	basic bread dough (*page 171*)	2½ lb
60 cl	olive oil	1 pint
500 g	tomatoes, skinned, seeded and chopped and cooked to a purée	1 lb
4	onions, thinly sliced	4
6	sweet red or green peppers, seeded and cut into strips	6
2	garlic cloves, chopped	2
6 tbsp	chopped parsley	6 tbsp
	salt and pepper	

Make the bread dough and leave it to rise in a warm place for 1 to 2 hours. The dough will be ready when small cracks appear on the surface. Gradually add ½ litre (16 fl oz) of the olive oil to the dough, kneading continually so that the oil is completely absorbed. Once the dough is smooth and elastic, it may either be divided into eight flans or used to make two large ones.

Roll out the dough into two 30 cm (12 inch) circles or eight 10 cm (4 inch) circles 1 cm (½ inch) thick. Place the circles on lightly oiled baking sheets, pinching the edges of the dough to make a decorative border. Cover the flans with a layer of tomato purée, and then arrange the onions and peppers on top. Scatter the garlic and parsley over these and season to taste. Pour on the remaining 12.5 cl (4 fl oz) of oil and bake the flans in an oven preheated to 180°C (350°F or Mark 4) until the dough is lightly browned and the vegetables are cooked—approximately 45 minutes for the large flans, 30 minutes for the small ones. Serve hot.

GLORIA ROSSI CALLIZO
LAS MEJORES TAPAS, CENAS FRÍAS Y PLATOS COMBINADOS

Buckwheat Flatbread

Tattarleipä

This traditional recipe from the province of Karelia, now partly in Finland and partly in the USSR, was often baked for special occasions in private homes by professional bakers.

To make one 20 cm (8 inch) flatbread		
250 g	buckwheat flour	8 oz
125 g	strong plain flour	4 oz
15 g	fresh yeast or 2 tsp dried yeast	½ oz
250 g	floury potatoes, scrubbed	8 oz
¾ litre	water	1¼ pints
2 tsp	sea salt	2 tsp
10 cl	buttermilk	3½ fl oz
1	egg, beaten, or 1 tbsp melted butter (optional)	1

To make the starter, boil the potatoes in their skins in the water with half a teaspoon of the salt, until they are soft. Drain them and reserve the cooking liquid. Peel and mash the potatoes thoroughly while still warm, and stir in ½ litre (16 fl oz) of the cooking liquid. Leave the mixture to cool.

Mix the yeast with 3 tablespoons of the potato cooking liquid cooled to tepid. Leave it for 5 minutes, until the mixture begins to foam. Then stir the yeast into the potato mixture. Add 125 g (4 oz) of the buckwheat flour. Cover and leave in a warm place for 6 to 7 hours or overnight, to allow the dough to ferment. It should become bubbly.

The next day, add the buttermilk and the rest of the buckwheat flour to the potato and buckwheat starter. Stir in the strong plain flour and the rest of the salt. Mix well until the dough has the consistency of thick porridge.

Butter a deep, circular baking dish, and pour in the dough, spreading it evenly to a depth of about 2.5 cm (1 inch). Bake the flatbread in a preheated 230°C (450°F or Mark 8) oven for 20 to 30 minutes. After it has been cooking for 10 to 15 minutes, the bread may be brushed with beaten egg or melted butter. When baked, cut it into squares and serve it warm.

ULLA KÄKÖNEN
NATURAL COOKING THE FINNISH WAY

Courgette Bread

The technique of making this bread is shown on page 50.

To make one 25 cm (10 inch) cylindrical loaf

600 g	strong plain flour	1¼ lb
20 g	fresh yeast or 2 tsp dried yeast	¾ oz
500 g	courgettes, washed and stalks trimmed off	1 lb
2 tbsp	salt	2 tbsp
30 cl	tepid water	½ pint
	olive oil or 1 egg yolk, beaten	

Coarsely grate the courgettes into a deep, wide bowl. When the courgettes cover the bottom of the bowl, sprinkle them with salt. Grate in another layer of courgettes and sprinkle again with salt. Repeat alternate layers of grated courgettes and salt until the courgettes are used up. Leave the courgettes for about 30 minutes so that the salt will draw out their excess moisture. Then squeeze out the moisture with your hands.

Dissolve the yeast in 8 tablespoons of the water. In another bowl, thoroughly mix the courgettes, the yeast and the flour; gradually add enough water to make a smooth but fairly firm dough. Knead the dough well for about 10 minutes. Return it to the bowl, cover it with plastic film and leave the dough to rise for about 1½ hours, until doubled in bulk. Knead the dough into a loose round, then shape it into a tapered cylinder. Lay it on a buttered baking sheet, cover it with a towel and leave it to prove in a warm place for about 45 minutes, until doubled in bulk again. Just before baking, brush the loaf with olive oil or egg yolk to prevent the pieces of courgettes on the surface from burning.

Bake the courgette bread in an oven preheated to 220°C (425°F or Mark 7) for about 45 minutes, until golden-brown. Cool the loaf on a wire rack.

PETITS PROPOS CULINAIRES IV

Pumpkin Bread

Pain de Citrouille

This recipe was first printed in France in 1654. The author was King Louis XIV's valet.

To make one 25 cm (10 inch) loaf

1 kg	strong plain flour	2½ lb
30 g	fresh yeast or 1 tbsp dried yeast	1 oz
850 g	pumpkin, peeled, seeded, scraped and cut into chunks	1¾ lb
3 tsp	salt	3 tsp

Bring a large pot of salted water to the boil; add the pumpkin, cover the pot and simmer gently for about 25 minutes or until the pumpkin is soft. Drain the pumpkin thoroughly, reserv-

ing the cooking liquid. Push the pumpkin through a close-meshed sieve to purée it and remove any remaining fibres. Cool the purée to tepid before mixing with the flour and salt.

Dissolve the yeast in about 6 tablespoons of the pumpkin cooking liquid, and leave it in a warm place until it foams—about 10 minutes. Then add the yeast to the pumpkin and flour mixture, and mix thoroughly to make a fairly firm dough. If the dough is too dry, add a few tablespoonfuls of pumpkin cooking liquid; generally, the pumpkin purée will contain enough liquid for the dough.

Knead the dough for 15 minutes and leave to rise until doubled in bulk—about 2 hours.

Knock back the dough, knead it lightly, and shape it into a slightly flattened ball. Leave it to rest for about 50 minutes or until well risen again.

With a razor blade or sharp knife, make a circular incision around the top of the ball about 10 cm (2 inches) from the curve at the edge. Bake in an oven preheated to 220°C (425°F or Mark 7) for about 50 minutes. You will obtain a very good bread which bakes to a rich golden colour and is very light to the stomach.

NICOLAS DE BONNEFONS
LES DELICES DE LA CAMPAGNE

Fruit Bread

Birewecke

The recipe given below comes from the Sitter patisserie in Colmar, Alsace. Fruit bread is traditionally eaten at Christmas, and is best made a week in advance. Serve in thin slices.

To make 3 small cylindrical loaves

175 g	strong plain flour	6 oz
175 g	basic bread dough (*page 171*)	6 oz
250 g	dried pears	8 oz
90 g	dried apples	3 oz
125 g	prunes	4 oz
125 g	dried figs, chopped	4 oz
250 g	orange and lemon peel, chopped	8 oz
100 g	raisins	3½ oz
10 cl	kirsch	3½ fl oz
175 g	walnuts	6 oz
125 g	almonds, blanched and split	4 oz
20 g	ground cinnamon	¾ oz
250 g	sugar	8 oz

Boil the dried pears, apples and prunes for about 20 minutes to soften them; drain and cut them into large pieces. Mix them with the figs and orange and lemon peel, add the raisins and leave to steep overnight in the kirsch.

The next day, add most of the walnuts and almonds, reserving a few for decorating the loaves, and mix in the cinnamon. Then stir in the sugar. Add this mixture to the bread dough, then add the flour. Shape into three cylindrical loaves, place them on buttered baking sheets and decorate with the reserved nuts. Bake in an oven preheated to 190°C (375°F or Mark 5) for 30 to 40 minutes, or until each loaf is golden-brown and sounds hollow when rapped.

CENTRE D'INFORMATION DU VIN D'ALSACE
FOOD AND WINES FROM ALSACE, FRANCE

Bremen Christmas Bread

Bremer Klaben

This bread is a variety of the sweet loaf called a stollen, *popular throughout the German-speaking world from Alsace to Czechoslovakia, but usually associated with Dresden.*

To make one 35 cm (14 inch) loaf

1 kg	strong plain flour	2½ lb
60 g	fresh yeast or 2 tbsp dried yeast	2 oz
½ litre	tepid milk	16 fl oz
½ tsp	salt	½ tsp
300 g	butter, melted and cooled to tepid	10 oz
350 g	raisins	12 oz
350 g	currants	12 oz
125 g	mixed candied peel, chopped	4 oz
1	lemon, rind grated	1
½ tsp	ground cinnamon	½ tsp
½ tsp	ground cloves	½ tsp
½ tsp	ground cardamom seeds	½ tsp
½ tsp	powdered mace	½ tsp
	semolina	

Dissolve the yeast in 15 cl (¼ pint) of the milk. Put the flour and salt in a large mixing bowl. Make a well in the centre, pour in the yeast mixture and the remaining milk and mix to make a dough. Knead the dough for 10 minutes, then leave it in a warm place to rise until it has doubled in bulk, about 1½ hours. Add the remaining ingredients to the risen dough and knead them in for about 5 minutes. Leave the dough to rise again for 2 to 3 hours until doubled in bulk.

Flatten the risen dough with your hands to make a thick rectangle about 35 by 30 cm (15 by 12 inches). Fold the rectangle in three lengthwise by flattening the half furthest from you with a rolling pin, then folding it towards the centre. Then fold these two thicknesses of dough over the third un-flattened portion so that the lowest edge protrudes slightly.

Seal the ends firmly, press the loaf lightly with a rolling pin and taper the ends to make the traditional *stollen* shape.

Dust a baking sheet with semolina, place the loaf on it and leave it to prove in a warm place for about 30 minutes, until doubled in bulk. Bake in an oven preheated to 180°C (350°F or Mark 4) for 1 hour or until the loaf is golden-brown.

MARIA ELISABETH STRAUB
GRÖNEN AAL UND RODE GRÜTT

Christmas Pear Bread

Birewecke

To make one 25 cm (10 inch) or two 20 cm (8 inch) cylindrical loaves

250 g	basic bread dough (page 171)	8 oz
200 g	dried pears, stalks and cores removed, coarsely chopped	7 oz
125 g	dried prunes, stoned and coarsely chopped	4 oz
50 g	raisins	2 oz
125 g	dried figs, coarsely chopped	4 oz
50 g	walnuts, chopped	2 oz
50 g	hazelnuts, chopped	2 oz
50 g	almonds, blanched and chopped	2 oz
4 tbsp	kirsch	4 tbsp
2	cloves, ground in a mortar, or a pinch of ground cloves	2
1	lemon, rind grated	1
1 tsp	ground cinnamon	1 tsp
30 g	candied citron peel, finely chopped	1 oz
1	egg yolk, beaten	1

Soak the pears and prunes in 30 cl (½ pint) of water overnight. The next day, cook them in the soaking liquid for 3 minutes and drain them. Soak the raisins for 10 minutes, then drain them. Mix all the dried fruits and the nuts together, and sprinkle them with the kirsch. Gradually incorporate this mixture into the bread dough, and add the cloves, grated lemon rind, cinnamon and candied peel. Prepare the bread dough in the usual way. Leave it to rise until doubled in bulk, then knock it back and knead thoroughly for about 10 minutes. Then shape it into one or two cylindrical loaves. Place the loaf or loaves on a buttered and floured baking sheet. Leave the dough to prove for about 30 minutes in a warm place, then glaze it with the beaten egg yolk.

Bake the dough in an oven preheated to 220°C (425°F or Mark 7) for about 30 minutes, or until it is brown and sounds hollow when rapped on the bottom.

NICOLE VIELFAURE AND A. CHRISTINE BEAUVIALA
FÊTES, COUTUMES ET GÂTEAUX

Christmas Bread

Vörtlimpor

To make three 25 cm (10 inch) loaves

700 g	rye flour	1½ lb
350 g	strong plain flour	12 oz
45 g	fresh yeast or 6 tsp dried yeast	1½ oz
8 tbsp	water	8 tbsp
60 g	lard or butter	2 oz
¾ litre	stout	1¼ pints
250 g	molasses	8 oz
1 tsp	salt	1 tsp
250 g	candied orange peel, chopped	8 oz
2 tbsp	ground aniseeds or fennel seeds	2 tbsp
2 tbsp	molasses, dissolved in 2 tbsp tepid water	2 tbsp

Dissolve the yeast in the water. Melt the fat, add the stout and heat them to lukewarm. Pour the fat and stout into a large bowl, add the molasses and half the rye and strong plain flours. Mix well. Then add the dissolved yeast, the salt, candied peel, seeds, the rest of the rye flour and all but 125 g (4 oz) of the strong plain flour. Beat well until the dough is smooth and firm. Cover it with a towel and allow it to rise in a warm place until almost doubled in bulk. Turn it on to a floured baking board and knead with the remaining flour until firm and glossy. Divide the dough into three parts and shape them into long loaves. Place the loaves on buttered baking sheets and cover them with a cloth. Leave them to rise for about 30 minutes. Prick the surfaces with a toothpick, and bake the loaves at 180°C (350°F or Mark 4) for 30 to 40 minutes or until golden-brown. When half done, brush them with the molasses and water glaze. Brush the loaves again with the glaze when they are done. Place the loaves between cloths while cooling to keep the crust soft.

SAM WIDENFELT (EDITOR)
FAVORITE SWEDISH RECIPES

Pear Bread

Birnbrot

This is a bread from the Glarus district of Switzerland.

If fresh pears are used instead of dried ones, they should be peeled, cored and sliced, and cooked in a scant 15 cl (¼ pint) of water with 60 g (2 oz) of sugar—with wine and butter if desired. Instead of the pastry, 850 g (1¾ lb) of basic bread dough (*page 171*) well mixed with 275 g (9 oz) of butter may be used. The loaves keep for a long time.

To make twelve 20 cm (8 inch) loaves

2.5 kg	basic bread dough (*page 171*)	5 lb
2.5 kg	dried pears	5 lb
15 cl	red wine (optional)	¼ pint
30 g	butter (optional)	1 oz
750 g	raisins, finely chopped	1½ lb
125 g	candied lemon peel, finely chopped	4 oz
350 g	walnuts, finely chopped	12 oz
70 g	ground cinnamon	2½ oz
15 g	ground cloves	½ oz
¼ litre	rose-water	8 fl oz
10 cl	kirsch	3½ fl oz

Rich pastry dough

1.5 kg	plain flour	3 lb
800 g	lard or butter	1 lb 10 oz
6	egg yolks	6
	salt	
	milk or water	
1	egg, beaten	1

Stalk and core the dried pears and soak them overnight. Cook them in about 30 cl (½ pint) of the soaking water and, if desired, the red wine and a knob of butter, for 20 minutes or until they are soft. When the pears are tender, pour off the remaining liquid. Pound or mash the pears and drain thoroughly. Add the raisins, candied lemon peel, walnuts, cinnamon, cloves, rose-water and kirsch. Leave overnight in a warm place.

Knead together the pear mixture and the bread dough and form 12 small oval loaves about 15 cm (6 inches) across. Mix the pastry dough and roll it out not too thinly—about half the thickness of a little finger. Divide it into 12 parts. Loosely wrap each small loaf in a piece of dough in such a way that the smooth surface is on top and the overlapping edges at the bottom. Prick the dough with a fork. Place the loaves on buttered, floured baking sheets, spacing them out well, and leave them to rise for 30 minutes. Brush them with beaten egg and bake in an oven preheated to 200°C (400°F or Mark 6) for 1 hour or until they are well browned and sound hollow when lightly rapped on the base.

EVA MARIA BORER
TANTE HEIDI'S SWISS KITCHEN

A Rich Scotch Bun

Scotch Bun, also called Black Bun, is said to have reached Scotland in the 16th century from Renaissance Italy. Once traditionally served on Twelfth Night, the bun is now baked for Hogmanay (New Year's Eve). This version is adapted from the 1841 edition of Mrs. Rundell's book, first published in 1806. The technique of making the bun is shown on page 54.

To make one 30 cm (12 inch) bun

1 kg	strong plain flour	2 lb
30 g	fresh yeast or 1 tbsp dried yeast	1 oz
45 cl	tepid water	$\frac{3}{4}$ pint
2 tsp	salt	2 tsp
350 g	butter, cut into 30 g (1 oz) pieces	12 oz
90 g	candied orange peel	3 oz
90 g	candied lemon peel	3 oz
1 tsp	whole allspice	1 tsp
1 tsp	peeled and chopped ginger root	1 tsp
3 or 4	cloves	3 or 4
90 g	almonds, blanched and chopped	3 oz
500 g	raisins	1 lb
500 g	currants	1 lb
$\frac{1}{2}$ tsp	grated nutmeg	$\frac{1}{2}$ tsp

To make the dough, dissolve the yeast in the water. Mix it with the flour and salt, using your hands to work it in, until all the ingredients are wetted. Turn the dough out on to a floured board, mix in the butter and knead for about 15 minutes until the dough is smooth and elastic. Put it into a warmed bowl, cover it with a tea towel and leave it in a warm place until it has doubled in bulk—about 2 hours.

To make the flavouring, soak the candied peels in very hot water for 1 minute to soften them and melt any excess sugar. Drain the peels and chop them finely. In a mortar, pound the allspice, ginger and cloves; mix the spices with the chopped peels and add the almonds, raisins, currants and nutmeg.

Punch down the dough and knead it briefly until the air has been expelled. Slice off one-third of the dough and reserve it. Flatten the larger piece of dough into a round about 3 cm (1 inch) thick. Sprinkle the flavouring mixture on to the dough. Then fold the dough over the flavouring, and knead well until the flavouring is evenly distributed. Lightly flour a working surface and roll out the remaining piece of dough into a 1 cm ($\frac{1}{2}$ inch) thick circle large enough to encase the fruit dough. Turn the circle of dough over and place the fruit dough in the centre. Pull the circle of plain dough round the fruit dough, folding any excess plain dough into pleats on top of the bun. Press the pleats together firmly, and turn the bun over. Gently flatten the bun until it is about 7 cm (3 inches) thick. Prick the bun all over right through to the bottom, to allow steam to escape during cooking.

Lay the bun on a buttered and floured baking sheet. Encircle the bun with a spring-form cake tin hoop or a ring of stiff cardboard, to ensure that the bun keeps its shape during cooking. The hoop or ring should be slightly larger than the bun to allow for expansion during cooking.

Bake the bun in an oven preheated to 190°C (375°F or Mark 5) for 1½ hours, removing the hoop or ring after 1 hour to let the sides of the bun brown.

MRS. MARIA ELIZA RUNDELL
A NEW SYSTEM OF DOMESTIC COOKERY

Walnut Bun

Tourte aux Noix

To make one 30 cm (12 inch) bun

400 g	strong plain flour	14 oz
10 g	fresh yeast or 1 tsp dried yeast	$\frac{1}{3}$ oz
200 g	walnuts, ground	7 oz
100 g	sugar	3½ oz
	salt	
80 g	butter, softened, or 3 tbsp oil	2½ oz
¼ litre	tepid water	8 fl oz
100 g	prunes, soaked in tea until plumped, then drained, stoned and cut into small pieces	3½ oz

Soften the yeast in half the water. Make a dough with the flour, sugar, salt, butter or oil and the yeast, adding just enough extra water to achieve the consistency of a bread dough. Knead the dough thoroughly—about 10 minutes—then incorporate the ground walnuts and chopped prunes. Shape the dough into a flat round, place on a buttered baking sheet and leave to rise in a warm place for about 1 hour or until it has doubled in bulk. Bake the bun in an oven preheated to 180°C (350°F or Mark 4) for about 45 minutes or until it is golden-brown.

ZETTE GUINAUDEAU-FRANC
LES SECRETS DES FERMES EN PÉRIGORD NOIR

Egg Breads

Swiss Plait

Schweizer Züpfe

A similar technique for plaiting three strands of dough is demonstrated on page 26.

To make one 25 cm (10 inch) plait

500 g	strong plain flour	1 lb
30 g	fresh yeast or 1 tbsp dried yeast	1 oz
30 cl	tepid milk	½ pint
1 tsp	sugar	1 tsp
75 g	butter, softened	2½ oz
2	eggs, each beaten in a separate bowl	2
2 tbsp	kirsch	2 tbsp
1 tsp	salt	1 tsp

Put the flour into a mixing bowl. Dissolve the yeast in half of the milk and leave it in a warm place until it is foaming, about 15 minutes. Make a well in the flour and pour in the yeast mixture and the sugar. Stir about 6 tablespoons of flour from the edges of the well into the yeast mixture, to make a yeast sponge. Cover the bowl with a cloth and leave the yeast sponge for 30 minutes, or until the sponge is foaming. Work in the rest of the flour, the butter, 1 egg, the remaining milk, the kirsch and salt, and knead the ingredients thoroughly until the dough is smooth and elastic.

Divide the dough into four pieces and, on a floured board, roll each piece into a strand as thick as your thumb. Place the strands parallel to each other, pinch them together at one end and braid the strands into a plait, pinching them together at the other end when finished. Place the four-strand plait on a buttered baking sheet and cover it with a tea towel. Fill a large saucepan or casserole three-quarters full of water and bring it to the boil. Lay the baking sheet on top of it and reduce the heat so that the water simmers.

Leave the loaf to rise there for 20 to 30 minutes, or until a dent remains in the dough when pressed. This procedure enables the loaf to prove quickly in a damp atmosphere.

Remove the baking sheet from the water, brush the top of the loaf with the remaining egg, and bake it in a preheated 220°C (425°F or Mark 7) oven for 30 to 40 minutes, or until the loaf sounds hollow when rapped on the base.

MARGRET UHLE AND ANNE BRAKEMEIER
EIGENBRÖTLERS BROTBACKBUCH

Blanche Frankehouser's Old-Fashioned Oatmeal Bread

To make two 20 by 10 cm (8 by 4 inch) loaves

700 g	strong plain flour	1½ lb
75 g	rolled oats	2½ oz
60 g	fresh yeast or 2 tbsp dried yeast	2 oz
½ litre	water	16 fl oz
75 g	butter	2½ oz
175 g	molasses	6 oz
4 tsp	salt	4 tsp
2	eggs, lightly beaten	2

Bring 35 cl (12 fl oz) of the water to the boil. Combine it with the oats, butter, molasses and salt. Cool the mixture to lukewarm. Heat the remaining water until it is tepid, then dissolve the yeast in it. Add the yeast to the oat mixture and mix well. Blend in the eggs and stir in the flour. The dough will be softer than a kneaded dough. Place the dough in a buttered bowl, cover it and store it in the refrigerator for at least 2 hours, or until needed.

Remove the chilled dough and knead it about 5 times (this helps to remove the air). Shape it into two loaves on a well-floured surface, place the loaves in two buttered 1 litre (2 lb) tins and cover them with a cloth. Let the loaves rise in a warm place until they double in bulk, about 2 hours.

Bake in an oven preheated to 190°C (375°F or Mark 5) for 1 hour, or until the loaves sound hollow when tapped.

BETTY GROFF AND JOSÉ WILSON
GOOD EARTH AND COUNTRY COOKING

Yeast Bread

Hefebrot

To make one 20 by 10 cm (8 by 4 inch) loaf

500 g	strong plain flour	1 lb
30 g	fresh yeast or 1 tbsp dried yeast	1 oz
¼ litre	tepid milk	8 fl oz
75 g	sugar	2½ oz
1	egg	1
125 g	butter, softened	4 oz
1	egg yolk, beaten	1

Dissolve the yeast in the milk with 1 teaspoon of the sugar and leave the mixture in a warm place for 10 minutes to froth. Sift about three-quarters of the flour into a bowl and add the yeast mixture, egg and softened butter. Blend them together, then knead them for about 10 minutes, until the dough forms a smooth ball that does not stick to the fingers. If the dough remains too sticky, sprinkle it with some of the remaining flour. Place the ball of dough in a bowl of tepid water and leave it until it floats on the surface, about 30 minutes. Remove the dough from the water and knead it again for about 10 minutes, incorporating the rest of the sugar and enough of the remaining flour to produce once more a smooth, elastic dough that does not stick to the fingers.

Butter and flour a baking sheet. Form the dough into a loaf shape about 20 by 10 cm (8 by 4 inches); brush the top with the beaten egg yolk. Bake the loaf in an oven preheated to 180°C (350°F or Mark 4) for about 45 minutes. The loaf will be done when a skewer stuck into it comes out clean.

DOROTHEE V. HELLERMANN
DAS KOCHBUCH AUS HAMBURG

Viennese Plait

Striezel

The technique of plaiting a loaf is demonstrated on page 26.

To make 1 plait

400 g	strong plain flour	14 oz
20 g	fresh yeast or 1 tbsp dried yeast	¾ oz
90 g	sugar	3 oz
20 cl	tepid milk	7 fl oz
¼ tsp	salt	¼ tsp
100 g	butter, softened	3½ oz
1	egg yolk	1
1	egg	1
1	lemon, rind grated	1
100 g	raisins	3½ oz
1	egg white, lightly beaten	1
	blanched, slivered almonds or coarse sugar (optional)	

Dissolve the yeast with the sugar in 4 tablespoons of the milk; leave it for about 10 minutes in a warm place until it foams. Warm the flour. To make the dough, combine the flour, yeast mixture, the remaining milk, salt, butter, egg yolk, egg and lemon rind. Knead well on a floured board for about 10 minutes to give a firm dough, then incorporate the raisins and knead for a further 5 minutes. Leave the dough in a warm place for about 1½ hours to rise until doubled in bulk.

Divide the dough into nine pieces and roll it out into sausage shapes of equal length, but in three different widths: three pieces the thickness of two fingers, three pieces the thickness of one finger and three pieces the thickness of half a finger. Plait each of the three sets of rolled dough. Brush the top of the medium-thick plait with egg white, and lay the

thinnest plait on top of it, making sure the two plaits are firmly stuck together. Then brush the top of the thickest plait with egg white and lay the assembled thin and medium plaits on top of the thick plait.

Place the resulting loaf on a buttered and floured baking sheet and leave it for a further 1½ hours in a warm place to rise until doubled in bulk. Glaze the whole loaf with egg white, and, if you like, sprinkle with slivered almonds or coarse sugar. Bake the plait in an oven preheated to 200°C (400°F or Mark 6) for 1 hour or until golden-brown.

OLGA HESS AND ADOLF FR. HESS
WIENER KÜCHE

Rusks

Zwieback

The author recommends omitting salt from the dough. Salt absorbs water from the atmosphere which makes the rusks soften more quickly. Rusks keep for months in an airtight tin.

To make about 72 rusks

1 kg	strong plain flour	2½ lb
60 g	fresh yeast or 2 tbsp dried yeast	2 oz
¾ litre	tepid milk	1¼ pints
120 g	sugar	4 oz
3	egg yolks	3
120 g	butter, melted and cooled	4 oz

Cream the yeast with 6 tablespoons of the milk and 1 teaspoon of sugar. Leave it in a warm place until foaming, about 15 minutes. Then add it to 250 g (8 oz) of the flour. Mix well, gradually adding up to 15 cl (¼ pint) of the remaining milk, to make a yeast sponge. Leave this sponge in a warm place to rise until doubled in bulk, about 1½ hours. Then stir in the egg yolks, sugar, butter and the rest of the flour and milk. Blend the mixture into a dough. Turn the dough out on to a floured surface and knead it thoroughly for about 15 minutes, or until it is smooth and elastic. Cover the dough with a damp cloth and leave it to prove for 30 minutes in a warm place.

Shape the dough into three 30 cm (12 inch) cylindrical loaves and sprinkle with a few drops of tepid water. Place the loaves on buttered baking sheets, allow them to prove for about 45 minutes, then bake in an oven preheated to 200°C (400°F or Mark 6) for 50 minutes or until light brown.

The next day, slice the loaves thinly with a very sharp knife. Place the slices on buttered baking sheets and bake them in an oven preheated to 170°C (325°F or Mark 3) for 30 minutes, until dry and evenly browned.

ELEK MAGYAR
KOCHBUCH FÜR FEINSCHMECKER

Egg Twist

To make three 37.5 cm (15 inch) loaves

550 g	strong plain flour	1 lb 2 oz
60 g	fresh yeast or 2 tbsp dried yeast	2 oz
¼ litre	water, half of it tepid	8 fl oz
4	eggs, beaten	4
60 g	sugar	2 oz
2 tsp	salt	2 tsp
4 tbsp	vegetable oil	4 tbsp
	Seed topping	
3 tbsp	poppy seeds or sesame seeds	3 tbsp
1	egg yolk, mixed with 2 tbsp water	1
	coarse salt	

Dissolve the yeast in the tepid water. When the yeast is soft, beat in the eggs, the rest of the water, the sugar, the salt and 250 g (8 oz) of the flour. Beat very well. Add the oil and another 250 g (8 oz) of the flour, and beat again. Sprinkle the rest of the flour on a board or working surface. Turn the dough on to the board or working surface and knead for a few minutes until smooth. Place the dough in a buttered bowl; cover it with a damp cloth and let it rise for 1 hour or until doubled in bulk. Punch the dough down, and divide it into nine pieces. Roll three of the pieces into lengths of at least 37.5 cm (15 inches).

Place three of the lengths on a buttered baking sheet or Swiss roll tin. Plait the dough as you would a pigtail. Brush the surface with one-third of the egg yolk and water mixture; sprinkle coarse salt and 1 tablespoon of the poppy or sesame seeds over the top. Repeat the process with another three lengths of dough, and then with the last three. Leave the loaves to rise for about 30 minutes. Bake them in an oven preheated to 180°C (350°F or Mark 4) for about 30 to 40 minutes, or until golden-brown. Remove the plaits from the tin and allow them to cool on a rack.

LIBBY HILLMAN
THE MENU-COOKBOOK FOR ENTERTAINING

Milk Rolls

Petits Pains au Lait

These little rolls are known as *fougasses* in the Paris region.

To make about 40 rolls

1 kg	strong plain flour	2½ lb
25 g	fresh yeast or 1 tbsp dried yeast	1 oz
½ litre	milk, 6 tbsp warmed to tepid	16 fl oz
2 tsp	salt	2 tsp
125 g	sugar	4 oz
2	eggs, lightly beaten	2
250 g	butter, softened	8 oz

Dissolve the yeast in the warmed milk. Leave it until it foams, about 10 minutes. Sift the flour and salt into a bowl. Make a well in the centre and pour in the yeast mixture, sugar, eggs and cold milk. Mix to a smooth dough, then lay it on a floured board and knead the dough until it is smooth and elastic, about 10 minutes. Incorporate the butter evenly, and return the dough to the bowl.

Cover the bowl, and leave the dough to rise until it has more than trebled in bulk—3 to 4 hours at room temperature, or overnight in the refrigerator.

Knock back the dough and leave it to rise again until it has doubled in bulk, about 1½ to 2 hours. Then divide the dough into small pieces, each weighing about 45 g (1¾ oz). Shape them into ovals or balls and lay them on floured baking sheets for the final rising, about 20 to 30 minutes.

Bake the rolls in a preheated 180°C (350°F or Mark 4) oven for 30 minutes, or until the rolls are golden-brown.

RAYMOND CALVEL
LA BOULANGERIE MODERNE

Muffins

To make 12 muffins

500 g	strong plain flour	1 lb
15 g	fresh yeast or 2 tsp dried yeast	½ oz
1	egg	1
30 cl	milk	½ pint
30 g	butter	1 oz
4 tbsp	tepid water	4 tbsp
1 tsp	salt	1 tsp

Break the egg into a bowl. Warm the milk and butter together to blood heat and beat them with the egg. Cream the yeast with the warm water.

Put the flour and salt into a warm bowl, and make a well in

the centre. Pour in the yeast, then the egg, butter and milk liquid. Knead thoroughly, adding more flour or more water if necessary. The dough should be soft but not sticky. Cover the bowl with a damp cloth and leave it in a warm place for about 1½ hours, or until the dough has doubled in size.

Roll out the dough to a 1 cm (½ inch) thickness on a floured board. Cut out the muffins with a large scone or biscuit cutter—about 6 cm (2½ inches) across. Knead the trimmings together and roll and cut them out in the same way.

Immediately you have finished cutting them out, start cooking the muffins on a lightly greased griddle, turning them over when they are floury and slightly brown on the base. Alternatively, cook the muffins for 15 minutes in a very hot oven, preheated to 230°C (450°F or Mark 8), turning them over after 6 to 7 minutes.

The muffins will rise and swell to look rather like a puffball fungus. They should not cook too fast, so the centre of the griddle may have to be avoided, and they should keep a floury look. Toast the muffins by the fire, then pull them apart and put a big knob of butter in the middle; muffins are never cut, always pulled apart. Keep them warm in a muffin dish, as you toast the rest, turning them over after a few minutes so that the butter soaks into both halves.

JANE GRIGSON
ENGLISH FOOD

Anchovy Loaf

La Pompe aux Anchois

This is an old Provençal recipe. Traditionally, the leaven consists of a piece of dough left over from the preceding week's batch of bread. It may be replaced by the basic bread dough.

To make two 25 cm (10 inch) loaves

1 kg	strong plain flour	2 to 2½ lb
500 g	leaven or basic bread dough (*page 171*)	1 lb
20	salt anchovies, soaked, filleted, rinsed and dried	20
10 cl	oil	3½ fl oz
100 g	butter, softened	3½ oz
4	eggs, lightly beaten	4
2 to 3 tbsp	brandy	2 to 3 tbsp

In a saucepan containing 8 cl (3 fl oz) of the oil, cook 18 of the filleted anchovies to a paste, taking care not to let them boil. Chop the remaining two anchovies finely and reserve them for the garnish.

Work the butter into the leaven or bread dough until it is completely absorbed. Add the cooked anchovies, the eggs, then the brandy and finally the flour. Knead until the dough

no longer sticks to your fingers. Leave the dough to rise in a warm place for 1½ hours, or until it has doubled in bulk.

Shape the risen dough into two round loaves. Pour the remaining oil into the bottom of two 25 cm (10 inch) tart tins, place the loaves in the tins, and sprinkle the tops of the loaves with the pieces of reserved anchovies. Press the pieces into place with your fingers.

Bake the loaves in an oven preheated to 200°C (400°F or Mark 6) for 25 minutes. Then turn the loaves upside down so that their bases will brown, and cook for a further 25 minutes, or until they are risen and golden-brown.

RODOLPHE BRINGER
LES BONS VIEUX PLATS DU TRICASTIN

Brentford Rolls

Richard Dolby, who published his book of recipes in 1830, was cook at the Thatched House Tavern, St. James's Street, London. Brentford, now a suburb of Greater London, was then a village by the Thames, about 8 miles west of the City.

To make 12 large rolls

1 kg	strong plain flour	2 lb
60 g	fresh yeast or 2 tbsp dried yeast	2 oz
60 cl	tepid milk	1 pint
60 g	castor sugar	2 oz
2	eggs, beaten	2
2 tsp	salt	2 tsp
125 g	butter, softened and cut into small pieces	4 oz

Dissolve the yeast in 6 tablespoons of the milk with 1 teaspoon of the sugar. Sift the flour, salt and the rest of the sugar into a bowl and work in the butter with your fingertips. Add the eggs, the yeast mixture and the rest of the milk. Mix the dough and knead it well for about 10 minutes. Set the dough aside in a warm place to rise, until doubled in bulk, about 1 hour. Divide the dough into 12 pieces, roll them into balls and place them on buttered baking sheets. Return the rolls to a warm place to rise, covered with a cloth, for about 30 minutes. When they have doubled in bulk, bake them in an oven preheated to 200°C (400°F or Mark 6) for 30 minutes, or until they are golden-brown.

RICHARD DOLBY
THE COOK'S DICTIONARY, AND HOUSE-KEEPER'S DIRECTORY

Marston Buns

The book from which this recipe is taken was published in 1694. Marston is in Derbyshire in the north of England.

To make 35 to 40 buns

1 kg	strong plain flour	2½ lb
30 g	fresh yeast or 1 tbsp dried yeast	1 oz
250 g	butter	8 oz
60 cl	tepid milk	1 pint
5	eggs, beaten	5
250 g	sugar	8 oz
350 g	currants or 2 tbsp caraway seeds	12 oz
	grated nutmeg	

Rub the butter into the flour. Mix the milk, yeast and eggs together and leave for 10 minutes, or until the yeast has begun to work. Then mix them into the flour, and leave the dough in a warm place to rise for 30 minutes. Add the sugar, currants or caraway seeds and grated nutmeg to taste, knead well, then put pieces of dough into buttered patty tins or shape into balls and place them on a buttered and floured baking sheet. Leave to rise for 30 minutes and bake in an oven preheated to 180°C (350°F or Mark 4) for 20 minutes or until golden-brown on top.

ANN BLENCOWE
THE RECEIPT BOOK OF ANN BLENCOWE

Cold Harbour Balls

There are more than 50 different places in the British Isles called Cold Harbour. This Cold Harbour is probably in Scotland, since Mrs. Dalgairns, who published her cookery book in 1829, lived in Edinburgh.

To make about 60 buns

2 kg	strong plain flour	4 lb
15 g	fresh yeast or 2 tsp dried yeast and 1 tsp sugar	½ oz
30 g	butter	1 oz
1.25 litres	milk	2 pints
½ tsp	salt	½ tsp
1	egg, beaten	1

Heat the butter in the milk to melt it, and leave the mixture to cool to lukewarm. Then stir it into the flour to form a stiff paste. Add the salt to the paste.

Dissolve the fresh yeast—or dried yeast and sugar—in the beaten egg, and leave them until foaming, about 10 minutes. Stir the yeast and egg mixture into the paste. Mix all the ingredients well together, knead for about 10 minutes, then

cover the dough with a cloth and leave it in a warm place for about 30 minutes or until doubled in bulk. Then make it into small round balls and bake them on buttered baking sheets in an oven preheated to 220°C (425°F or Mark 7) for about 20 minutes or until the buns are golden-brown.

MRS. DALGAIRNS
THE PRACTISE OF COOKERY

Shrove Tuesday Buns

Semlor

If bitter almonds are not available, add to both the dough and the filling an extra 15 g (½ oz) of ground almonds and a few drops of bitter almond flavouring.

In Sweden on Shrove Tuesday, and on every Tuesday during Lent, *semlor* are traditionally served for pudding at dinner. They are eaten in soup plates, with hot milk flavoured by chopped, blanched almonds and a little vanilla sugar.

To make 24 buns

900 g	strong plain flour	1 lb 14 oz
40 g	fresh yeast or 2 tbsp dried yeast	1½ oz
60 cl	tepid milk	1 pint
125 g	sugar	4 oz
150 g	butter	5 oz
2 tbsp	ground almonds, including 5 bitter almonds	2 tbsp
2	eggs, each beaten in a separate bowl	2
	icing sugar (optional)	
Almond paste		
175 g	almonds, ground	6 oz
8	bitter almonds, ground	8
300 g	icing sugar	10 oz
1 to 2 tbsp	cold water	1 to 2 tbsp
5 to 6 tbsp	whipped cream (optional)	5 to 6 tbsp

Sift all but 60 g (2 oz) of the flour into a bowl. Dissolve the yeast in half the milk with 1 teaspoon of the sugar. Pour this mixture into the flour, and stir in the rest of the milk. Work the dough to a smooth and glossy consistency, kneading it for about 10 minutes. Leave it, covered by a cloth, in a warm place, to rise to twice its size. Stir together the butter and sugar until they are light and fluffy, mix in the ground almonds and one of the eggs, and work the mixture well into the dough. If necessary, work in some or all of the reserved flour to make the dough firmer. Leave the dough to rise again for about 1 hour or until it has doubled in size. Turn the dough on to a floured board, knead it well for about 5 minutes, and then divide it into 24 portions. Shape the portions into round buns, arrange them on well-buttered baking sheets, brush them with the remaining egg, and leave them to rise quickly, preferably by placing the sheets over boiling water. Bake the buns in a preheated, 220°C (425°F or Mark 7) oven for 10 to 15 minutes, or until they are golden. Cool them on a wire rack.

To prepare the filling, beat the ground almonds, sugar and enough water together to make a smooth paste. Whipped cream, mixed into the paste just before using it, makes it very delicious. When the buns are cool, slice off their tops, scoop out a little of the inside dough, fill them with the almond paste and replace the tops. Dust the buns with the icing sugar.

INGA NORBERG
GOOD FOOD FROM SWEDEN

Minorcan Buns

Ensaimadas Menorquinas

Ensaimadas, *snail-shaped buns which are a speciality of the Balearic Islands off the coast of Spain, use very little yeast but need a long proving time. This method is well suited to the hot, dry climate of the Islands and, although unusual, it works extremely well. Traditionally the buns, eaten at breakfast, are about the size of a saucer. Even larger* ensaimadas *are eaten at lunch or dinner, topped with bacon or* sobresada *sausage.*

To make 60 buns

2.25 kg	strong plain flour	4 lb 10 oz
30 g	fresh yeast or 1 tbsp dried yeast	1 oz
30 cl	tepid water	½ pint
6	eggs, beaten	6
300 g	sugar	10 oz
125 g	butter or lard, softened	4 oz
6 tbsp	castor sugar	6 tbsp

Dissolve the yeast in the water and set it aside until it foams, about 20 minutes. Put the eggs into a large bowl and mix them well with the sugar. Stir in the yeast mixture, then gradually add enough flour to make a firm but not stiff dough.

Grease the bowl and your hands, then knead the dough thoroughly while it is still in the bowl, continually pushing the dough from the sides to the middle of the bowl.

Gradually work in half of the fat. When the mixture is well kneaded, roll it into a ball and place it in another greased bowl, spreading the dough as thinly as possible on the bottom. Brush the dough with the remaining fat and cover the bowl by inverting a second bowl of the same size over it. Then wrap the bowls in a blanket; leave the dough to rise overnight.

Next morning, knead the dough again and cover as before. Repeat the process at midday and again at night, leaving the dough to rise again overnight. On the third day, the buns can be made, usually without kneading the dough any further. But if the dough appears to have risen too much, it can be kneaded one last time before immediately shaping into buns.

There are two methods of making Minorcan buns: in both cases, the hands must be well greased. One method consists simply of making small portions of the dough into balls, rolling them flat—not too flat—and allowing them to find their own shape. The traditional method is to roll the dough into a long sausage—the thickness of a pencil—and to wind it into a coil. When a large enough coil is obtained, cut off the end of the spiral and begin again, until all the dough is used up. Dip a spoon handle in water and use it to accentuate the coils, so that the outlines do not run together while baking.

Grease your baking sheets liberally with butter or lard and place the buns on them, well spaced apart; cover them with a towel and leave them in a warm place until they have risen again—about 20 minutes. Bake the buns in an oven preheated to 200°C (400°F or Mark 6) for 20 minutes or until they are brown. Remove from the oven and sprinkle them with castor sugar while they are still hot.

PEDRO BALLESTER
DE RE CIBARIA

Yorkshire Cakes

These cakes must be buttered hot out of the oven, or cut in two when cold, toasted brown and buttered.

To make 10 to 15 cakes

1 kg	strong plain flour	2 lb
30 g	fresh yeast or 1 tbsp dried yeast	1 oz
125 g	butter	4 oz
60 cl	milk	1 pint
2	eggs, beaten	2

In a saucepan, warm the butter and milk together until the butter has melted. Remove from the heat and leave to cool until the milk is tepid. Then add the eggs and yeast to the liquid. Leave for 10 minutes or until the yeast begins to foam, then add the yeast mixture to the flour. Mix well together; leave to rise in a warm place for 1 hour or until doubled in bulk. Knead the mixture thoroughly, then break off pieces of dough and shape them into cakes about 2 cm (¾ inch) thick and 15 cm (6 inches) square. Put the cakes on a buttered baking sheet to rise and leave in a warm place for 1 hour or until slightly less than doubled in bulk. Bake in an oven preheated to 180°C (350°F or Mark 4) for 30 to 40 minutes or until nicely browned on top.

DUNCAN MACDONALD
THE NEW LONDON FAMILY COOK

Walnut Loaf

Pain aux Noix

This loaf should be eaten when a few days old, thinly sliced and well buttered. It is perfect with tea.

To make one 17 by 9 cm (7 by 3½ inch) loaf

250 g	strong plain flour	8 oz
10 g	fresh yeast or 1 tsp dried yeast	⅓ oz
150 g	walnuts, chopped	5 oz
¼ litre	tepid milk	8 fl oz
1	egg, beaten	1
200 g	sugar	7 oz
	salt	

Mix the yeast with the milk. Stir in the beaten egg and add the sugar, flour, walnuts and a pinch of salt. Transfer the mixture to a buttered ½ litre (1 lb) loaf tin and leave to rise in a warm place for about 30 minutes. Bake in an oven preheated to 190°C (375°F or Mark 5) for about 40 minutes, or until the loaf is golden-brown.

ZETTE GUINAUDEAU-FRANC
LES SECRETS DES FERMES EN PÉRIGORD NOIR

Southern Irish Potato "Box" Scones

This quaint concoction is often known as "tea-biscuits", "split-opens", etc. Rolls may be made from the same dough.

To make about twenty-five 5 cm (2 inch) double-decker scones

750 g	strong plain flour	1½ lb
30 g	fresh yeast or 1 tbsp dried yeast	1 oz
3	potatoes, peeled, boiled and well mashed	3
30 g	lard, melted	1 oz
175 g	butter, softened	6 oz
75 g	sugar	2½ oz
1¼ tsp	salt	1¼ tsp
35 cl	tepid milk	12 fl oz
1	egg, beaten	1
1	egg yolk, beaten	1

Beat the lard, 125 g (4 oz) of the butter, and the sugar and salt into the potatoes. Dissolve the yeast in 4 tablespoons of the milk. Add the remaining milk, with the yeast solution, to the potato mixture. Add the whole egg and the yolk; fold in the flour. Knead the dough until it becomes springy and place in a large greased bowl to rise. When doubled in bulk—about 1 hour—remove to a floured board and work it into a smooth dough. Roll it out to about 1 cm (½ inch) thick, and cut it into rounds with a biscuit cutter. Melt the remaining butter and brush each round with it. Place one round on top of another to make double-decker scones and put on buttered baking sheets. Bake in a preheated 230°C (450°F or Mark 8) oven for 20 to 30 minutes or until well risen and golden.

MARION BROWN
THE SOUTHERN COOK BOOK

Plum Slices

Placek ze Śliwkami

To make 40 slices

500 g	strong plain flour	1 lb
30 g	fresh yeast or 1 tbsp dried yeast	1 oz
30 cl	milk	½ pint
40 g	sugar	1½ oz
40 g	butter	1½ oz
2	egg yolks	2
1	egg	1
¼ tsp	salt	¼ tsp
Plum and cinnamon topping		
1 kg	ripe plums, washed, stalks removed	2 lb
1 tsp	powdered cinnamon	1 tsp
2 tbsp	icing sugar	2 tbsp

Sift half the flour into a bowl. Bring half the milk to the boil. Reserve 1 tablespoon of this milk and leave it to cool to tepid. Pour the rest of the boiled milk over the flour, stirring well to avoid forming lumps.

Cream the yeast with the tablespoon of tepid milk, 1 tablespoon of the flour and 1 teaspoon of the sugar. Allow this mixture to rise by leaving it in a warm place for 15 to 20 minutes. Heat the remaining milk with the butter. Remove from the heat when the butter has melted. Pour it into the flour mixture, then add the rest of the flour and the sugar, the egg yolks and the egg. Beat well, then add the salt. When the dough has cooled to tepid, add the yeast mixture. Beat the dough until it is smooth and shiny, about 15 minutes. Put it in a warm place, covered with a tea towel, to rise for 40 minutes, or until it has doubled in bulk.

To prepare the topping, slit the plums almost in half—until the two halves are joined only by the skin—and remove the stones. Make a small notch in each half, at the stem on one half of the plum and at the tip on the other, to keep the skin from splitting during baking.

Roll out the dough into a rectangle to fit a buttered 38 by 30 cm (15 by 12 inch) baking dish. Cover the dough completely with the plums, the halves opened out like a book, cut sides uppermost. Cover the dish with a cloth and leave the dough to rise once more for 1 hour. Mix the icing sugar and cinnamon and sieve them over the plums. Bake the cake in an oven preheated to 220°C (425°F or Mark 7) for 20 to 25 minutes or until the dough is pale golden and the plums are completely cooked. Cut the cake into rectangular slices before serving.

LILI KOWALSKA
COOKING THE POLISH WAY

Corsican Raisin and Walnut Buns

U Pan di i Morti o "Uga Siccati"

These buns are often served after funerals, hence their rather macabre Corsican name.

To make 20 buns

1.6 kg	strong plain flour	3¼ lb
60 g	fresh yeast or 2 tbsp dried yeast	2 oz
500 g	raisins	1 lb
500 g	walnuts, chopped	1 lb
4 tbsp	tepid water	4 tbsp
250 g	butter, softened	8 oz
4	eggs	4
	salt	
500 g	sugar	1 lb
1	lemon rind, grated	1
1 tbsp	oil	1 tbsp

Dissolve the yeast in the tepid water. Make a yeast sponge by adding about 100 g (3½ oz) of the flour to the dissolved yeast. Cover the sponge with a cloth and leave it in a warm place to rise for about 2 hours.

Pour the rest of the flour on to a work surface. Make a well in the centre and add the butter, eggs, a pinch of salt, the sugar and grated lemon rind. Knead the mixture into a dough and then add the well-risen yeast sponge. Knead the dough thoroughly for about 10 minutes, or until smooth and elastic. Add the raisins and walnuts and knead until they are well incorporated into the dough. Put the dough in an earthenware bowl, cover it with a cloth and leave it to prove for about 1 hour.

Divide the dough into 20 pieces and shape them into balls. Place the balls on three or four lightly oiled baking sheets. Bake in an oven preheated to 220°C (425°F or Mark 7) for about 40 minutes, or until the buns are golden-brown.

CHRISTIANE SCHAPIRA
LA CUISINE CORSE

Crispies

To make 24 buns

350 g	strong plain flour	12 oz
30 g	fresh yeast or 1 tbsp dried yeast	1 oz
4 tbsp	tepid water	4 tbsp
100 g	butter, softened	3½ oz
4 tbsp	milk	4 tbsp
175 g	sugar	6 oz
½ tsp	salt	½ tsp
1	egg, beaten	1
125 g	nuts, finely chopped	4 oz

In a bowl, dissolve the yeast in the water. Warm 60 g (2 oz) of the butter in the milk until the butter has dissolved. Remove the mixture from the heat and cool to lukewarm. To the yeast and water add 100 g (3½ oz) of the flour, the milk and butter, 60 g (2 oz) of the sugar and salt. Beat the egg and 4 tablespoons of flour into the batter, then add the rest of the flour to make a stiff dough. Turn it out on to a floured surface, and knead it until smooth—about 10 minutes. Return the dough to the bowl. Melt the remaining butter and use half of it to brush the top of the dough. Leave the dough to rise until doubled in bulk—about 1 hour.

Punch the dough down, and let it rise a second time for 45 minutes. Punch it down again, turn it on to a lightly floured surface, and roll it out to a 23 by 45 by 1 cm (9 by 18 by ½ inch) rectangle. Brush the top again, using the rest of the butter.

Combine the nuts and the rest of the sugar then sprinkle half of this mixture over the dough. Roll the dough up from the long side, as for a Swiss roll, and seal the edges by pressing them together with a little water. Cut the roll into 2 cm (1 inch) slices, sprinkle the remaining sugar and nut mixture on to the kneading surface, place each slice of dough on it and flatten it lightly with a rolling pin to make a 7 cm (3 inch) round. Turn the flattened Crispie over and press it into the sugar and nuts, so that both top and bottom are well coated.

Butter two baking sheets and place the Crispies on them carefully. Cover the buns and leave to rise in a warm place for about 30 minutes. Bake in an oven preheated to 190°C (375°F or Mark 5) for about 10 minutes or until brown.

GRACE FIRTH
STILLROOM COOKERY

Prune Bread

Pognons aux Peurniaux

This egg bread is traditionally made for festivals and christenings in the countryside around Lyons, in eastern France.

To make one 20 cm (8 inch) loaf

200 g	basic bread dough (*page 171*)	7 oz
150 g	prunes	5 oz
2	eggs, beaten	2
100 g	sugar	3½ oz
100 g	butter, softened and cut into small pieces	3½ oz
30 cl	water	½ pint

Mix the bread dough in the usual way; knead it, leave it to rise and punch it down. Gradually knead in the eggs and half of the sugar, then add the butter. Knead the dough thoroughly, until it is smooth. Leave it to rise in a warm place for 2 to 3 hours, or until almost doubled in bulk.

Cook the prunes in the rest of the sugar and the water for 30 minutes or until they are soft. Allow them to cool. Drain, stone and chop the fruit and knead it into the dough. Shape the dough into a round, and put it either in a buttered brioche mould or on a buttered baking sheet. Bake the bread in a preheated 190°C (375°F or Mark 5) oven for about 30 minutes, or until it is golden-brown.

NICOLE VIELFAURE AND A. CHRISTINE BEAUVIALA
FÊTES, COUTUMES ET GÂTEAUX

Algerian Orange-Flavoured Loaves

Mounas

To make four 20 cm (8 inch) loaves

1 kg	strong plain flour	2½ lb
30 g	fresh yeast or 1 tbsp dried yeast	1 oz
8 cl	tepid water	3 fl oz
5	eggs	5
300 g	sugar	10 oz
2	sugar cubes, rubbed over the rind of an orange	2
8 cl	olive oil	3 fl oz
75 g	butter, cut into pieces	2½ oz
1	egg yolk, beaten with 3 tbsp water	1
3 tbsp	icing sugar	3 tbsp

Dissolve the yeast in the water. Add it to 125 g (4 oz) of the flour. Cover this yeast sponge and leave it for 1 hour or until it has doubled in bulk. In a bowl, combine the eggs and sugar and add the sugar cubes. Add the oil and butter. Gradually beat in the remaining flour. Add the yeast sponge, then knead the dough for 15 minutes, or until it is smooth and elastic. Put it in a floured bowl, cover it with a cloth and leave it in a warm place for 3 hours or until doubled in bulk.

Shape the dough into four rounds or cylinders, each weighing about 400 g (14 oz). Place them on a floured baking sheet, cover them and leave them to prove for 1½ hours. When the loaves have doubled in bulk, use a sharp knife or razor blade to make incisions in the tops. Glaze the loaves with the egg yolk diluted with water, sprinkle them with the icing sugar and bake in an oven preheated to 180°C (350°F or Mark 4) for 50 minutes or until they sound hollow when rapped.

IRÈNE AND LUCIENNE KARSENTY
LA CUISINE PIED-NOIR

Austrian Potato Bread

Erdäpfelbrot

To make one 20 cm (8 inch) loaf or one 25 cm (10 inch) cylindrical loaf

450 g	strong plain flour	1 lb
30 g	fresh yeast or 1 tbsp dried yeast	1 oz
90 g	mashed potato	3 oz
About ¼ litre	tepid milk	About 8 fl oz
100 g	butter, cut into pieces	3½ oz
40 g	sugar	1½ oz
3	egg yolks, beaten	3
	salt	
100 g	sultanas	3½ oz
1	egg, lightly beaten	1

Cream the yeast with about 4 tablespoons of the milk, and stir in just enough flour to give the mixture the consistency of a thin batter. Leave the mixture in a warm place for about 20 minutes, until it becomes spongy.

Sift the rest of the flour into a bowl. Rub in the butter, then the mashed potato, and add the sugar. Incorporate the egg yolks, a good pinch of salt, the sultanas, the yeast mixture and enough of the remaining milk to make a fairly firm dough. Knead the dough briefly, for about 5 minutes, and then leave it to rise in a warm place for 1 hour or until doubled in bulk.

Shape the dough into a cylindrical or round loaf and leave it to prove in a warm place for 20 to 30 minutes or until it is just beginning to rise again. Brush the top of the loaf with the egg, and bake it in an oven preheated to 180°C (350°F or Mark 4) for about 50 minutes or until it sounds hollow when rapped.

EVA BAKOS
MEHLSPEISEN AUS ÖSTERREICH

Hunting Bread

This recipe is from an anonymous cookery book published in about 1827. Although the book is an excellent and comprehensive work, it was never republished, and the author's identity has never been discovered.

To make about 40 cakes

750 g	strong plain flour, sifted	1½ lb
15 g	fresh yeast or 2 tsp dried yeast	½ oz
500 g	sugar	1 lb
1 to 2 tsp	caraway seeds	1 to 2 tsp
1 to 2 tsp	coriander seeds	1 to 2 tsp
17.5 cl	tepid rose-water	6 fl oz
6	egg yolks, lightly beaten	6
4	egg whites	4

Mix the flour, sugar and caraway and coriander seeds, as many as may be thought proper. Dissolve the yeast in all but 4 tablespoons of the rose-water. Beat the egg yolks and egg whites with the rest of the rose-water. Strain the egg and rose-water mixture through a sieve into the flour. Add the dissolved yeast and knead the mixture into a firm dough. Turn out the dough on to a lightly floured board and roll it out thin, about 1 cm (½ inch) thick. Cut it into pieces like lozenges, and place them on buttered baking sheets. Bake the cakes in an oven preheated to 200°C (400°F or Mark 6) for 15 to 20 minutes or until they are golden-brown. Remove them from the baking sheets to cool.

THE NEW LONDON COOKERY AND COMPLETE DOMESTIC GUIDE

Old Maids

If coarse cornmeal is not obtainable, use coarse semolina.

To make about twenty-five 7.5 cm (3 inch) cakes

800 g	strong plain flour	1 lb 10 oz
90 g	coarse cornmeal	3 oz
30 g	fresh yeast or 1 tbsp dried yeast	1 oz
12.5 cl	tepid water	4 fl oz
1 tsp	sugar	1 tsp
¼ litre	tepid milk	8 fl oz
30 g	butter, softened	1 oz
1 tsp	salt	1 tsp
3	eggs, beaten	3

Dissolve the yeast in the water and sugar and let it stand for 5 minutes or until it is frothy. Add the milk, butter and salt. Stir in the beaten eggs and 550 g (1 lb 2 oz) of the flour to make a moist dough. Turn the dough on to a floured board and knead in the remaining flour. Beat and knead the dough until the surface glows and it becomes elastic—about 20 minutes. Roll it out until the dough is 1 cm (½ inch) thick and cut it into rounds with a coffee cup. Sprinkle the cornmeal on the board and press each round into the meal to give an interesting gritty surface. Allow the Old Maids to rise for 1 hour, then fry them in a heavy, lightly buttered frying pan over a low heat until straw-coloured and ringed with brown on both sides.

GRACE FIRTH
STILLROOM COOKERY

Sweet Pretzels

Homburger Prezeln

The technique of making pretzels is shown on page 34.

To make about 40 pretzels

750 g	strong plain flour	1½ lb
50 g	fresh yeast or 2 tbsp dried yeast	2 oz
20 cl	tepid milk	7 fl oz
1	lemon, rind grated	1
	salt	
375 g	butter, softened	13 oz
4	egg yolks, beaten	4
3	eggs, beaten	3
3 tbsp	castor sugar	3 tbsp

Dissolve the yeast in half the milk. Add about one-third of the flour and leave the mixture in a warm place until the resulting yeast sponge is well risen, about 1 hour.

In a bowl, sift the rest of the flour with the lemon rind, salt, the rest of the milk, the butter, egg yolks and 2 of the eggs. Blend in the yeast sponge. Knead the dough vigorously for 10 minutes, or until it is fairly stiff and bubbles appear in it. Divide the dough into about 40 pieces and roll each into a strip the length and thickness of a finger. Twist the strips of dough and lay the pretzels on three buttered baking sheets. Cover and leave the pretzels in a warm place to rise for about 30 minutes. Then brush the pretzels with the remaining egg and bake them in an oven preheated to 180°C (350°F or Mark 4) for about 20 minutes or until golden-brown. Sprinkle the pretzels with sugar while they are cooling on wire racks.

SOPHIE WILHELMINE SCHEIBLER
ALLGEMEINES DEUTSCHES KOCHBUCH FÜR ALLE STÄNDE

Irish Spice Bread

Bairn Brack

This is an 1829 version of the spice bread better known as barm brack or barmbrack (barm meaning home-made yeast) which was once popular throughout the British Isles. It is now eaten chiefly in the Isle of Man and in Southern Ireland. The author of this recipe recommends toasting the bairn brack if it is not eaten immediately.

To make one 40 by 25 cm (16 by 10 inch) bread

1.5 kg	strong plain flour, sifted	3 lb
60 g	fresh yeast or 2 tbsp dried yeast	2 oz
60 g	caraway seeds	2 oz
	grated nutmeg	
60 cl	tepid milk	1 pint
500 g	soft brown sugar	1 lb
500 g	butter	1 lb
8	eggs, well beaten	8

Cream the yeast in 15 cl ($\frac{1}{4}$ pint) of the milk with 1 teaspoon of the brown sugar and leave the mixture in a warm place until foaming, about 10 minutes. Dissolve the butter in the rest of the milk. Remove from the heat, cool to lukewarm, then mix with the flour. Add the eggs, the rest of the sugar, the caraway seeds and a good pinch of nutmeg, and beat to form a fairly moist dough. Beat the dough for about 10 minutes, cover it with a cloth and set it in a warm place to rise for about 1 hour, or until doubled in bulk. When the dough is well risen, transfer it to a deep buttered baking tin about 40 by 25 cm (16 by 10 inches) and bake it in an oven preheated to 200°C (400°F or Mark 6) for 50 minutes or until a skewer inserted into the centre of the bread comes out clean.

MRS. DALGAIRNS
THE PRACTISE OF COOKERY

Poppy Seed or Walnut Roll

To make two 30 cm (12 inch) rolled breads

350 g	strong plain flour, sieved	12 oz
15 g	fresh yeast or 2 tsp dried yeast	$\frac{1}{2}$ oz
1 tbsp	tepid milk	1 tbsp
	salt	
2 tbsp	soured cream	2 tbsp
150 g	butter, melted or 125 g (4 oz) lard, melted	5 oz
1	egg, beaten	1

Walnut filling

200 g	walnuts, ground	7 oz
150 g	sugar	5 oz
2 to 3 tbsp	milk	2 to 3 tbsp
$\frac{1}{2}$	lemon, rind grated	$\frac{1}{2}$
2 to 3 tbsp	apricot jam, apple purée or 1 to 2 apples, peeled and grated	2 to 3 tbsp

Poppy seed filling

125 g	poppy seeds, ground	4 oz
150 g	sugar	5 oz
15 to 20 cl	milk	5 to 7 fl oz
$\frac{1}{2}$	lemon, rind grated	$\frac{1}{2}$
1 to 2 tbsp	apple purée or 1 to 2 apples, peeled and grated	1 to 2 tbsp

Cream the yeast in the milk, and leave it to stand in a warm place until foaming, about 10 minutes. Put the flour and salt into a bowl, and add the yeast mixture. Pour in the soured cream and melted butter or lard cooled to tepid, and mix to a stiff dough. Knead for about 10 minutes, until the dough is smooth. Let it stand for 15 minutes, or until it begins to rise.

To prepare the walnut filling, make a syrup by dissolving the sugar in the milk. Simmer for 2 minutes. Add the walnuts, lemon rind and the jam, purée or grated apple.

To prepare the poppy seed filling, make a syrup by dissolving the sugar in the milk. Simmer for 2 minutes. Add the poppy seeds and bring to the boil. Remove from the heat and stir in the lemon rind and apple purée or grated apple.

Divide the dough in two, and roll out each piece into a rectangle the thickness of a matchstick. Cover one piece of rolled-out dough with the walnut filling and the other with the poppy seed filling. Roll up the dough like a Swiss roll and place in buttered and floured baking tins. Brush the rolls with the beaten egg and prick them in a few places with a larding needle. Allow the rolls to stand for 10 minutes, then brush again with the beaten egg. Bake them in an oven preheated to 180°C (350°F or Mark 4) for 1 hour or until golden-brown.

JÓZSEF VENESZ
HUNGARIAN CULINARY ART

Bread of the Dead

Pan de Muerto

If pink sugar crystals are not available, coffee sugar or hundreds and thousands may be substituted.

It is traditional in Mexico for people to visit their family graves on November 2, All Souls' Day, as a mark of love and respect. They take with them this special bread that is decorated with a cross made of pieces of baked dough in the form of alternating tear drops and bones with a knob in the centre, the whole covered with pink sugar crystals.

To make anise water, boil 1 teaspoon of anise seeds in 3 tablespoons of water for 2 to 3 minutes. Cool and strain.

To make two 17 cm (7 inch) loaves		
500 g	strong plain flour	1 lb
30 g	fresh yeast or 1 tbsp dried yeast	1 oz
10 cl	tepid water	4 fl oz
1 tsp	salt	1 tsp
125 g	sugar	4 oz
250 g	butter, melted and cooled to tepid	8 oz
6	eggs, lightly beaten	6
1 tbsp	orange flower water	1 tbsp
2 tbsp	anise water	2 tbsp
1	orange, rind grated	1
125 g	icing sugar, sifted	4 oz
5 tbsp	boiling water or milk	5 tbsp
30 g	pink sugar crystals	1 oz

Dissolve the yeast in the tepid water. Add 175 g (6 oz) flour to make a light dough. Knead it, shape it into a ball, and put it in a warm place to double in bulk—about 1 hour.

Sift the remaining flour with the salt and sugar. Work in the butter, eggs, orange flower water, anise water and the grated orange rind. Knead the dough well on a lightly floured board until smooth, about 10 minutes. Then add the yeast sponge, and knead again until the texture is satiny. Cover the dough with a cloth, and let it rest in a warm place for about 1½ hours, or until it has doubled in bulk. Set aside about a quarter of the dough and shape the rest into two round loaves.

Place the loaves on a greased baking sheet and decorate each with a cross made of pieces of the remaining dough, alternately shaped like bones and teardrops. Roll two small pieces of dough into knobs. Allow these to rise for about 20 minutes, and attach them to the centre of each loaf before baking. Cover the loaves, and leave them in a warm place until doubled in bulk, about 30 minutes. Bake the loaves in a preheated 190°C (375°F or Mark 5) oven for about 30 minutes or until they sound hollow when rapped. Allow to cool.

To make the frosting, add icing sugar to the boiling water or milk until it is of the right consistency for spreading. Frost the loaves, and sprinkle them with the pink sugar crystals.

ELISABETH LAMBERT ORTIZ
THE COMPLETE BOOK OF MEXICAN COOKING

Scalded Yeast Roll

Strucle Parzone

Alternative fillings for these rolls are listed on page 173.

To make two 20 cm (8 inch) rolls		
600 g	strong plain flour	1¼ lb
30 g	fresh yeast or 1 tbsp dried yeast	1 oz
30 cl	milk	½ pint
90 g	butter, softened	3 oz
3	eggs	3
60 g	sugar	2 oz
1	lemon, rind grated	1
	salt	
	milk or beaten egg for brushing	
Poppy seed and sultana filling		
175 g	poppy seeds	6 oz
60 g	sultanas	2 oz
60 g	butter	2 oz
90 g	sugar	3 oz
1	egg, beaten	1

Put 125 g (4 oz) of flour in a mixing bowl. Heat half the milk to boiling point and pour it over the flour, stirring well to prevent lumps from forming. Leave the mixture to cool to lukewarm. Warm the rest of the milk until it is tepid and mix it with the yeast. Leave the yeast mixture to rise in a warm place for 15 minutes, or until it shows bubbles.

To make the filling, melt the butter over a low heat and add the poppy seeds, sultanas and sugar. Simmer for 5 minutes, until the sugar has completely dissolved. Allow the mixture to cool and then beat in the egg.

Cream together the butter, eggs, sugar, lemon rind and a pinch of salt. Add the scalded flour, yeast mixture, remaining milk and flour and knead the dough until it feels spongy and stops sticking to your fingers, about 10 minutes.

Divide the dough in half, roll out each piece on a floured board into a rectangle about 25 by 20 cm (10 by 8 inches) and 1 cm (½ inch) thick. Spread each half with filling, leaving a 2.5 cm (1 inch) margin all round the edge, and roll up each rectangle like a Swiss roll. Lay the rolls on a buttered, floured baking sheet. Cover with a cloth and leave them to rise in a warm place for about 30 minutes or until doubled in bulk.

Brush the rolls with milk or egg and bake them in an oven preheated to 180°C (350°F or Mark 4) for 35 to 40 minutes until pale golden. Allow to cool before serving.

LILI KOWALSKA
COOKING THE POLISH WAY

Russian Easter Cake

Kulitsch

The simple egg dough preparation on page 58 can also be used to make this cake, in which case it should be baked for 1 hour at 190°C (375°F or Mark 5).

The *kulitsch* is baked in the shape of a pyramid, symbolizing Mount Golgotha—the site of the crucifixion.

To make one 20 cm (8 inch) cake

1 kg	strong plain flour, sifted and slightly warmed	2 lb
60 g	fresh yeast or 2 tbsp dried yeast	2 oz
¼ litre	tepid milk	8 fl oz
300 g	butter, softened	10 oz
5	egg yolks, beaten	5
200 g	sugar	7 oz
	salt	
1	lemon, rind grated	1
½ tsp	crushed cardamom seeds	½ tsp
1 tsp	powdered saffron	1 tsp
150 g	raisins	5 oz
125 g	currants	4 oz
150 g	almonds, blanched and coarsely chopped	5 oz
1	egg, beaten	1

Dissolve the yeast in the milk and leave it in a warm place until it is foaming, about 10 minutes. Add the yeast mixture to one-third of the flour and mix well to make a yeast sponge. Leave the sponge to rise until doubled in bulk, about 1 hour.

Blend the butter and egg yolks with the sugar, a pinch of salt, lemon rind, cardamom and saffron and beat until foaming. Fold this mixture and the remaining flour into the yeast sponge and knead the dough thoroughly for about 10 minutes. Add the raisins, currants and half of the almonds to the dough. Cover the dough and leave it to rise for about 2 hours.

Roll out the dough to the thickness of a finger. Cut out a 20 cm (8 inch) circle of dough and place it on a buttered baking sheet. Next, cut out a circle with a slightly smaller diameter and place it on top of the first circle. Continue in the same way, building up progressively smaller rounds of dough forming a pyramid shape until all of the dough is used up.

Leave the *kulitsch* to prove for about 45 minutes, then brush it all over with the beaten egg. Sprinkle it with the remaining almonds and bake it in an oven preheated to 220°C (425°F or Mark 7) for 45 to 60 minutes or until the *kulitsch* is golden-brown. The initial high temperature ensures that the cake does not sink during baking; if the *kulitsch* appears to be browning too quickly the heat may be reduced.

GRETE WILLINSKY
KULINARISCHE WELTREISE

New Year Sweet Bread

Vassilopitta

To make one 30 cm (12 inch) bread

625 g	strong plain flour	1 lb 5 oz
30 g	fresh yeast or 1 tbsp dried yeast	1 oz
17.5 cl	tepid milk	6 fl oz
5	eggs	5
1 tsp	salt	1 tsp
175 g	sugar	6 oz
1	lemon, rind grated	1
125 g	butter, melted and cooled to tepid	4 oz
1 tbsp	sesame seeds or blanched, halved almonds	1 tbsp

Dissolve the yeast in the tepid milk. Add about 200 g (7 oz) of the flour and beat the batter until it is smooth. Cover and set it in a warm place for about 1 hour.

Beat together over hot water 4 of the eggs, the salt, sugar and lemon rind, until the sugar has melted. Stir the mixture into the batter; add the remaining flour and knead, gradually adding the butter, until the dough is smooth and elastic, about 10 minutes. Cover with a cloth and let it rise in a warm place until doubled in bulk, about 2 hours. Knead the dough and put it in a buttered, deep baking dish. Cover and leave in a warm place until almost doubled in bulk, about 30 minutes.

Brush the dough with the remaining egg, lightly beaten, and sprinkle with sesame seeds, or garnish with blanched, halved almonds. Bake the loaf in a preheated 180°C (350°F or Mark 4) oven for about 45 minutes, until it is golden-brown.

CHRISSA PARADISSIS
THE BEST BOOK OF GREEK COOKERY

Sugar Flan

Tarte au Sucre

To make one 25 cm (10 inch) flan

250 g	strong plain flour	8 oz
15 g	fresh yeast or 2 tsp dried yeast	½ oz
15 g	sugar, dissolved in 10 cl (3½ fl oz) tepid milk	½ oz
130 g	butter	4½ oz
2	eggs	2
	salt	
100 g	soft brown sugar	3½ oz

Melt 100 g (3½ oz) of the butter and then leave it to cool to lukewarm. Dissolve the yeast in the sugared milk and leave it in a warm place until foaming, about 15 minutes. Sift the flour into a bowl, make a well in the centre and break in the eggs. Add a pinch of salt and the cooled butter. Add the yeast mixture and work the ingredients together. Knead the dough thoroughly for about 10 minutes, cover, then leave it to rise in a warm place until doubled in bulk, about 2 hours.

Roll out the dough to a thickness of about 1 cm ($\frac{1}{2}$ inch) to fit a buttered tart or flan tin. Lay the dough in the tin, sprinkle it with the brown sugar and dot it with the rest of the butter, cut into pieces. Leave the dough to prove for about 30 minutes in a warm place. Then bake in an oven preheated to 220°C (425°F or Mark 7) for 15 to 20 minutes or until golden-brown and the sugar and butter have melted together. Serve hot or cold.

NICOLE VIELFAURE AND A. CHRISTINE BEAUVIALA
FÊTES, COUTUMES ET GÂTEAUX

Italian Easter Bread with Cheese

Crescia di Pasqua col Formaggio

To make four 20 by 10 cm (8 by 4 inch) loaves

500 g	basic bread dough (*page 171*)	1 lb
1 kg	strong plain flour	2 lb
30 g	fresh yeast or 1 tbsp dried yeast	1 oz
300 g	Parmesan cheese, grated	10 oz
100 g	Gruyère cheese, diced	3½ oz
¼ litre	tepid water	8 fl oz
½ litre	tepid milk	16 fl oz
10	eggs	10
150 g	butter, softened	5 oz
50 g	lard, softened	2 oz
1 tbsp	salt	1 tbsp

On the evening before making the bread, prepare a sourdough leaven by mixing the bread dough with the water and half the milk. Then sift the flour on to a work surface, and make a well in the centre. Pour the softened bread dough into the well and gradually work the flour into it, kneading for about 10 minutes to make a firm, elastic dough. Form the dough into a ball. With a sharp knife, make two cuts in the shape of a cross in the ball of dough to help the rising process. Cover and leave the dough in a warm place overnight.

The next day, dissolve the yeast in the rest of the milk, and leave until slightly foaming, about 10 minutes. Knead the yeast mixture into the leavened dough. In a large bowl, beat the eggs and add the Parmesan and Gruyère cheeses, the butter, lard and the salt. Mix them all together thoroughly, then work them into the leavened dough, kneading until the mixture is soft and smooth, about 10 minutes.

Butter four 1 litre (2 lb) bread tins. Divide the dough into four, shape these into cylinders and put them in the tins. The dough should reach no more than half way up the sides. Leave the loaves in a warm place to prove for 30 minutes, or until the dough has risen to about 1 cm ($\frac{1}{2}$ inch) above the rims of the tins. Bake the loaves in an oven preheated to 200°C (400°F or Mark 6) for 50 minutes, or until the loaves are golden-brown and sound hollow when they are rapped.

PIERO LUIGI MENICHETTI AND LUCIANA MENICHETTI PANFILI
VECCHIA CUCINA EUGUBINA

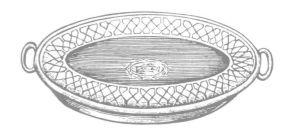

Riom Brioche

Gâteau ou Brioche de Riom

This brioche is typical of Riom-les-Montagnes in the Auvergne district of south-eastern France. The dough should be very soft, and is traditionally left to rise in a woven straw basket, to give the brioche a lattice pattern on the outside.

To make one 25 cm (10 inch) brioche

300 g	strong plain flour	10 oz
15 g	fresh yeast or 2 tsp dried yeast	½ oz
2 tbsp	tepid water	2 tbsp
40 g	sugar	1½ oz
150 g	butter, softened	5 oz
3	eggs	3
	salt	
4 tbsp	tepid milk	4 tbsp

Cream the yeast in the water with 1 teaspoon of the sugar, and leave it in a warm place until foaming, about 15 minutes. Then stir in 60 g (2 oz) of the flour. In a large bowl, sift the rest of the flour and mix with the rest of the sugar, butter, eggs and a pinch of salt. Beat in the yeast and flour mixture, and knead this firm dough thoroughly for about 10 minutes, or until smooth. Leave the dough, covered, in a warm place for 3 to 4 hours, or until it has doubled in bulk.

Soften the dough by kneading in the milk. Place it in a buttered brioche mould, ensuring that the dough does not fill more than one-third of the mould. Leave the brioche in a warm place to prove for about 1 hour. Bake it in an oven preheated to 190°C (375°F or Mark 5) for 40 minutes or until the brioche is golden and well risen. Cool it on a wire rack.

NICOLE VIELFAURE AND A. CHRISTINE BEAUVIALA
FÊTES, COUTUMES ET GÂTEAUX

Sausage in Brioche

Saucisson Brioché

The authors recommend using a truffled cervelas sausage, but any good boiling sausage can be substituted. The technique for making a sausage in brioche according to the method used below is demonstrated on page 66.

An alternative method of making a sausage in brioche is to bake the brioche in a 20 by 10 cm (8 by 4 inch) loaf tin. In this case, divide the dough into two pieces, one two-thirds larger than the other. Roll out the larger piece to a thickness of 1.5 to 2 cm (½ to ¾ inch) in a shape to fit the tin, and line the tin with it. Dust the cooked sausage with flour and place it in the centre of the dough. Roll out the other piece of dough to cover it. Dampen and seal the edges then glaze the dough with the egg yolk diluted in a little water. Leave the brioche in a warm place to prove for about 2 hours. Glaze it again and bake it in the loaf tin set on a baking sheet in a preheated 220°C (425°F or Mark 7) oven for 45 to 50 minutes, or until the brioche is well browned. Remove the brioche and unmould it while still hot.

To make one 25 cm (10 inch) brioche

500 g	rich egg dough (*page 172*)	1 lb
1	500 g (1 lb) boiling sausage, pricked thoroughly with a fork	1
About 2 litres	stock or water	About 3½ pints
60 g	flour	2 oz
1	egg yolk, beaten with 2 tbsp water	1

Heat the stock or water, skim it and bring it to the boil. Drop the sausage into the liquid, and reduce the heat immediately, so that the cooking liquid is at a bare simmer. Cook the sausage for 30 to 40 minutes, depending on its thickness. Remove it from the cooking liquid and skin it carefully by making a long incision down its length and pulling the skin away to either side. Dust the hot sausage lightly with flour.

Roll out and trim the dough into two long strips approximately 5 cm (2 inches) wide. Wrap the sausage by winding the dough strips round it in a spiral. Seal the ends and joins of the dough with a little water. Put the brioche on a greased baking sheet, brush the dough with the egg yolk and set the brioche aside in a warm place to prove for about 2 hours.

Glaze the dough again and bake the brioche for 35 to 45 minutes in a preheated 220°C (425°F or Mark 7) oven. It should be golden-brown and well risen. Transfer the brioche to a serving dish and eat it hot.

A. DELPLANQUE AND S. CLOTEAUX
LES BASES DE LA CHARCUTERIE

Neapolitan Rustic Brioche

Brioche Rustica

If provolone cheese is not available, Gruyère or Cheddar may be used instead with equally good results.

The well in the centre of the brioche can be filled while still warm with peas or beans in a white sauce.

To make one 25 cm (10 inch) brioche

500 g	rich egg dough (*page 172*)	1 lb
100 g	prosciutto, coarsely chopped	3½ oz
150 g	*provolone* cheese, diced	5 oz
150 g	Bel Paese cheese, diced	5 oz
	freshly ground pepper	
100 g	Parmesan cheese, grated	3½ oz

Prepare the brioche dough in the usual way, but before the final rising, add the prosciutto, diced cheeses, pepper and grated Parmesan. Put the dough in a fluted 25 cm (10 inch) brioche mould with a central funnel; the dough should only half fill the mould. Leave the dough to prove in a warm place for 1 hour, or until doubled in bulk.

Bake the brioche in an oven preheated to 150°C (300°F or Mark 2) for about 45 minutes or until well risen and golden-brown. Rest the brioche for about 10 minutes after removing it from the oven, then turn it out on to a serving dish.

JEANNE CARÒLA FRANCESCONI
LA CUCINA NAPOLETANA

Cheese Brioche

Brioche au Fromage

To make one 20 cm (8 inch) brioche

250 g	rich egg dough (*page 172*)	8 oz
100 g	Gruyère cheese, 50 g (2 oz) grated and the rest diced	3½ oz
	salt and pepper	
1	egg, beaten	1

Prepare the rich egg dough in the usual way. Leave it to rise, then punch it down and mix in the grated and diced Gruyère cheese and a pinch of salt and pepper. Let the dough prove until doubled in bulk again, about 1 hour. Butter a brioche or savarin mould or a baking sheet. Put the dough into the mould or shape into a ring if baking it on a baking sheet. With a sharp knife or razor blade, make two or three shallow diagonal incisions in the dough. Glaze the brioche with the beaten egg and bake it in an oven preheated to 200°C (400°F or Mark 6) for 30 minutes or until it is well risen and golden-brown.

PIERRE ANDROUET
LA CUISINE AU FROMAGE

Polish Festival Bread

Polnisches Feiertagsbrot

To make one 23 cm (9 inch) loaf

500 g	strong plain flour	1 lb
30 g	fresh yeast or 1 tbsp dried yeast	1 oz
8 cl	tepid water	3 fl oz
½ tsp	salt	½ tsp
½ tsp	ground cinnamon	½ tsp
90 g	sugar	3 oz
25 g	raisins	1 oz
25 g	mixed nuts, chopped	1 oz
1	lemon, rind grated	1
¼ litre	yogurt	8 fl oz
3	egg yolks, lightly beaten	3
100 g	butter, melted and cooled to tepid	3½ oz

In a warm bowl mix the flour, salt, cinnamon, sugar, raisins, nuts and lemon rind and then gently fold in the yogurt and egg yolks. Dissolve the yeast in the water. If using dried yeast, add 1 teaspoon of sugar. Leave the yeast mixture in a warm place until it foams, about 15 minutes. Add the yeast to the other ingredients, then stir in the butter and beat thoroughly until smooth. Cover with a cloth, and leave in a warm place until the dough has doubled in bulk, about 2 hours.

Knock back the dough and knead it again for about 10 minutes, adding a little additional flour if the dough feels too sticky. Shape it into an oval ball and lay it on a buttered baking sheet. Leave the loaf in a warm place to prove for about 50 minutes. Bake it in an oven preheated to 220°C (425°F or Mark 7) for about 40 to 50 minutes, until golden-brown.

JUTTA KÜRTZ
DAS BROT BACKBUCH

—◆—

Butter Cake

Butterkuchen

The coarse sugar here is hagelzucker, *large sugar crystals used throughout central Europe for decorating cakes and buns. Coffee sugar or other large sugar crystals can be used.*

To make one 50 by 40 cm (20 by 16 inch) cake

500 g	strong plain flour	1 lb
30 g	fresh yeast or 1 tbsp dried yeast	1 oz
200 g	butter, softened	7 oz
15 cl	tepid milk	¼ pint
6	egg yolks	6
60 g	sugar	2 oz

Almond topping		
125 g	almonds, blanched and chopped	4 oz
1	egg, beaten	1
30 g	coarse sugar	1 oz
60 g	butter	2 oz

Mix the yeast with the milk and 300 g (10 oz) of the flour; leave this sponge to rise for 2 hours in a warm place until doubled in bulk. Add the remaining flour, yolks, butter and sugar. Knead well for 10 minutes, then leave for 30 minutes to prove.

Roll out the dough to fit a 50 by 40 cm (20 by 16 inch) Swiss roll tin. Lay it in a well-buttered tin, brush it with the beaten egg, sprinkle it with the almonds and coarse sugar and dot it with the butter. Bake the cake in an oven preheated to 180°C (350°F or Mark 4) for 45 minutes or until golden.

DOROTHEE V. HELLERMANN
DAS KOCHBUCH AUS HAMBURG

—◆—

Yeast Coffee Cake

Babka Drożdżowa

To make one 25 cm (10 inch) cake

500 g	strong plain flour	1 lb
15 g	fresh yeast or 2 tsp dried yeast	½ oz
150 g	butter	5 oz
90 g	sugar	3 oz
3	egg yolks	3
90 g	sultanas	3 oz
15 cl	tepid milk	¼ pint
	salt	
30 g	almonds, slivered	1 oz
	icing sugar	

Cream the butter until soft, then work in the sugar. Continue stirring and add the egg yolks, one by one. Add the sultanas.

Dissolve the yeast in 1 tablespoon of the milk and stir it until it is smooth. Allow it to stand in a warm place for 10 minutes. Add a pinch of salt to the butter and egg mixture and stir in the yeast, flour and remaining milk. Beat very well with a wooden spoon until the dough develops bubbles and looks smooth and glossy, about 15 minutes. Butter and flour a brioche mould and stick slivered almonds against the fluted sides for decoration. Put in the dough and leave it to rise in a warm place until doubled in bulk, about 30 to 40 minutes.

Bake the cake in an oven preheated to 220°C (425°F or Mark 7) for 10 minutes. Reduce the heat to 190°C (375°F or Mark 5) and bake for a further 50 minutes. Leave the cake to cool and sprinkle it with icing sugar.

LILI KOWALSKA
COOKING THE POLISH WAY

French Sally Lunn Cake

Solilemme

The rich egg bread known variously as Solilemme, Solimene *and* Solimeme *is said to have originated in Alsace in eastern France. The meaning of the name is obscure. However, the dough and serving method are so similar to the English Sally Lunn cake that there are grounds for believing that they share a common origin. There was a pastry cook named Sally Lunn, in Bath in the 18th century, but she may well have adopted the French* Solilemme *and altered its name simply because it was so similar to her own.*

To make one 20 cm (8 inch) brioche

375 g	strong plain flour	13 oz
15 g	fresh yeast or 2 tsp dried yeast	½ oz
5 tbsp	tepid water	5 tbsp
1 tsp	salt	1 tsp
30 g	castor sugar	1 oz
4	egg yolks	4
300 g	butter, softened	10 oz
10 cl	double cream	3½ fl oz
1	egg, beaten	1

Sift 100 g (3½ oz) of the flour into a bowl and make a well in the centre. Dissolve the yeast in 3 tablespoons of the water and mix it into the flour. Add the rest of the water and beat the mixture into a smooth, soft dough. Cover with a cloth and leave in a warm place to double in bulk, about 1 hour.

Sift the rest of the flour into a large bowl, together with the salt and sugar, and make a well in the centre. Mix in the egg yolks, 150g (5 oz) of the butter, and the cream. Knead the mixture for about 10 minutes, until it is smooth and elastic and no longer sticks to the bowl. Knead in the yeast dough.

Butter a 20 cm (8 inch) brioche mould or *kugelhopf* mould and put the dough into it—it should only half fill the mould. Cover the mould with a cloth and leave it in a warm place to double in bulk—about 30 minutes.

Using a pastry brush, glaze the top of the dough with the beaten egg. Bake the bread in an oven preheated to 200°C (400°F or Mark 6) for 1 hour, until it is golden-brown and a toothpick inserted into the centre comes out clean. Remove the bread from the oven and unmould it; slice it immediately in two horizontally, turn the top half upside-down and season each half with a pinch of salt. Melt the rest of the butter and pour it over each cut half of the bread. Put the two halves together again and serve the bread hot.

CÉLINE VENCE AND ROBERT J. COURTINE
THE GRAND MASTERS OF FRENCH CUISINE

Currant Bread

Bara Brith

To make two 20 by 10 cm (8 by 4 inch) loaves

1 kg	strong plain flour	2 lb
30 g	fresh yeast or 1 tbsp dried yeast	1 oz
175 g	currants	6 oz
350 g	butter, cut into pieces	12 oz
175 g	soft brown sugar	6 oz
12.5 cl	tepid milk	4 fl oz
¼ tsp	grated nutmeg or mixed spice	¼ tsp
½ tsp	salt	½ tsp
175 g	sultanas	6 oz
90 g	raisins	3 oz
60 g	mixed candied peel, chopped	2 oz
2	eggs, well beaten	2
2 tsp	black treacle	2 tsp
35 cl	tepid water	12 fl oz

Put the flour in a mixing bowl and allow it to stand in a warm place for a short while. Rub the butter into the flour, add all the other dry ingredients except 1 teaspoon of the sugar and mix thoroughly. Cream the yeast with the remaining sugar in a smaller basin and blend it with the milk. Make a well in the centre of the dry ingredients, pour the yeast mixture into it and sprinkle a little additional flour over it. Cover the dough and allow it to stand in a warm place for a few minutes, until just beginning to rise. Pour the beaten eggs on to the dough and proceed to knead to a soft dough.

Melt the treacle in the tepid water and gradually add it to the dough, while kneading. Cover the bowl with a cloth and allow the dough to rise in a warm place for 1½ hours or until it has doubled in bulk. Then turn it out on to a well-floured board, divide it in half and put it into two well-buttered 1 litre (2 lb) loaf tins. Leave the loaves to prove in a warm place for about 30 minutes, or until they have nearly risen to the rims of the tins. Then bake the loaves in an oven preheated to 180°C (350°F or Mark 4) for 1 to 1½ hours, so that the tops are browned and the loaves sound hollow when rapped.

S. MINWEL TIBBOTT
WELSH FARE

Sally Lunns

Sally Lunn, who was born and lived in Bath, in south-west England, in the 18th century, is reputed to have made the tea-cakes which took her name from her own private recipe. She sent them hot (maybe carried them herself) to all the important tea-parties in Bath. A special round Sally Lunn tin, 6 cm (2½ inches) deep, is still used for these hot delicacies. When baked, the cake is cut into horizontal slices and the slices toasted and buttered; then the slices are put together again and the Sally Lunn is served hot in its original form. Sometimes in the past the cakes appear to have been spread with hot scalded cream in place of butter.

To make one 16 cm (6 inch) cake

175 g	strong plain flour, sifted	6 oz
15 g	fresh yeast or 2 tsp dried yeast dissolved in 3 tbsp tepid water	$\frac{1}{2}$ oz
20 cl	tepid single cream	7 fl oz
	salt	
3 tsp	castor sugar	3 tsp
2	egg yolks, beaten	2
75 g	butter, softened	$2\frac{1}{2}$ oz
About 1 tbsp tepid milk		About 1 tbsp

Put about a quarter of the flour into a basin and set the rest aside in another bowl in a warm place. Mix 4 tablespoons of the cream with yeast, and leave in a warm place for 10 minutes until the yeast begins to foam. Work the cream and yeast mixture into the small amount of flour until a light dough is formed. Put this into a warm place and let it rise to twice its original bulk.

To the larger quantity of flour, add a pinch of salt, the sugar, egg yolks, butter and the remaining cream. Work together for 4 to 5 minutes, making a light mixture. Then add the yeast mixture and work together for 5 to 6 minutes.

Butter and flour a 20 cm (8 inch) Sally Lunn or cake tin about 6 to 8 cm ($2\frac{1}{2}$ to 3 inches) deep. Half fill the tin with the dough and stand it on a baking tin in a warm place until the contents rise to the top of the tin. Then brush the top with the tepid milk and bake in an oven preheated to 230°C (450°F or Mark 8) for about 15 minutes or until golden-brown.

When cooked, turn the cake out of the tin and let it cool on a rack if not wanted at once.

GERTRUDE MANN
A BOOK OF CAKES

Curly Murly

The technique of plaiting dough is demonstrated on page 26.

To vary the recipe, omit the citron peel and nuts from the batter, and sprinkle 60 g (2 oz) of shredded, blanched almonds mixed with 60 g (2 oz) of castor sugar equally over the wreaths. When hazelnuts are in season, sprinkle one or two shredded hazelnuts over the rolls as they are iced. Sometimes, Curly Murlies used to be filled with an almond paste before plaiting. To make the paste, beat 40 g ($1\frac{1}{2}$ oz) of butter to a cream with 125 g (4 oz) of castor sugar, then stir in 150 g (5 oz) of ground almonds, a pinch of grated lemon rind, and one lightly beaten egg. Roll the strips very thinly. Spread the filling down the middle. Wet the edges. Fold in two and plait.

To make two 22 cm (9 inch) wreaths

560 g	strong plain flour	1 lb 2 oz
60 g	fresh yeast or 2 tbsp dried yeast	2 oz
$\frac{1}{4}$ litre	tepid milk	8 fl oz
125 g	castor sugar	4 oz
275 g	butter, softened	9 oz
3	eggs	3
$\frac{3}{4}$ tsp	salt	$\frac{3}{4}$ tsp
$1\frac{1}{2}$ tsp	grated lemon rind	$1\frac{1}{2}$ tsp
30 g	citron peel, chopped	1 oz
125 g	hazelnuts, chopped	4 oz
	Royal icing	
125 g	icing sugar, sifted	4 oz
2 tbsp	boiling water	2 tbsp
$\frac{1}{2}$ tsp	vanilla extract or $\frac{3}{4}$ tsp lemon juice	$\frac{1}{2}$ tsp

Dissolve the yeast in the milk. Sift the flour. Stir 125 g (4 oz) of the flour into the milk. Cover the mixture and stand it in a warm place for about 30 minutes, until it is spongy. Sift the sugar. Beat the sugar with 250 g (8 oz) of the butter until creamy. Then beat in 1 egg at a time. Add the yeast sponge, salt and lemon rind and beat well, then gradually stir in the remaining flour. Beat for 5 minutes. Add the citron peel and nuts. Cover the dough with a cloth and leave it in a warm place until it has doubled its bulk—about 2 hours.

Then divide the dough into two equal portions. Roll each portion out into three long strips. Plait each set and shape it, wetting the ends and moulding them neatly together into a wreath about 22 cm (9 inches) in diameter. Place the two wreaths on a buttered baking sheet. Cover the wreaths and leave them in a warm place to rise for 30 minutes. Melt the remaining butter and use it to brush the tops of the wreaths. Bake them in an oven preheated to 180°C (350°F or Mark 4) until golden-brown—about 30 minutes. Cool them on a wire rack. To prepare the icing, mix the sifted icing sugar with the boiling water and add either vanilla extract or lemon juice. Cover the wreaths with the icing.

ELIZABETH CRAIG
THE SCOTTISH COOKERY BOOK

Poppy Seed Kugelhopf

Gugelhupf mit Mohnfülle

Any of the fillings given on page 173 may be substituted for the poppy seed in this recipe.

To make one 20 cm (8 inch) kugelhopf

500 g	strong plain flour	1 lb
30 g	fresh yeast or 1 tbsp dried yeast	1 oz
150 g	sugar	5 oz
¼ litre	tepid milk	8 fl oz
125 g	butter, softened	4 oz
6	egg yolks	6
¼ tsp	salt	¼ tsp
1	lemon, rind grated	1
60 g	almonds, blanched and split	2 oz
30 g	rusk or biscuit crumbs	2 oz
	icing sugar	

Poppy seed filling

125 g	poppy seeds, ground	4 oz
¼ litre	milk	8 fl oz
60 g	sugar	2 oz
1 tsp	vanilla sugar	1 tsp
	ground cinnamon	
30 g	butter	1 oz

Cream the yeast with 1 teaspoon of sugar, 2 tablespoons of milk and 1 teaspoon of flour and leave this sponge in a warm place until it foams, about 15 minutes. Beat all but 30 g (1 oz) of the butter and the rest of the sugar together, gradually incorporating the egg yolks. Add the salt, grated lemon rind and the yeast sponge. Gradually stir in the rest of the tepid milk alternately with the rest of the flour. Beat the dough well with a wooden spoon for about 10 minutes, cover and leave in a warm place to rise until it has doubled in bulk.

Meanwhile, prepare the filling. In a saucepan, simmer the poppy seeds, milk, sugar, vanilla sugar, a pinch of cinnamon and butter, stirring constantly until the butter has melted.

Butter a *kugelhopf* mould and sprinkle it with the crumbs. Scatter in the almonds and then put in half of the dough. Pour in the poppy seed filling and cover it with the rest of the dough. Leave the mould in a warm place, covered with a cloth, for the dough to prove for a further 30 minutes. Brush the top of the dough with the remaining 30 g (1 oz) of butter and bake the *kugelhopf* in an oven preheated to 200°C (400°F or Mark 6) for 45 minutes or until a skewer inserted into the *kugelhopf* comes out clean. Turn the *kugelhopf* out of the tin while still warm and dust it with icing sugar.

JOZA BRÍZOVÁ AND MARYNA KLIMENTOVÁ
TSCHECHISCHE KÜCHE

Old-Fashioned Viennese Kugelhopf

Alt-Wiener Patzerlgugelhupf

The name patzerlgugelhupf *derives from the* patzerln, *or slices of dough, used to fill the* kugelhopf *mould. The basic technique for making this type of* kugelhopf *is demonstrated on page 68. A list of alternative fillings is given on page 173.*

To make two 20 cm (8 inch) kugelhopfs

600 g	strong plain flour	1¼ lb
40 g	fresh yeast or 2 tbsp dried yeast	1½ oz
10 cl	tepid milk	3½ fl oz
100 g	sugar	3½ oz
30 g	vanilla sugar	1 oz
	salt	
4	eggs, beaten	4
2 tbsp	rum	2 tbsp
1 tsp	grated lemon rind	1 tsp
150 g	unsalted butter, in small pieces	5 oz
	icing sugar	

Walnut filling

90 g	walnuts, finely chopped	3 oz
1 tbsp	biscuit crumbs	1 tbsp
¼ tsp	ground ginger	¼ tsp
3 tbsp	milk	3 tbsp
40 g	sugar	1½ oz
15 g	butter	½ oz
2 tbsp	rum	2 tbsp

In a small bowl, dissolve the yeast in the milk. Put the flour, sugar, vanilla sugar and salt into a bowl. Make a well in the centre and add the yeast, eggs, rum and lemon rind. Mix these ingredients together. Turn the dough out on to a work surface.

Knead it vigorously for about 10 minutes, then knead in the butter until well mixed. Place the dough in a bowl, cover it with a towel and leave it to rise in a warm place until the dough has trebled in bulk, about 1½ hours.

While the dough is rising, make the filling. Mix the walnuts with the biscuit crumbs and add the ginger. Heat the milk with the sugar and butter until they have dissolved, and add the rum. Pour this over the walnut mixture. Allow the filling to cool to tepid.

Generously butter a 4 litre (7 pint) *kugelhopf* mould and dust it with flour. On a floured surface, roll the dough into a thick sausage shape, about 10 cm (4 inches) in diameter. Slice it into 25 pieces, and spread a little of the filling over each slice, pressing the filling well down into the dough. Cover the bottom of the mould with the slices. Add another layer of slices, arranging them so that they cover the spaces between the first layer; in this manner continue to layer slices until the mould is half full. Cover the mould and leave the dough to prove in a warm place for about 1 hour, or until it has almost risen to the rim of the mould.

Bake the *kugelhopf* on the centre shelf of an oven preheated to 180°C (350°F or Mark 4) for 45 to 50 minutes, or until the dough has slightly shrunk away from the sides of the mould and the top is well browned. Leave the *kugelhopf* to cool in the mould for a few minutes, then turn it out on to a wire rack and dust it with icing sugar.

EVA BAKOS
MEHLSPEISEN AUS ÖSTERREICH

Viennese Kugelhopf

Germgugelhupf

To make one 20 cm (8 inch) kugelhopf

350 g	strong plain flour	12 oz
30 g	fresh yeast or 1 tbsp dried yeast	1 oz
15 cl	tepid milk and water in equal quantities	¼ pint
	salt	
125 g	butter	4 oz
175 g	sugar	6 oz
1	small egg	1
2	egg yolks	2
60 g	sultanas	2 oz
4 tbsp	castor sugar or vanilla sugar	4 tbsp

Make a yeast sponge by dissolving the yeast in the milk and water, and then adding 1 teaspoon of the sugar and a quarter of the flour. Leave for about 20 minutes until it is frothy.

Sieve the rest of the flour into a large bowl with a pinch of salt. In another bowl, cream together the butter, sugar, egg and egg yolks. As soon as the yeast sponge is ready, add it to the rest of the flour, together with the butter and egg mixture. Knead the dough for about 10 minutes and leave it to rise until doubled in bulk, about 1½ hours.

Butter a 20 cm (8 inch) *kugelhopf* mould; sprinkle it with the sultanas and a little flour. Put the dough into the mould and leave it to prove for about 30 minutes, or until the dough reaches the rim.

Bake the *kugelhopf* in an oven preheated to 200°C (400°F or Mark 6) for about 45 minutes, or until the cake begins to shrink from the sides of the mould. Test it with a skewer. If the skewer comes out clean, turn off the oven. Leave the cake in the oven for a few minutes. Then take it out and turn it out on to a plate. Sprinkle the *kugelhopf* with castor or vanilla sugar, and leave it to cool before cutting.

ROSL PHILPOT
VIENNESE COOKERY

Alsatian Kugelhopf

Kougelhopf

This recipe for the classic Alsatian version of the kugelhopf *was selected by the Club Prosper Montagné.*

To make one 20 cm (8 inch) kugelhopf

1 kg	strong plain flour	2 lb
30 g	fresh yeast or 1 tbsp dried yeast	1 oz
½ litre	tepid milk	16 fl oz
150 g	castor sugar	5 oz
1 tsp	salt	1 tsp
3	eggs	3
300 g	butter, softened	10 oz
150 g	sultanas, soaked in 15 cl (¼ pint) water or 5 tbsp of kirsch	5 oz
5 tbsp	kirsch (optional)	5 tbsp
75 g	almonds, blanched and split	2½ oz

Dissolve the yeast in half of the milk with 1 teaspoon of the castor sugar and leave it in a warm place until it is frothy, about 15 minutes. Then add about 250 g (8 oz) of the flour to make a sponge. Leave this sponge in a warm place to rise until doubled in bulk, about 1 hour.

In a separate bowl, mix the remaining flour with the salt, eggs and the rest of the milk, and knead energetically for about 15 minutes, lifting the mixture with the hands until it becomes smooth and elastic. Cream the butter and the rest of the sugar together and add them to the mixture. Then work in the yeast sponge, and knead the dough thoroughly for 5 minutes or until it is very silky and springy. Place the dough in a bowl, cover it with a cloth and leave it to rise in a warm place for about 1 hour or until doubled in bulk. Knead it again, break open the dough and mix in the sultanas—if soaked in water, the kirsch may be added now, if desired.

Butter a 20 cm (8 inch) *kugelhopf* mould and decorate the bottom with the almonds, then put the dough into the mould. The dough should not come more than two-thirds of the way up the sides of the mould. Leave the dough to prove once more for about 30 minutes, or until it reaches the rim of the mould. Bake the *kugelhopf* in an oven preheated to 180°C (350°F or Mark 4) for about 45 minutes or until golden-brown. If it browns too quickly, cover with a sheet of greaseproof paper.

FOOD AND WINES FROM ALSACE, FRANCE

Leek Pie

Porrata

Pancetta *is salt pork belly, a speciality of Parma. If it is not available, substitute green or boiled ham.*

To make one 25 cm (10 inch) pie

375 g	strong plain flour	13½ oz
60 g	fresh yeast or 2 tbsp dried yeast	2 oz
¼ litre	tepid water	8 fl oz
2	eggs	2
1½ tsp	salt	1½ tsp
	Leek and pancetta filling	
2 kg	leeks, rinsed, sliced into rings, soaked for 10 minutes in cold water and rinsed several times in fresh water to remove all the grit	4 lb
175 g	*pancetta*, chopped	6 oz
3 tbsp	olive oil	3 tbsp
15 g	butter	½ oz
	salt and pepper	
4	eggs, beaten	4

To make the filling, heat the olive oil and butter in a large fireproof casserole. When the butter is melted, add the leeks and sprinkle them with salt and pepper. Cover the casserole and cook very slowly until the leeks are soft (30 to 40 minutes), stirring frequently with a wooden spoon. Remove the casserole from the heat and let the leeks stand until they are cold (about 1 hour).

Meanwhile, make the pie crust. Dissolve the yeast in the water. Place all but 2 tablespoons of the flour in a mound on a floured board. Make a well in the flour, then pour in the dissolved yeast and add the eggs and salt. Mix with a wooden spoon, incorporating the flour from the inside rim of the well, little by little. When the dough is firm, start kneading. Knead it very thoroughly for about 20 minutes.

Sprinkle the dough with the remaining flour and cover it with a tea towel. Let it stand in a warm place, away from draughts, until doubled in size (about 1½ hours).

Place the 4 beaten eggs in the casserole with the leeks and mix well with a wooden spoon. Oil a 25 cm (10 inch) spring-form tin. When the dough has risen, gently roll it, using a rolling pin, into a large sheet about 1 cm (½ inch) thick. Fit the dough into the tin, letting excess dough hang over the edges.

Sprinkle the *pancetta* over the dough, then, using a perforated spoon, fill the crust with the leek mixture. With a knife, cut off the dough round the edges of the tin. Turn the edges inwards over the leeks, to make a decorative border round them, but do not cover them completely. Sprinkle the top of the dish liberally with pepper, then place the pie in an oven preheated to 200°C (400°C or Mark 6) for 45 to 50 minutes, or until the filling has set and the dough is golden-brown.

Remove the leek pie from the oven and allow it to cool for 15 minutes before opening the spring-form tin. Remove the pie from the tin and transfer it to a serving dish.

GIULIANO BUGIALLI
THE FINE ART OF ITALIAN COOKING

Polish Rice and Mushroom Kulibiak

Kulebiak z Ciasta Krucho-Drozdzowego z Rýzem i Grzybami

The kulibiak *can be filled with any number of sweet or savoury mixtures. Savoury fillings include fish and chopped hard-boiled egg, minced meat and* viaziga—*the dried spinal cord of the sturgeon which is sold in dried form. Sweet fillings consist of fruit in season.*

To make one 20 by 15 cm (8 by 6 inch) pie

250 g	strong plain flour	8 oz
15 g	fresh yeast or 2 tsp dried yeast	½ oz
1 tsp	sugar	1 tsp
75 g	butter	2½ oz
2	egg yolks, beaten	2
2	eggs, beaten	2
	salt	
4 tbsp	double cream	4 tbsp
	Rice and mushroom filling	
200 g	rice	7 oz
30 g	dried mushrooms, washed and soaked for 4 hours in 15 cl (¼ pint) water	1 oz
	salt and pepper	
40 g	butter	1½ oz
50 g	onion, finely chopped	2 oz
2	eggs, hard-boiled and chopped	2

First prepare the filling. Simmer the dried mushrooms in the soaking liquid for 20 minutes or until they are tender. Rinse the rice thoroughly, drain it and put it in a saucepan with twice its volume of liquid—use the water in which the mushrooms were cooked, made up to the right quantity with boiling water. Season the rice and liquid with salt, add half the butter and bring the mixture to boiling point. Simmer it for 20 minutes or until all the liquid has been absorbed. Fry the onion to a light golden colour in the remaining butter. Add the hard-boiled eggs to the cooked rice, together with the mushrooms, onion, salt and pepper.

To make the dough, mix the yeast with the sugar and leave for 2 to 3 minutes until the mixture liquefies (if using dried yeast, add 3 tablespoons of tepid water). Sieve the flour on to a board. Using a knife, blend the butter with the flour. Add the egg yolks, 1 egg, a pinch of salt, the yeast mixture and the cream. Continue chopping and folding the mixture with the knife, until it sticks together. Knead the dough quickly until it is smooth, about 5 minutes, and roll it out into a long rectangle about 30 by 20 cm (12 by 8 inches) and 1 cm ($\frac{1}{2}$ inch) thick. Lay it on a greased and floured baking sheet.

Spread the filling down the centre of the dough rectangle. Fold over the two longer sides of the rectangle to the centre, pinching them together firmly between thumb and finger, to make a raised, decorative centre.

Leave the *kulibiak* in a warm place for about 1$\frac{1}{2}$ hours until it has doubled in bulk, and brush it with the egg. Bake it in a preheated 180°C (350°F or Mark 4) oven for about 1 hour until it is lightly browned. Place the *kulibiak* on a long serving dish and slice it into portions.

HELENA HAWLICZKOWA
KUCHNIA POLSKA

Cabbage and Mushroom Kulibiak

Kulebiak z Kapusta i Grzybami

To make one 25 by 20 cm (10 by 8 inch) pie

500 g	rich egg dough (*page 172*)	1 lb
1	medium-sized cabbage	1
30 g	dried mushrooms, washed and soaked for 4 hours in 15 cl ($\frac{1}{4}$ pint) water	1 oz
30 g	butter	1 oz
1	medium-sized onion, sliced	1
3	eggs, hard-boiled and chopped	3
	salt and pepper	
1	egg, beaten	1

Prepare the rich egg dough. To make the filling, parboil the whole cabbage in salted water for 5 minutes, drain and shred it. In a saucepan, melt the butter and add the cabbage and onion and stew until the cabbage is tender, about 10 minutes. Cook the mushrooms in as little water as possible without scorching until done, about 5 minutes, then chop them and add them to the cabbage. Add the hard-boiled eggs. Season to taste and mix thoroughly.

When the rich egg dough has had its final rising, divide it in half and roll each piece into a 25 by 20 cm (10 by 8 inch) rectangle. Lay one rectangle on a floured baking sheet. Spread the filling over it, leaving a 5 cm (2 inch) margin all round the dough. Cover the mixture with the second rectangle and press the edges firmly together. Brush the *kulibiak* with the egg. Bake it in a preheated 220°C (425°F or Mark 7) oven for about 20 minutes or until golden-brown.

MARJA OCHOROWICZ-MONATOWA
POLISH COOKERY

Jewish Bagels

Bagels originated in Austria, where they were called beugeln, *meaning "rings". An alternative method of shaping bagels to the one described below is shown on page 79.*

Bagels are best served sliced through the middle (toasted, if liked) and buttered. Good with cream cheese or smoked fish, they also make an unusual breakfast roll.

To make 24 bagels

400 g	strong plain flour	14 oz
15 g	fresh yeast or 2 tsp dried yeast	$\frac{1}{2}$ oz
$\frac{1}{4}$ litre	milk	8 fl oz
50 g	butter	2 oz
30 g	castor sugar	1 oz
$\frac{1}{2}$ tsp	salt	$\frac{1}{2}$ tsp
1	egg, yolk separated from white, yolk beaten with 1 tsp cold water	1
	poppy seeds, sesame seeds or coarse salt crystals (optional)	

Bring the milk to the boil, remove the pan from the heat and add the butter and sugar. Stir until the butter has dissolved. Pour the milk mixture into a bowl and cool it to tepid. Then stir in the yeast, and leave the mixture aside for about 10 minutes, until it is frothy.

Beat the egg white and the salt into the yeast liquid and then gradually work in the flour. Mix together to form a smooth, soft dough. Turn the dough out on to a lightly floured surface and knead it until it is smooth and no longer sticky, about 15 minutes. Form the dough into a ball and place it in an oiled or buttered polythene bag; leave it aside in a warm place for about 1 hour, or until it has doubled in bulk.

Divide the dough into 24 pieces and roll each piece into a strip about the length of a pencil and the width of your finger, tapering the strips slightly at both ends. Shape the strips into rings, pinching the ends together firmly. Leave the rings on the floured surface until they begin to rise, about 10 minutes.

Bring a large pan of water to the boil, place the bagels a few at a time into the boiling water and cook for about 15 seconds, until they puff up. (Overcooking will cause the bagels to break up and lose their shape, so remove them quickly and carefully with a slotted spoon.)

Place the bagels on a buttered baking sheet. Use the diluted egg yolk to brush over the bagels before baking. If liked, they may be sprinkled with poppy seeds, sesame seeds or a very few coarse salt crystals. Bake the bagels in a preheated 200°C (400°F or Mark 6) oven for about 20 minutes, until brown and crisp. Cool them on a wire rack.

LORNA WALKER AND JOYCE HUGHES
THE COMPLETE BREAD BOOK

Yeast Puff Pastry

Viennese Filled Croissants

Croissants Viennois Fourrés

Another method of making and shaping croissants is demonstrated on pages 70-72. Sweet croissants can also be filled with jam, in which case they are not iced but glazed with egg yolk before baking and dusted with icing sugar afterwards.

The croissant arose from a battle. In 1689, the Ottoman Turks laid siege to Vienna. They devised a plan to tunnel into the heart of the city by night, and would have succeeded, had not the bakers, working through the night, heard them. They raised the alarm and saved the city. For their valour, the bakers were allowed to make a crescent-shaped bun, representing the Ottoman crescent moon.

To make 12 croissants

500 g	strong plain flour	1 lb
15 g	fresh yeast or 2 tsp dried yeast	½ oz
200 g	butter, softened	7 oz
About 8 cl	tepid milk	About 3 fl oz
1 tsp	salt	1 tsp
1 tbsp	sugar	1 tbsp

Almond cream filling

50 g	almonds, blanched and ground	2 oz
1	egg	1
2	egg yolks	2
75 g	sugar	2½ oz
30 g	flour	1 oz
½ litre	milk, boiled with a piece of vanilla pod for 3 minutes	16 fl oz
30 g	butter	1 oz

Iced almond topping

100 g	almonds, blanched and slivered	3½ oz
1	egg white, lightly beaten	1
About 150 g	icing sugar	About 5 oz

First prepare a yeast sponge by diluting the yeast with 2 to 3 tablespoons of the tepid milk. Blend in one-third of the flour to make a soft dough. Cover the mixture and leave it to rise for 30 minutes in a warm place. Mix the rest of the flour with half of the butter, the salt, sugar and the rest of the milk. Knead until a smooth, elastic dough is obtained. Mix this with the well-risen yeast sponge. Roll the dough into a ball, cover, and leave it to rise in a cool place for at least 2 hours, or preferably overnight in the refrigerator until well risen.

Roll out the ball of dough into a rectangle. Divide the rest of the butter into small pieces and dot them over the dough. Fold the sides of the rectangle into the middle, enclosing the butter as if it were in a purse.

Roll out the dough again and fold it in three, then give the dough a quarter turn and roll it out again. Fold it in three, cover, and leave it to rest for 20 minutes in the refrigerator.

Repeat this rolling and folding method twice more, letting the dough rest, covered, for 20 minutes in the refrigerator between each rolling. Then roll the dough out a final time into a rectangle about 3 mm (⅛ inch) thick. Slice the rectangle into 12 equilateral triangles with 15 cm (6 inch) sides. Roll up each triangle, starting from the base and rolling towards the apex, then bend the ends slightly to make a crescent shape. Place the croissants on lightly buttered baking sheets and leave them to prove. The time needed will depend on the temperature of the room—20 minutes in a warm place, several hours in a cool one or left overnight in the refrigerator.

Bake the croissants in an oven preheated to 190°C (375°F or Mark 5) for about 20 minutes, or until they are well risen and browned on the bottom.

Remove the croissants from the oven and cool them on wire racks. While they are cooling, make the filling and the icing. To make the filling, mix the egg and the egg yolks with the sugar, flour and ground almonds. Gradually add the milk, stirring constantly. Put the mixture in a pan and simmer it over a gentle heat, stirring constantly until the mixture begins to bubble. Remove it from the heat and stir in the butter. Mix until the butter has dissolved and leave to cool.

Split the croissants lengthwise. Fill them with the cream filling and sandwich them together again.

Beat the egg white and sugar to form a stiff icing. Toast the almonds in an ungreased frying pan until they are lightly browned all over. Ice the croissants while the icing is still soft, stick the slivered almonds into the icing, and leave it to set.

B. DESCHAMPS AND J.-CL. DESCHAINTRE
LE LIVRE DE L'APPRENTI PÂTISSIER

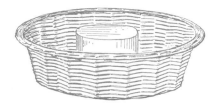

Danish Pastries

Wienerbrød

Despite the name given to this yeast puff dough in English-speaking countries, in Denmark, Danish pastry is called Wienerbrød, reflecting its true origin. About 100 years ago, the bakers of Copenhagen went on strike. Their employers retaliated by importing bakers from Vienna, and the Viennese method of folding cold butter into yeast dough became popular. The technique of rolling and folding butter into the dough is shown on page 70. Ways of making the cockscomb and alternative shapes are shown on pages 74-77.

To make 12 pastries (6 of each shape)

250 g	strong plain flour	8 oz
15 g	fresh yeast or 2 tsp dried yeast and ½ teaspoon sugar	½ oz
8 cl	tepid water	3 fl oz
1	egg, beaten	1
1 tsp	sugar	1 tsp
	salt	
30 g	lard	1 oz
150 g	butter, slightly salted	5 oz

Fruit snail filling

1	egg, beaten	1
30 g	butter, softened	1 oz
30 g	castor sugar	1 oz
1 tsp	ground cinnamon	1 tsp
30 g	sultanas	1 oz
60 g	icing sugar	2 oz
1 tsp	water	1 tsp

Cockscomb filling

30 g	butter, softened	1 oz
30 g	castor sugar	1 oz
30 g	macaroons, crushed, or 3 tbsp apple purée or lemon curd	1 oz
1	egg, beaten	1
15 g	almonds, blanched and chopped	½ oz

Blend the fresh yeast into the tepid water. If using dried yeast, dissolve the sugar in the water and then sprinkle the yeast on the mixture. Leave until frothy, 15 to 20 minutes.

Add the beaten egg to the yeast liquid. In a large mixing bowl, mix the flour, sugar and salt. Rub the lard into the flour, add the yeast liquid and mix to a soft dough. Turn the dough out on to a floured board and knead it until it is smooth and elastic, about 10 minutes. Place the dough in a lightly oiled polythene bag and refrigerate it for about 10 minutes.

With a palette knife, soften the butter and shape it into a rectangle about 1 cm (½ inch) thick. On a floured work surface, roll out the dough to approximately 25 cm (10 inches) square. Spread the butter down the centre of the square to within 2.5 cm (1 inch) of the edges. Fold the sides over the butter to overlap in the middle by about 1 cm (½ inch); seal the bottom and top. Roll out the dough into a rectangle about 45 by 15 cm (18 by 6 inches). Fold it evenly in three. Return the dough to the polythene bag and allow it to rest in the refrigerator for 10 minutes. Then return it to the floured work surface and roll it out in the opposite direction. Repeat the rolling, folding and resting process twice more, ensuring that the dough is rolled in a different direction each time. Return the dough to the polythene bag and refrigerate it for at least 4 hours, or overnight. The dough will then be ready for use.

To make the fruit snails, roll out half the dough into a 35 by 15 cm (15 by 6 inch) rectangle. Brush the two short ends with beaten egg to give a 2.5 cm (1 inch) beaten egg margin at both ends. Cream the butter with the sugar and cinnamon. Spread this mixture on the dough and sprinkle it with sultanas. Roll up the dough from one short end to make a fat Swiss roll shape. Slice this roll into six pieces and place them on a buttered baking sheet. Flatten them slightly with your palm and brush with beaten egg. Leave to prove in a warm place for 30 minutes, or until well risen, before baking.

To make the cockscombs, roll out the rest of the dough into a 30 by 20 cm (12 by 8 inch) rectangle. Slice the dough into six 10 cm (4 inch) squares. Cream the butter with the castor sugar and fold in the macaroons, or the apple purée or lemon curd. Place a little of this filling in the centre of each square. Brush the rest of the surface of the dough square with a little of the beaten egg, fold the square in half and make 6 to 8 incisions along one edge. Bend each "comb" so that the "teeth" fan out. Brush the combs with the rest of the egg and scatter chopped almonds on them. Transfer the cockscombs to a buttered baking sheet and leave them to prove for 20 to 30 minutes, or until they are well risen.

Bake the snails and cockscombs in an oven preheated to 200°C (400°F or Mark 6) for 10 minutes. Then reduce the heat to 180°C (350°F or Mark 4) and bake for a further 10 to 15 minutes, or until the pastries are golden-brown.

Cool the pastries on a wire rack. To ice the fruit snails, sieve the icing sugar, blend in the water and beat the mixture until it is smooth. Trickle the icing over the pastries.

PAULINE VIOLA AND KNUD RAVNKILDE
COOKING WITH A DANISH FLAVOUR

Yugoslav Walnut Crescents

Kiflice od Sala

A method for shaping crescent rolls is shown on page 72.

To make 32 croissants

500 g	strong plain flour	1 lb
15 g	fresh yeast or 2 tsp dried yeast	½ oz
250 g	beef suet, chilled and chopped finely	8 oz
8 cl	tepid milk	3 fl oz
1	lemon rind, grated	1
1 tsp	salt	1 tsp
40 g	icing sugar	1½ oz
2	egg yolks	2

Vanilla and walnut filling

200 g	walnuts, ground	7 oz
1 tsp	vanilla sugar	1 tsp
200 g	castor sugar	7 oz
8 cl	milk	3 fl oz

Walnut topping

60 g	walnuts, ground	2 oz
1	egg yolk, beaten	1
45 g	vanilla sugar	1½ oz

In a bowl, mix 200 g (7 oz) of the flour and the suet. Divide the mixture into three equal parts and leave for 30 minutes.

Dissolve the yeast in the milk and add it to the remaining flour in a warmed mixing bowl, together with the lemon rind, salt, icing sugar and the egg yolks, and knead well. Let the dough rest for 15 minutes.

Roll the dough out into a rectangle 5 mm (¼ inch) thick. Take one-third of the suet and flour mixture and spread it in an even layer over two-thirds of the dough. Fold the suet-covered portion of the dough in half, then fold the plain dough over the top. Let the dough stand for 30 minutes. Give the dough a quarter turn, roll out again, sprinkle it with another portion of reserved suet mixture; fold as before. Rest the dough for 30 minutes, then repeat the process, leaving the dough to rest for another 30 minutes.

Divide the dough into four equal pieces. Roll each into a round 28 cm (11 inches) across. Cut each round in half, then in quarters, then in eighths, making a total of 32 triangles.

Prepare the filling by mixing the walnuts with the castor sugar and vanilla sugar. Boil the milk, stir it into the mixture and allow it to cool until tepid. Put a teaspoonful of the walnut filling at the base of each triangle of dough and roll up the triangle towards the apex. Form crescents by bending the ends slightly. Place the crescents, spaced well apart, on three buttered and floured baking sheets. Brush the crescents with the egg yolk and sprinkle with ground walnuts. Leave the crescents to stand for about 30 minutes or until doubled in bulk. Bake the crescents in an oven preheated to 240°C (475°F or Mark 9) for about 20 minutes. Dust them while still hot with the vanilla sugar and serve warm.

SPACENIJA-PATA MARKOVIĆ
YUGOSLAV COOKBOOK

Flatbreads with Rillons and White Wine

Pogacice Sa Ovarcima I Belim Vinon

To prepare *rillons*, take 350 g (12 oz) of pork belly, dice it and place it in a large pan. Add 12.5 cl (4 fl oz) of milk and cook the pork belly over a brisk heat. When the small pieces of pork have turned a nice, light brown colour, drain off the rendered fat. Season the *rillons* with salt before they cool.

To make six 5 cm (2 inch) flatbreads

250 g	strong plain flour	8 oz
15 g	fresh yeast or 2 tsp dried yeast	½ oz
250 g	*rillons*, finely chopped	8 oz
15 cl	dry white wine	¼ pint
8 cl	tepid milk	3 fl oz
3	egg yolks, 1 beaten	3
	salt and pepper	
100 g	lard	3½ oz

Dissolve the yeast in the milk and leave until foaming, about 20 minutes. Sieve the flour on to a work surface, make a well in the centre and pour in the yeast mixture. Add the *rillons*, 2 of the egg yolks and a pinch each of salt and pepper. Mix to a dough, adding the wine to moisten. Knead the dough thoroughly for about 10 minutes, or until smooth and elastic. Leave it in a warm place to rise for about 30 minutes.

Roll out the dough with a rolling pin into a square about 1 cm (½ inch) thick. Smear the dough with the lard, fold it in half like a book and then roll it out again. Rotate the square through a quarter turn, and roll it out again. Repeat this process twice more, leaving the dough to rest for 30 minutes between rollings. Now roll out the dough to a thickness of about 2 cm (¾ inch) and using a biscuit cutter or a glass, cut the dough into six rounds about 5 cm (2 inches) across.

Grease a baking sheet with lard and place the rounds on it. With the tip of a knife, trace a grid pattern on the top of each round. Brush them with the beaten egg yolk and bake them in an oven preheated to 220°C (425°F or Mark 7) for about 25 minutes or until they turn golden-brown. Serve hot.

SPACENIJA-PATA MARKOVIĆ
YUGOSLAV COOKBOOK

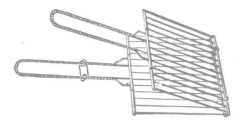

Chelsea Buns

To make 10 to 12 buns

600 g	strong plain flour	1¼ lb
15 g	fresh yeast or 2 tsp dried yeast	½ oz
15 cl	tepid milk	¼ pint
1 tsp	salt	1 tsp
2 tbsp	sugar	2 tbsp
250 g	butter, softened	8 oz
2	eggs, beaten	2
1	lemon, rind grated	1
1 tsp	ground cinnamon or mixed spice	1 tsp
30 g	castor sugar	1 oz
2 tbsp	milk, mixed with 2 tbsp castor sugar	2 tbsp
	Chelsea bun filling	
90 g	butter, cut into pieces	3 oz
90 g	currants, warmed	3 oz
90 g	soft brown sugar	3 oz

Pour half the milk over the yeast, and leave the mixture to foam. Mix the flour with the salt and sugar, then rub in the softened butter. Add the yeast and the eggs, lemon rind and spices, then mix to a fairly stiff dough with the rest of the milk. Cover the bowl and leave it in a warm place for about 2 hours, until the dough has risen very high and is extremely light and puffy.

Break down the dough, knead it well, and divide it into two equal portions. Roll each into a rectangle. Spread each rectangle of dough with an equal quantity of butter, warmed currants and brown sugar. Fold each rectangle in three by folding one third over a second third and folding the remaining third on top of the other two. Turn the rectangles through a quarter-circle, then roll them out again into rectangles approximately 20 by 25 cm (8 by 10 inches). Now roll up each piece of dough firmly, like a jam roll. Seal the edges with water. Cut these rolls into slices from 3 to 5 cm (1 to 2 inches) thick, according to the size you need your buns to end up, remembering that by the time they have been proved and baked, they will have doubled in volume.

Arrange the slices in even rows on a greased baking sheet—seven to a row used to be the rule of professional bakers—with a space of about 3 cm (1 inch) between each bun. The spacing is important, for during the proving period and as the buns grow in volume, so that they almost merge, they begin to assume the characteristically square shape. (If they are too far apart they remain round.) When they are all but touching, sprinkle them with the castor sugar. They are now ready for the oven. Bake them in an oven preheated to 220°C (425°F or Mark 7) for 15 minutes. During baking, the merging process is completed. As soon as you take the buns from the oven, brush them with the milk and sugar glaze. Separate them only after they have cooled for a few minutes.

ELIZABETH DAVID
ENGLISH BREAD AND YEAST COOKERY

Bulgarian Cheese Bread

Tootmanik s Gotovo Testo

This typical Bulgarian bread is often made with lard instead of butter. Sirene cheese is the Bulgarian equivalent of the Greek feta cheese, which may be substituted.

To make one 25 by 20 cm (10 by 8 inch) loaf		
500 g	basic bread dough (*page 171*)	1 lb
250 g	*sirene* cheese, grated	8 oz
150 g	butter, melted and cooled to lukewarm	5 oz
3	eggs, lightly beaten	3

Make the bread dough in the usual way and leave it to rise. When it has risen, divide it into nine pieces. Roll out each piece into a circle about 20 cm (8 inches) across. Spread six of the dough circles with half of the butter. Stack the buttered dough circles in pairs, buttered sides uppermost, then top each pair with an unbuttered dough circle. Roll out each "sandwich" into a sheet 25 by 20 cm (10 by 8 inches).

Reserve half of the beaten eggs for brushing the top of the bread, and mix the remainder with the grated cheese. Butter the tin with 2 tablespoons of the reserved melted butter. Place a sheet of dough in the tin, spread the surface with butter and spoon over half of the cheese and egg mixture. Cover with another sheet of dough, spread it with some more of the butter and spoon over the remaining cheese and egg mixture. Put the third sheet of dough on top and spread it with the rest of the butter. Prove the bread in a warm place for 1 to 1½ hours or until the dough has more than doubled in bulk.

Bake the bread in the upper part of an oven preheated to 180°C (350°F or Mark 4) for about 30 minutes. Remove the bread from the oven, brush the surface with the reserved egg, and bake for another 10 to 15 minutes, or until the crust is deep golden and shiny. Serve warm or cold, with tea or yogurt.

PENKA I. CHOLCHEVA
KNIGA ZA VSEKI DEN I VSEKI DOM

Aberdeen Butter Rolls

Buttery Rowies

To make about 20 rolls

500 g	strong plain flour	1 lb
30 g	fresh yeast or 1 tbsp dried yeast	1 oz
175 g	butter, softened	6 oz
1 tbsp	castor sugar	1 tbsp
1 tsp	salt	1 tsp
45 cl	tepid water	$\frac{3}{4}$ pint
175 g	lard, softened	6 oz

Sift the flour into a warm bowl. Mix the yeast with the sugar and salt, and add it to the flour along with the water. Mix well, cover the dough with a warm, damp towel and leave in a warm place until the dough rises to twice its bulk.

Beat the butter and lard together until they are thoroughly blended; then divide the mixture into three equal portions. On a floured board, roll out the dough (which is the better for being chilled after it has risen) into a strip three times as long as it is wide. Place small pats of the butter mixture all over the strip until the first portion is used up. Fold the dough in three and roll it out. Repeat this process twice, at intervals of 30 minutes, keeping the dough refrigerated or in a cool place during the intervening periods.

Divide the dough into about 20 pieces and shape each of these into ovals. Place the ovals a little apart on two greased and floured trays, and prove in a warm place for another 30 minutes. Bake in an oven preheated to 200°C (400°F or Mark 6) for 20 to 25 minutes, or until golden-brown.

F. MARIAN McNEILL
THE SCOTS KITCHEN

Breton Butter Loaf

Kouing-Aman

This Breton bread is served as a dessert or at teatime. It is baked in a tin placed on top of two baking sheets to prevent the bottom of the loaf burning before the bread is ready.

To make one 25 cm (10 inch) loaf

300 g	basic bread dough (*page 171*)	10 oz
1 tbsp	strong plain flour	1 tbsp
180 g	slightly salted butter, softened	6 oz
180 g	castor sugar	6 oz

Make the basic bread dough in the usual way then, after the first rising, knock it back and roll it out on a floured board into a rectangle about 1 cm ($\frac{1}{2}$ inch) thick. Spread it with all but 30 g (1 oz) of the butter, leaving an unbuttered 2 cm (1 inch)

margin round the edge of the dough. Sprinkle the butter with all but 1 tablespoon of the sugar. Fold the dough in three lengthwise then in three crosswise, until it is a little parcel. Roll out the dough again, trying not to let the butter and sugar escape. Fold the dough again, but in two this time, instead of in three. Then roll it out again, and shape it into a round about 25 cm (10 inches) across, and 1 cm ($\frac{1}{2}$ inch) thick.

Butter a 25 cm (10 inch) spring-form tin with the reserved butter and lay the dough on it. Leave it to prove for 20 minutes, then place it in an oven preheated to 220°C (425°F or Mark 7) on top of two baking sheets, and bake it for about 20 minutes, or until the bread is golden and caramelized on top. Remove it from the tin while it is still hot and sprinkle it with the reserved sugar. Serve it warm. The bread can be reheated in a 180°C (350°F or Mark 4) oven for about 10 minutes.

LES DESSERTS DE NOS PROVINCES

Austrian Coffeetime Crescents

Kaffeekipferln

To make about 16 to 20 rolls

450 g	strong plain flour	1 lb
30 g	fresh yeast or 1 tbsp dried yeast	1 oz
About $\frac{1}{4}$ litre	tepid milk	About 8 fl oz
200 g	butter, cut into small pieces	7 oz
	salt	
2	egg yolks	2
2 tbsp	double cream	2 tbsp
1	egg, lightly beaten	1
	Nut and sultana filling	
100 g	walnuts, chopped	$3\frac{1}{2}$ oz
100 g	sultanas	$3\frac{1}{2}$ oz
100 g	candied peel, finely chopped	$3\frac{1}{2}$ oz
$\frac{1}{8}$ tsp	ground ginger	$\frac{1}{8}$ tsp

Mix the yeast with a little of the tepid milk. Rub the butter into the flour until the mixture resembles breadcrumbs. Add a pinch of salt, the egg yolks, cream and just enough of the remaining milk to form a stiff dough. Knead for a few minutes, then roll out the dough on a floured surface into a rectangle, three times as long as it is wide. Fold over the ends of the rectangle so that they meet in the centre. Turn the dough through a quarter circle, so that a long side of this rectangle is facing you, then roll out the dough again. Repeat the process four times. Cover the dough and leave it in a warm place for about 1 hour or until it doubles in bulk. Knock it back, roll it out to about 5 mm ($\frac{1}{4}$ inch) thick and slice it into 16 to 20 squares.

To make the filling, mix all the ingredients together. Place a teaspoonful of the filling on one corner of each square of dough and, starting from the corner with the filling, roll up each square diagonally. The corner opposite to the filling should end up on the underside of the roll. Bend the ends of each roll slightly to form a crescent shape.

Lay the rolls on well-buttered baking sheets and leave them to rise in a warm place for 20 to 30 minutes. When the rolls have doubled in bulk, brush them with the beaten egg. Bake them near the top of an oven preheated to 200°C (400°F or Mark 6) for about 20 minutes or until well browned.

EVA BAKOS
MEHLSPEISEN AUS ÖSTERREICH

Salted Crescent Rolls

Sörkifli

To make 32 small rolls

500 g	strong plain flour	1 lb
20 g	fresh yeast or 2 tsp dried yeast	$\frac{3}{4}$ oz
30 to 40 cl	tepid milk	$\frac{1}{2}$ to $\frac{3}{4}$ pint
1 tsp	sugar	1 tsp
1 tsp	salt	1 tsp
60 g	butter, softened	2 oz
1	egg yolk, beaten	1
	Salted caraway topping	
1 tsp	sea or rock salt, coarsely crushed	1 tsp
2 tbsp	caraway seeds	2 tbsp

Start the yeast working with 3 to 4 tablespoons of the milk, mixed with the sugar. Leave in a warm place until the yeast foams on the surface of the milk, about 10 minutes. Pour the liquid into the flour, add the salt and enough of the remaining milk to make a rather soft dough.

Work the dough thoroughly with a wooden spoon, then knead it with your hands, dusting them with flour if necessary to make the dough easier to handle. Divide the dough into four portions. Roll each portion into a thin round about 25 cm (10 inches) in diameter, and spread each with the softened butter. Divide each round into eight wedges like a cake, and roll up each of these triangular wedges firmly, starting from the base of the triangle. Bend the rolls slightly to form crescents, and lay them on three buttered baking sheets, allowing plenty of room between the crescents.

Leave the crescents to rise in a warm place for about 2 hours, or until double in size. Then brush them with the beaten egg yolk. Mix the caraway seeds with the coarse salt, and sprinkle the crescents with the mixture.

Bake the crescents in a preheated 200°C (400°F or Mark 6) oven for 10 to 15 minutes or until golden-brown.

FRED MACNICOL
HUNGARIAN COOKERY

Breads without Yeast

Boston Cornbread

Cultured buttermilk can be used instead of soured milk.

To make 2 large loaves

500 g	cornmeal	1 lb
125 g	strong plain flour	4 oz
2 tsp	bicarbonate of soda	2 tsp
250 g	molasses	8 oz
$\frac{1}{4}$ litre	milk	8 fl oz
$\frac{1}{2}$ litre	soured milk	16 fl oz

Sift together the flour and bicarbonate of soda, and stir in the cornmeal. Add the molasses, the milk and the soured milk.

Grease two 1 litre (1$\frac{3}{4}$ pint) metal basins and divide the batter between them. Cover the basins with buttered foil and tie the covers on well. Fill a large saucepan with enough boiling water to half-submerge the basins, place the basins in the pan side by side and steam them on top of the stove for 3 hours, adding more boiling water as necessary.

Remove the tops from the basins and place the basins in an oven preheated to 180°C (350°F or Mark 4) for about 10 minutes or until the loaves are browned on top.

THE BUCKEYE COOKBOOK

Buttermilk Oaten Bread

To make four 21 by 12 by 12 cm (8$\frac{1}{2}$ by 5 by 5 inch) wedges

200 g	fine oatmeal, steeped overnight in 30 cl ($\frac{1}{2}$ pint) buttermilk or soured milk	7 oz
275 g	plain flour	9 oz
$\frac{1}{2}$ tsp	bicarbonate of soda	$\frac{1}{2}$ tsp
$\frac{1}{2}$ tsp	salt	$\frac{1}{2}$ tsp

Mix the flour, soda and salt together in a bowl. Stir in the oatmeal. If necessary, add a little more buttermilk or soured milk to make the mixture into a soft dough. Knead the dough until it is smooth—about 10 minutes.

Roll out the dough into a circle about 5 cm (2 inches) thick, and lay it on a well-buttered baking sheet. With a sharp knife, cut it in quarters. Bake in an oven preheated to 190°C (375°F or Mark 5) for about 25 minutes, until the bread is golden.

IRISH RECIPES TRADITIONAL AND MODERN

Soda Bread (White)

Yogurt may be used if cultured buttermilk or soured milk are not available. A baking tin may be substituted for an iron pot.

To make one 20 cm (8 inch) bread

500 g	plain flour	1 lb
½ tsp	bicarbonate of soda	½ tsp
½ tsp	salt	½ tsp
30 cl	buttermilk or soured milk	½ pint

Heat the oven to 200°C (400°F or Mark 6). Butter a 20 cm (8 inch) cast-iron pot and place it in the oven to warm.

Sieve the flour, bicarbonate of soda and salt into a bowl. Mix them into a loose dough with the buttermilk or soured milk. Turn the dough out on to a floured board and knead it with a pushing and pulling motion until smooth. Remove the pot from the oven and lay the dough in it, floured side up. With a sharp knife, cut a cross into the top of the bread. Cover the pot with a tight-fitting lid or with aluminium foil and return it to the preheated oven for about 40 minutes or until the soda bread is golden-brown.

IRISH RECIPES TRADITIONAL AND MODERN

Brown Oatmeal Bread

Wheatmeal flour is 85 per cent wholemeal flour. Cultured buttermilk or yogurt can be substituted for the soured milk.

To make two 20 cm (8 inch) flatbreads

500 g	wheatmeal flour	1 lb
4 tbsp	coarse oatmeal	4 tbsp
1 tsp	bicarbonate of soda	1 tsp
1 tsp	salt	1 tsp
60 g	lard	2 oz
About 30 cl	soured milk	About ½ pint

Sieve together the salt, bicarbonate of soda and flour and mix very thoroughly. Rub in the fat until it has the consistency of fine breadcrumbs, then mix in the oatmeal. Make a well in the centre of the mixture, and add enough soured milk to produce a dry but spongy dough—a sticky dough will make the bread heavy. Turn the dough out on to a floured board, divide it in half and, with your palms, quickly pat and roll the dough into two flat cakes. Place these on two floured baking sheets. Score each bread lightly into four quarters with a sharp knife and bake the breads in a preheated, 220°C (425°F or Mark 7) oven for 30 minutes, or until the breads are brown and crisp.

ANN PASCOE
CORNISH RECIPES OLD AND NEW

Cheesy Bread

To make 10 buns

250 g	plain flour	8 oz
1 tbsp	baking powder	1 tbsp
125 g	Cheddar cheese, finely grated	4 oz
1 tsp	salt	1 tsp
125 g	cooked potatoes, mashed and sieved	4 oz
12.5 cl	milk	4 fl oz

Sieve together the flour, baking powder and salt, making sure there are no lumps remaining, particularly of the baking powder. Gradually add the cheese and potatoes, blending the mixture quickly with your fingertips. Add the milk to make a soft, dry dough and shape it into 10 small balls, handling the dough as little as possible. Place the balls on a floured baking sheet and bake them in an oven preheated to 230°C (450°F or Mark 8) for about 15 minutes or until they are golden-brown. Eat them while they are still warm.

ANN PASCOE
CORNISH RECIPES OLD AND NEW

Boston Brown Bread

You may freeze this bread tightly wrapped and reheat it in aluminium foil for about 20 minutes in an oven preheated to 180°C (350°F or Mark 4), or slice it and toast it. Delicious with cream cheese and jam.

To make two 15 cm (6 inch) loaves

175 g	fine cornmeal	6 oz
175 g	rye flour	6 oz
1 tsp	bicarbonate of soda	1 tsp
½ tsp	salt	½ tsp
½ litre	milk	16 fl oz
1	egg, well beaten	1
12.5 cl	molasses, warmed	4 fl oz
150 g	raisins (optional)	5 oz

Sift the cornmeal, rye flour, bicarbonate of soda and salt together. Stir the milk and egg into the molasses. Combine all the ingredients and mix them well. Add the raisins, if used.

Butter two 1.25 litre (2 pint) moulds, pudding basins or 500 g (1 lb) coffee tins. Make tight lids for them out of foil which you tie on securely so that no steam escapes. Pour the batter into the moulds, filling them not more than three-quarters full to allow for rising. Cover them tightly.

Pour water into a Dutch oven or large casserole to a depth of 2.5 cm (1 inch). Cover the pan tightly and bring the water to the boil. Place the moulds in the water and re-cover the pan tightly. Steam the bread for 3 hours, checking occasionally to be sure that the water does not boil away, and continue to add enough water to maintain the 2.5 cm (1 inch) level in the pan.

To serve the bread, let the covered moulds stand on a rack for about 5 minutes to permit the steam to subside. Then simply remove the covers and upend the moulds on to a plate. Cut the bread into 1½ cm (¾ inch) slices while it is still hot. Slice only as much as you will need for a meal and serve with butter.

JANE MOSS SNOW
A FAMILY HARVEST

Bury Simnel

The Simnel bread is one of the oldest English sweet breads. Although it has traditionally been baked for Mothering Sunday (the fourth Sunday in Lent) as a gift from children to their parents, its origins are probably pre-Christian, since the name may well derive from the Roman white flour called simila. *This fine, white flour was used to bake a cake decorated with balls for the Roman feast of Matronalia, a Roman version of Mother's Day; the Shrewsbury Simnel Cake is similarly garnished with marzipan balls to represent the Twelve Apostles. This Simnel recipe comes from Bury, in Lancashire, and is closer to medieval versions of the bread.*

To make one 20 to 17 cm (8 to 7 inch) cake

150 g	plain flour	5 oz
½ tsp	baking powder	½ tsp
30 g	butter	1 oz
30 g	lard	1 oz
90 g	castor sugar	3 oz
½ tsp	ground cinnamon	½ tsp
¼	small nutmeg, freshly grated	¼
250 g	currants	8 oz
30 g	candied peel, chopped	1 oz
1	egg, lightly beaten	1
2 to 3 tbsp	milk	2 to 3 tbsp
	whole blanched almonds or walnuts	
	cherries	
	thinly sliced candied citron peel	

Rub the butter and lard into the flour and then add the sugar, cinnamon, nutmeg, currants and candied peel, mixing well. Add the egg, and mix all the ingredients into a very stiff dough, adding a small quantity of milk if necessary. Form the dough into a round flat cake, and place it on a buttered baking sheet. Decorate the cake with the nuts, cherries and citron peel, and bake in an oven preheated to 200°C (400°F or Mark 6) for 30 minutes, or until golden-brown.

MARGARET BATES
THE SCOTTISH AND IRISH BAKING BOOK

Raspberry Buns

To make 8 to 10 buns

125 g	plain flour	4 oz
½ tsp	baking powder	½ tsp
8 to 10 tsp	raspberry jam	8 to 10 tsp
	salt	
125 g	ground rice	4 oz
60 g	butter	2 oz
60 g	sugar	2 oz
2 to 3 tbsp	lukewarm milk	2 to 3 tbsp
1	egg, beaten	1

Mix the flour, salt, baking powder and ground rice together. Rub in the butter, and then work in the sugar. Add the milk to the egg and incorporate them into the dry ingredients.

Form the mixture into 8 to 10 balls and place them on a buttered baking sheet. Make a well in each with the finger and put 1 teaspoon of raspberry jam into the well. Fold the dough over the well to seal it, and bake the buns in an oven preheated to 200°C (400°F or Mark 6) for 20 or 25 minutes or until golden-brown. Leave to cool on a wire rack.

ABERDEEN SCHOOL OF DOMESTIC SCIENCE
PLAIN COOKERY RECIPES

Kneaded Cream Cakes

Gâteaux d'Etampes ou Fraiser

The quantities given here are very large because the author of the recipe, who lived in the 17th century and was valet to King Louis XIV of France, was used to catering for banquets. The amounts can, of course, be reduced.

To make about thirty-five 10 cm (4 inch) cakes

2 kg	plain flour	4 lb
15 cl	double cream, whipped	¼ pint
400 g	butter, softened	14 oz
125 g	Gruyère cheese, grated	4 oz
1	egg, beaten	1

Add the whipped cream to the flour and mix well. Then work in the butter and grated cheese. The dough should be fairly firm. Knead it well for about 10 minutes. Form the dough into about 35 flat, round cakes. Lay the cakes on a floured baking sheet and glaze them with the beaten egg. Bake them in an oven preheated to 200°C (400°F or Mark 6) for about 20 minutes, or until they are golden-brown.

NICOLAS DE BONNEFONS
LES DÉLICES DE LA CAMPAGNE

Italian Speckled Bread

Pan Striáa

To make one 25 cm (10 inch) bread

500 g	plain flour	1 lb
500 g	fine cornmeal	1 lb
2	large onions, thinly sliced	2
200 g	grapes, sliced, pips removed	7 oz
200 g	dried figs, sliced	7 oz
300 g	apples, peeled, cored and sliced	10 oz
½ litre	milk	16 fl oz

In a large bowl, mix all the ingredients thoroughly and leave them to stand for 1 hour. Butter a cake tin about 8 to 10 cm (3 to 4 inches) deep. Pour in the mixture. Bake in an oven preheated to 220°C (425°F or Mark 7) for 30 to 40 minutes or until the bread is golden-brown and sounds hollow when rapped. Eat the bread as soon as it cools.

OTTORINA PERNA BOZZI
VECCHIA BRIANZA IN CUCINA

Spanish Nut Bread

Pan de Nueces

*To make one 17 by
9 cm (7 by 3½ inch) loaf*

275 g	plain flour	9 oz
1 tsp	baking powder	1 tsp
125 g	walnuts, coarsely chopped	4 oz
20 g	butter, softened	¾ oz
1	egg, beaten	1
200 g	sugar	7 oz
¼ litre	milk	8 fl oz
75 g	raisins, soaked in water to cover for 20 minutes, drained and dried on a paper towel	2½ oz

In a bowl, beat together the butter, egg and sugar until creamy. Add half the flour alternately with the milk, then add the raisins and nuts, and finally the rest of the flour mixed with the baking powder. Turn out the dough on to a floured work surface and knead lightly with your fingers for about 10 minutes. Butter and flour a ½ litre (1 lb) loaf tin. Put in the dough and leave it to rise in a warm place for 30 minutes or until it has doubled in bulk.

Bake the loaf in an oven preheated to 170°C (325°F or Mark 3) for 1 hour or until a skewer inserted into the loaf comes out clean. If the bread browns too quickly, cover the top with

greaseproof paper to prevent burning. The flavour will be improved if the loaf is wrapped after cooling in a clean cloth or aluminium foil and left in a cool dry place for 24 hours.

SIMONE ORTEGA
MIL OCHENTA RECETAS DE COCINA

Cream Scones

The technique for making these scones is demonstrated on page 86. If a sweeter scone is preferred, a little castor sugar may be added to the mixture.

To make 8 scones

250 g	plain flour	8 oz
1 tbsp	baking powder	1 tbsp
	salt	
30 g	butter, softened	1 oz
1	egg	1
15 cl	soured cream	¼ pint

Sieve the flour, baking powder and a pinch of salt into a mixing bowl. Rub in the butter with your fingertips, until the mixture resembles fine breadcrumbs.

Make a well in the centre of the flour mixture. Beat together the egg and soured cream and pour them into the flour, mixing from the centre outwards until the dough is smooth and free from lumps.

Turn the dough out on to a floured board and knead it lightly for 1 minute, or until it is free from cracks. Roll it out to a thickness of about 1 cm (½ inch). Using a glass or a pastry cutter, cut it into eight rounds about 5 cm (2 inches) in diameter. Place the rounds on a buttered baking sheet and bake in a preheated 190°C (375°F or Mark 5) oven for 15 to 20 minutes or until lightly browned.

The scones can also be baked on top of the stove on a greased griddle. Brown the scones for 10 minutes on one side then on the other until they are cooked through.

FLORENCE B. JACK
COOKERY FOR EVERY HOUSEHOLD

Mrs. Macnab's Scones

Mrs. Macnab was the wife of a farmer who lived near Ballater in the Grampian highlands. Such was her reputation as a baker that King Frederick of Prussia and other distinguished guests at Balmoral used frequently to go over and have tea with her. It is not possible to impart Mrs. Macnab's lightness of touch, or the wine-like air of these regions, which doubtless contributed to her visitors' enjoyment; but here, at least, is the recipe for her celebrated scones.

The secret of success lies in not working the dough with the hands except just once kneading it.

To make 15 to 20 scones

500 g	plain flour	1 lb
1 tsp	bicarbonate of soda	1 tsp
2 tsp	cream of tartar	2 tsp
1 tsp	salt	1 tsp
60 g	butter, softened and cut into pieces	2 oz
1	egg, beaten	1
30 cl	buttermilk	$\frac{1}{2}$ pint

In a bowl mix thoroughly the flour, bicarbonate of soda, cream of tartar and salt. Rub in the butter. Gradually stir in the egg and buttermilk. Turn out the dough on to a floured board, flour the top, and knead with the hand as little as possible. Cut off pieces of dough about the size of hens' eggs and flatten them with the knuckles, but do not roll them out at all. Prick each scone with a fork and cut it into quarters. Butter and flour a baking sheet and place the scones on it. Bake in an oven preheated to 200°C (400°F or Mark 6) for 10 to 15 minutes, or until lightly browned.

F. MARIAN McNEILL
THE SCOTS KITCHEN

Granary and Onion Scones

Granary meal is a proprietary name for a blend of wholemeal, rye flour and pieces of malted grain, also known as sprouted wheatflakes. The soured milk or fresh milk plus cream of tartar can also be replaced by cultured buttermilk.

To make 8 scones

250 g	granary meal	8 oz
1 tsp	bicarbonate of soda	1 tsp
1	large onion, thinly sliced	1
40 g	butter	1$\frac{1}{2}$ oz
1 tsp	fine sea salt	1 tsp
1 tbsp	chopped thyme	1 tbsp
15 cl	soured milk, or fresh milk plus $\frac{1}{2}$ tsp cream of tartar	$\frac{1}{4}$ pint

Brown the onion in 15 g ($\frac{1}{2}$ oz) of the butter. Put the granary meal, salt, bicarbonate of soda and thyme into a mixing bowl and rub in the remaining butter. Mix in the browned onion. Make a well in the centre and pour in the soured milk or the fresh milk mixed with cream of tartar. Mix everything to a

soft dough. Turn it on to a floured board and knead it lightly for 10 minutes. Divide the dough into eight pieces and shape them into rounds about 2 cm ($\frac{3}{4}$ inch) thick. Lay them on a floured baking sheet and bake them in an oven preheated to 200°C (400°F or Mark 6) for 25 minutes or until golden.

GAIL DUFF
GAIL DUFF'S VEGETARIAN COOKBOOK

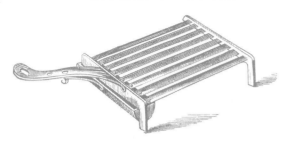

Singing Lilly

This is a variation of the Singing Hinnie—an economical and substantial scone created by miners' wives in the north-east of England, and so called because it "sings" when cooked on a griddle. You can't hear it from the oven. But if you wish you can prepare the dough without the sugar, and cook it on a griddle lightly greased with lard. During cooking, some of the fat will ooze out of the pastry and start to fry, humming and buzzing in the process. Cook over a moderate heat for 3 to 4 minutes on each side, or until the Hinnie stops "singing" and is a pretty golden colour.

To make one 20 cm (8 inch) scone

250 g	plain flour	8 oz
$\frac{1}{4}$ tsp	salt	$\frac{1}{4}$ tsp
125 g	cold lard, firm but not hard, or 60 g (2 oz) each unsalted butter and lard or cooking fat, cut into small pieces	4 oz
250 g	currants or other dried fruit, roughly chopped	8 oz
30 g	castor sugar	1 oz
4 to 6 tbsp	cold milk	4 to 6 tbsp

Sift the flour with the salt into a mixing bowl. Rub in the fat, until the mixture resembles fine breadcrumbs. Stir in the chopped fruit and castor sugar. Mix with just enough cold milk to make a stiff paste.

Turn the dough out on to a floured work surface. Roll it out into a round about 5 mm ($\frac{1}{4}$ inch) thick. Place it on a lightly greased baking sheet and bake in a preheated 200°C (400°F or Mark 6) oven for about 20 minutes or until pale golden.

Leave it on the baking sheet to cool, then slice it into wedges and serve it spread with butter.

PETITS PROPOS CULINAIRES I

Griddle Cake

Cacen Gri

To make one 20 cm (8 inch) cake

250 g	plain flour	8 oz
½ tsp	bicarbonate of soda	½ tsp
¼ tsp	salt	¼ tsp
125 g	butter	4 oz
60 g	sugar	2 oz
60 g	currants	2 oz
1	egg, well beaten	1
12.5 cl	buttermilk or milk	4 fl oz

Put the flour into a bowl with the salt. Rub in the butter. Add the sugar and currants and mix thoroughly. Make a well in the centre of the mixture. Dissolve the soda in the buttermilk or milk, and pour this mixture into the dry ingredients. Then add the egg. Blend well and knead the mixture to a soft dough. Turn the dough out on to a well-floured board, shape it into a ball, and flatten it with the palm of the hand to form a round, flat cake about 1 cm (½ inch) thick. Bake the cake on a lightly greased griddle or large, heavy-bottomed frying pan over a moderate heat until nicely browned, about 10 minutes on each side. Split the griddle cake in half when warm and spread it thickly with butter.

S. MINWEL TIBBOTT
WELSH FARE

Granny's Oatcakes

The beef dripping called for is the fat melted from a roasting joint; dripping bought from a butcher is beef fat rendered by frying and is not comparable in flavour.

These oatcakes are always best made in small batches. If a large quantity is to be made, keep repeating the small batches. Never substitute porridge oats for the oatmeal.

To make ten to twelve 8 cm (3 inch) oatcakes

175 g	fine or medium oatmeal	6 oz
¼ tsp	bicarbonate of soda	¼ tsp
2 tsp	beef dripping	2 tsp
2 to 3 tbsp	boiling water	2 to 3 tbsp
	salt	

Melt the beef dripping in the water, then add this to the oatmeal along with the bicarbonate of soda and a pinch of salt. Work the mixture into a stiff dough. Roll out the dough very thinly on a board sprinkled with oatmeal. Cut the dough into rounds with an 8 cm (3 inch) biscuit cutter or a breakfast cup,

and place the rounds a few at a time on a hot, lightly greased griddle or heavy-based frying pan. Cook them until the edges curl, about 3 minutes. Do not turn them over, but transfer them to a baking sheet and put them under the grill for 2 or 3 minutes to brown the tops lightly.

PETITS PROPOS CULINAIRES I

French Spice Bread

Pain d'Épice

French spice bread should be made with rye flour, but ordinary wheat flour can be used. Rheims has long been thought to produce the best spice bread, but Dijon and Orléans are also very famous for their spice bread.

To make one 35 by 28 cm (14 by 11 inch) flatbread or two 17 cm (7 inch) breads

500 g	rye flour or plain flour	1 lb
2 tsp	baking powder	2 tsp
1 tsp	bicarbonate of soda	1 tsp
500 g	honey	1 lb
100 g	castor sugar	3½ oz
60 g	almonds, blanched and chopped	2 oz
60 g	mixed candied citrus peel, chopped	2 oz
1 tsp	aniseeds (optional)	1 tsp
1 tsp	ground cinnamon (optional)	1 tsp
1 tsp	ground cloves (optional)	1 tsp
½ tbsp	grated lemon or orange rind (optional)	½ tbsp
4 tbsp	milk	4 tbsp
2 tbsp	sugar	2 tbsp

Heat the honey to boiling point; skim the froth on the surface, remove it from the heat and cool to lukewarm. Sieve the flour into a bowl, make a well in the centre and pour in the honey. Mix with a wooden spoon until a firm paste is obtained. It may be necessary to add additional flour, as some flours are more absorbent than others. Shape the paste into a ball, wrap it in a cloth and leave it to rest for 1 hour. Then beat in the sugar, baking powder, bicarbonate of soda, chopped almonds and candied peel. Beat in the aniseeds, cinnamon, ground cloves and grated rind, if using. Knead the dough vigorously for about 10 minutes to give it body.

Roll out the dough to the desired thickness and place it on a buttered Swiss roll tin or divide it between several tins. Bake the spice bread in an oven preheated to 180°C (350°F or Mark 4) for 1 hour. As soon as the bread is cooked, brush the surface quickly with the milk heated to a syrup with the 2 tablespoons of sugar and return it to the oven for a few seconds to set the glaze. Cool the cake before serving.

PROSPER MONTAGNÉ
NEW LAROUSSE GASTRONOMIQUE

Bran Muffins

Either cultured buttermilk or plain yogurt can be used in this recipe instead of soured milk.

To make 12 muffins

125 g	plain flour, sifted	4 oz
1 tsp	bicarbonate of soda	1 tsp
60 g	bran breakfast cereal	2 oz
60 g	butter	2 oz
60 g	sugar	2 oz
1	egg, beaten	1
½ tsp	salt	½ tsp
¼ litre	soured milk	8 fl oz
100 g	raisins or dates, chopped (optional)	3½ oz

Cream the butter with the sugar. Add the egg and beat well. Mix the dry ingredients—bran breakfast cereal, flour, bicarbonate of soda and salt—and add them alternately with the soured milk. Stir in raisins or dates, if desired. Fill buttered muffin tins two-thirds full. Bake the muffins in an oven preheated to 200°C (400°F or Mark 6) for 20 to 25 minutes, or until golden-brown.

CHEZZETCOOK HISTORICAL SOCIETY

Dodgers, Dabs or Cornmeal Puffs

To make 12 puffs

250 g	fine cornmeal	8 oz
8 cl	boiling water	3 fl oz
1 tsp	butter, softened	1 tsp
1 tsp	sugar	1 tsp
½ tsp	salt	½ tsp
2 to 3 tbsp	milk	2 to 3 tbsp
2	eggs, yolks separated from whites, yolks beaten, whites stiffly beaten	2

Scald the cornmeal with the boiling water so that the meal is all wet but not soft. Add the butter, sugar, salt and milk. When the mixture is cold, add the yolks and fold in the whites. The batter should drop easily from the spoon, neither thin enough to pour nor stiff enough to be scraped from the bowl.

Have your bun tins well buttered and hissing hot. Drop a tablespoon of the batter into each compartment of the tins and bake in an oven preheated to 200°C (400°F or Mark 6) for about 20 minutes or until brown and puffy.

MRS. MARY J. LINCOLN
THE BOSTON COOK BOOK

Blueberry or Cranberry Muffins

If blueberries or cranberries are not available, bilberries can be substituted. You can substitute ordinary baking powder for the double-acting baking powder if you add one teaspoonful of tartaric acid. The technique of making these muffins is demonstrated on page 88.

To make about thirty 5 cm (2 inch) muffins

250 g	plain flour, sifted	8 oz
2 tsp	double-acting baking powder	2 tsp
150 g	blueberries, lightly floured or 125 g (4 oz) cranberries, chopped	5 oz
¾ tsp	salt	¾ tsp
60 g	sugar	2 oz
2	eggs, beaten	2
60 g	butter, melted	2 oz
17.5 cl	milk	6 fl oz
1 tsp	grated orange or lemon peel (optional)	1 tsp

Combine the flour, baking powder, tartaric acid, salt and sugar. Stir in the eggs, butter and most of the milk in a few swift strokes; fold in the fruit and the peel, if used, and add the rest of the milk. Be sure to hold the mixing to an absolute minimum, a light stirring of 10 to 20 seconds, which will leave some lumps. Ignore them. The dough should not be mixed to the point of pouring, ribbon-like, from the spoon, but should break in coarse globs.

Butter the cups of muffin tins and fill them about two-thirds full. Bake at once in an oven preheated to 200°C (400°F or Mark 6) for 20 to 25 minutes. If muffins are left in the tins a few moments after leaving the oven, they will be easier to remove. They are really best eaten at once.

IRMA S. ROMBAUER AND MARION ROMBAUER BECKER
JOY OF COOKING

Cheese Popovers

The technique of making popovers is demonstrated on page 88. In the United States, special popover tins are sold; they are wider at the top than at the bottom. Deep patty pans or castle pudding tins could be used instead.

To make about 9 popovers

125 g	plain flour	4 oz
125 g	strong Cheddar or Parmesan cheese, grated	4 oz
¼ litre	milk	8 fl oz
15 g	butter, melted	½ oz
¼ tsp	salt	¼ tsp
2	eggs, beaten	2
	paprika or cayenne pepper	

Beat the milk, butter, flour and salt together, just until smooth. Add 1 egg at a time, but do not overbeat; the batter should be no heavier than whipping cream. Add a pinch of paprika or cayenne pepper to the grated cheese. Butter deep muffin tins or custard cups; dust them with grated cheese. Pour a scant tablespoon of batter into each cup and cover it with a few teaspoons of cheese, then add more batter until the cups are two-thirds full. Bake at once in an oven preheated to 230°C (450°F or Mark 8) for 15 minutes, then reduce the heat to 180°C (350° or Mark 4) and bake for about 20 minutes more.

To test for doneness, remove a popover to be sure the side walls are firm. If not cooked long enough, the popover will collapse. You may insert a sharp paring knife gently into the other popovers to allow the steam to escape after baking.

IRMA S. ROMBAUER AND MARION ROMBAUER BECKER
JOY OF COOKING

Popovers

Popovers, which are similar to Yorkshire puddings, are baked in American muffin tins which have wells like the standard patty pans. They are deeper and narrower at the bottom than at the top. Ramekins, dariole moulds, castle pudding tins or deep patty pans can be used instead. The technique of making popovers is demonstrated on page 88.

To make 12 popovers

125 g	plain flour, sifted	4 oz
½ tsp	salt	½ tsp
¼ litre	cold milk	8 fl oz
3	large eggs	3
15 g	butter, melted	½ oz

Sift the flour and salt together. Generously butter 12 wells in a muffin tin and place the tin in an oven preheated to 230°C (450°F or Mark 8) for 3 minutes while you mix up the batter.

Whisk the milk into the flour in small additions, beating each addition well. This method will prevent the flour from lumping. Beat in the eggs one at a time. Beat in the butter. The batter should be smooth and evenly mixed. Do not continue beating the batter beyond this point.

Remove the muffin tin from the oven and distribute the batter evenly among the wells. Each well should be three-quarters full. Place the tin in the centre of the lower part of the oven. Bake the popovers for 15 minutes, then reduce the heat to 180°C (350°F or Mark 4) and bake for a further 20 minutes.

Do not open the oven door even a crack during the baking time, or you will cause the collapse of your popovers. Remove the popovers from the oven and serve at once.

KATHLEEN THORNE-THOMSEN AND LINDA BROWNRIDGE
WHY THE CAKE WON'T RISE AND THE JELLY WON'T SET

Jamaican Banana Bread

If pecans are not available, walnuts can be substituted.

To make one 20 by 10 cm (8 by 4 inch) loaf

250 g	plain flour	8 oz
1 tbsp	baking powder	1 tbsp
500 g	large, ripe bananas	1 lb
125 g	unsalted butter, softened	4 oz
125 g	sugar	4 oz
1	egg	1
½ tsp	salt	½ tsp
½ tsp	freshly grated nutmeg	½ tsp
1 tsp	vanilla extract	1 tsp
90 g	seedless raisins, tossed with 1 tsp flour	3 oz
4 tbsp	coarsely chopped pecans	4 tbsp

Cream the butter and sugar together in a mixing bowl until they are light and fluffy. Add the egg and beat the mixture thoroughly. In another bowl, sift the flour, baking powder, salt and nutmeg. Mash the bananas and add the vanilla extract. Add the sifted ingredients and the banana alternately to the egg, butter and sugar mixture, beating after each addition until everything is thoroughly blended. Add the raisins with the pecans to the batter, mixing well. Pour the batter into a buttered 1 litre (2 lb) loaf tin. Bake the loaf in a preheated 180°C (350°F or Mark 4) oven for about 1 hour or until a skewer inserted into the loaf comes out clean.

ELISABETH LAMBERT ORTIZ
CARIBBEAN COOKING

Spiced Apple Bread

Guernsey Gâche Melée

This traditional bread from Guernsey in the Channel Islands is partly leavened by the action on the flour of the malic acid which is present in the apples.

To make one 30 by 20 cm (12 by 8 inch) loaf

500 g	wholemeal flour	1 lb
500 g	cooking apples, peeled, cored and chopped into small pieces	1 lb
250 g	butter, softened	8 oz
500 g	soft dark brown sugar	1 lb
1 tsp	ground cinnamon	1 tsp
2 tsp	grated nutmeg	2 tsp
3	eggs, beaten	3

Mix the flour and apples thoroughly and leave them to stand in a warm place for 3 hours. Cream the butter with the sugar and add the cinnamon and grated nutmeg. Mix all the ingredients together, add the eggs and mix again thoroughly. Pour the mixture into a greased baking tin about 30 by 20 cm (12 by 8 inches) and bake in an oven preheated to 170°C (325°F or Mark 3) for 1½ hours or until a knife dipped into the bread comes out clean.

J. STEVENS COX (EDITOR)
GUERNSEY DISHES OF BYGONE DAYS

Whole Wheat Griddle Breads

Chappati and Phulka

Chappatis are unleavened Indian breads. Phulkas are smaller versions of the same bread. Griddles of various sizes can be bought from Indian cookware shops.

Chappati dough can be made and cooked within a few minutes. Personally, I like to leave the dough overnight in the refrigerator, covered with a damp muslin cloth. A few tablespoons of milk can be used in the dough, and the addition of a tablespoon of clarified butter will make the dough more elastic and the bread more supple.

To make eight 12 cm (5 inch) flatbreads

250 g	wholemeal flour	8 oz
1 tsp	salt	1 tsp
About 20 cl	water	About 7 fl oz

Mix the flour and salt and place on a pastry board. Sprinkle some of the water in the middle and gradually work until the flour has absorbed most of the water. Stop as soon as the dough is supple and elastic. The exact quantity of water required will vary according to the flour and the prevailing weather. Knead the dough well—the longer the better. Ten minutes gives a specially light finish, but on average 5 minutes is adequate. Cover with a wet muslin cloth and leave for 30 minutes at least. Knead lightly again before shaping the dough. If the dough is left for a longer period of time, it should be kept in a cool place.

Form the dough into small, round balls and flatten them with the palm of your hand. Dust the rounds with a little flour on each side, place them on a board and roll each of them out as thin as a sheet of parchment paper. They should be the same size as your griddle; use a smaller griddle for a *phulka* and a larger one for a chappati. Have the griddle at medium heat (a little hotter if the griddle is very thick) and turn a flatbread on to it. Wait until the first bubbles rise in the bread, about 3 minutes. Turn it over, using a spatula or your hand. After a minute or so, press on the edges a little and gently rotate the bread. Now pick up the bread with the spatula and, if you are using gas, hold the bread steady over a high flame. Otherwise, leave the bread under a hot grill for a few seconds. In both cases, the bread should puff up and will then be ready to eat.

To serve, heat a deep dish, line it with hot napkins and stack the bread. Keep covered, and take it to the table.

DHARAMJIT SINGH
INDIAN COOKERY

Whole Wheat Buttered Griddle Bread

Paratha

To make six 18 cm (7 inch) breads

200 g	wholemeal flour	7 oz
30 g	butter, melted	1 oz
¾ tsp	salt	¾ tsp
12 to 16	lovage seeds, roughly bruised	12 to 16
¼ litre	milk and water in equal quantities	8 fl oz

Sift the flour and salt on to a board with the lovage seeds and make a well in the centre. Pour in the milk and water to make a very soft dough, almost a batter. Knead it until it is smooth. Cover with a damp cloth and leave it to rest for at least 1½ hours, but preferably for 8 hours or overnight.

Roll out the dough into six perfect circles, about 18 cm (7 inches) across and brush them with a little melted butter. Fold the circles in half and then fold again to make triangles. Roll them out again to their former size. Brush them with melted butter and repeat the folding process. Do this at least three times more. The more times you repeat the process, the crisper your bread will be.

Cook the *parathas* one by one on a lightly buttered griddle or heavy-based frying pan until they are pale brown and mottled. Turn them over and cook on the other side. Serve hot.

DHARAMJIT SINGH
INDIAN COOKERY

Telemark Flatbread

This crispbread keeps indefinitely if stored in an airtight tin.

To make one 25 cm (10 inch) flatbread

150 g	rolled oats	5 oz
150 g	barley flour	5 oz
200 g	light rye flour	7 oz
250 g	plain flour	8 oz
½ litre	water	16 fl oz
½ tsp	salt	½ tsp

Mix all the ingredients together and work them into a pliant dough. Roll out the dough into a thin, 25 cm (10 inch) circle and cook on a buttered griddle until the flatbread is crisp, about 10 minutes on each side.

ELISE SVERDRUP
NORWAY'S DELIGHT: DISHES AND SPECIALITIES

Norman Flatbread

La Foncée

This traditional Norman flatbread is almost identical to those eaten in Scandinavia, and can thus almost certainly be traced back to the Normans' Viking ancestors.

To make one 25 cm (10 inch) flatbread

250 g	plain flour	8 oz
2	eggs, beaten	2
	salt	
250 g	butter, softened and cut into pieces	8 oz
¼ litre	double cream	8 fl oz
1	egg yolk, beaten	1

Put the flour into a bowl. Make a well in the centre and pour in the eggs. Add a pinch of salt, the butter and the cream. Knead well with your fingertips to obtain a smooth dough. Leave the dough to stand for 30 minutes.

Roll out the dough and fold it in four. Roll out the dough again and repeat the process. Then make the dough into a ball and leave to rest, covered, for 15 minutes before rolling it out into a round the thickness of a finger. Lay this round on a buttered baking sheet. Score a cross with the point of a sharp knife to divide the dough lightly into quarters. Brush the round with the egg yolk. Bake in an oven preheated to 220°C (425°F or Mark 7) for about 30 minutes or until brown.

MARIE BISSON
LA CUISINE NORMANDE

Stuffed Parathas

Garam masala, *a mixture of ground spices, usually peppercorns, coriander seeds, cumin seeds, cloves, cinnamon and cardamom, can be bought from Indian shops.*

Stuffed *parathas* are served with vegetable or meat dishes and are very tasty eaten with yogurt.

To make about 10 parathas

300 g	wholemeal flour	10 oz
½ tsp	salt	½ tsp
17.5 cl	water	6 fl oz
90 g	*ghee*	3 oz

Potato stuffing		
2	large potatoes	2
15 g	*ghee*	½ oz
1	small onion, finely chopped	1
2 tbsp	chopped fresh coriander	2 tbsp
1 cm	ginger root, peeled and finely chopped	½ inch
1½ tsp	salt	1½ tsp
1 tsp	*garam masala*	1 tsp
½ tsp	chili powder (optional)	½ tsp
1 tbsp	pulped mango or 2 tsp lemon juice	1 tbsp

Put 250 g (8 oz) of the flour into a bowl with the salt and gradually add the water to make a loose dough. Pound and knead with the hands for several minutes: the more it is kneaded, the lighter the bread will be. Leave the dough for at least one hour, then knead it once again and, if necessary, sprinkle a little more water on it.

Warm the *ghee* and have it by you. Break off a piece of the dough, shape it into a ball and, with a little of the reserved flour, roll it out into a round (not too thin) to about 5 mm (¼ inch) thick. Using a spoon, spread some of the warm *ghee* on the dough, then fold it over and spread a little more *ghee* on the fresh layer. Do this two or three times and then roll the *paratha* out fairly thinly, to make either a round or a V-shape. Repeat the process with the rest of the dough.

To make the potato stuffing, boil the potatoes in their jackets; when cool, peel and mash them. Heat the *ghee* in a frying pan and fry the onion, coriander and ginger slowly for a few minutes. Add the salt, *garam masala*, chili powder if used, and the mango or lemon juice. Mix in the mashed potato and let the mixture sizzle for two to three minutes. Remove it from the heat and allow it to cool.

Spread another layer of warm *ghee* on the rolled-out *parathas* and place a tablespoon or more of the potato stuffing in the centre of each. Fold the dough over the stuffing to enclose it. Using some of the reserved flour, roll the *paratha* out as thinly and as round as you can.

Grease a hot-plate or heavy frying pan well with butter or extra *ghee* and put a *paratha* on it. When one side is partially cooked—about 5 minutes—turn it over and spread *ghee* liberally on it; do the same to the other side. When ready, the *parathas* should be of golden-brown colour and well soaked in *ghee*. They should be served piping hot.

SAVITRI CHOWDHARY
INDIAN COOKING

Finnish Potato Flatbread

Perunarieska

To make one 25 cm (10 inch) flatbread

40 g	plain flour	1½ oz
125 g	barley flour	4 oz
250 g	mealy potatoes, scrubbed	8 oz
¼ litre	water	16 fl oz
1 tsp	sea salt	1 tsp

Boil the potatoes in their skins in the water until soft. Drain them and reserve the cooking liquid. Peel the potatoes and mash them while they are still hot. Add ¼ litre (8 fl oz) of the cooking liquid. Mix well and let the potatoes cool. Put the potatoes in the refrigerator to chill.

Add the salt to the potatoes, mix in the plain flour and beat the mixture well. Knead in the barley flour. Knead the dough for 10 to 15 minutes, or until it is perfectly smooth. Then shape the dough into a ball. Dip your hands in cold water if the dough is hard to handle.

Butter a large baking sheet or grease it with oil. Put the dough ball on it and pat it down until it becomes a large, thin round or oval that almost completely covers the baking sheet. The dough should be about 5 mm (¼ inch) thick. Prick this flatbread all over with a fork. Bake it in a preheated, 230°C (450°F or Mark 8) oven for 15 to 20 minutes. When done, the bread should have dark brown flecks all over it, and the edges should be dark brown and crisp, almost burnt.

Remove the bread from the oven and cover it with a cloth for 10 to 20 minutes to soften it a little. Cut it into squares and serve it with butter while still warm.

ULLA KÄKÖNEN
NATURAL COOKING THE FINNISH WAY

Cornbread with Black Truffle

Focaccia di Farina Gialla al Tartufo

Instead of the one small black truffle used here, you can substitute a small tin of truffle peelings, chopped, and add the liquid from the tin to the batter.

To make one 20 cm (8 inch) bread

100 g	fine cornmeal	3½ oz
1	small black truffle, grated	1
½ litre	milk	16 fl oz
	salt	
60 g	Parmesan cheese, grated	2 oz
4 tbsp	oil	4 tbsp
4	eggs, yolks separated from whites, whites stiffly beaten	4
	freshly ground black pepper	
20 g	butter	¾ oz

Boil the milk with a pinch of salt in a large saucepan. Remove the milk from the heat and slowly add the cornmeal, mixing constantly. Cook over a low heat for 45 minutes, stirring frequently, until the mixture is thick. Remove it from the heat and add the Parmesan cheese and the oil. Allow the mixture to cool completely. Add the egg yolks to the pan, followed by the whites. Season with a pinch of pepper and add the truffle. Pour the mixture into a deep, buttered baking dish and smooth its surface with a spoon. Bake in an oven preheated to 220°C (425°F or Mark 7) for 30 minutes or until the bread is set and just beginning to brown. Serve hot.

ILARIA RATTAZZI (EDITOR)
TANTE COSE CON IL PANE

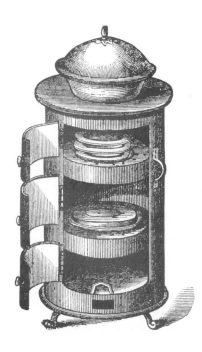

Barley Flatbread

Ohrarieska

Pearl barley is whole barley with the husks removed. It can be bought in health food shops.

This is a thick, chewy flatbread with a subtly sour taste. It is good with soups, or as a snack, or it can be eaten as a coffee bread spread with butter.

To make one 20 cm (8 inch) square flatbread		
30 g	barley flour	1 oz
200 g	pearl barley	7 oz
60 cl	buttermilk	1 pint
1	egg, lightly beaten	1
1½ tsp	sea salt	1½ tsp
1 tbsp	oil or melted butter	1 tbsp

Let the barley flour and pearl barley soak in the buttermilk for 7 to 8 hours or overnight at room temperature.

Butter a square or rectangular glass baking dish. Add the egg and the salt to the barley and buttermilk mixture and blend well. Pour the mixture into the baking dish and bake it in an oven preheated to 180°C (350°F or Mark 4) for 30 minutes, then brush the top of the flatbread with oil or butter. Continue baking the bread for 30 minutes to 1 hour or until the top and sides are brown and crisp. Serve warm or cold.

ULLA KÄKÖNEN
NATURAL COOKING THE FINNISH WAY

Spider Corncake

This American cornbread recipe comes from Connecticut. A spider is a North American word for a cast-iron frying pan. The original spiders had long legs and were used standing over coals in a hearth.

To make one 22 cm (9 inch) bread		
175 g	fine cornmeal	6 oz
60 g	flour	2 oz
1 tsp	bicarbonate of soda	1 tsp
¼ litre	buttermilk	8 fl oz
½ litre	milk	16 fl oz
2 tsp	sugar	2 tsp
½ tsp	salt	½ tsp
30 g	rendered bacon fat or butter	1 oz

Combine the cornmeal, flour and bicarbonate of soda in a mixing bowl. Add the buttermilk, half of the milk, the sugar and the salt. Stir to blend well.

Meanwhile put the bacon fat or butter in a 22 cm (9 inch) cast-iron frying pan with a metal handle, or in a heavy baking dish, and place it in an oven preheated to 180°C (350°F or Mark 4). When the frying pan is thoroughly hot, remove it from the oven and pour in the cornmeal batter. Carefully pour the remaining milk over the top. Bake for 50 minutes, or until the cake is firm and the top is golden.

JEAN HEWITT
NEW ENGLAND HERITAGE COOKBOOK

Bacon Spoonbread

The technique of making this cornbread is shown on page 84.

To make one 20 cm (8 inch) bread		
90 g	fine cornmeal	3 oz
250 g	bacon, fried and chopped into small pieces	8 oz
35 cl	water	12 fl oz
225 g	strong Cheddar cheese, coarsely grated	7½ oz
60 g	butter	2 oz
2	garlic cloves, crushed to a paste	2
½ tsp	salt	½ tsp
¼ litre	milk	8 fl oz
4	eggs, yolks separated from whites, whites stiffly beaten	4

Stir the cornmeal into the cold water in a saucepan and place over a medium heat. Bring to a bubbling boil, stirring constantly. When the cornmeal is thick—perhaps 60 seconds—remove the pan from the heat. Stir in the grated Cheddar cheese, butter, garlic and salt. When the cheese melts, pour in the milk. Stir in the egg yolks and bacon bits. Fold the beaten egg whites into the batter.

Butter a 1.5 litre (3 pint) casserole or soufflé dish. Pour the mixture in. Level the batter with a rubber spatula. Bake in an oven preheated to 170°C (325°F or Mark 3) for 1 hour or until a knife inserted into the centre comes out clean. Serve hot.

BERNARD CLAYTON, JR.
THE COMPLETE BOOK OF BREADS

Bulgarian Village Cornbread

Prosenik

This bread is usually served with yogurt, soft white cheese or fried haricot beans.

To make four 15 cm (6 inch) cornbreads

600 g	fine cornmeal	1¼ lb
200 g	plain flour	7 oz
1 tsp	salt	1 tsp
About 60 cl	tepid water	About 1 pint

Sift the cornmeal with the salt into a bowl. Add enough water to form a smooth, soft, wet dough which holds its shape. Add the flour and knead the dough on a floured work surface until all the flour is absorbed.

Divide the dough into four pieces. Roll the pieces into balls and pat them into rounds about 4 cm (1½ inches) thick. Bake the rounds on greased baking sheets in an oven preheated to 170°C (325°F or Mark 3) for about 1 hour, or until the crusts have turned a deep golden colour.

DR. L. PETROV, DR. N. DJELEPOV, DR. E. IORDANOV AND S. UZUNOVA
BULGARSKA NAZIONALNA KUCHNIYA

Italian Sweet Cornbread

Pizza di Polenta

If citron is not available, used chopped mixed peel.

To make one 25 by 20 cm (10 by 8 inch) bread

400 g	fine cornmeal	14 oz
50 g	plain flour	2 oz
50 g	butter, softened	2 oz
8 cl	oil	3 fl oz
30 g	sugar	1 oz
	salt	
45 cl	hot water	¾ pint
150 g	sultanas	5 oz
100 g	pine-nuts	3½ oz
50 g	candied citron, chopped	2 oz

Put the cornmeal and flour in a large mixing bowl, make a well in the centre and add the butter, oil, sugar and a pinch of salt. Mix all the ingredients together and bind them with the water to form a batter the consistency of thick cream. Add the sultanas, pine-nuts and candied citron peel and incorporate them well and evenly into the dough.

Butter and flour a baking tin. Gently pour the mixture into the tin and bake in a preheated 190°C (375°F or Mark 5) oven for about 30 minutes until the edges are golden-brown.

LUIGI VOLPICELLI AND SECONDINO FREDA (EDITORS)
L'ANTIARTUSI: 1000 RICETTE

Bulgarian Cornbread

Kerkelek

This cornbread comes from Vratza, a town in the wine-making region of northern Bulgaria. It is usually served cold, cut into bite-sized pieces, topped with milk, sauerkraut juice or madzhun (grape syrup).

To make one 45 cm (18 inch) square cornbread

1 kg	coarse cornmeal	2 lb
About 5 litres	water	About 8 pints
2 tsp	salt	2 tsp
100 g	butter	3½ oz

Pour the water into a large, heavy-based saucepan. Add the salt and bring to the boil. Gradually pour in the cornmeal, stirring with a wooden spoon or spatula. Cook over a low heat, stirring frequently, for at least 1 hour, or until you have a smooth, thick mass that comes away from the sides of the pan.

Melt the butter in a baking tin about 45 cm (18 inches) square and 9 cm (3½ inches) deep. Swirl the butter so that the tin is well greased. Pour the cornmeal mush into the tin; wet the back of a spoon and use it to smooth the surface of the mush. Bake the cornbread in an oven preheated to 170°C (325°F or Mark 3) for about 1 hour, or until the surface turns golden and the cornbread starts to shrink from the sides of the tin. Remove the bread from the tin and slice it immediately, using a strong cotton thread held taut between both hands.

DR. L. PETROV, DR. N. DJELEPOV, DR. E. IORDANOV AND S. UZUNOVA
BULGARSKA NAZIONALNA KUCHNIYA

Josephine's Batter Bread

Josephine was for years the cook for the Cucullu family of Lynchburg, Virginia. This is the recipe for her delicious old-fashioned batter bread.

To make one 20 by 10 cm (8 by 4 inch) bread

125 g	fine cornmeal, sifted	4 oz
1 tsp	baking powder	1 tsp
1 tsp	sugar	1 tsp
½ litre	milk	16 fl oz
3	eggs	3
60 g	butter, melted	2 oz

Mix the dry ingredients; beat the milk and eggs together and add them. In a 1 litre (2 lb) loaf tin, swish the melted butter round the tin so that the sides are evenly coated. Pour the batter into the loaf tin. Bake for about 30 minutes in an oven preheated to 180°C (350°F or Mark 4), or until a knife comes out clean from the centre of the bread. Do not let it cook until it is too dry. Serve the bread with butter.

MARION BROWN
THE SOUTHERN COOK BOOK

Lombard Corn Rolls

Pan de Mei alla Lombarda

These rolls are traditionally served in Milan as a dessert on St. George's Day (23rd April). Dried elderberries can be bought at shops specializing in home wine-making. If dried elderberries are not available, currants can be substituted.

To make four 7.5 cm (3 inch) rolls

100 g	coarse cornmeal	3½ oz
100 g	plain flour	3½ oz
1 tsp	baking powder	1 tsp
4	egg yolks	4
100 g	sugar	3½ oz
100 g	butter, softened	3½ oz
	salt	
4 tsp	dried elderberries	4 tsp
¼ litre	fresh single cream, chilled	8 fl oz

Beat the egg yolks and the sugar in a bowl for about 10 minutes, until they no longer stream down in a continuous ribbon when the spoon is raised. Add the butter; sieve the flour, cornmeal, baking powder and salt and mix well. The result should be a soft dough. Divide the dough into four equal parts. Form these into balls, flatten them slightly and lay them well separated on a buttered baking sheet. Sprinkle the rolls with the dried elderberries.

Bake the rolls in an oven preheated to 150°C (300°F or Mark 2) for 10 to 15 minutes or until they are golden. Cool them on a wire rack and serve them with the chilled cream.

IL MONDO IN CUCINA: I DOLCI

Serbian Cornbread

Srpska Proja

This cornbread is always served warm as an entrée with soft cheese or sauerkraut dishes.

To make one 30 by 20 cm (12 by 8 inch) bread, cut into squares

850 g	cornmeal	1¾ lb
1 tsp	salt	1 tsp
¼ litre	oil or melted butter	8 fl oz
5	eggs, beaten	5
½ litre	milk	16 fl oz

Sift the cornmeal with the salt and add the oil or melted butter, eggs and half the milk. Mix well for 15 minutes. Add the rest of the milk and mix again. Grease or oil a baking dish and put in the mixture.

Bake the cornmeal in an oven preheated to 190°C (375°F or Mark 5). When it starts getting a nice golden colour, take it out of the oven; cut it into squares and return it to the oven to finish baking. The cornbread should have a nice crust when baked. The total baking time is 50 to 60 minutes.

SPACENIJA-PATA MARKOVIĆ
YUGOSLAV COOKBOOK

Rice Bread

Pain de Riz

To make one 20 cm (8 inch) bread

125 g	boiled rice, cooled and sieved or cold leftover rice, sieved	4 oz
250 g	cornmeal, sieved	8 oz
2½ tsp	baking powder	2½ tsp
60 cl	milk	1 pint
3	eggs, well beaten	3
1 tsp	salt	1 tsp
15 g	butter, melted	½ oz

Gradually pour the milk into the eggs while mixing. Mix the salt and baking powder with the cornmeal and add it to the milk and eggs. Beat well. Then add the melted butter and the rice. Mix all thoroughly and beat until very light. Then grease the bottom of a shallow pan and turn the mixture in and bake for 30 minutes in a preheated 200°C (400°F or Mark 6) oven, or until a skewer inserted in the centre comes out clean. Serve hot, buttering the slices freely.

THE PICAYUNE CREOLE COOK BOOK

Old-Fashioned Indian Bread

If soured milk is not available, either cultured buttermilk or fresh milk to which 2 teaspoons of cream of tartar have been added can be substituted.

To make one 30 cm (12 inch) square bread

500 g	cornmeal	1 lb
120 g	plain flour	4 oz
1 tsp	bicarbonate of soda	1 tsp
1 tsp	salt	1 tsp
250 g	sugar	8 oz
1 litre	milk	1¾ pints
½ litre	soured milk	16 fl oz

Mix together all the ingredients until well blended. Pour them into a buttered, square baking tin and bake in an oven preheated to 150°C (300°F or Mark 2) for 1½ hours or until a knife inserted in the centre comes out clean.

LINDA KENNEDY ROSSER (EDITOR)
PIONEER COOKERY AROUND OKLAHOMA

Grandmother's Corn Pone

Sometimes the term "corn pone" also referred to these same ingredients with milk or molasses and baked in the oven. In parts of southern United States these fried pones were referred to as hoe cakes, because they were fried over open fires on hoes. Settlers who came from the north might have called them "johnny cakes", probably derived from journey cake.

To make about five 7.5 cm (3 inch) cakes

125 g	cornmeal	4 oz
1 tsp	salt	1 tsp
¼ litre	boiling water	8 fl oz
60 g	rendered bacon fat	2 oz

Mix together the salt and the cornmeal. Pour the water over them and stir well. Immediately wet your hands in cool water and form the mixture into rounds about 7.5 cm (3 inches) across. Heat the bacon fat in a frying pan, and fry the rounds until they are golden-brown on each side.

LINDA KENNEDY ROSSER (EDITOR)
PIONEER COOKERY AROUND OKLAHOMA

Philpy

This is a traditional rice bread from Charleston, South Carolina; rice was first introduced into North America when Captain John Thurber brought a bag of Madagascar rice with him to Charleston in 1680.

To make one 25 cm (10 inch) loaf

125 g	fine cornmeal	4 oz
125 g	rice, boiled and cooled	4 oz
¼ litre	milk	8 fl oz
2	eggs, beaten	2
15 g	butter, melted	½ oz
½ tsp	salt	½ tsp

Mix the rice with the milk, cornmeal, eggs, butter and salt. Beat well and pour into a well-buttered 25 cm (10 inch) pie dish. The mixture should be thin. Bake in an oven preheated to 190°C (375°F or Mark 5) until nicely browned—about 30 minutes. Break into pieces and serve with butter.

HELEN BROWN
HELEN BROWN'S WEST COAST COOK BOOK

Standard Preparations

Modern Sourdough Starter

Either the modern or the traditional sourdough starter can be used when a sourdough starter is called for in this Anthology. Any type of strong wheat or rye flour or a mixture of these flours can be used as a base for this starter. Where the Anthology recipe calls for strong plain flour, use strong plain flour as the base for the starter.

To make enough starter to leaven 1 kg (2½ lb) dough

250 g	flour	8 oz
15 g	fresh yeast or 2 tsp dried yeast	½ oz
60 cl	tepid water	1 pint

Mix the yeast with the water. If you are using dried yeast, leave the mixture for about 15 minutes to dissolve. Sprinkle the flour on to the yeast mixture and whisk it in to form a thick batter. It is not essential for the batter to be smooth: the action of the yeast will break down any lumps. Pour the mixture into a bowl, cover it with plastic film and leave it at warm room temperature for at least 24 hours, when it should be frothy.

The starter can be used immediately, but it will have a better sourdough flavour if it is left for at least another three days. After that, if the sourdough starter has not been used, or if it needs replenishing after use, it must be "fed" daily. Simply add to the mixture a handful of flour and enough water to restore it to a thick batter when beaten. The starter should then be covered with plastic film and left overnight in a warm place, after which it will again be ready for use. The starter can be refrigerated for up to one week; refrigeration will inhibit fermentation and prevent the sourdough flavour from becoming too strong, but the starter must be reactivated by adding more flour and water and leaving it overnight in a warm place before use.

When making bread with a sourdough starter, use four parts flour to one part starter.

Traditional Sourdough Starter

Either the traditional or the modern sourdough starter can be used when a sourdough starter is called for in the Anthology. Traditional sourdough starters are leavened by the natural yeasts that are present in the atmosphere. Although this recipe contains a large amount of sugar, it merely serves to feed the yeast and encourage its growth, and will not give the starter a sweet flavour. Any type of strong wheat or rye flour can be used as a base for this starter; rice, buckwheat and barley flours, cornmeal and oatmeal, or a mixture, are also suitable. Where the Anthology recipe calls for strong plain flour, use strong plain flour as the base for the starter.

To make enough starter to leaven 2.5 kg (5 lb) dough

500 g	flour	1 lb
1	medium-sized potato	1
About 90 cl	water	About 1½ pints
250 g	sugar	8 oz

Boil the potato in water to cover. Reserve the cooking liquid. Peel the potato and mash it thoroughly. Add enough tepid water to the cooled cooking liquid to make it up to 90 cl (1½ pints) of liquid, and stir it with the mashed potato, flour and sugar to make a thick batter. Pour the mixture into a bowl. Cover the bowl with plastic film and fold it in a large towel or blanket. Put the sourdough starter in a warm place—next to a stove, for example, or in an airing cupboard—for three days. The mixture is ready when it is bubbly and has a sour smell. If liquid has formed on the top it should be stirred in before use. If the mixture has no bubbles or has turned reddish or orange in colour, throw it away and make a new batch.

Where the starter is not to be used immediately, or it needs replenishing after some has been used, add a handful of flour and enough tepid water to make a thick batter when beaten. Cover the bowl with plastic film and wrap it in a towel or a blanket and leave it in a warm place for 24 hours before use. The starter can be stored in a refrigerator for up to one week.

When making bread with a sourdough starter, use four parts flour to one part starter.

Rye Sourdough Starter

Although any sourdough starter which includes rye flour can be used to leaven rye bread, the following recipe gives the most authentic sour rye flavour.

To make enough starter to leaven 2.5 kg (5 lb) dough

500 g	rye flour	1 lb
30 g	fresh yeast or 1 tbsp dried yeast	1 oz
¾ litre	tepid water	1¼ pints
1	small onion, peeled and halved	1

In a bowl, dissolve the yeast in ½ litre (16 fl oz) of the water, then whisk in half the flour, beating until no lumps remain. Add the onion, cover the mixture loosely with a cloth, and let it stand at room temperature for 24 hours.

Remove the onion. Whisk in the remaining water and the rest of the flour. Cover the mixture again and let it stand for three days; the starter should be bubbly and have a sour smell. If it is flat or has changed colour, it must be discarded.

Starter that is not to be used immediately it is ready or that needs replenishing after use should be "fed" daily with a handful of flour and enough tepid water to make a thick batter when beaten. The bowl should be covered and left overnight or for up to 24 hours in a warm place, by which time the starter will again be ready for use. Leftover rye starter can be refrigerated for up to two weeks, but must be replenished and left in a warm place for 24 hours before use.

When making a rye loaf with a sourdough starter, use four parts flour to one part starter.

Basic Bread Dough

Wherever basic bread dough is called for in the recipe section of this book, this method can be followed, using strong plain flour. For a more rustic flavour, a small amount of rye, wholemeal or barley flour can be substituted for the same amount of strong plain flour. The same recipe can be followed for a mixture of wheat flours.

To make 2.5 kg (5 lb) bread dough
or two 30 cm (12 inch) loaves

1.5 kg	strong plain flour	3 lb
30 g	fresh yeast or 1 tbsp dried yeast	1 oz
1 tbsp	salt	1 tbsp
90 cl	tepid water	1½ pints
	coarse semolina	

Sift the salt and flour into a bowl. Mix the yeast with the water; if you are using dried yeast, leave it to soften for about 15 minutes. Pour the yeast mixture into the flour. Mix the flour and liquid together into a stiff, sticky dough. Put the dough on to a floured board and knead it thoroughly, until it is elastic and glossy—about 15 minutes.

Shape the dough into a ball and return it to the bowl. Cover the bowl with plastic film and leave the dough to rise until doubled in bulk—1½ to 2½ hours, depending on temperature and humidity. The dough is ready when a finger pressed into it leaves a dent that does not immediately smooth itself out.

Put the dough on a working surface and divide it in half. Knead each half into a ball, cover it with a cloth, and leave it to rest for 10 to 15 minutes. Reshape the dough into two balls. Lay the loaves on a board sprinkled with coarse semolina and cover them with a cloth. Leave them to prove until doubled in bulk again, about 45 minutes to 1 hour. With a razor blade or sharp knife, cut a cross about 1 cm (½ inch) deep in each loaf.

Preheat the oven to 230°C (450°F or Mark 8). Put an ungreased baking sheet in the centre of the oven. Lay a wide dish on the oven floor and pour hot water into it so that steam is released into the oven as the water heats. Slide the loaves off the board and on to the baking sheet. Using a plant sprayer, spray water all over the inside of the oven. Bake the loaves for about 45 minutes. After 20 minutes, remove the wide dish containing water. Bake for a further 15 minutes, then reduce the oven temperature to 200°C (400°F or Mark 6) for the rest of the baking time. The loaf is baked if it sounds hollow when rapped on the bottom with the knuckles.

Cool the loaves on wire racks. Do not slice them until they are cold, preferably the next day.

Basic bread dough with olive oil. Suitable for pizza or other breads with surface flavourings. Add 1 to 2 tablespoons olive oil when mixing the liquid with the flour and salt.

Butter and Milk Dough

This dough is suitable for making rolls (*pages 30-33*), tin or sandwich loaves (*page 36*) or a plaited loaf (*page 26*).

To make 2 kg (4 lb) dough or two 20 by 10 cm
(8 by 4 inch) tin loaves or about 15 rolls

1 kg	strong plain flour	2½ lb
15 g	fresh yeast or 2 tsp dried yeast	½ oz
2 tsp	salt	2 tsp
About ¾ litre	tepid milk	About 1¼ pints
100 g	butter, softened	3½ oz

Place the flour and salt in a bowl. Dissolve the yeast in the milk; if you are using dried yeast leave it in a warm place for about 15 minutes. Pour the liquid into the flour and salt and work in the softened butter until a sticky dough is obtained. Turn the dough out on to a floured board, and knead it vigorously for 10 to 15 minutes or until the dough is elastic, smooth and glossy. The dough should be fairly firm; add more flour if necessary.

Put the dough into a clean, dry bowl, cover the bowl with plastic film and leave the dough to rise until doubled in bulk, about 1½ to 2½ hours, depending on the temperature and humidity. The dough is ready when a finger pressed into it leaves a dent which does not immediately smooth itself out.

Knead the dough again and shape it into the required shape or put it into two 1 litre (2 lb) loaf tins. Cover the bread with a cloth and leave it to rise until doubled in bulk again, or until it has risen to the rims of the tins, about 45 to 60 minutes.

Bake the bread in an oven preheated to 230°C (450°F or Mark 8) for about 20 minutes if making rolls, or 45 minutes if making loaves. The bread is ready when golden-brown and when, turned out of the tin, it sounds hollow when the base is rapped with your knuckles. Cool the bread on wire racks before slicing or storing.

Simple Egg Dough

This dough can be baked in tins or shaped into a fancy bread such as a ring (*page 58*). It can be used for a kulibiak (*pages 148-149*), or to replace rich egg dough in a sausage brioche (*page 66*). To make a pyramid (*page 60*) or a plait (*page 26*), reduce the quantity of milk to 20 cl (7 fl oz).

To make 1 kg (2½ lb) dough

750 g	strong plain flour	1½ lb
30 g	fresh yeast or 1 tbsp dried yeast	1 oz
¼ litre	tepid milk	8 fl oz
1 tbsp	sugar	1 tbsp
3	eggs	3
250 g	butter, softened	8 oz
1½ tsp	salt	1½ tsp
1	egg yolk, beaten with 2 tbsp water	1

Dissolve the yeast in the milk; if you are using dried yeast, leave in a warm place for about 15 minutes. Then whisk in the sugar and about 200 g (7 oz) of the flour, until the mixture has the consistency of a thick batter. Cover the bowl with plastic film and leave it in a warm place until this yeast sponge has doubled in bulk, about 1 hour. Whisk the eggs into the sponge.

Add the softened butter in walnut-sized pieces. Gradually add the rest of the flour, a handful at a time, stirring it in until the dough has a firm consistency. Lumps of butter will remain in the dough, but this does not matter, as they will be incorporated during the kneading process.

Turn out the dough on to a floured board, and knead thoroughly until it is smooth, glossy and elastic, 10 to 15 minutes. Return it to a clean, dry bowl, and leave it covered in a warm place to rise until it is three to four times its previous bulk, 1½ to 2½ hours.

Punch down the dough and give it the required shape. Cover it with a cloth and lay it on a buttered baking sheet or in a greased loaf tin for the final proving: it should double in bulk again after about 45 minutes. Glaze the dough with the egg yolk. Bake the bread in an oven preheated to 200°C (400°F or Mark 6) for 50 minutes to 1 hour, or until the loaf is golden-brown. Leave it to cool on a wire rack before cutting.

Rich Egg Dough

Rich egg dough is the standard dough for the brioche. Individual or large brioches may be baked in the fluted, large brioche mould (*page 64*). Alternatively, when the dough is formed into a ring and the surface cut with scissors, it is known as a *brioche couronne* (crown brioche). Brioche dough is also baked as a plaited loaf (*page 26*) or wrapped around a poaching sausage (*page 66*).

To make 1 kg (2 lb) rich egg dough

500 g	strong plain flour	1 lb
20 g	fresh yeast or 2 tsp dried yeast	¾ oz
3 to 4 tbsp	tepid water	3 to 4 tbsp
60 g	sugar	2 oz
1 tsp	salt	1 tsp
6	eggs	6
300 g	unsalted butter, softened	10 oz
1	egg yolk, beaten with 2 tsp water	1

Mix the yeast in the tepid water; if you are using dried yeast, leave for 15 minutes. Put the flour, sugar and salt into a bowl. Add the yeast mixture and break in the eggs. Mix the eggs and yeast, gradually pulling flour from the sides of the well, until all the flour has been wetted.

Turn the dough out on to a cool working surface. It should be very soft and sticky. Using your hands and a dough scraper, knead the dough thoroughly until it looses its stickiness and becomes smooth and elastic, about 10 minutes.

Break off walnut-sized pieces of the butter and, using a dough scraper or spatula, fold them one at a time into the dough. Fold in the butter and knead until the dough is smooth. Put the dough into a bowl, cover it with plastic film, and leave in a warm place until it has trebled in bulk, 3 to 4 hours.

Punch the dough down several times to expel the air, then knead it lightly for 2 to 3 minutes. Cover the bowl again with plastic film and leave the dough to rise again. For best results, the dough should be left to rise in the refrigerator for 6 to 8 hours or overnight. Otherwise, leave the dough to rise at room temperature until doubled in bulk—3 to 4 hours—and then leave it to chill for at least half an hour before shaping.

Shape the dough as required and put it in a well-buttered mould or loaf tin. Cover the mould with a cloth or an inverted bowl and leave the dough to rise at room temperature until doubled in bulk, 1½ to 2 hours. Glaze the top of the dough with the egg yolk beaten with water. If making a large moulded or plaited brioche, do not glaze at the seams where two pieces of dough join, as this will impede the rising during baking. A large loaf should be baked in an oven preheated to 220°C (425°F or Mark 7) for 10 minutes, and the heat then reduced to 190°C (375°F or Mark 5) and the loaf baked for a further 30 to 40 minutes. Individual brioches are baked in an oven preheated to 220°C (425°F or Mark 7) for about 15 minutes, or until golden-brown. To test for doneness, insert a skewer into the centre of the bread. If it comes out clean, the bread is ready. Unmould and cool it on a wire rack for at least 15 minutes before serving.

Yeast Puff Dough

Yeast puff dough is used for rich breads and cakes such as croissants (*page 70*) and Danish pastries (*pages 74-77*). The yeast puff pastry recipes in this Anthology are variations on the method below, but may contain egg and fold the dough in different ways to incorporate the fat. The basic rule for this type of pastry is to use cold fat and sandwich it into the dough.

To make about 750 g (1½ lb) dough

500 g	strong plain flour	1 lb
15 g	fresh yeast or 2 tsp dried yeast	½ oz
30 cl	tepid milk	½ pint
1 tsp	salt	1 tsp
1 tsp	sugar	1 tsp
250 g	butter, softened	8 oz

Dissolve the yeast in the milk. If you are using dried yeast, leave it for 15 minutes in a warm place to soften. Place the flour and salt in a bowl. Make a well in the flour and pour the yeast into it. Add the sugar and 60 g (2 oz) of the butter, cut into pieces, and gradually incorporate flour from the sides of the well into the liquid until all the flour is wet and the mixture is a soft, sticky dough.

Knead the dough for about 5 minutes, cover it with plastic film then leave it to rise at room temperature until doubled in bulk, from 1½ to 2½ hours. Punch the dough down to expel the bubbles of air, cover it and leave it to rise again, either at room temperature for 1 hour then chilled for another hour or overnight in the refrigerator.

Flatten the dough on a cool, floured surface. Roll it out into a rectangle about 1 cm (½ inch) thick and twice as long as it is wide. With a palette knife, spread two-thirds of the rectangle with the rest of the butter, leaving an unbuttered margin about 2 cm (¾ inch) wide. Fold the unbuttered third of the dough over half of the buttered section, then fold the other buttered section over the top. The dough will thus form three layers, with two thicknesses of butter between them. With a rolling pin, press the edges of the dough to seal in the butter. Turn the dough and, with a folded side facing towards you, roll it out lightly; too much pressure would force the butter out. Continue rolling the dough until it is about twice as long as it is wide.

Fold the dough into thirds again. Wrap it in plastic film and chill it for 1 hour. Place the rectangle on the work surface with one of its short sides facing you. Roll it out lengthwise and fold

as before. Repeat the rolling and folding, wrap it in plastic film and return the dough to the refrigerator. After an hour, the dough is ready for shaping, proving and baking.

Yeast Dough Fillings

These fillings are suitable for Danish pastries, croissants, *kugelhopf* cakes, buns or any other filled yeast dough.

Cinnamon butter. Spread about 125 g (4 oz) of softened butter over the surface of the dough to be filled. Sprinkle with 125 g (4 oz) of castor sugar and 2 teaspoons of ground cinnamon.
Cheese and egg. Sieve 250 g (8 oz) of *ricotta* or curd cheese. Beat an egg into the cheese, then blend in 125 g (4 oz) of grated Parmesan and a pinch of cayenne pepper.
Poppy seed. In a saucepan, combine 250 g (8 oz) of ground poppy seeds and ¼ litre (8 fl oz) of milk and simmer for 5 minutes, stirring constantly. Stir in 125 g (4 oz) of sugar, 30 g (1 oz) of butter, 1 teaspoon of vanilla sugar, half a teaspoon of ground cinnamon and half a teaspoon of grated lemon rind. Simmer for another 5 minutes, stirring constantly. Stir in 2 tablespoons of grated chocolate, honey or jam, and reduce over a high heat if necessary to produce a thick purée. One tablespoon of rum may be added, if desired.
Apple and cinnamon. Simmer 250 g of peeled and diced apples with 125 g (4 oz) of sugar, 6 tablespoons of water, 1 tablespoon of lemon juice, half a teaspoon of grated lemon rind and a quarter teaspoon of ground cinnamon. When the apples are soft, in about 10 minutes, rub the mixture through a sieve or mash it with a fork. Add 1 tablespoon of rum. Reduce over a high heat if the mixture is too liquid.
Almond paste. In a bowl, mix 250 g (8 oz) of ground almonds, 100 g (3½ oz) of castor sugar, 125 g (4 oz) of icing sugar and the grated rind of 1 lemon. Stir the ingredients well. Add 1 lightly beaten egg white, and stir to form a thick paste.

Recipe Index

English recipe titles are listed by categories such as "Brioche", "Filling", "Oatmeal", "Rye Bread" and "Walnut", and within those categories alphabetically. Foreign recipe titles are listed alphabetically without regard to category.

Almond:
Cream Filling, 150
Iced, Topping, 150
Paste, 132
Paste Filling, 173
in Shrove Tuesday Buns, 132
Topping, 143
see also Fruit; Nut
Alt-Wiener Patzerlgugelhupf, 146
Anchovy:
Endive, Olive and, Filling, 112
Loaf, 131
and Tomato Filling, 122
and Tomato Flan, 122
Apple:
and Cinnamon Filling, 173
Spiced, Bread, 163

Babka Droźdźowa, 143
Bacon Spoonbread, 166
Bagels, Jewish, 149
Bairn Brack, 138
Banana Bread, Jamaican, 162
Bara Brith, 144
Barley Meal:
in Finnish Potato Flatbread, 165
Flatbread, 166
Hertfordshire, Bread, 102
in Telemark Flatbread, 164
BASIC BREADS, 94-107
Batavian Endive:
Neapolitan, and Black Olive Bread, 108
and Olive Filling, 108
see also Endive
Batter Bread, Josephine's, 168
Beer:
Bread, 98
German Malt, Bread, 99
Bicarbonate of Soda, *see* Crumpets; Soda Bread
Birewecke, 124, 125
Birnbrot, 126
Blueberry or Cranberry Muffins, 161
Bortellina Bettolese, 106
Bran Muffins, 161
Bread, Plain:
Annadamma, 101
Beer, 98
Black Rye, 96
Boston Brown, 156
Boston Cornbread, 155
Brown Oatmeal, 156
Bulgarian Cornbread, 167

Bulgarian Village Cornbread, 167
Buttermilk Oaten, 155
Dutch Brown, 96
German Household, 99
German Malt Beer, 99
German Sourdough Cornbread, 101
German Sourdough Rye Loaf, 99
German Whole Rye, 98
Grant Loaf, The, 95
Hertfordshire Barley, 102
Home-Made Italian Milk, 94
Household, 96
Josephine's Batter, 168
Oatmeal, 103
Philpy, 169
Rice, 169
with Rolled Oats, 103
Salt-Rising, 94
Salt-Rising Leaven for, 94
Serbian Cornbread, 168
Soda, (White), 156
Sour-Rye, with Caraway Seeds, 97
Sourdough, 95
Sourdough Starter for, 170
Spanish Household, 94
Swedish Tin Loaves, 98
see also Egg-Enriched Bread; Flatbread; Filled Bread; Flavoured Bread; White Bread; individual flours, shapes, etc.
BREADS WITHOUT YEAST, 155-169
Bremer Klaben, 125
Brioche:
Cheese, 142
Neapolitan Rustic, 142
Riom, 141
Sausage in, 142
see also Egg-Enriched Bread
Brioche:
au Fromage, 142
Rustica, 142
Broas de Torresmos de Souzel, 120
Brown Bread *see* Wholemeal Bread
Bruin Brood, 96
Buckwheat:
Flatbread, 123
Polish Flatbread, 102
Buns:
Cheesy Bread, 156
Chelsea, 153
Chelsea, Filling, 153
Cold Harbour Balls, 132
Corsican Raisin and Walnut, 135
Crispies, 135
Dodgers, Dabs or Cornmeal Puffs, 161
Huffkins, 104
Marston, 132
Minorcan, 133
Raspberry, 157
Rich Scotch, A, 127
Shrove Tuesday, 132
Walnut, 127
Butter:
Aberdeen, Rolls, 154
Breton, Loaf, 154

Cake, 143
Italian Flatbread with, 109
and Milk Dough, 171
Butterkuchen, 143
Buttery Rowies, 154

Cabbage and Mushroom Kulibiak, 149
Cacen Gri, 160
Cake:
Bury Simnel, 157
Butter, 143
French Sally Lunn, 144
Griddle, 160
Onion, 110
Russian Easter, 140
Sally Lunns, 144
Yeast Coffee, 143
Cakes:
Granny's Oat, 160
Kneaded Cream, 157
Old Maids, 137
Yorkshire, 133
Caraway:
Crustless, Bread, 120
in Hunting Bread, 137
in Irish Spice Bread, 138
Salted, Topping, 155
Sour Rye Bread with, Seeds, 97
Swedish Limpé, 121
Chappati and Phulka, 163
Chausson à la Napolitaine, 113
Cheese:
Bread, 122
Brioche, 142
Bulgarian, Bread, 153
Cheesy Bread, 156
Cream, Bread, 114
and Egg Filling, 173
Italian Easter Bread with, 141
in Neapolitan Rustic Brioche, 142
and Olive Filling, 107
and Onion Topping, 113
Popovers, 162
Sheep's, Bread, 122
Swiss, Flan, 113
Chocolate Rolls, 115
Cinnamon:
Apple and, Filling, 173
Butter Filling, 173
Plum and, Topping, 134
Coca de Trampó Mallorquina, 123
Coffee Cake, Yeast, 143
Coriander, in Hunting Bread, 137
Cornbread:
Bacon Spoonbread, 166
with Black Truffle, 165
Boston, 155
Bulgarian, 167
Bulgarian Village, 167
German Sourdough, 101
Italian Sweet, 167
Serbian, 168
Spider Corncake, 166
see also Cornmeal

Cornmeal:
    Annadamma Bread, 101
    Bacon Spoonbread, 166
    Boston Brown Bread, 156
    Boston Cornbread, 155
    Bulgarian Cornbread, 167
    Bulgarian Village Cornbread, 167
    Corn Sandwich Muffins, 101
    Dodgers, Dabs or, Puffs, 161
    German Sourdough Cornbread, 101
    Grandmother's Corn Pone, 169
    Italian Speckled Bread, 158
    Italian Sweet Cornbread, 167
    Josephine's Batter Bread, 168
    Lombard Corn Rolls, 168
    Miniature, Loaves, 121
    Old-Fashioned Indian Bread, 169
    in Old Maids, 137
    Philpy, 169
    in Pumpernickel Bread, 117
    in Rice Bread, 169
    Serbian Cornbread, 168
    Spider Corncake, 166
Courgette Bread, 124
Crackling:
    Neapolitan, Pizza, 109
    Portuguese, Loaf, 120
Cranberry Muffins, Blueberry or, 161
Cream:
    Kneaded, Cakes, 157
    Scones, 158
Crescents:
    Austrian Coffeetime, 154
    Salted, Rolls, 155
    Yugoslav Walnut, 152
    see also Croissants; Rolls
Crescia di Pasqua col Formaggio, 141
Crispies, 135
Croissants:
    Viennese Filled, 150
    Yugoslav Walnut Crescents, 152
Croissants Viennois Fourrés, 150
Crumpets, 105, 106
    Flannel, 106
    Pikelets, 106
Currant Bread, 144
    see also Fruit

Danish Pastries, 151
Dough:
    Basic Bread, 171
    Basic Bread, with Oil, 171
    Butter and Milk, 171
    Rich Egg, 172
    Rich Pastry, 126
    Simple Egg, 172
    Yeast, Fillings, 173
    Yeast Puff, 173

Egg:
    Cheese and, Filling, 173
    Rich Dough, 172
    Simple Dough, 172
    Twist, 130

EGG BREADS, 128-149
Egg-Enriched Bread:
    Algerian Orange-Flavoured Loaves, 136
    Anchovy Loaf, 131
    Austrian Potato, 136
    Blanche Frankehouser's Old-Fashioned
        Oatmeal, 128
    Bread of the Dead, 138
    Cheese Brioche, 142
    Curly Murly, 145
    Currant, 144
    Dough for, 172
    Egg Twist, 130
    French Sally Lunn Cake, 144
    Hunting, 137
    Irish Spice, 138
    Italian Easter Bread with Cheese, 141
    Neapolitan Rustic Brioche, 142
    New Year Sweet, 140
    Plum Slices, 134
    Polish Festival, 143
    Poppy Seed or Walnut Roll, 138
    Prune, 136
    Riom Brioche, 141
    Sally Lunns, 144
    Sausage in Brioche, 142
    Swiss Plait, 128
    Viennese Plait, 129
    Walnut Loaf, 134
    Yeast, 128
    Yeast Coffee Cake, 143
    see also Cakes; Filled Bread; Flavoured
    Bread; Kugelhopf; Kulibiak; etc.
Endive:
    Neapolitan, Pie, 112
    Olive and Anchovy Filling, 112
    and Olive Filling, 108
    see also Batavian Endive
Ensaimadas Menorquinas, 133
Erdäpfelbrot, 136

Feines Gesäuertes Roggenbrot, 99
Fennel:
    Rings, 121
    Swedish Limpé, 121
Filled Bread:
    Anchovy and Tomato Flan, 122
    Bulgarian Cheese, 153
    Cabbage and Mushroom Kulibiak, 149
    Cream Cheese Bread, 114
    Leek Pie, 148
    Mallorcan Onion and Tomato Flan, 123
    Marrakesh "Pizza", 111
    Neapolitan Batavia and Black Olive, 108
    Neapolitan Endive Pie, 112
    Neapolitan Rustic Brioche, 142
    Neapolitan Turnover, 113
    Old-Fashioned Quiche Lorraine, 111
    Old-Fashioned Viennese Kugelhopf, 146
    Olive, 107
    Onion Cake, 110
    Onion Flatbread, 110
    Picnic Loaf, A, 114
    Polish Rice and Mushroom Kulibiak, 148

Poppy Seed Kugelhopf, 146
Poppy Seed or Walnut Roll, 138
Sausage in Brioche, 142
Scalded Yeast Rolls, 139
Swiss Cheese Flan, 113
    see also Filling; Pizza
Filling:
    Almond Cream, 150
    Almond Paste, 132, 173
    Anchovy and Tomato, 122
    Apple and Cinnamon, 173
    Cheese and Egg, 173
    Cheese and Olive, 107
    Chelsea Bun, 153
    Chocolate Rolls, 115
    Cinnamon Butter, 173
    Cockscomb, 151
    Endive and Olive, 108
    Endive, Olive and Anchovy, 112
    Fruit Snail, 151
    Leek and Pancetta, 148
    Nut, 115
    Nut and Sultana, 154
    Poppy Seed, 138, 146, 173
    Potato Stuffing, 164
    Rice and Mushroom, 148
    Vanilla and Walnut, 152
    Walnut, 138, 146
    Yeast Dough, 173
    see also Topping
Fiouse è lè Flemme, 111
Flan:
    Anchovy and Tomato, 122
    Cream Cheese Bread, 114
    Mallorcan Onion and Tomato, 123
    Sugar, 140
    Swiss Cheese, 113
    see also Filled Bread; Quiche; Tart
Flatbread:
    Barley, 166
    Buckwheat, 123
    Finnish Potato, 165
    Fried, 106
    Italian, with Butter, 109
    Italian, with Ham, 112
    Italian Sausage Bread, 114
    Marrakesh "Pizza", 111
    Norman, 164
    Oatmeal Bread, 103
    with Oil and Salt, 109
    Onion, 110
    Pitta Bread, 103
    Polish Buckwheat, 102
    with Rillons and White Wine, 152
    Sage, 110
    Stuffed Parathas, 164
    Telemark, 164
    Wholemeal Buttered Griddle Bread, 163
    Wholemeal Griddle Breads, 163
    see also Pizza
Flavoured Bread:
    Algerian Orange, 136
    Alsatian Kugelhopf, 147
    Anchovy Loaf, 131

Austrian Potato, 136
Bread of the Dead, 138
Bremen Christmas, 125
Breton Butter Loaf, 154
Buckwheat Flatbread, 123
Bury Simnel, 157
Cheese, 122
Cheese Brioche, 142
Christmas, 126
Christmas Pear, 125
Courgette, 124
Crustless Caraway Bread, 120
Fennel Rings, 121
Flatbread with Oil and Salt, 109
Fruit, 124
Hermit's Rice, The, 117
Hunting, 137
Irish Spice, 138
Italian Easter, with Cheese, 141
Italian Flatbread with Butter, 109
Italian Flatbread with Ham, 112
Italian Sausage Bread, 114
Miniature Cornmeal Loaves, 121
Nut Roll, 115
Pear, 126
Portuguese Crackling Loaf, 120
Potato, 116
Prune, 136
Pumpernickel, 117
Pumpkin, 124
Raisin Nut Bread, 119
Republican Potato, 116
Rich Scotch Bun, A, 127
Rosemary, 118
Sage Flatbread, 110
Sheep's Cheese, 122
Sourdough Onion, 118
Swedish Limpé, 121
Ulm, 118
Vegetable, 116
Viennese Kugelhopf, 147
Walnut Bun, 127
Walnut Loaf, 134
Walnut and Onion, 120
Walnut Wholemeal, 119
see also Egg-Enriched Bread; Fruit;
    individual flavours
FLAVOURED AND FILLED BREADS, 107-127
Focaccia:
    di Farina Gialla al Tartufo, 165
    all'Olio con Sale, 109
    alla Salvia, 110
Foncée, La, 164
Forron, 114
Fruit:
    Bread, 124
    Bremen Christmas Bread, 125
    Bury Simnel, 157
    Christmas Pear Bread, 125
    Currant Bread, 144
    Italian Speckled Bread, 158
    Pear Bread, 126
    Polish Festival Bread, 143
    Prune Bread, 136

Rich Scotch Bun, A, 127
Russian Easter Cake, 140
Snail Filling, 151
see also individual fruits

*G*âteau ou Brioche de Riom, 141
Gâteaux d'Etampes ou Fraiser, 157
Germgugelhupf, 147
Gialletti, 121
Glazes:
    Milk and Sugar, 115
    Molasses, 126
    see also Topping
Gnocco al Forno, 112
Granary and Onion Scones, 159
Griddle:
    Cake, 160
    Wholemeal, Breads, 163
    Wholemeal Buttered, Bread, 163
Guernsey Gâche Melée, 163
Gugelhupf mit Mohnfülle, 146

*H*am, Italian Flatbread with, 112
Hausmannsbrot, 99
Hefebrot, 128
Homburger Prezeln, 137
Huajuan, 104
Huffkins, 104

*K*affeekipferln, 154
Käswähe, 113
Kauraleipä, 103
Kerkelet, 167
Khboz Bishemar, 111
Khubz (Eish Shami), 103
Kiflice od Sala, 152
Kougelhopf, 147
Kouing-Aman, 154
Kraftbrot mit Haferflocken, 103
Kugelhopf:
    Alsatian, 147
    Old-Fashioned Viennese, 146
    Poppy Seed, 146
    Viennese, 147
Kulebiak:
    z Ciasta Krucho-Drożdżowego z Rýzem i
        Grzybami, 148
    z Kapusta i Grzybami, 149
Kulibiak:
    Cabbage and Mushroom, 149
    Polish Rice and Mushroom, 148
Kulitsch, 140
Kümmelbrot (Ohne Rinde), 120

*L*eaven, Salt-Rising, 94
Leek Pie, 148
    and Panceta Filling, 148

*M*aisbrot mit Sauerteig, 101
Malzbierbrot, 99
Milk:
    Butter and, Dough, 171
    Home-Made Italian, Bread, 94
    Rolls, 130

and Sugar Glaze, 115
Mounas, 136
Muffins, 130
    Blueberry or Cranberry, 161
    Bran, 161
    Corn Sandwich, 101
    see also Popovers
Mushroom:
    Cabbage and, Kulibiak, 149
    Polish Rice and, Kulibiak, 148
    Rice and, Filling, 148

*N*ut:
    Filling, 115
    Roll, 115
    and Sultana Filling, 154
    see also Almond; Walnut

*O*atmeal:
    Blanche Frankehouser's Old-Fashioned,
        Bread, 128
    Bread, 103
    Brown, Bread, 156
    Buttermilk Oaten Bread, 155
    Granny's Oatcakes, 160
    in Hertfordshire Barley Bread, 102
    see also Rolled Oats
Ohrariesta, 166
Oil:
    Basic Bread Dough with, 171
    Flatbread with, and Salt, 109
    Pizza, 111
Olive:
    Batavia and, Filling, 108
    Bread, 114
    Cheese and, Filling, 107
    Endive, and Anchovy Filling, 112
    Neapolitan Batavia and Black, Bread, 108
    Tart, 107
Øllebrød, 98
Onion:
    Cake, 110
    Cheese and, Topping, 113
    Flatbread, 110
    Granary and, Scones, 159
    Mallorcan, and Tomato Flan, 123
    Sourdough, Bread, 118
    Walnut and, Bread, 120
Orange, Algerian, Flavoured Loaves, 136

*P*ain:
    de Citrouille, 124
    d'Épice, 160
    au Levain, 95
    de Ménage, 96
    aux Noix, 134
    de Noix, Le, 119
    à la Pomme de Terre, 116
    de Riz, 169
Pan:
    Casero, 94
    de Mei alla Lombarda, 168
    de Muerto, 138
    de Nueces, 158

Striáa, 158
Pancetta, Filling, Leek and, 148
Pane:
    al Latte Fatto in Casa, 94
    di Rosmarino, 118
    con Salsicce, 114
Paratha, 163
Parathas, Stuffed, 164
Pastry, *see* Dough
Pear:
    Bread, 126
    Christmas, Bread, 125
Pepper Wreaths, Neapolitan, 100
Perunarieska, 165
Petits Pains:
    au Chocolat, 115
    au Lait, 130
Pie:
    Leek, 148
    Neapolitan Endive, 112
Pikelets, 106
Pissaladiera Niçoise, 108
Pistolets, Les, 104
Pizza:
    Basic Bread Dough with Oil for, 171
    Marrakesh, 111
    Neapolitan Crackling, 109
    Oiled, 111
    Provençal, 108
    see also Filled Bread; Flatbread
Pizza:
    di Polenta, 167
    Rustica, 112
    di Scarola, 112
Placek ze Śliwkami, 134
Plain Flour, *see* White Bread
Plait:
    Curly Murly, 145
    Egg Twist, 130
    Swiss, 128
    Viennese, 129
Plum Slices, 134
    and Cinnamon Topping, 134
Pogacice Sa Ovarcima I Belim Vinon, 152
Pognons aux Peurniaux, 136
Polnisches Feiertagsbrot, 143
Pompe aux Anchois, La, 131
Popovers, 162
    Cheese, 162
    see also Muffins
Poppy Seed:
    Egg Twist, 130
    Filling, 138, 146, 173
    Kugelhopf, 146
    and Sultana Filling, 139
    Topping, 130
Porrata, 148
Potato:
    Austrian, Bread, 136
    Bread, 116
    in Buckwheat Flatbread, 123
    Finnish, Flatbread, 165
    Republican, Bread, 116
    Southern Irish, "Box" Scones, 134

Stuffing, 164
    in Traditional Sourdough Starter, 170
    see also Kulibiak
Pretzels:
    Salted, 100
    Sweet, 137
Prosenik, 167
Prune Bread, 136
Puffs, Dodgers, Dabs or Cornmeal, 161
Pumpkin Bread, 124
Pyza z Hreczanej Mąki, 102

Quiche, Old-Fashioned, Lorraine, 111

Raisin:
    Corsican, and Walnut Buns, 135
    Nut Bread, 119
Raspberry Buns, 157
Rice:
    Bread, 169
    Hermit's Bread, The, 117
    and Mushroom Filling, 148
    Philpy, 169
Rillons, Flatbreads with, and White Wine, 152
Rings:
    Fennel, 121
    Jewish Bagels, 149
Roll:
    Nut, 115
    Poppy Seed or Walnut, 138
    Scalded Yeast, 139
Rolled Oats:
    Blanche Frankehouser's Old-Fashioned
        Oatmeal Bread, 128
    Bread with, 103
    in Sourdough Onion Bread, 118
    in Telemark Flatbread, 164
    see also Oatmeal
Rolls:
    Aberdeen Butter, 154
    Austrian Coffeetime Crescents, 154
    Brentford, 131
    Chocolate, 115
    Flower, 104
    Lombard Corn, 168
    Milk, 130
    Salted Crescent, 155
    Split, 104
Rosemary Bread, 118
Rusks, 129
    German, 102
Rye Bread:
    Beer, 98
    Black, 96
    Christmas Bread, 126
    French Spice, 160
    German Household, 99
    German Malt Beer, 99
    German Sourdough, Loaf, 99
    German Whole, 98
    Pumpernickel, 117
    Sour, with Caraway Seeds, 97
    Sourdough Onion, 118
    Sourdough Starter for, 170

Swedish Limpé, 121
Swedish Tin Loaves, 98
Telemark Flatbread, 164

Sage Flatbread, 110
Salé du Bugey, Le, 120
Sally Lunns, 144
    French Cake, 144
Salt:
    Crescent Rolls, 155
    Flatbread with Oil and, 109
    Pretzels, 100
    Rising Bread, 94
    Rising Leaven, 94
    Swedish, Sticks, 107
    Topping, 107
Saltstänger, 107
Salzbrezeln, 100
Sardenaira, 122
Saucisson Brioché, 142
Sauerteig-Zwiebelbrot, 118
Sausage:
    in Brioche, 142
    Italian, Bread, 114
Schafskäsebrot, 122
Schiacciata:
    col Burro, 109
    con la Cipolla, 110
Schrotbrot, 98
Schwarzbrot, 96
Schweizer Züpfe, 128
Scones:
    Cream, 158
    Granary and Onion, 159
    Mrs. Macnab's, 158
    Singing Lilly, 159
    Southern Irish Potato "Box", 134
Semlor, 132
Slices, Plum, 134
Soda Bread:
    Boston Brown, 156
    Boston Cornbread, 155
    Brown Oatmeal, 156
    Buttermilk Oaten, 155
    French Spice, 160
    Griddle Cake, 160
    Old-Fashioned Indian Bread, 169
    Salt-Rising, 94
    (White), 156
    see also Muffins; Scones
Solilemme, 144
Sörkifli, 155
Sourdough Bread, 95
    Black Rye, 96
    German, Cornbread, 101
    German Household, 99
    German Malt Beer, 99
    German, Rye Loaf, 99
    German Whole Rye, 98
    Onion, 118
    Sour Rye, with Caraway Seeds, 97
Sourdough Starter:
    Modern, 170
    Rye, 170

Traditional, 170
Spice:
 Apple Bread, 163
 French, Bread, 160
 Irish, Bread, 138
Srpska Proja, 168
STANDARD PREPARATIONS, 170-173
Stiacciata con l'Olio, 111
Striezel, 129
Strucla Drożdżowa z Masą Orzechową, 115
Strucle Parzone, 139
Stuffing, *see* Filling
Sugar:
 Flan, 140
 Milk and, Glaze, 115
Sultana:
 Nut and, Filling, 154
 Poppy Seed and, Filling, 139
 in Yeast Coffee Cake, 143
 see also Fruit

T*aloa*, 101
Taralli:
 con i Finocchietti, 121
 a Sugna e Pepe, 100
Tart:
 Olive, 107
 see also Quiche
Tarte:
 aux Olives, 107
 au Sucre, 140
Tattarleipä, 123
Tomato:
 Anchovy and, Flan, 122
 Mallorcan Onion and, Flan, 123
Tootmanik s Gotovo Testo, 153
Topping:
 Almond, 143
 Cheese and Onion, 113

Iced Almond, 150
Plum and Cinnamon, 134
Poppy Seed, 130
Royal Icing, 145
Salt, 107
Salted Caraway, 155
Seed, 130
Walnut, 152
 see also Glazes
Tortano con i Cicoli o Pizza Stracciata, 109
Tourte aux Noix, 127
Truffle, Cornbread with Black, 165
Turnover, Neapolitan, 113
Twist, *see* Plait

U *Pan di i Morti o "Uga Siccati"*, 135
Ulmer Brot, 118

Vanilla and Walnut Filling, 152
Vassilopitta, 140
Vegetable Bread, 116
Vörtlimpor, 126

Walnut:
 Bun, 127
 Corsican Raisin and, Buns, 134
 Filling, 138, 146
 Loaf, 134
 Nut Roll, 115
 Nut and Sultana Filling, 154
 and Onion Bread, 120
 Poppy Seed or, Roll, 138
 Raisin Nut Bread, 119
 Spanish Nut Bread, 158
 Topping, 152
 Vanilla and, Filling, 152
 Wholemeal Bread, 119
 Yugoslav, Crescents, 152
 see also Nut

White Bread:
 Hermit's Rice Bread, The, 117
 Household, 96
 Neapolitan Pepper Wreaths, 100
 Salt-Rising, 94
 Soda Bread (White), 156
 Sourdough, 95
 see also Bread; Egg-Enriched Bread; Filled
  Bread; Flatbread; Flavoured Bread;
  Plait
Wholemeal Bread:
 Brown Oatmeal, 156
 Buttered Griddle, 163
 Dutch Brown, 96
 Grant Loaf, The, 95
 Griddle, 163
 Spanish Household, 94
 Spiced Apple, 163
 Stuffed Parathas, 164
 Vegetable, 116
 Walnut, 119
 see also Bread; Rye Bread; White Bread
Wienerbrød, 151
Wine, Flatbreads with Rillons and White, 152
Wreaths:
 Curly Murly, 145
 Neapolitan Pepper, 100
 see also Plait

Yeast:
 Bread, 128
 Coffee Cake, 143
 Dough Fillings, 173
 Puff Dough, 173
 Scalded, Roll, 139
YEAST PUFF PASTRY, 150-155

Zwieback, 102, 129
Zwiebelkuchen zum Neuen Wien, 110

General Index/Glossary

Included in this index are definitions of many of
the culinary terms used in this book: definitions
are in italics. The recipes in the Anthology are
listed in the Recipe Index on page 174.

Acid, with bicarbonate of soda, 81
Acton, Eliza, 6
Allspice: *the dried berry—used whole or
ground—of a member of the myrtle family.
Called allspice because it has something of the
aroma of clove, cinnamon and nutmeg
combined;* 54
Almonds, 54, 57, 60; paste, 73, 74
Anchovies, as topping, 7, 45, 46
Antiphanes, 6
Apples, 48, 90
Apricots, 46, 90; jam, 74

Aristophanes, 6
Aromatics: *all substances—such as
vegetables, herbs and spices—that add aroma
and flavour to food when used in cooking.*
Avocados, 90
Bacon, 88; in spoonbread, 84-85; as topping,
45, 46-47
Bagels, 57, 78-79
Baking, the basic bread, 14, 16; early methods,
5-6; at home, 6-7; with steam, 7, 14, 16
Baking powder, 81, 86, 88, 90
Baking tins, for bread, 36-37; for fruit bread,
90; for muffins, 88-89
Bananas, in fruit bread, 90-91
Barley, 50
Barley flour, 6, 9; in non-yeast doughs, 81, 82,
84
Bashing, dough for cottage loaf, 18-19
Basil, 46
Batavian endive, as filling, 48

Batters, baking in moulds, 36; for cornbread,
92; for crumpets, 40-41; for muffins, 88-89; for
popovers, 88-89; preliminary, 58; for
spoonbread, 85; for wholemeal bread, 38
Beef, minced, as topping, 46
Beer, 5, 52
Beetroot, 50
Bicarbonate of soda, 9, 40-41, 81, 86, 88, 92
Bins, for storing bread, 7
Blanch: *to plunge food into boiling water for a
short period. Done for a number of reasons: to
remove strong flavours, such as the excess
saltiness of some bacon; to soften vegetables
before further cooking; to facilitate the removal
of skins or shells. Another meaning is "to
whiten".*
Blanched almonds: *almonds that have been
peeled by blanching (q.v.)*
Bleached flour, 6, 8
Blender, 7

Blueberries, in muffins, 88
Bolting, 6
Bran, 8; nutrition, 6
Bread, basic yeast, 13-43; courgette, 50-51; dark, 45, 52-53; flaky, 70-72, 82, 83; flavoured and filled, 45-55; history, 5-6; home-baking, 6-7; pudding, 7; pumpkin, 50-51; rich, 57-79; rich dark, 52-53; slicing, 17; sourdough, 17; stale, 7; storing, 7; white, 14-16; wholemeal, 38-39
Breadcrumbs, 7
Brick ovens, 6, 7
Brioche, 7, 57, 62-65; kugelhopf, 68-69; sausage filled, 66-67
Brown bread, 6
Brown rice, 50
Buckwheat flour, 9; in unleavened bread, 82
Buns, fruit and nut, 54-55; Scotch black, 44, 45, 54-55
Butter, in batter, 88, 90; as dough enrichment, 27, 30, 38, 57, 58-59, 60, 62; glaze, 30, 33; in paratha dough, 83; in puff dough, 57, 70-71
Buttermilk: *a by-product of churning cream to make butter, buttermilk is used in cheese-making and with leavening agents in baking. Nowadays, it is also made by thickening skimmed milk with a bacterial culture;* 86, 92
Cake hoop, 54-55
Candied peel, 68
Capers, 48
Caraway seeds, 34, 35, 52, 78
Carbon dioxide, as leavening agent, 10, 81, 86
Cardamom, 60
Carrots, 50
Casseroles, 7
Cervelas, 57, 66
Chappatis, 81, 82-83
Chard, 48
Cheddar cheese, in spoonbread, 84
Cheese, 7, 28, 88; for fillings, 45, 48, 73, 76; see also individual cheeses
Chequerboard loaf, 18, 19
Cherries, 46, 48
Chili peppers: *numerous varieties of small, finger-shaped hot peppers, native to tropical America and the West Indies.*
Chinese flower-rolls, 42-43
Chocolate, 45; in petit pain au chocolat, 48; in rich dark bread, 52
Cigar rolls, 30, 32
Cinnamon, 7, 46, 76
Citrus peel, 52; candied, 68; see also Lemon peel, Orange peel
Cloverleaf rolls, 30-31
Cloves, 54
Cluster rolls, 38-39
Cockscombs, pastries, 75
Cooling, loaves, 7
Copper bowl, for beating egg whites, 84
Cornbread, 92
Cornmeal flour, 9; in cornbread, 92; in non-yeast doughs, 81, 82, 84; in rich dark bread, 52-53; in spoonbread, 84-85
Cottage loaf, 18-19
Courgettes, shredded, in dough, 45, 50-51

Cracked wheat, as garnish, 39
Cracklings: *crisp pieces of rind and connective tissue obtained by frying or rendering (q.v.) beef, pork, goose or duck fat; 88*
Cranberries, 88
Cream, to enrich dough, 26; to marble cornbread, 92; as topping, 45, 46-47; see also Soured cream
Cream of tartar, 86
Cream cheese, 46, 68; eaten with bagels, 78
Croissants, 70-72
Croûtons: *small cubes of bread fried in butter and used as garnish; 7*
Crumpets, 40-41
Crust, scissor cuts, 20-21, 25; scored, 14, 16, 18, 19, 22-23, 25, 28, 31, 37, 87, 88
Cumin, 34
Currants, 54, 60, 73, 76
Cylinder loaf, 20-21; baked in a mould, 36-37
Danish pastries, 57, 73, 74, 75
Dark breads, 45; pumpernickel, 52-53
David, Elizabeth, 7
Dough, 13; with egg white and butter, 57, 78-79; with eggs and butter, 57, 58-59, 60, 62; incorporating flavours, 45, 52-53, 54-55; kneading, 15; with milk and butter, 26, 27, 30, 32, 33, 36, 38; mixing, 14; with olive oil, 28, 48; puff, 57, 70-71, 73, 74, 75, 76; rising time, 10, 13; without yeast, 81, 82-83, 86
Dried fruits, 45, 68, 76, 88; see also Currants, Raisins, Sultanas
Dried yeast, preparation, 10
Earthenware, loaf mould, 38
Egg white, in almond paste, 73; to enrich dough, 57, 78; glazes, 49, 53; as leaven, 81, 84-85
Egg yolk, glazes, 26-27, 64, 72, 73, 74, 75, 77, 79
Eggs, in batters, 85, 88, 90; as binder, 48; in doughs, 57, 58-59, 60, 62, 86; filling for pastries, 73, 75, 76; glazes, 23, 30, 33, 35, 38, 60, 66; hard-boiled, as filling, 66; see also Egg white, Egg yolk
Electric food processor, 7
Electric mixer, 13
Embryo, see Germ
Endive, 45; Batavian, 48
Endosperm, 6, 8, 9; vitamin content, 6
English Bread Book, The, 6
Envelopes, pastry, 73
Épi, 24
Fennel seeds, 34
Fermentation, sourdough starters, 11; yeast, 5
Fermipan, 10
Feta: *a Greek curd cheese made from sheep's milk.*
Filled breads, 45-55
Fillings, 45, 48-49, 57; for brioche, 66; for kugelhopf, 68; for muffins, 88; for pastries, 73, 76; for pittas, 28; for unleavened bread, 82
Fish, 46, 66; see also Anchovies, Smoked salmon
Flaky breads, croissants, 70-72; parathas, 82, 83

Flatbreads, 5, 28-29
Flavoured breads, 45-55
Flours, keeping qualities, 9; milling, 6; range of, 8-9; see also individual flours
Flower-rolls, 42-43
Folding, Parker House rolls, 32; puff dough, 70-71
Freezing, bread, 7
French toast, 7
Fruit, puréed, in fruit bread, 90-91; in spoonbread, 84; see also Dried fruits, individual fruits
Fruit bread, 90-91
Garlic, 45, 46, 48, 84
Garnishes, 7
Germ, 8, 9; oil, 9
Ghee: *Indian cooking fat; either clarified butter or made from vegetable fats. It can be bought from Indian grocers and will keep for up to one year if refrigerated.*
Ginger, ground, in kugelhopf, 68; root, 54
Glazes, butter, 30, 33; egg, 23, 30, 33, 35, 38, 60, 66; egg white, 49, 53; egg yolk, 26-27, 64, 72, 73, 74, 75, 77, 79; milk, 23; olive oil, 49
Gluten, 8, 9, 10
Goat cheese, 46
Grains, added to dough, 50
Green bacon: *unsmoked bacon; see Bacon*
Griddle, 6; for chappatis, 82; for crumpets, 40-41; for parathas, 83; for scones, 87
Ham, 68
Hard flour, 8
Herbs, 45, 82, 88
Home baking, 6
Honeycomb crumb, 40
Husk, 6, 8; see also Bran
Keeping qualities, bread, 7; flour, 9; rich dark bread, 52
Kneading, 8, 13, 15, 55, 63
Knot rolls, 30, 33
Kugelhopf, 57, 68-69
Lamb, minced, as topping, 46
Leavens, non-yeast, 81; sourdough, 11; yeast, 10
Lemon peel, 54
Lemon rind, 60, 68, 73
Loaves, chequerboard, 19; cottage, 18-19; cylinder, 20-21, 36-37; flat, 5, 28-29; long, 24-25; in moulds, 36-37; plaited, 26-27; tapered cylinder, 22-23; in tins, 36-37, 90; turban, 24
Long loaves, 24-25
Malt extract: *a product, available in dried or thick liquid form, made from fermented barley or other grain and used in brewing and bread-making.*
Marbled crumb, 68
Meals (grain), keeping qualities, 9; range of, 8-9
Meat, 28; leftover, 7; minced, as filling, 82; see also Beef, Lamb, Pork
Milk, in batters, 40, 58, 85, 88; and butter dough, 26, 27, 30, 32, 33, 36, 38; in egg white and butter dough, 78; glaze, 23; to marble cornbread, 92; see also Soured milk

Milling, 6, 7, 8
Molasses: *uncrystallized syrup drained from crude, unrefined sugar; similar to treacle and usually interchangeable with treacle in bread-making;* 45; in rich, dark bread, 52
Moulds, for baking bread, 36-37; for kugelhopf, 68-69; for popovers, 88-89
Mozzarella: *soft, kneaded cheese from southern Italy, traditionally made from buffalo's milk, but now also made from cow's milk;* 48-49
Muffins, 88-89
Mushrooms, 66
Notching, see Scoring
Nutmeg, 7, 54, 91
Nutrition, 6
Nuts, 45; chopped, 73, 88; see also Almonds, Pecans, Pine-nuts, Walnuts
Oatmeal flour, 9; in non-yeast doughs, 81, 82, 92
Oil, in the germ, 9; see also Olive oil, Sesame-seed oil
Olive oil, 46, 47, 48; glazes, 49; in pitta dough, 28
Olives, in filling, 48; in topping, 45, 46-47
Onions, 50, 88; as topping, 7, 45, 46-47, 78; see also Spring onions
Orange peel, 54
Oregano, 46
Ovens, 5, 6; brick, 6, 7; first purpose-built, 5
Pain perdu, 7
Parathas, 82, 83
Parker House rolls, 30, 32-33
Parmentier, Antoine-Auguste, 5
Parmesan, 48, 75, 76
Parsley, 48
Parsnips, 50
Pastries, 57; cheese plait, 76-77; croissants, 70-72; Danish, 73-75; fruit and spice, 76-77
Pecans, 90
Pecorino: *hard, yellow cheese from Italy, made from sheep's milk, similar to Parmesan, but sharper.*
Peppers, see Chili peppers, Sweet peppers
Persimmons, 90
Petit pain au chocolat, 48
Pine-nuts, 45, 48
Pinwheels, pastry, 74
Pissala, 46
Pissaladiera, 7, 45, 46-47
Pittas, 28-29
Plaiting, dough, 26-27, 76-77
Plaits, 26-27; pastry, 76-77
Plums, 46, 48
Poaching, bagels, 57, 78
Poor Knights of Windsor, 7
Popovers, 88-89
Poppy seeds, 23, 31, 38, 78
Pork cracklings, 88; see also Cracklings
Potatoes, 50; in rich dark bread, 52-53; in sourdough starter, 11; see also Sweet potatoes
Pretzels, 34-35
Prosciutto: *Italian unsmoked ham, here refers to prosciutto crudo (raw ham e.g. Parma ham).*

Protein, 8
Proving, dough, 14, 19
Provolone: *a hard, cream-coloured curd cheese from Italy.*
Puff dough, 57, 70-71, 73, 74, 75, 76-77
Pumpernickel, 52-53
Pumpkin, 90; puréed, in dough, 45, 50-51
Quiche Lorraine, 46-47
Racks, for cooling loaves, 7
Raisins, 54, 57, 60, 90
Redcurrants, 88
Refrigerating, dough, 6, 13; sourdough starter, 11; yeast, 10
Render: *to refine fat by melting the pure fat out of the fleshy tissues. Rendered fat, such as that from pork or goose, is used for cooking.*
Rice, 50, 66
Ricotta: *soft, mild, white cheese from Italy, made from either cow's or sheep's milk;* 48, 75, 76
Ring, pastry, 76-77
Rolling out dough, 28, 46-47; for chappatis, 82; for knots, 33; for pretzels, 34; for puff dough, 70-71
Rolls, 7, 30-33; cigar, 30, 32; cloverleaf, 30-31; in clusters, 38-39; flower, 42-43; fresh, for breakfast, 6-7; knot, 30, 33; Parker House, 30, 32-33
Roquefort, 46
Rose-water: *commercially produced flavouring from rose petals; available from chemists and good grocers.*
Roughage, 6
Rum, 68, 84
Rye, 50
Rye flour, 6, 9, 11; bread, sourdough leavened, 10; in rich dark bread, 52-53; in unleavened bread, 82
Saffron: *spice, from a species of crocus, used to impart a distinctive aroma and yellow colour to certain dishes. Sold in thread or powdered form;* 57, 60
Salad, 28
Salami, as filling, 45, 48-49
Salmon, see Smoked salmon
Salt, on bagels, 78; to demoisturize courgettes, 50; on pretzels, 35
Sausage-meat, 73
Sausages, cervelas, 57, 66; as filling, 7; as topping, 46; wrapped in brioche, 66-67
Scald: *to heat milk or other liquid to near boiling-point.*
Scissor cuts, cylinder loaf, 20-21; pastry ring, 76; turban loaf, 25
Scones, 86-87
Scoring, chequerboard loaf, 19; cottage loaf, 18, 19; flat loaf, 28; long loaf, 25; rolls, 30, 31, 32; tapered cylinder loaf, 22-23; white bread, 14, 16
Scotch black bun, 44, 45, 54-55
Self-raising flour, 8
Sesame-seed oil, 42
Sesame seeds, 23, 78
Simmer: *to cook in liquid at just below boiling-*

point, so that the surface of the liquid trembles but bubbles do not burst violently.
Slashing, see Scoring
Smoked salmon, eaten with bagels, 78
Soda bread, 86-87
Soft flour, 8
Soups, bread, 7
Sourdough, loaf, 17; starter, 10-11
Soured cream, in scone dough, 86
Soured milk, 81
Spices, 52, 82, 88
Spinach, 48
Spoonbreads, 7, 84-85
Spring onions, 42
Steam, in baking, 5-6, 7, 14, 16; as leavening agent, 5, 81, 82, 84
Steaming, rolls, 42-43
Sticks, bread, 34-35
Storing, flour, 9
Stretching dough, for cylinder loaves, 21; for long loaves, 24
Strong flour, 8
Suet: *hard fat from beef or lamb kidneys or loins, used to enrich dough.*
Sugar, in almond paste, 73; to enrich dough, 26; in kugelhopf, 68
Sultanas, 45, 48
Swedes, 50
Sweet peppers: *used to distinguish red or green bell peppers from the hotter chili pepper (q.v.) varieties of the pepper family;* 46
Sweet potatoes, 50
Tapered cylinder loaf, 22-23
Tartaric acid, 88
Tins, see Baking tins
Toast, 7
Tomatoes, sauce, in dough, 50; as topping, 46
Toppings, 46-47
Treacle, 52
Turban loaf, 24
Turnips, 50
Twists, pastry, 74-75
Unleavened dough, 82
Vanilla sugar: *sugar which is flavoured by storing it with a vanilla pod in a closed jar;* 90
Vegetables, mixed with dough, 48, 50; puréed, as filling, 82; see also individual vegetables
Vitamins, 6, 8
Walnuts, 68; chopped, 75
Wheat, 6; cracked, 39; grains, 8, 50; hard and soft, 8
Wheatmeal flour, 9
White bread, 6, 14-16
White flour, 6, 8
Whole wheat flour, see Wholemeal flour
Wholemeal flour, 8-9; batter for bread, 38-39; in chappati dough, 82; in dark bread dough, 52-53; in paratha dough, 83; in sourdough, 17
Wild yeasts, starters, 10-11
Yeast, in basic dough, 13, 14-16; in batters, 40, 58; dried, 10; in egg and butter dough, 58; fermentation, 5; in flavoured doughs, 50, 52, 53; fresh, 10; in lightly enriched dough, 27; in rich dough, 62, 78; wild, 10-11

Recipe Credits

The source for the recipes in this volume are shown below. Page references in brackets indicate where the recipes appear in the Anthology.

Aberdeen School of Domestic Science, *Plain Cookery Recipes*. Published by Robert Gordon's Technical College, Aberdeen, 1913 (*page 157*).

Acton, Eliza, *The English Bread-Book for Domestic Use*. Published by Longman, Brown, Green, Longmans, & Roberts, London, 1857 (*page 116*).

Adam, Hans Karl, *Das Kochbuch aus Schwaben*. © Copyright 1976 by Verlagsteam Wolfgang Hölker. Published by Verlag Wolfgang Hölker, Münster. Translated by permission of Verlag Wolfgang Hölker (*pages 110 and 118*).

Åkerström, Jenny, *Prinsessornas Kokbok*. © 1945 Albert Bonniers Boktryckeri, Stockholm. Published by Albert Bonniers Förlag, Stockholm. Translated by permission of Albert Bonniers Förlag A.B. (*page 107*).

Androuet, Pierre, *La Cuisine au Fromage*. © 1978, Éditions Stock. Published by Éditions Stock, Paris. Translated by permission of Éditions Stock (*pages 113, 114 and 142*).

Artocchini, Carmen (Editor), *400 Ricette della Cucina Piacentina*. Published by Gino Molinari, Piacenza. Translated by permission of the author (*page 106*).

Artusi, Pellegrino, *La Scienza in Cucina e l'Arte di Mangiar Bene*. Copyright © 1970 Giulio Einaudi Editore S.p.A., Torino. Published by Giulio Einaudi Editore S.p.A., Turin (*page 121*).

Bakos, Eva, *Mehlspeisen aus Österreich*. Copyright © 1975 by Verlag Carl Ueberreuter, Wien/Heidelberg. Published by Salzer-Ueberreuter, Vienna. Translated by permission of Verlag Carl Ueberreuter (*pages 136, 146 and 154*).

Ballester, Pedro, *De Re Cibaria. Cocina, Pastelería, Repostería Menorquinas*. Published by Editorial Sintes S.A., Barcelona, 1973. Translated by permission of Editorial Sintes S.A. (*page 133*).

Banfield, Walter T., *"Manna". A Comprehensive Treatise on Bread Manufacture*. Published by Maclaren & Sons, Ltd., London, 1937. By permission of Applied Science Publishers Ltd., Barking (*page 105*).

Bates, Margaret, *The Scottish and Irish Baking Book*. Copyright © Pergamon Press Ltd. Published in 1965 by Pergamon Press Ltd., London. By permission of Pergamon Press Ltd. (*page 157*).

Bisson, Marie, *La Cuisine Normande*. © Solar, 1978. Published by Solar, Paris. Translated by permission of Solar (*page 164*).

Blencowe, Ann, *The Receipt Book of Ann Blencowe. A.D. 1694*. Published by Guy Chapman, The Adelphi, London, 1925 (*page 132*).

Bonnefons, Nicolas de, *Les Délices de la Campagne*. 1655 (*pages 124, 157*).

Borer, Eva Maria, *Tante Heidi's Swiss Kitchen*. English text copyright © 1965 by Nicholas Kaye Ltd. First published under the title "Die Echte Schweizer Küche" by Mary Hahns Kochbuchverlag, Berlin W., 1963. By permission of Kaye & Ward Ltd., London (*page 126*).

Bozzi, Ottorina Perna, *Vecchia Brianza in Cucina*. © 1975 by Giunti Martello Editore, Firenze. Published by Aldo Martello-Giunti Editore S.p.A., Florence. Translated by permission of Aldo Martello-Giunti Editore S.p.A. (*page 158*).

Bringer, Rodolphe, *Les Bons Vieux Plats du Tricastin*. Published by Les Amis du Tricastin. Reprinted by Éditions Daniel Morcrette, Luzarches. Translated by permission of Éditions Daniel Morcrette (*page 131*).

British Columbia Women's Institutes, *Adventures in Cooking*. Published by British Columbia Women's Institutes, British Columbia, 1958. By permission of British Columbia Women's Institutes (*page 94*).

Brízová, Joza and Klimentová, Maryna, *Tschechische Küche*. © Joza Brízová & Maryna Klimentová, 1977. Published by Verlag Práca, Prague and Verlag für die Frau, Leipzig. Translated by permission of DILIA, Authors' Agency, Prague, for the authors (*page 146*).

Brown, Helen, *Helen Brown's West Coast Cook Book*. Copyright 1952 by Helen Evans Brown. Published by Little, Brown and Company, Boston. By permission of Little, Brown and Company (*page 169*).

Brown, Marion, *The Southern Cook Book*. © 1968 The University of North Carolina Press. Published by The University of North Carolina Press, Chapel Hill. By permission of The University of North Carolina Press (*pages 134, 168*).

Buckeye Cookbook, The: Traditional American Recipes. As published by the Buckeye Publishing Co., 1883. Republished by Dover Publications, Inc., New York, 1975 (*page 155*).

Bugialli, Giuliano, *The Fine Art of Italian Cooking*. Copyright © 1977 by Giuliano Bugialli. Published by Times Books, a division of Quadrangle/The New York Times Book Co., Inc., New York. By permission of Times Books, a division of Quadrangle/The New York Times Book Co., Inc. (*pages 114, 148*).

Calvel, Raymond, *La Boulangerie Moderne*. © 1978 Eyrolles. Published by Éditions Eyrolles, Paris, 1978. Translated by permission of Éditions Eyrolles (*pages 104, 130*).

Casella, Dolores, *A World of Breads*. Copyright © 1966 by Dolores Casella. Published by David White Company, New York. By permission of David White Inc., Port Washington (*page 121*).

Cavazzuti, Giorgio (Editor), *Il Mangiarfuori: Almanacco della Cucina Modenese*. Published by Camera di Commercio, Modena, 1965. Translated by permission of Camera di Commercio Industria Artiginato e Agricoltura (*page 112*).

Chamberlin-Hellman, Maria (Editor), *Food Notes*. © Copyright 1974, The Rudolf Wittkower Fellowship Fund. Published for the benefit of The Rudolf Wittkower Fellowship Fund, Department of Art, History and Archaeology, Columbia University, New York. By permission of Maria Chamberlin-Hellman (*page 101*).

Chezzetcook Historical Society, *Chezzetcook Historical Society Cookbook*. Published by Women's Clubs Publishing Co. Inc., Chicago, c. 1973 (*page 161*).

Cholcheva, Penka I., *Kniga za Vseki Den i Vseki Dom*. Published by the State Publishing House "Technika", 1979. Translated by permission of Jusautor Copyright Agency, Sofia, for the author (*page 153*).

Chowdhary, Savitri, *Indian Cooking*. Copyright © Savitri Chowdhary 1954, 1975. Published by André Deutsch, London, 1954 and Pan Books, London, 1975. By permission of André Deutsch (*page 164*).

Clayton, Jr., Bernard, *The Breads of France*. Copyright © 1978 by Bernard Clayton, Jr. Published by The Bobbs-Merrill Company, Inc., Indianapolis/New York. By permission of The Bobbs-Merrill Company, Inc. (*page 101*).

Clayton, Jr., Bernard, *The Complete Book of Breads*. Copyright © 1973 by Bernard Clayton, Jr. Published by Simon & Schuster, a division of Gulf & Western Corporation, New York. By permission of Simon & Schuster (*pages 117, 166*).

Corsi, Guglielma, *Un Secolo di Cucina Umbra*. Published by Tipografia Porziuncola, Assisi, 1968. Translated by permission of Tipografia Porziuncola (*pages 110, 112*).

Cox, J. Stevens (Editor), *Guernsey Dishes of Bygone Days*. © James and Gregory Stevens Cox. Published by The Toucan Press, St. Peterport, Guernsey, 1974. By permission of Gregory Stevens Cox (*page 163*).

Craig, Elizabeth, *The Scottish Cookery Book*. © Elizabeth Craig, 1956. Published by André Deutsch, London, 1956. By permission of André Deutsch (*page 145*).

Dalgairns, Mrs., *The Practise of Cookery*. Printed for Cadell & Co., Edinburgh, 2nd edition, 1829 (*pages 132, 138*).

David, Elizabeth, *English Bread and Yeast Cookery*. Copyright © Elizabeth David, 1977. Published by Penguin Books Ltd., London, 1979. By permission of Penguin Books Ltd. (*pages 115, 153*).

Davidis, Henriette, *Henriette Davidis Illustriertes Praktisches Kochbuch*. Newly revised by Helene Faber. Published by Schreitersche Verlagsbuchhandlung, Berlin, W. 35 (*page 99*).

Delplanque, A. and Cloteaux S., *Les Bases de la Charcuterie*. © 1975 Éditions Jacques Lanore C.L.T. Published by Éditions Jacques Lanore C.L.T., Malakoff. Translated by permission of

Éditions Jacques Lanore C.L.T. (*page 142*).

Deschamps, B. and Deschaintre J.-Cl., *Le Livre de l'Apprenti Pâtissier.* © 1978 Éditions Jacques Lanore C.L.T. Published by Éditions Jacques Lanore C.L.T., Malakoff. Translated by permission of Éditions Jacques Lanore C.L.T. (*page 150*).

Desserts de nos Provinces, Les. © Hachette, 1974. Published by Librairie Hachette, Paris. Translated by permission of Librairie Hachette (*page 154*).

Disslowa, Maria, *Jak Gotowac.* Copyright by Maria Disslowa. Published by Instytut Gospodarstwa Domowego, Wydawnictwo Rybitwa, Warsaw. Translated by permission of Agencja Autorska, Warsaw, for the author (*page 102*).

Dolby, Richard, *The Cook's Dictionary, and House-Keeper's Directory.* Published by Henry Colburn and Richard Bentley, London, 1830 (*page 131*).

Duff, Gail, *Gail Duff's Vegetarian Cookbook.* © Gail Duff 1978. Published by Macmillan London Limited, 1978 and Pan Books Ltd., London, 1979. By permission of Macmillan, London and Basingstoke (*page 159*).

Edmonds, Anna G. (Editor), *An American Cook in Turkey.* Published by Redhouse Press, Istanbul, 1961, 1966, 1971, 1978. By permission of Anna Edmonds for Redhouse Press (*page 119*).

Ellis, W., *The Country Housewife's Family Companion.* Published in London, 1750 (*page 102*).

Firth, Grace, *Stillroom Cookery.* Copyright © 1977 Grace Firth. Published by EPM Publications, Inc., McLean. By permission of EPM Publications, Inc. (*pages 135, 137*).

Food and Wines from Alsace, France. Published by Centre d'Information du Vin d'Alsace, Colmar, 1979. By permission of Centre d'Information du Vin d'Alsace (*pages 124, 147*).

Francesconi, Jeanne Caròla, *La Cucina Napoletana.* Copyright 1965 by Casa Editrice Fausto Fiorentino, Napoli. Published by Fausto Fiorentino Editore, Naples. Translated by permission of the author (*pages 112, 121 and 142*).

Franch, Rosa Sola, *De qué Va la Alimentación Natural.* © Las Ediciones de la Piqueta, Madrid, 1979. Published by Las Ediciones de la Piqueta, Madrid. Translated by permission of Las Ediciones de la Piqueta (*page 94*).

Grant, Doris, *Your Daily Food: Recipe for Survival.* © Doris Grant 1973. Published by Faber & Faber Limited, 1973. By permission of Faber & Faber Limited (*page 95*).

Grigson, Jane, *English Food.* Copyright © 1974 Jane Grigson. Published by Macmillan London Limited, 1974. By permission of Macmillan, London and Basingstoke (*pages 106, 130*).

Groff, Betty and Wilson, José, *Good Earth & Country Cooking.* Published by Stackpole Books, Harrisburg, Pennsylvania, 1974. By permission of Stackpole Books (*page 128*).

Groot, Roy Andries de, *The Auberge of the Flowering Hearth.* Copyright © 1973 by Roy Andries de Groot. Published by The Bobbs-Merrill Company, Inc., Indianapolis/New York. By permission of Robert Cornfield, Agent for the author (*page 119*).

Guinaudeau-Franc, Zette, *Les Secrets des Fermes en Périgord Noir.* © 1978, Éditions Serg, Paris. Published by Éditions Serg, Paris. Translated by permission of the author (*pages 127, 134*).

Haitsma Mulier-van Beusekom, C.A.H. (Editor), *Culinaire Encyclopedie.* Published by Elsevier © 1957. Revised edition 1974 by N.V. Uitgeversmaatschappij Elsevier Nederland and E.H.A. Nakken-Rovekamp. Translated by permission of B.V. Uitgeversmaatschappij Elsevier Focus, Amsterdam (*page 96*).

Hawliczkowa, Helena, *Kuchnia Polska.* (Editor: Maria Librowska). Published by Panstowe Wydawnictwo Ekonomiczne, Warsaw, 1976. Translated by permission of Agencja Autorska, Warsaw, for the author (*page 148*).

Hellermann, Dorothee v., *Das Kochbuch aus Hamburg.* © copyright 1975 by Verlagsteam Wolfgang Hölker. Published by Verlag Wolfgang Hölker, Münster. Translated by permission of Verlag Wolfgang Hölker (*pages 128, 143*).

Hess, Olga and Adolf Fr., *Wiener Küche.* 37th edition 1977. Copyright © by Franz Deuticke, Vienna, 1963. Translated by permission of Franz Deuticke (*page 129*).

Hewitt, Jean, *New England Heritage Cookbook.* Copyright © 1972 and 1977 by New York Times Company. Introduction © 1977 by Jean Hewitt. Published by G. P. Putnam's Sons, New York. By permission of Curtis Brown Ltd., New York (*page 166*).

Hillman, Libby, *The Menu-Cookbook for Entertaining.* Copyright © 1968 by Libby Hillman. Published by Hearthside Press Incorporated Publishers, New York. By permission of the author (*page 130*).

Irish Recipes Traditional and Modern. Published by Mount Salus Press Limited, Dublin. By permission of Mount Salus Press Limited (*pages 155, 156*).

Jack, Florence B., *Cookery for Every Household.* Published by Thomas Nelson & Sons, Ltd., London and Edinburgh, 1934. By permission of Thomas Nelson & Sons Ltd. (*page 158*).

Jensen, Ingeborg Dahl, *Wonderful, Wonderful Danish Cooking.* Copyright © 1966 by Ingeborg Dahl Jensen. Published by Simon & Schuster, a division of Gulf & Western Corporation, New York. By permission of Simon & Schuster (*page 98*).

Käkönen, Ulla, *Natural Cooking the Finnish Way.* Copyright © 1974 by Ulla Käkönen. Published by Quadrangle/The New York Times Book Company, New York. By permission of Times Books, a division of Quadrangle/The New York Times Book Company (*pages 103, 123, 165 and 166*).

Karsenty, Irène and Lucienne, *La Cuisine Pied-Noir* (Cuisines du Terroir). © 1974, by Éditions Denoël, Paris. Published by Éditions Denoël, Paris. Translated by permission of Éditions Denoël (*pages 96, 107 and 136*).

Kiehnle, Hermine and Hädecke, Maria, *Das Neue Kiehnle-Kochbuch.* © Walter Hadecke Verlag (vorm. Süddeutsches Verlagshaus), Weil der Stadt, 1960. Published by Walter Hadecke Verlag, Weil der Stadt. Translated by permission of Walter Hadecke Verlag (*pages 96, 103 and 120*).

Klever, Eva and Ulrich, *Selber Brot Backen.* © by Grafe und Unzer GmbH., München. Published by Grafe und Unzer GmbH., Munich. Translated by permission of Grafe und Unzer GmbH. (*page 100*).

Kowalska, Lili, *Cooking the Polish Way.* © Paul Hamlyn Limited 1964. Published by Paul Hamlyn Limited, London. By permission of The Hamlyn Publishing Group Limited (*pages 115, 134, 139 and 143*).

Kürtz, Jutta, *Das Brot Backbuch.* © Copyright 1975 by Verlag Wolfgang Hölker. Published by Verlag Wolfgang Hölker, Münster. Translated by permission of Verlag Wolfgang Hölker (*pages 99, 101, 122 and 143*).

Lazarque, E. Auricoste de, *Cuisine Messine.* Published by Sidot Frères, Libraires-Éditeurs, Nancy, 1927. Reprinted by Laffitte Reprints, Marseilles, 1979. Translated by permission of Laffitte Reprints (*page 111*).

Lincoln, Mrs. Mary J., *The Boston Cook Book.* Published in 1912 by Little, Brown, and Company, Boston (*page 161*).

Llanover, The Right Hon. Lady, *Good Cookery.* Published by Richard Bentley, London, 1867 (*page 117*).

Macdonald, Duncan, *The New London Family Cook (or Town and Country Housekeeper's Guide).* Published by Albion Press for J. and J. Cundee, London, 1812 (*page 133*).

Macnicol, Fred, *Hungarian Cookery.* Copyright © 1978 by Fred Macnicol. Published by Penguin Books Ltd., London. By permission of Penguin Books Ltd. (*page 155*).

Magyar, Elek, *Kochbuch für Feinschmecker.* © Dr. Magyar Balint. © Dr. Magyar Pal. Originally published in 1967 under the title "Az Inyesmester Szakacs Konyve" by Corvina Verlag, Budapest. Translated by permission of Artisjus, Literary Agency, Budapest (*page 129*).

Mann, Gertrude, *A Book of Cakes.* © Gertrude Mann, 1957. Published 1957 by André Deutsch, London. By permission of André Deutsch (*page 144*).

Marković, Spacenija-Pata, *Yugoslav Cookbook.* Fourth edition 1977. Published by Publicisticko-Izdavacki Zavod "Jugoslavija", Belgrade. Original title in Serbo-Croatian "Jugoslovenska Kuhinja". By permission of Jugoslovenska Autorska Agencija, Belgrade, for the author (*pages 152, 168*).

Mascarelli, Benoît, *La Table en Provence & sur la Côte d'Azur.* Copyright 1946, by Jacques Haumont, Paris. Published by Jacques Hau-

mont, Paris, 1947 (*page 108*).
McNeill, F. Marian, *The Scots Kitchen*. Second edition 1963. Published by Blackie and Son Limited, London and Glasgow. By permission of Blackie and Son Limited (*pages 154, 158*).
Menichetti, Piero Luigi and Panfili, Luciana Menichetti, *Vecchia Cucina Eugubina*. Published by Tipolitografia Rubini e Petruzzi, Città di Castello, 1976. Translated by permission of Piero Luigi Menichetti, Gubbio (*page 141*).
Mérigot, Madame, *La Cuisinière Républicaine*. Published by Mérigot jeune, Libraire, Paris, in the third year of the Republic (1795) (*page 116*).
Mondo in Cucina, II: I Dolci. Copyright © 1969, 1971 by Time Inc. Jointly published by Sansoni/Time Life (*page 168*).
Monod, Louis, *La Cuisine Florentine*. Published by Éditions Daniel Morcrette, B.P. 26, 95270 Luzarches, 1977. Translated by permission of Éditions Daniel Morcrette (*page 111*).
Montagné, Prosper, *New Larousse Gastronomique*. © Copyright English text The Hamlyn Publishing Group Limited 1977. Originally published under the title "Nouveau Larousse Gastronomique" © Copyright Librairie Larousse, Paris 19, 1960. By permission of The Hamlyn Publishing Group Limited (*page 160*).
New London Cookery and Complete Domestic Guide, The, By a Lady. Published by G. Virtue, Bristol, c. 1827 (*pages 116, 137*).
Norberg, Inga, *Good Food from Sweden*. Published by Chatto and Windus, London, 1935. By permission of Curtis Brown Ltd., London, Agents for the author (*pages 98, 132*).
Ochorowicz-Monatowa, Marja, *Polish Cookery. Uniwersalna Książka Kucharska*. Translated by Jean Karsavina. © 1958 by Crown Publishers, Inc., New York. By permission of Crown Publishers, Inc. (*page 149*).
Olney, Judith, *Comforting Food*. Copyright © 1979 by Judith Olney. Published by Atheneum Publishers, Inc., New York. By permission of Atheneum Publishers, Inc. (*page 95*).
Olney, Judith, *Summer Food*. Copyright © 1978 by Judith Olney. Published by Atheneum Publishers, Inc., New York. By permission of Atheneum Publishers, Inc. (*page 114*).
Ortega, Simone, *Mil Ochenta Recetas de Cocina*. © Simone K. de Ortega, 1972. © Alianza Editorial, S.A., Madrid, 1972. Published by Alianza Editorial, S.A. Translated by permission of Alianza Editorial, S.A. (*page 158*).
Ortiz, Elisabeth Lambert, *Caribbean Cooking*. Copyright © Elisabeth Lambert Ortiz, 1973, 1975. Published by Penguin Books Ltd., London. By permission of Penguin Books Ltd. (*page 162*).
Ortiz, Elisabeth Lambert, *The Complete Book of Mexican Cooking*. Copyright © 1967 by Elisabeth Lambert Ortiz. Published by M. Evans and Company, Inc., New York. By permission of Paul R. Reynolds Inc., Literary Agents, New York (*page 139*).
Paradissis, Chrissa, *The Best Book of Greek Cookery*. Copyright © 1976 P. Efstathiadis &

Sons. Published by Efstathiadis Group, Athens, 1976. By permission of P. Efstathiadis & Sons S.A. (*page 140*).
Pascoe, Ann, *Cornish Recipes Old and New*. Published by Tor Mark Press, Truro, Cornwall. By permission of Tor Mark Press (*page 156*).
Petits Propos Culinaires 1. February, 1979. Copyright © Prospect Books 1979. Published by Prospect Books, London and Washington D.C. By permission of the publisher (*pages 159, 160*).
Petits Propos Culinaires 4. February, 1980. Copyright © Prospect Books 1980. Published by Prospect Books, London and Washington D.C. By permission of the publisher (*page 124*).
Petrov, Dr. L., Djelepov, Dr. N., Iordanov, Dr. E. and Uzunova, S., *Bulgarska Nazionalna Kuchniya*. Copyright © by the four authors, 1978, c/o Jusautor, Sofia. Published by Zemizdat. Sofia, 1978. Translated by permission of Jusautor Copyright Agency, Sofia, for the authors (*page 167*).
Philpot, Rosl, *Viennese Cookery*. Copyright © 1965 by Rosl Philpot. Published by Hodder & Stoughton Limited, London. By permission of Hodder & Stoughton Limited (*page 147*).
Picayune Creole Cook Book, The. First published in 1901 as "The Original Picayune Creole Cook Book". Reprinted in 1971 by Dover Publications, Inc., New York (*page 169*).
Rattazzi, Ilaria (Editor), *Tante Cose con il Pane*. © 1978 Fratelli Fabbri Editori S.p.A.—Milano. Published by Fratelli Fabbri Editori S.p.A., Milan. Translated by permission of Fratelli Fabbri Editori S.p.A. (*pages 110, 165*).
Robbins, Ann Roe, *The Seven-Ingredients Cookbook*. Copyright © 1968 by Ann Roe Robbins. Published by Chilton Book Company, New York. By permission of Chilton Book Company (*page 122*).
Roden, Claudia, *A Book of Middle Eastern Food*. Copyright © Claudia Roden, 1968. Published by Penguin Books Ltd., London, 1970. By permission of the author (*page 103*).
Rombauer, Irma S. and Becker, Marion Rombauer, *Joy of Cooking*. Copyright © 1931, 1936, 1941, 1942, 1943, 1946, 1951, 1952, 1953, 1962, 1963, 1964, 1975 by The Bobbs-Merrill Company, Inc. Published by the Bobbs-Merrill Company, Inc., Indianapolis/New York, 1975. By permission of The Bobbs-Merrill Company, Inc. (*pages 161, 162*).
Rosser, Linda Kennedy (Editor), *Pioneer Cookery around Oklahoma*. Copyright 1978 Linda Kennedy Rosser. Published by Omniplex (Oklahoma Science and Arts Foundation, Inc.), Oklahoma City, 1978. By permission of Linda Kennedy Rosser (*page 169*).
Rossi Callizo, Gloria, *Las Mejores Tapas, Cenas Frías y Platos Combinados*. © Editorial De Vecchi, S.A., Barcelona, 1978. Published by Editorial De Vecchi, S.A. Translated by permission of Editorial De Vecchi, S.A. (*page 123*).
Rossi, Emmanuele (Editor), *La Vera Cuciniera Genovese*. Published by Casa Editrice Bietti,

Milan, 1973. Translated by permission of Casa Editrice Bietti (*page 109*).
Rundell, Mrs. Maria Eliza, *A New System of Domestic Cookery*. First published 1806. 65th edition remodelled and improved, by the addition of nearly one thousand entirely new receipts (contributed by Mrs. Emma Roberts), 1841 (*page 127*).
Schapira, Christiane, *La Cuisine Corse*. © Solar, 1979. Published by Solar, Paris. Translated by permission of Solar (*page 135*).
Scheibler, Sophie Wilhelmine, *Allgemeines Deutsches Kochbuch für alle Stände*. Published in Leipzig, 1896 (*pages 102, 137*).
Schrecker, Ellen, *Mrs. Chiang's Szechwan Cookbook*. Copyright © 1976 by Chiang Jung-Feng, John E. Schrecker and Ellen W. Schrecker, Trustees. Published by Harper & Row, Publishers, Inc., New York. By permission of Deborah Rogers Ltd., London, Literary Agents (*page 104*).
Singh, Dharamjit, *Indian Cookery*. Copyright © Dharamjit Singh, 1970. Published by Penguin Books Ltd., London, 1970. By permission of Penguin Books Ltd. (*page 163*).
Snow, Jane Moss, *A Family Harvest*. Copyright © 1976 by Jane Moss Snow. Published by The Bobbs-Merrill Company, Inc., Indianapolis/New York. By permission of Collier Associates, New York, for the author (*page 156*).
Straub, Maria Elisabeth, *Grönen Aal und Rode Grütt*. © LN-Verlag Lübecker Nachrichten GmbH., Lübeck 1971. Sixth edition 1977. Published by LN-Verlag Lübecker Nachrichten GmbH. Translated by permission of LN-Verlag Lübecker Nachrichten GmbH. (*page 125*).
Sverdrup, Elise, *Norway's Delight: Dishes and Specialities*. © Elise Sverdrup 1957. Published by Johan Grundt Tanum Forlag, Oslo, 1968. By permission of Forlaget Tanum/Norli A/S., Oslo (*page 164*).
Tendret, Lucien, *La Table au Pays de Brillat-Savarin*. Published by Librairie Dardel, Chambéry, 1934. Translated by permission of Jacques Grancher, Éditeur, Paris (*page 120*).
Thorne-Thomsen, Kathleen and Brownridge, Linda, *Why the Cake Won't Rise and the Jelly Won't Set*. Copyright © 1979 by Kathleen Thorne-Thomsen and Linda Brownridge. Published by A. & W. Publishers, Inc., New York. By permission of International Literary Agents Ltd., New York, for the authors (*page 162*).
Tibbott, S. Minwel, *Welsh Fare*. © National Museum of Wales (Welsh Folk Museum). Published by National Museum of Wales (Welsh Folk Museum), 1976. By permission of National Museum of Wales (Welsh Folk Museum) (*pages 144, 160*).
Tschirky, Oscar, *The Cook Book by "Oscar" of the Waldorf*. Copyright 1896 by Oscar Tschirky. Published by The Werner Company, Chicago and New York (*page 106*).
Uhle, Margret and Brakemeier, Anne, *Eigenbrötlers Brotbackbuch*. © 1975 Mosaik Verlag

GmbH., München. Published by Verlagsgruppe Bertalsmann GmbH., Vienna. Translated by permission of Mosaik Verlag GmbH. (*pages 98, 99, 118 and 128*).

Uttley, Alison, *Recipes from an Old Farmhouse*. © Alison Uttley 1966, 1972. Published by Faber and Faber Limited, London, 1973. By permission of Faber and Faber Limited (*page 106*).

Valente, Maria Odette Cortes, *Cozinha Regional Portuguesa*. Published by Livraria Almedina, Coimbra, 1973. Translated by permission of Livraria Almedina (*page 120*).

Vence, Céline and Courtine, Robert, *The Grand Masters of French Cuisine*. Copyright © 1978 by G. P. Putnam's Sons. Published by G. P. Putnam's Sons, New York. Originally published in France as ''Les Grands Maîtres de la Cuisine Française'', copyright © 1972 by Bordas. By permission of G. P. Putnam's Sons (*page 144*).

Venesz, József, *Hungarian Culinary Art*. © Mrs. József Venesz. Originally published by Corvina, Budapest, 1958. By permission of Artisjus, Literary Agency, Budapest, for Mrs. Venesz (*page 138*).

Vielfaure, Nicole and Beauviala, A. Christine, *Fêtes, Coutumes et Gâteaux*. © Christine Bonneton Éditeur. Published by Christine Bonneton Éditeur, Le Puy-en-Velay. Translated by permission of Christine Bonneton Éditeur (*pages 125,*
136, 140 and 141).

Viola, Pauline and Ravnkilde, Knud, *Cooking with a Danish Flavour*. Copyright © 1978 by Pauline Viola and Knud Ravnkilde. Published by Elm Tree Books for Danish Agricultural Producers, London. By permission of Hamish Hamilton Ltd., London (*page 151*).

Volpicelli, Luigi and Freda, Secondino (Editors), *L'Antiartusi: 1000 Ricette*. © 1978 Pan Editrice, Milano. Published by Pan Editrice, Milan. Translated by permission of Pan Editrice (*pages 122, 167*).

Walker, Lorna and Hughes, Joyce, *The Complete Bread Book*. © Copyright The Hamlyn Publishing Group Limited 1977. Published by The Hamlyn Publishing Group Limited, London, 1977. By permission of The Hamlyn Publishing Group Limited (*page 149*).

White, Florence, *Good English Food*. Published by Jonathan Cape Ltd., London, 1952. By permission of Jonathan Cape Ltd. (*page 104*).

Widenfelt, Sam (Editor), *Favorite Swedish Recipes*. Published by Dover Publications, Inc., New York, 1975. By permission of Dover Publications, Inc. (*page 126*).

Willinsky, Grete, *Kulinarische Weltreise*. © 1961 by Mary Hahns Kochbuchverlag, Berlin W. Published by Büchergilde Gutenberg, Frankfurt/Main. Translated by permission of
Mary Hahns Kochbuchverlag, Munich (*pages 113, 140*).

Witty, Helen and Colchie, Elizabeth Schneider, *Better than Store-Bought*. Copyright © 1979 by Helen Witty and Elizabeth Schneider Colchie. Published by Harper & Row, Publishers, Inc., New York. By permission of Harper & Row Publishers, Inc. (*page 97*).

Wolfert, Paula, *Couscous and Other Good Food from Morocco*. Copyright © 1973 by Paula Wolfert. Published by Harper & Row, Publishers, Inc., New York. By permission of the author (*page 111*).

Wolfert, Paula, *Mediterranean Cooking*. Copyright © 1977 by Paula Wolfert. Published by Quadrangle/The New York Times Book Company Inc., New York. By permission of the author (*page 108*).

Zaniboni, Maria Rivieccio, *Cucina e Vini di Napoli e della Campania*. © Copyright 1975 Ugo Mursia Editore, Milano. Published by Ugo Mursia Editore, Milan. Translated by permission of Ugo Mursia Editore S.p.A. (*pages 100, 109*).

Zuliani, Mariù Salvatori de, *La Cucina di Versilia e Garfagnana*. Copyright © by Franco Angeli Editore, Milano. Published by Franco Angeli Editore, Milan, 1969. Translated by permission of Franco Angeli Editore (*pages 94, 109 and 118*).

Acknowledgements and Picture Credits

The Editors of this book are particularly indebted to Peter Ort, Master Baker, Leighton Buzzard, Bedfordshire; Gail Duff, Maidstone, Kent; Dr. R. H. Smith, Aberdeen; and Ann O'Sullivan, Deya, Mallorca.

They also wish to thank the following: Christine Adams, London; Mary Attenborough, Chelmsford, Essex; Liz Clasen, London; Emma Codrington, Petersham, Surrey; Department of Home Economics and Nutrition Education, The Flour Advisory Bureau Ltd., London; Mimi Errington, London; Fayal Greene, London; Maggie Heinz, London; Stella Henvey, London; Brenda Jayes, London; Maria Johnson,
Hatfield, Hertfordshire; Rosemary Klein, London; Sue McFarland, Milton Keynes; Pippa Millard, London; Sonya Mills, Canterbury, Kent; Michael Moulds, London; Dilys Naylor, London; Fiona Tillett, London; Tina Walker, London; Nigel Warrington, London; Tiggi Wood, Eastbourne, Sussex.

Photographs by Tom Belshaw: 10, 11—top centre and bottom, 27—top right, 40—top, 41—top, 44,46, 47—top,50, 51,52—top and bottom left, 53—top and bottom right, 54, to 56, 58—top, 59—top, 60—top, 62 to 79, 84 to 89.
Photographs by Alan Duns: cover, 4, 8, 9, 11—top left, 12, 14, 15, 17—top, 18 to 24, 26, 27—top left,
top centre and bottom, 28 to 36, 37—top and bottom left, 38, 39, 40—bottom, 41—bottom, 42, 43—bottom, 47—bottom, 52—bottom right, 53—bottom left, 58—bottom, 59—bottom.

Other photographs (alphabetically): David Davies, 48, 49, 82,83. John Elliott, 16,17—bottom, 25, 37—bottom right, 43—top, 60—bottom, 61, 92. Louis Klein, 2. Bob Komar, 11—top right, 80,90, 91.

Line cuts from Mary Evans Picture Library and private sources. Diagram on page 8 by Mary Staples.

Colour separations by Gilchrist Ltd.—Leeds, England
Typesetting by Camden Typesetters—London, England
Printed and bound by Brepols S.A.—Turnhout, Belgium.